LATIN AMERICAN
RELIGION IN MOTION

LATIN AMERICAN RELIGION IN MOTION

EDITED BY
CHRISTIAN SMITH AND
JOSHUA PROKOPY

ROUTLEDGE
NEW YORK AND LONDON

Published in 1999 by
Routledge
29 West 35th Street
New York, NY 10001

Published in Great Britain by
Routledge
11 New Fetter Lane
London EC4P 4EE

Norget, Kristin. "Progressive Theology and Popular Religiosity in Oaxaca, Mexico." Copyright © 1997. From *Ethnology*, Winter 1997, pp. 67–84. Reprinted with permission of publisher.

Printed in the United States of America on acid-free paper.

Library of Congress Cataloging-in-Publication Data

Latin American religion in motion / [edited by] Christian Smith and Joshua Prokopy.
     p.   cm.
   ISBN 0-415-92105-8 (alk. paper). — ISBN 0-415-92106-6 (pbk. : alk. paper)
    1. Latin America—Religion.   I. Smith, Christian (Christian Stephen), 1960– . II. Prokopy, Joshua.
  BL2540.L37 1999
  200'.98—DC21   98-28932
                                    CIP

CONTENTS

INTRODUCTION

Joshua Prokopy and Christian Smith

As the twentieth century passes into the twenty-first, we are witnessing numerous upheavals and transformations within Latin America's myriad religious traditions. Much of the recent research on this tumultuous period has focused on the rise and fall of liberation theology and the explosive growth of Protestantism across the continent. Important as these two issues are, they do not capture the full range or nature of the changes that have occurred. Latin America is experiencing a genuine and profound pluralization of faith. The Catholic Church has been internally divided by conflicts between more radical liberation theologians, progressives, conservatives bent on rebuilding the institutional church, and charismatics who mirror the emotional worship style of the Pentecostals. Protestants are even more deeply divided, as the historical denominations, like the Lutherans and Baptists, compete with hundreds of conservative evangelical and Pentecostal churches. At the same time, Afro-Brazilian spiritist religions, new ageism, Buddhism, and indigenous creole faiths are also on the rise in many parts of the continent. An adequate assessment of these transformations will have to take a broad view, and play close attention to unexpected and counterintuitive developments which raise questions about some of the conventional wisdoms in this field.

To understand these major religious changes in a continent that was once viewed as uniformly Catholic in both culture and religious tradition, we might do well to make use of new theoretical lenses that have recently been developed for the study of religion in North America. In this introduction, we will give an overview of the theory of religious economies and of subcultural identity theory, and use them to reanalyze the process of religious pluralization in Latin America. We will then look at the Catholic response to these changes, and at the pluralization which has taken place within the Church itself.

RELIGIOUS ECONOMIES

Roger Finke and Rodney Stark (1992: 17), proponents of the theory of religious economies, state that: religious economies are like commercial economies in that they consist of a market made up of a set of current and potential customers and a set of firms seeking to serve that market. The relative success of religious bodies (especially when they are confronted with an unregulated economy) will depend upon their polity, their clergy, their religious doctrine, and their evangelization techniques.

Finke and Stark argue that as state-imposed religious monopolies are lifted and religious markets become unregulated, pluralism increases, because a single religious tradition is inherently unable to meet all religious consumers' needs and tastes. As they put it (1992: 18):

> Pluralism arises because of the inability of a single religious organization to be at once worldly and otherworldly, strict and permissive, exclusive and inclusive, while the market will always contain distinct consumer segments with strong preferences on each of these aspects of faith.

As a result, religious faith can never be fully monopolized. Even when a religious organization receives the backing of the state as the "official religion," it will be surrounded by sects, heretical movements, and religious dissent. While such dissent may be forced underground through repression, it will continue to survive, only to flourish once the repression is relaxed. When people whose needs are not met by the official religion are unable or unwilling to dissent or join a heretical movement, they are likely to become indifferent to religion until such time as it becomes possible for them to find a version of faith that does meet their needs. According to Finke and Stark, this subverts the long-held belief that religious faith is actually weakened by pluralistic religious environments.

In applying this theory of religious economies to the study of religion in Latin America, we must begin by going back to the time of the Conquest. The Catholic Church has long maintained that Latin America is an essentially Catholic culture, and that before the arrival of Protestant missionaries the people of Latin America were almost entirely Catholic. The truth, however, is much more in keeping with the theory that religious monopolies, like the Catholic Church, are always surrounded by heresy and dissent. Catholicism was, after all, an immigrant faith, brought to the New World by Spanish and Portuguese missionaries and explorers. Its history in the region extends back much further than that of the various Protestant denominations, but it is in no sense an indigenous religion. The Spanish and Portuguese came to a New World that was already teeming with all manner of religions. In addition to the state religions of the Incas, Mayas, and Aztecs, hunter-gatherer societies and indigenous peasants throughout the continent maintained their own various folk beliefs and practices. Catholicism became but one part of this milieu, adopted by some, rejected by others, and creolized by many. Creolization meant that even within the Church there was a difference between the formal Catholicism of the clergy and upper classes, and the folk Catholicism practiced by the majority (in which Catholic practices were mixed with indigenous beliefs and rituals).

As David Martin (1990) has noted, over the course of the last five hundred years, numerous other religious faiths have been added to the mixture, despite state support of the Catholic Church. African slaves, imported to Brazil and the Caribbean, carried with them their own religious traditions. These were maintained in varying forms over time, and have now come to form the basis for Umbanda, Candomble, Voodoo, and other such Afro-Brazilian and Caribbean traditions. South Asian immigrants came to Trinidad, Guyana, and Surinam, bringing forms of Islam and Hinduism with them. Japanese immigrants settled in Peru and Brazil, and introduced Buddhism to the region. Non-Catholic European migrants seeking work and greater religious freedom also made their way to Latin America. Lithuanian Baptists came to Brazil and Russian Mennonites to Paraguay. German economic migrants, along with smaller numbers of Scandinavian and Scottish immigrants, set up Protestant churches in Brazil, Chile, Argentina, and Guatemala. Add to this the recent reemergence of indigenous religions and cultures throughout the continent, and the fact that, even among the Hispanic and Creole populations, Catholic doctrine and practice was often reinterpreted to fit local circumstances, and it becomes obvious that the foundation of religious pluralism has long been present in Latin America (Martin 1992: 55-57).

The stage was set for change (and further pluralization) during the nineteenth-century struggles for political independence. The Catholic Church sided with the Spanish Crown, the institution which had long protected its interests in the New World. The new liberal regimes, which came to power following independence, reacted by severing the traditional ties of support between Church and state. They worked to reduce the power and privilege of the Church, opening the way for rival religious organizations, which no longer had to fear state-sponsored repression for challenging the Catholic Church. Thus, non-Catholic religious beliefs and practices that had earlier remained limited and localized were often given the freedom to expand.

It was not until the early twentieth century, however, that pluralization really began in earnest. Increased pluralization was propelled by the spread of urbanization and industrialization. Rural communities of the early part of the century were fairly socially comprehensive and were dominated by the landed elite. Because of the relative cultural continuity found in these communities, there was less diversity of religious needs than then there are today. Some individuals may well have been dissatisfied with the religious options provided by the single, unified Catholic Church, but it was difficult for them to act on their dissatisfaction because the Church was supported and defended by the landed elite. The dominant position of the landed elite, and their desire to keep out any beliefs or ideas which might threaten the social status quo, generally deterred people from introducing new belief systems (Ireland 1993, Gill 1993). Thus, while the states had often reduced their support of the Catholic Church, pluralization remained at a low level because local elites took over the functional role of the state in rural communities across the continent. In other words, dissent and alternative belief systems existed, but they could not spread as long as the Catholic Church had the support and backing of either the state or the local elite. The available supply of unregulated alternative religions was severely restricted (compare to Wuthnow 1989: 52-156).

It was not until masses of Latin Americans began moving out of the villages, escaping the power of the landed elite by migrating to the cities, that religious pluralization was able to begin in earnest. As people moved to the cities, and sought new religions to meet their rapidly diversifying religious needs, new religious entrepreneurs moved in to meet those needs. According to Gill (1993: 187), as peasants flooded into La Paz, Bolivia, the Catholic Church found itself unable to meet the new demands. Protestants and Pentecostals filled the gap by moving into neighborhoods where the Catholic presence was weak. This was possible because Protestant pastors did not require long periods of training: Local men who received "the calling" set up their own storefront churches with the support of small groups of followers. Some of the most successful Pentecostal churches were established by local men who broke away from missionary control. Such leaders developed their own particular interpretations of the scriptures and could conduct worship services in Aymara if they needed to communicate with new migrants from the countryside.

These local religious entrepreneurs were simply responding to the expressed religious needs of the new migrants. They often came out of the local community, spoke the local language, and could more easily identify with the needs and fears of the new migrants than could the foreign-born Catholic priests.

SUBCULTURAL IDENTITY THEORY

Christian Smith et al.'s (1998) subcultural identity theory may also help in making sense of how religious faith is shaped by a pluralizing cultural and religious environment. Their basic argument, analogous to that of Finke and Stark, is that faith thrives on plurality, tension, and conflict. They base their argument on a set of general sociological principles. Smith et al. begin with the rather simple premise that humans are inescapably moral creatures whose identities are constructed through engagement with others in identifiable social groups. That engagement, they argue, is facilitated through the creation of symbolic cultural markers which separate "insiders" from "outsiders," and determine who people will measure themselves against both positively and negatively. By categorizing and labeling themselves and others, people are able to contrast themselves with those whom they feel that they are unlike, while identifying with those whom they feel that they resemble. People also create rules and markers to identify who is part of the insider group, and carefully police that boundary. In any pluralistic environment, there will be an abundance of outsider groups, which can then be used to strengthen the morally-orienting collective identity of the insiders.

Using these principles, Smith et al. argue against secularization theorists, who maintain that social and cultural pluralization leads to a decline in faith. In response to the belief that a plurality of religious choices diminishes any one tradition's aura of objective truth by relativizing faith, they contend that people do not evaluate their beliefs by the norms of outsiders. Instead, they compare them to the beliefs of both specific reference groups whose opinions they value, and negative reference groups which represent what they don't want to be or to believe. Those people who are not a part of one of these reference groups can usually be ignored. Things which challenge people's belief systems may only serve to strengthen their faith. They become external enemies that unite believers in their faith, give them strength, and highlight what separates them from outsiders.

Finally, in response to the argument that urbanization leads to a breakdown of community and a subsequent decline in faith, Smith et al. maintain that modern community is not best conceived of as a physical place. Rather, it is a set of relationships that bind people together. When people move to the city, they may lose the traditional version of community based on local geography and close kinship networks. In a city, with all of its diversity of people and cultures, people are forced to create new networks and sets of community relationships. Religion often offers one of the most readily accessible means of doing this.

For example, when poor migrants move into cities, we might suppose that they often find themselves living in slum communities made up of other recent migrants with whom they may have no preexisting bonds of kinship or community. In order to rebuild their vital human relationships, they may seek connections with others through religion. They may search for religions that can both meet their need for moral identity and provide them with a renewed sense of community in an otherwise unfamiliar environment.

To maintain that sense of community in a crowded and diverse urban setting, where many people must coexist with one another, each new religious community is likely to construct strong symbolic markers. This is necessary so that people can differentiate themselves from everyone else and maintain a sense of the special nature of their particular community and the inherent truth of their doctrine and practices. As such markers are constructed in an already plural environment, they only reinforce the sense of difference between groups. This furthers competition between them and leads to greater pluralization. Thus, according to this theory, rather than leading to an inevitable decline in faith, urbanization can actually spur a renewal and rediscovery of faith that results in religious pluralization and strength.

This can help us to explain the rapid pluralization of faith in Latin America that began in the 1930s with the acceleration of urbanization and industrialization. Between 1930 and 1940, the urban population of Latin America increased by 39 percent. Then it grew again by another 61 percent from 1940 to 1950. That same period was also the time when industry began expanding faster then agriculture (Smith 1991: 73-74). The Great Depression caused a sharp decline in imported manufactured goods, prompting Latin American entrepreneurs to begin investing in domestic industry, especially in Mexico and the Southern Cone. This led to a rapid increase in manufacturing jobs. "In Brazil, for example, the number of industrial workers almost tripled between 1920 and 1940, and during the 1950s industry continued to expand almost twice as fast as agriculture"(Smith 1991: 74).

Urban migrants entered a situation in which the traditional community and kinship and patronage ties were often disrupted. There was little central unifying force to draw them together. As they began to live and work in an urban environment, they also developed a more diverse set of wants, needs, and problems than might have been the case in their old villages, where people's positions in society were more clearly defined and understood. Religion often provided them with a means of addressing these problems. According to Gill (1993: 189), for Indian migrants living in the barrios of La Paz:

Affiliating with an organized religion is just one of a number of ways that people try to establish bonds in this crisis-ridden milieu and construct new explanations of their personal history. Aymara immigrants have to contend with the stigma of their rural Indian origins as they struggle to forge new identities and build supportive networks in the city. Worship services offer them an institutional base for developing significant ties to other people. Churches also provide rituals and beliefs to validate these social bonds, creating a new sense of community.

According to the logic of subcultural identity theory, to attract more congregants in this highly competitive religious environment, pastors and their followers would have to differentiate themselves from other religious alternatives. They would have to create distinguishing features of doctrine, worship, or lifestyle in order to compete, and they would have to make sure that believers within their congregations respected these boundaries. As more people migrate to the cities, and their range of needs and problems continue to expand, more and more congregations, both small and large, would develop to meet those needs. This would further increase the level of religious competition, and the need to set and patrol boundaries. Rowan Ireland provides a clear illustrative description of the impact of urbanization and industrialization on the rural community of Campo Alegre in Brazil:

By mid-century, the local sugar industry was dying, urban transport networks made Recife much more accessible, and Campo Alegre's institutional focus on [Catholic] brotherhood patronage relationships, though still sought by many Campo Alegrenses, was increasingly difficult to maintain. Not only had the elite become more diverse and less locked into Campo Alegre, but the town's population was newer and the range of relationships with the central institution of the town was much more varied than in previous decades. The inner coherence and outer boundaries of the town were becoming less well defined. By the 1970s there was no one institution, and certainly not the brotherhood of old, that could integrate the urban diversity that Campo Alegre had become. When Campo Alegre was still dominated by the sugar industry, the town's institutional focus was provided by the Catholic Church, which was controlled by the local elite. The Church provided the poor with a meager level of charity, and also organized festivals for religious holidays. Most important of all, however, was the fact that the Church's governing board controlled access to the town's patrimonial land, which the elite patrons would distribute among their clients. As the sugar industry died, and the town became increasingly tied into the local capitalists of Recife, however, the poor found other means of employment and the elite found other ways to invest their wealth. The patron-client ties that ran through the Church became harder to maintain, and the control exercised by the local elite decreased. As a result, the Catholic Church no longer met everyone's needs (both spiritual and material), and there was less risk attached to leaving the Church for another religion. In a relatively short period of time, the Catholic Church had to compete with popular Catholicism, the pentecostal Assemblies of God, and various Afro-Brazilian groups (Ireland 1993: 46-7).

Another example of this trend towards pluralization comes from Caracas, Venezuela. The late 1950s and early 1960s saw a major increase in migration to Caracas. Between 1958 and 1962 alone, more than 200,000 of the rural poor moved there. This was accompanied by a significant increase in the level of Protestant activity in the city. Between 1960 and 1990, the number of Catholic parishes in Caracas declined from 233 to 217, while the number of evangelical churches rose from 75 to 239 (Froehle 1995: 131-32).

PLURALIZATION AND THE CATHOLIC RESPONSE

Part of the reason for this vast pluralization of faith has been the Catholic Church's understandable inability to provide for people's ever-expanding and diversifying needs, problems, and wants. This should not be seen as a failure on the part of the Church, however. As Anthony Gill points out in his contribution to this volume, the Catholic Church is still the largest religious institution on the continent. It wields a great deal of influence, continues to meet the needs of many of its parishoners, and is actively involved in efforts to reverse the trend towards pluralization. This will, however, be a difficult struggle for the Church, as Latin America has been caught up in a worldwide trend of expanding social, spiritual, and economic needs, and decreasing religious hegemony. As the theory of religious economies makes clear, this is a process that almost inevitably leads to pluralization and the rise of alternative religious faiths.

In Latin America, as state support for the Catholic Church decreased, and the expansion of urban industry and urban values led to an inevitable decline in the power of the landed elite, the way was open for greater religious pluralization. For the first time, the Church really had to compete vigorously with other faiths and traditions. In the new urban environment of the barrios and shantytowns, however, the Church was at a distinct disadvantage compared to the Protestant denominations.

To help understand the reasons for this disadvantage, it is helpful to return to Finke and Stark (1992). Their theory of religious economies maintains that religious monopolies breed lazy clergies. When clergy don't have to compete for a living, when they are the only religious representatives available, they have less reason to be active and innovative. In contrast, within a pluralistic environment the clergy will be both more numerous and more active. They will also be more specialized, creating niches for themselves within the wider religious field. As religious organizations specialize, they are, collectively, able to attract a much larger proportion of the population.

In Latin America, the Catholic Church has suffered from a severe shortage of clergy, which has often prevented it from expanding into the vast new shantytowns and squatter settlements that sprang up on the edges of the cities. In most countries, the numbers of clergy continue to dwindle, and many of the Catholic priests are foreign born and educated (Smith 1991). There are often barely enough new priests to replace those who have died, and certainly far too few to keep up with population growth. Between 1973 and 1990, the number of priests on the continent fell from 1.6 to 1.2 per 10,000 residents (Daudelin and Hewitt 1995: 183).

One study conducted by Froehle (1995) in Caracas, Venezuela, for example, showed a steady decline in the size of the clergy. Between 1970 and 1990, the average number of priests per parish fell from 3.46 to 1.99. In addition, it has been difficult to recruit priests to serve in the poorer neighborhoods: "Not only are social conditions difficult, but one's opportunities for ecclesiastical promotion are considerably lower than in the parishes of wealthier neighborhoods" (1995: 133). The poorer neighborhoods are more often served by vicarages run by nuns, but there are not yet enough of these to meet the growing need. As a result, by 1990 the Catholic Church was still concentrated primarily in the upper- and middle-class neighborhoods of the city. Froehle showed that only 13 percent of Catholic religious groups, 12 percent of parish offices, and 25 percent of parish territories were located in the neighborhoods occupied by the poorest 44 percent of the population. Only 13 percent of Catholic parishioners came from these neighborhoods. The average number of people in each parish located in the neighborhoods occupied by the poorest 25 percent of the population was 42,830, compared to 17,668 people per parish in the neighborhoods occupied by the richest 25 percent. Thus, even as late as 1990 the Church has had difficulty expanding into the slums and ministering to the newest urban migrants.

In addition to a lack of priests, the Catholic Church has also had trouble adapting to Latin America's rapidly changing socioeconomic environment. In most countries, 85 percent of the clergy are foreign born, and the Church's doctrine continues to be determined by Rome, leaving individual priests and nuns constrained in their ability to refashion it to better fit their local context. As a result, many people have increasingly discovered that the priests cannot identify with them, and that sometimes the Church can offer them neither helpful explanations for their problems nor helpful solutions.

In this sense, the evangelical and Pentecostal denominations are organizationally far better adapted for survival in a pluralistic environment. Their churches tend to be smaller, less centralized, and far more fragmented. They are often little more than storefronts. This means that they have more autonomy than the Catholic Church affords to its congregations. Some of the Pentecostal churches are independent of any denomination, and even those that are part of a denomination often reinterpret scripture as necessary to fit local needs and changing cultural values. According to Mariz, in her contribution to this volume, protestants in Brazil have adapted their teachings to the changes in sexual morality and gender relations that have permeated the rest of the country, while Haas points out how the official Catholic hierarchy in Chile has retrenched itself and has continued to defend its traditional teachings on culture and morality. This also makes it easier for Protestant parishoners to construct symbolic markers and cultural barriers to differentiate themselves from members of competing churches and denominations.

In many countries of Latin America, Pentecostal and evangelical pastors are actually more numerous than Catholic priests, which is especially significant given that there are still far fewer Protestant than Catholic believers. As mentioned above, one reason for this is that evangelical pastors don't need to receive the same kind of special training as priests, nor must they abide by the rules of celibacy. Anyone who feels 'the call' may become an evangelical pastor, and try to establish his or her own congregation. As a result, pastors are more likely to come from the local community, to speak the local language, and to understand the local culture and problems than the often foreign-born and highly educated priests. Their evangelization techniques are also highly experiential and aggressive, focusing on healing, emotional prayer, and active outreach.

One result of this organizational structure and doctrinal flexibility is that competition and pluralization within evangelicalism and Pentecostalism has also become quite intense (though as Marostica points out in his contribution to this volume, there have been tentative movements toward more evangelical unity in some parts of Latin America). While there are still only about a dozen major evangelical denominations, such as the Assemblies of God, there are perhaps thousands of smaller denominations and independent churches. Each time a new believer feels the call and begins to preach, they do so in competition with other local pastors, and must therefore create symbolic identity markers to differentiate themselves and attract congregants.

Non-Christian Pluralization

While Protestants represent the most prominent challenge to the Catholic Church in Latin America, pluralization has also spread to numerous non-Christian faiths. As the power of the Church has weakened, and rapid socioeconomic changes have created an ever-widening range of new social, spiritual, and economic needs and desires, an increasing number of Latin Americans have begun to look beyond the traditional bounds of Christianity for answers.

In many countries with large indigenous populations, the past thirty years have seen a significant increase in cultural consciousness, and a revival of indigenous religious beliefs. Traditional Mayan ceremonies, for example, are now performed openly in the highlands of Guatemala, and there have been vocal, and often violent, movements for indigenous rights there. As Siebers points out in his contribution to this volume, these traditional beliefs and practices have also had an influence on the way in which the indigenous peoples of Guatemala practice Christianity. Afro-Brazilian religions have also undergone a revival, and a return to their African roots (they are 'reafricanizing' themselves, as Jensen puts it in her contribution to this volume). Because of the stigma that still hangs over the Afro-Brazilian religions, it is difficult to know just how many people are practitioners. Many Christians visit spirit mediums, but are reluctant to admit it to others. According to Burdick (1993: 14), of 100 people with whom he talked in the Brazilian community of São Jorge, "at least half admitted to having consulted with a medium at some time or another, and a fifth were either regular participants or mediums." There were two Umbanda centers in São Jorge at the time, but most of the locals who wanted to consult a medium would travel to other towns, where they could visit the centers in more anonymity (p. 47). Burdick even noted that many of the spirit mediums themselves were also Catholics. They and their followers are intermingling these faiths to create something new of their own.

While Afro-Brazilian spiritism has become something of an indigenous religion, there are also new non-Christian faiths making their way into Latin America from other parts of the world. One of the more prominent of these, according to Clarke (1995), has been Buddhism, which is on the rise in both Brazil and Mexico. While Buddhists in Brazil were once primarily Japanese, the Japanese, in an attempt to assimilate, have begun to abandon Buddhism and adapt their culture and language to the rest of Brazilian society.

As of 1964, only 19 percent of third- and fourth-generation Japanese immigrants were still Buddhist. The rest had converted to Catholicism and other Christian religions. On the other hand, many non-Japanese have begun practicing Buddhism. By 1988, there were some 2,800,000 Buddhists in Brazil, the vast majority of non-Japanese descent. Of the 2,400,000 followers of Seicho no ie, for example, 85 percent were non-Japanese (Clark 1995). According the Robert Carpenter's chapter in this volume, there has also been a growing interest in "New Age" writings and philosophies among the Brazilian upper class. In both São Paulo and Rio de Janeiro, there are more than 1,000 New Age groups and establishments.

The point is that while most of the scholarly and media attention on religious pluralization in Latin America has focused on the rise of Protestantism, people are actually converting to a whole range of new religious faiths. The process of pluralization, and the diversification of material, social and spiritual needs that fuels it, means that the religious environment can, and will, spread increasingly beyond the confines of Christianity.

TRANSFORMATION WITHIN THE CATHOLIC CHURCH

This process of pluralization has also led to new changes and tensions within the Latin American Catholic Church. If the Church was ever a monolithic institution, it is now becoming somewhat decentralized, despite the best efforts of the Vatican to reverse the process. This process of decentralization is in part a result of the Church's own attempts to resist pluralization.

In the 1930s, partly as a means to halt the growth of Protestantism in the region, the Latin American Catholic Church introduced the strategy of "New Christendom." The Church became an advocate of "progress," "science," and "modernity," and tried to mobilize the laity for "religiously informed" participation in politics and the economy. The Church encouraged the establishment of Christian Democratic parties, used the radio to broadcast Church teachings, engaged in economic development, promoted lay leadership, and commissioned theological reflections on socioeconomic development. By the 1960s, however, this strategy had begun to falter. Religious pluralization increased, the Christian Democratic parties failed to curb military violence and promote genuine democracy, and governments across the continent fell to military dictatorships.

Where "New Christendom" had tried to maintain the Church's hegemony by Christianizing the world, the Catholic Church in the wake of Vatican II took a more humble position. The Church focused on promoting the betterment of humanity and building alliances with the masses and placed an emphasis on developing local initiative and reducing hierarchical control over the priesthood. As part of this, Smith (1982: 17) notes, "Condemnation of modern secular values and movements, such as freedom of conscience, religious toleration, liberalism, communism, socialism, articulated by the nineteenth-century Church were conspicuously absent in Vatican II's treatment of the mission of the Church in the world today."

The Church became more open to learning from the world in order to help make it a better place for the majority. This encouraged the development of the liberation theology movement in Latin America, which held that the institutional Church was in decline because it no longer met the needs of the masses. Liberation theologians called for the establishment of base communities, in which lay members would reinterpret the Bible according to their local situation, and use it to help them address pressing socioeconomic and political problems.

The liberation theologians referred to this as a "new way of being church," a way that focused on local autonomy and empowerment. The base communities enabled the Church to meet people's ever diversifying needs. But they did not stem the tide of pluralization. There are three possible reasons for this. For one thing, as numerous studies have pointed out, base community members do not tend to be drawn from the poorest classes. Instead, they are often artisans, shopkeepers, white-collar workers and community leaders (Burdick 1993). Burdick noted several reasons for this fact. First of all, the base community emphasis on small-group interaction made class differences within the group increasingly visible. This made the poorer members of the community more uncomfortable. The base community movement's new emphasis on having groups read and interpret the Bible had the same effect by creating a division between the literate and illiterate members of the community. Thus, while one of the goals of the base community movement was to open up the Church and transcend class barriers, in practice it often served only to strengthen the barriers. This has caused many of the poor to look for new religious options.

Another reason may be found in the possibility that the focus of liberation theology was so firmly set on sociopolitical and economic change that it overlooked people's need for religious mystery. According to Miguez's chapter in this volume, one of the women in his study left the Catholic Church because the church community with which she was involved placed so much emphasis on helping her to raise her economic status and feed her family that she received no spiritual nourishment. Burdick (1993: 78) makes a similar point when he notes that many of the illiterates who left the local base community group converted to the Pentecostal church because of the Pentecostal emphasis on experience and mystery rather than political and intellectual understanding (according to Smilde's contribution to this volume, however, some evangelical and Pentecostal churches are becoming more politically active and aware). A similar sentiment was found among the Umbandistas of São Jorge. According to one Umbanda spirit medium, the Catholic priests denounce Umbanda because they are jealous: "[T]hey have all their learning, and that has killed the spiritual part. They want to get it back and have it like us" (Burdick 1993: 52).

More importantly, however, the base communities were now part of a pluralistic religious environment in which they were but one of many options. While the base communities had more autonomy than the institutional Church, and an increased capacity to respond to people's individual needs, they were in competition with many other religious movements capable of doing the same thing. Given the small number of pastoral workers available to put the base community concept into practice—compared to the often much larger number of Protestant pastors—it was difficult for the base communities to compete in the long run. The level of competition was perhaps further increased by Vatican II's message that the Church needed to learn from the world and work alongside other organizations for the betterment of humanity. This new attitude helped to create an atmosphere of openness in which pluralism could more easily survive and grow.

The current retrenchment of the Church is in part a reaction to the base community movement's inability to stem the tied of pluralization. It is a reaction to the openness of Vatican II, an attempt to reassert the authority of the hierarchical Church, and, according to Haas' contribution to this volume, an attempt to defend traditional Catholic morality and values in a changing world. But at the very time that the Church is trying to do this, its own internal divisions appear to be widening. Conservatives now compete with liberationists, progressives, and the Catholic charismatics who have begun imitating the emotional style of worship promoted by the Pentecostals. As Marjo de Thieje makes clear in her contribution to this volume, the growing diversity within the Catholic Church has even lead to strange new permutations in which people become both Catholic charismatics and members of a base community. The tide of pluralization is thus spreading among the ranks of the Catholic Church itself, bringing with it the near inevitability of further change.

This emphasis on the explosion of pluralization, and the retrenchment of the institutional Catholic Church could almost lead one to believe that the Catholics have somehow failed and are now a minority religion in Latin America. Thus, it is important to emphasize that the majority of Latin Americans still consider themselves Catholic, and that the Church has not failed in its mission. It has simply become part of a religious and cultural process in which people seek diverse faiths to meet a range of material, social, and spiritual needs that have been expanding rapidly as a result of urbanization and industrialization.

It is also important to reemphasize the fact that the progressive Catholic Church remains alive and well in Latin America, despite the decline of the base community movement. As Kristin Norget and Sarah Brooks make clear in their contributions to this volume, the progressive church has been transformed in accordance with changes in the local religious and political environment. Progressive priests have changed their strategies, and perhaps even their theological interpretations, but the progressive movement as a whole has continued.

To summarize, Latin America is experiencing a major pluralization of religious faith. This is a phenomenon that extends far beyond the more commonly recognized explosion of Protestantism, and the alleged demise of liberation theology, to include a growing range of non-Christian faiths. These developments have even affected the very fabric of the Catholic Church itself, and are promoting growing competition within the already diverse Protestant community. According to Finke and Stark, once the process of pluralization begins, the only way in which it might be reversed is through external repression and the promulgation of a single official faith. Barring such an event, the religious environment of Latin America is likely to become more pluralized in the future. The changes that began in the nineteenth century are likely to have a very long–lasting impact.

With such rapid and profound changes taking place within this pluralistic Latin American religious environment, our understanding of religion in the region requires continual reconsideration and updating. Some of our existing beliefs and assumptions about religion there are obsolete. The chapters in this volume represent one part of the larger scholarly attempt to delve into this rapidly changing field, broaden our perspectives, and update old knowledge and ideas. Most importantly, by bringing together articles on a variety of religious movements and traditions, we hope to convey a better sense of the magnitude and complexity of this process of pluralization, and to encourage further exploration of some traditions that have thus far been relatively understudied.

REFERENCES

Burdick, John. 1993. *Looking for God in Brazil*. Los Angeles: University of California Press.

Clarke, Peter. 1995. "The Cultural Impact of New Religions in Latin America and Central America and the Caribbean with Special Reference to Japanese New Religions." In *Journal of Latin American Cultural Studies*, 4 (1), 117-126.

Daudelin, Jean and Hewit, W. E. 1995. "Latin American Politics: Exit the Catholic Church?" In Satya Pattnayak (ed.) *Organized Religion in the Political Transformation of Latin America*. New York: University Press of America.

Finke, Roger and Stark, Rodney. 1992. *The Churching of America, 1776-1990: Winners and Losers in Our Religious Economy*. New Brunswick, NJ: Rutgers University Press.

Froehle, Bryan. 1995. "Religious Competition in Contemporary Venezuela." In Satya Pattnayak (ed.) *Organized Religion in the Political Transformation of Latin America*. New York: University Press of America.

Gill, Lesley. 1993. "Religious Mobility and the Many Words of God in La Paz, Bolivia." In Virginia Garrard-Burnett and David Stoll (eds.) *Rethinking Protestantism in Latin America*. Philadelphia: Temple Unviersity Press.

Ireland, Rowan. 1993. "The *Crentes* of Campo Alegre and the Religious Construction of Brazilian Politics." In Virginia Garrard-Burnett and David Stoll (eds.) *Rethinking Protestantism in Latin America*. Philadelphia: Temple Unviersity Press.

Martin, David. 1990. *Tongues of Fire: The Explosion of Protestantism in Latin America*. Cambridge, MA: Basil Blackwell.

Smith, Brian. 1982. *The Church and Politics in Chile: Challenges to Modern Catholicism*. Princeton, NJ: Princeton University Press.

Smith, Christian. 1991. *The Emergence of Liberation Theology: Radical Religion and Social Movement Theory*. Chicago: University of Chicago Press.

Smith, Christian, et al. 1998. *American Evangelicalism: Embattled and Thriving*. Chicago: University of Chicago Press.

Wuthnow, Robert. 1989. *Communities of Discourse*. Cambridge: Harvard University Press.

ONE

THE STRUGGLE TO BE SOUL PROVIDER
CATHOLIC RESPONSES TO PROTESTANT GROWTH
IN LATIN AMERICA

Anthony Gill[1]

Since the publication of landmark works by David Stoll (1990) and David Martin (1990), the focus of scholarship on Latin America's religious landscape has shifted away from the study of Catholicism, most notably the progressive Church, to the rapid expansion of evangelical Protestantism. While research on this "new" phenomenon[2] has taught us a great deal about the socioeconomic and political effects that Protestantism has had on Latin American society (cf. Hallum 1996, Brusco 1995, Mariz 1994), it generally has ignored how Protestantism has affected the Roman Catholic Church directly.[3] This is unfortunate given that the Catholic Church remains the largest *single* religious institution within the region and continues to wield a great deal of political and social clout. If we are to get a full picture of how religious practice and belief is being transformed, as well as how religion is influencing social and political relations more generally, we need to understand how the Roman Catholic Church has responded to what may be perhaps the greatest challenge to its cultural hegemony—evangelical Protestantism.

Using the analogy of a monopoly firm reacting to increased market competition, this essay will argue that the hierarchy of the Catholic Church, as represented by its top ecclesiastic leaders (i.e., the pope and bishops), has developed a two-pronged strategy to deal with the growth of evangelical Protestantism (*evangélicos*) and other non-Catholic religions.[4] First, bishops have sought government assistance in dealing with this competitive "threat." Similar to older industries seeking tariff protection and public subsidies to deal with more efficient upstarts, the Catholic hierarchy has asked national and local governments to implement policies that raise the costs of proselytizing for non-Catholic denominations while subsidizing the evangelizing activities of their own institution. Second, Church officials have pursued a strategy of institutional restructuring to become more efficient at maintaining parishioners and converting nominal Catholics into active participants in the faith. Like a corporate firm trying to retool, this is a long-term and costly strategy for the Church. However, while the former strategy is a more attractive and less costly option in the short run, the ability of the Catholic Church to retain a dominant presence in Latin American society rests upon the latter. Ironically, the increase in religious pluralism and competition likely will result in a Catholic Church that is institutionally stronger and more connected to the needs of its parishioners than at any time during its 500-year history in the Western Hemisphere. Empirical evidence supporting this argument will be culled from general trends across the region with specific attention to Argentina and Mexico, two countries that were comparatively immune from evangelical Protestant growth until the 1980s.

PROTESTANTISM: A THREAT TO CATHOLICISM?

Before examining Catholic responses to Protestant growth in detail, it is first necessary to establish whether, and to what extent, Catholic leaders perceive evangelical Protestantism as a credible threat to their religious hegemony. At its foundation, the Catholic Church is an evangelizing religion that wants to reach a universal audience with its holy message (cf. Conferencia Episcopal Argentina 1987, 9; Conferencia Episcopal Latinoamericana 1991, 301). To the extent that other religious organizations present a message contrary to Catholicism, they represent an implicit challenge to that universal, evangelizing mission. This challenge is aggravated to the degree that non-Catholic religions aggressively seek converts among nominal (and active) Catholic populations. Even in the post–Vatican Council II era, when cultivating ecumenical relations with non-Catholic faiths has taken on greater importance, denominations that actively recruit members from the Catholic Church quickly raise the ire of bishops and priests.

That Catholic officials consider Protestantism to be a serious regional threat is evident from statements made by various members of the Church hierarchy, from the pontiff to the parish clergy. Addressing the Fourth General Conference of Latin American Bishops in Santo Domingo (1992), Pope John Paul II referred to *evangélicos* as nothing short of predators:

> Like the Good Shepherd, you [the Latin American bishops] are to feed the flock entrusted to you and defend it from *rapacious wolves*. A source of division and discord in your ecclesial communities are—as

you well know—the sects and "psuedospiritual" movements mentioned in the Puebla Conclusions, whose aggressiveness and expansion must be faced (John Paul II 1993, 47-48, emphasis added).[5]

Papal concern is not new. As early as 1955, Pope Pius XII publicly stated that the advance of Protestantism was one of the "mortal dangers" facing Latin America (Vitalis 1969, 3/1). That the spread of *evangélicos* generates substantial attention within the Holy See (Comisión Nacional de Ecumenismo 1989, 96-97) indicates that it is a topic that is taken seriously among Church strategists.

Regionally, the Latin American Bishops' Conference (CELAM) understands this phenomenon in terms of direct competition for the souls of the population. In an extensive document directly addressing the "invasion of the sects," CELAM stated that "[t]he presence and increasing advance of various sects or religious groups in Latin America represents a grave pastoral problem" (Conferencia Episcopal Latinoamericana 1984, 276). At the national level, Catholic episcopacies show even greater awareness of the competitive threat posed by *evangélicos*, often accusing these movements of destroying the religious culture of their countries. For example, the Mexican "Catholic hierarchy accused the 'sects' of being 'de-nationalisers, propagators of an alien faith, and destroyers of national values and civic duties'" (Latin American Weekly Report 1991, 9). The official pastoral plan of the Mexican bishops' conference for 1996-2000 explicitly states that *evangélicos* "constitute a serious pastoral concern," and that "it is necessary to lead Catholics to a personal devotion to Christ and for the Church to *respond to the attack of the sects and new religious groups*" (Conferencia del Episcopado Mexicano 1996, emphasis added).

Statements and pastoral activities at the parish level further underscore how serious the Catholic Church takes Protestantism as a competitive threat. Local priests urge parishioners to put signs on their doors declaring "*hogar Católica*" (Catholic home) so as to discourage door-to-door recruitment by certain denominations (e.g., Mormons). Catholic parishes in Mexico provide small pamphlets at the entrance of their buildings warning parishioners of the dangers of Protestantism (see various pamphlets by Sembrador, n.d.), a practice common in many other Latin American countries. The Catholic hierarchy in Bolivia has prepared a manual to instruct pastoral workers and laity how to deal with the "challenge of the sects" (Damen 1988). All told, the Catholic Church views Protestantism as an increasingly serious threat to its religious, cultural, and institutional presence in Latin America. Given this perception, the question now arises: how can the Church best respond to this challenge?

CATHOLIC RESPONSES TO PROTESTANTISM

To understand how Catholic leaders have responded to Protestant expansion in the region, it is useful to view the Church through the lens of microeconomic theory as a monopoly firm reacting to the presence of more efficient entrants into the market for religious goods and services.[6] At first, such an approach seems misplaced given that religious leaders deal with "otherworldly" concerns and not the more "materialistic" concerns of economics. With regards to this observation, a group of economists who study the medieval Catholic Church note that there exists a

> long-standing tradition that asserts that religious organizations are principally motivated by "other-worldly" interests (e.g., salvation). In this older intellectual tradition, the internal workings of religious organizations are treated as "epiphenomena," or outside the interests of self-interested maximization, primarily because religious belief is defined as a fundamental, faith-driven commitment to a system of ideas, norms, and values that lie beyond the calculus of rational choice. Spiritual considerations notwithstanding, decisions within religious organizations are made by human beings living in a worldly environment (Ekelund et al. 1996, 4).

This "worldly environment" imposes certain constraints on individuals, namely the constraint of resource scarcity. Religious organizations, like the Catholic Church, do not have limitless financial and human resources at their disposal to apply toward their evangelizing mission. As such, leaders of these organizations will have to decide how to use their available resources to meet their institutional objectives in the best (i.e., most efficient) way possible. Religious organizations that waste valuable resources will be less effective in evangelizing a population relative to organizations that are more efficient, *ceteris paribus*.[7] To the extent that bishops respond to institutional incentives such as preserving and expanding their organization—and there is good reason to believe they do—economic theory will be useful in understanding at least some portion of ecclesiastic decision-making.

As noted above, one of the most fundamental objectives of the Church is to provide salvation, its principal product,[8] to as many people as possible. Economically speaking, Catholic bishops are market share maximizers. For most of its existence, the Latin American Church has existed as a monopoly, frequently with the explicit guarantee of the state. For a firm primarily interested in maximizing market share, a guaranteed monopoly can have deleterious effects on the *quantity* and *quality* of the product it delivers to its customer base (Iannaccone 1991, 159). The Latin American Catholic Church is no exception. Historically, it has failed to provide regular services to a substantial portion of its parishioners. This problem has been related inextricably to the low quantity of priests in the region (Poblete 1965). It was (and is) not uncommon for a priest to visit a rural village once every six to twelve months. This represents a serious shortfall in the supply of religious goods (e.g., the sacraments) to consumers.

Maryknoll priest William J. Coleman, commenting on the 1953 Chimbote Conference of Catholic Action leaders, noted that it was not just a low supply of religious personnel that was a problem, but that the *quality* of religious services had suffered as well.

> [T]he average person in Latin America receives only an appalling minimum of religious instruction, and is a nominal Catholic for that reason. Though born and baptized and even reared in the Catholic Faith, he inherits a traditional and devitalized form of Catholicism, often with a curious mixture of religious sentiments and practices that bears no relation to the real substance of his Faith. [T]here is a lack of clergy and other means of giving the proper amount of instruction; but the [Chimbote] delegates agreed that the problem is deeper than this lack of means. It is a question of the kind of religious instruction that is given—and much religious instruction is actually given. The caliber of religious teaching is low, much lower than that current in the other intellectual disciplines (Coleman 1958, 21).

As indicated here, the monopoly status of the Latin American Church provided only a nominal veneer of Catholicism for a large portion of the population. The quantity and quality of the "religious product" suffered, making it vulnerable to upstart competitors.

The entrance of alternative religious providers (e.g., evangelical Protestants) into Latin America exposed the weakness and inefficiencies of the monopoly Church to the clergy and bishops. As one Chilean priest observed in the 1940s,

> One of the causes of the success of [the Protestant] campaign in Chile is the lack of religious cultivation of our popular masses. They are sheep without pastors. . . . The responsibility for the success of the Protestant campaign in Chile belongs to the Catholics who have not knowingly cultivated their church. . . . Protestantism in Chile lives on our errors: it grows where Catholic life has been uncared for and nourishes the Christian nature of our people (Hurtado 1992, 83, 91).

Cardinal Raúl Silva of Chile also made the connection between the monopoly status of the Church, the consequent poor quantity and quality of Catholic religious services, and the growth of evangelical Protestantism.

> We can attribute such increase [in Protestantism] to several reasons. One is the genuine need of the masses for religious experience, which

our own ministry has not been able to satisfy fully because of the scarcity of priests at times; because of the aloofness with which some pastors deal with the laity at other times; and mostly because we have based our pastoral action on the assumption that ours is a secure Christianity (Quoted in Vitalis 1969, 8/7).

These concerns have been echoed by others with first hand knowledge of the region's religious landscape (cf. Conferencia Episcopal de Chile 1992; Damen 1988; Poblete 1965).

Given the Catholic Church's laxity in satisfying religious demand in their countries, Protestants, once they turned their attention to the region, found it fairly easy to expand. In terms of their ability to proselytize, Protestants possess a number of advantages over the Catholic Church. First, several Protestant missionary organizations receive funds and personnel from foreign sources. Early missionary movements such as the Latin American Mission, as well as ones that are active currently (e.g., the Mormons, Jehovah's Witnesses), are prime examples of groups supported externally. Catholic bishops consider this to be a prime advantage for *evangélicos* (Conferencia Episcopal Latinoamericana 1984, 35). However, the majority of evangelical growth in the region is among indigenous churches, mostly Pentecostal, that have minimal connections with foreign organizations. As Hurtado observed as far back as the 1930s, the "majority of the money that they [Pentecostals] earn in Chile is from Chileans. The Pentecostals . . . do not rely solely on foreign pastors and they cover all their expenses with tithes and offerings gathered from among their faithful" (Hurtado 1992, 84). Berryman (1994, 9) also notes that *evangélicos* receive most of their financial support from domestic parishioners, more so than the Catholic Church, which receives substantial resources from the United States and Europe.[9] Since the vast majority of Protestant growth in Latin America represents indigenous variations of Pentecostalism, the Church is primarily faced with a problem of domestic competition, a situation that will have a dramatic impact on how national Catholic episcopacies respond to the situation.

Another significant advantage for *evangélicos* is their decentralized nature. While some denominations (e.g., Assemblies of God, Universal Church) maintain umbrella organizations for their ministries (Lehmann 1996, 128-29), many Pentecostal churches operate as independent units with no (or minimal) overarching bureaucratic organization. These individual churches often have lower overhead costs pertaining to such things as building maintenance and personnel. Catholic leaders are well aware of these advantages. Writing for the regional bishops' conference, Fathers Osvaldo Santagada and Humberto Muñoz protested separately that evangelical "groups are not obligated to maintain ancient colonial church buildings, as many Catholic parishes must" while Pentecostal "chapels or 'temples' are almost always very humble" (Conferencia Episcopal Latinoamerica 1984, 35 and 148). Pentecostals are also advantaged by low training costs for their clergy, which allows them to field more pastoral workers in less time than the Catholic Church (Gill 1995a). By 1985, and over the course of just a few decades, the number of Protestant pastors exceeded the number of Catholic priests in Brazil, the world's most populous "Catholic" nation (Martin 1990, 50-51). A greater number of ministers and worship sites helps to explain why *evangélicos* have been able to recruit more active parishioners than the Catholic Church in a relatively short period of time (see Stewart-Gambino 1992, 14-15). In Brazil, the number of active Protestants equals, if not exceeds, the number of practicing Catholics (Berryman 1994, 7).

Thus, in many respects, evangelical Protestants represent a more efficient, domestic competitor to the Catholic Church. When faced with more efficient competition, less efficient monopoly firms have two fundamental responses at their disposal. First, they can ask for government assistance in either prohibiting competitors from entering (or imposing exceedingly high costs on competitive entry) or subsidizing the production costs of the less efficient, monopoly firm. The use of tariff barriers, import quotas and other regulatory measures has an immediate impact in limiting foreign competitive pressure faced by domestic firms. Subsidies likewise allow the firm to stay afloat in the short term until a more permanent solution to deal with increased competition can be found. The second alternative available to less efficient firms is to restructure their organizations in such a way that they are as efficient or more efficient than their competitors. Such a strategy usually involves high costs that firms simply cannot bear due to lack of investment capital. Moreover, the lengthy time frame involved in institutional restructuring presents a substantial risk that by the time the process is completed, the competition may have destroyed the consumer base of the firm. This is especially true for complex organizations with entrenched bureaucratic interests. As members of bureaucracies often have a stake in preserving the status quo, they have a strong incentive to resist changes that threaten their institutional position. In reality, firms are likely to pursue both strategies, hoping for support in the short term to ease the costs of institutional restructuring and shore up a competitive advantage in the long run. To the extent that the Roman Catholic Church can be viewed as a firm, particularly one interested in maximizing market share as compared to financial profit,[10] we should expect to see Catholic bishops pursuing a similar mixed strategy of government protection/subsidization as well as organizational restructuring. The long-term success of these strategies depends both upon endogenous factors—namely, the ability of the Church to overcome institutional barriers to restructuring—and exogenous factors—the relative efficiency of competitive denominations at recruiting parishioners and the preferences of religious consumers.

CATHOLIC RESPONSE I:
SEEKING PROTECTION AND SUBSIDIZATION

The initial expansion of evangelical Protestantism in Latin America came from foreign faith missions in the early twentieth century. The opportunity for these groups to gain entry into the region actually developed in the 1800s when liberal governments introduced freedom of worship into national constitutions. Protestants were slow in coming since they considered the region already to be Christian and focussed instead on Asia. As political conflict heated up in Asia during the 1930s and 1940s, raising the costs of proselytizing in that region, missionary activities were redirected to Latin America (Gill 1998, 82). For its part, the Catholic Church responded to this influx by asking governments to restrict the entry of foreigners seeking to proselytize. Brazilian president Getúlio Vargas withheld visas from U.S. missionaries during the 1940s at the behest of the nation's episcopacy (Pierson 1974, 177). In similar manner, the Colombian government complied with the request of bishops by signing a Concordat with the Vatican in 1953 guaranteeing that more than three-fourths of the country would be designated for Catholic evangelization only (Goff 1968, 3/27-36). During most of Juan Perón's administration in Argentina (1945-55), Catholic bishops saw an opportunity to limit the expansion of non-Catholic missionary organizations. A pastoral letter issued on January 25, 1945 by the Argentine bishops declared:

> The right of Protestants and dissidents to have their religious exercise respected and not be persecuted does not give them the right to proselytize. These religious civil liberties and tolerance of all religions, guaranteed in the Constitution for all inhabitants of the country, is something very distinct from [the] absolute religious liberty claimed by Protestant missionaries (Canclini 1972, 107).

The government responded to Catholic requests to make Protestant missionary activity a more costly endeavor by forbidding non-Catholic evangelization among native populations, by prohibiting evangelical radio broadcasting, and by increasing the monitoring of non-Catholic religious activities (Canclini 1972, 73-154).[11]

While Protestant growth in the first half of the twentieth century was driven mostly by foreigners, and hence could be dealt with by restricting missionary entry and activities in a country, Protestantism established itself as a mostly domestic phenomenon in the latter half of the 1900s. This presented a new dilemma for the Catholic Church since governments had less incentive to evict their own citizens. In fact, many governments saw Protestant activity as beneficial in that these groups often provided social welfare to many among the poor and were largely apolitical (until recently).[12] Nonetheless, Catholic Church leaders exerted substantial pressure on various governments throughout the region to enact legislation that would raise the cost of proselytizing for these domestic Protestant churches. Since the success of Protestant evangelists is dependent upon their ability to contact potential converts, anything preventing pastor-parishioner contact slows their progress, something the Catholic hierarchy knew very well and sought via government regulation of evangelical churches.

The legislation being pushed by the Catholic Church have commonly included registration laws and restrictions on property rights (for buildings or media). Mexico, a country that has seen an expansion of evangelical Protestantism in the past decade, offers a clear example of this strategic response to increased competition.

> The Mexican government has begun strictly to enforce registration laws among Protestant evangelical churches in the central state of Hidalgo. On March 13 [1991] the state's director of government, Beatriz Franco, notified Aroldo Espinoza, president of the 1,000-congregation Independent Pentecostal Christian Church, that all evangelical church buildings lacking proper registration documents as religious centers would be closed within two weeks. Mexico's constitution states that all churches and any structure used to perform the sacraments of a religious faith, even private homes, must be registered with the government. After registration they become property of the state, and unregistered facilities are subject to confiscation. . . . [Espinoza] said churches have not registered because the process involved is often very laborious and time-consuming. Some churches are forced into securing construction permits as educational centers first, then soliciting status as religious centers (Christian Century 1991, 648).

This crackdown on churches in Mexico came at a time when the Catholic Church, led by papal nuncio Gerónimo Prigione, was negotiating a change in religious laws that would allow for greater liberty for the Catholic Church (Gill 1995b). Msgr. Prigione, a long time opponent of Mexican evangelicals, was quoted by one news source as saying that the "sects, like flies, have to be removed" (Scott 1992, 14). The Mexican government, seeking episcopal endorsement of the controversial North American Free Trade Agreement and political support more generally, obliged the Church's wishes.

> [T]he Roman Catholic hierarchy has been making a determined effort to attract the state's support in its contest with the evangelicals—mainly by playing on the old theme of Catholic radicals and leftwingers generally, that the 'sects' are part of a CIA-sponsored plot to impose the 'American way of life'. . . . As 1990 came to a close, the Catholic bishops seemed to be succeeding. Officials at the interior ministry announced that the government would be sponsoring a campaign to counter the 'pernicious' influence of 'some sects' (Latin American Weekly Report 1991, 9).

Although the national government has listened to the concerns of evangelical organizations, religiously motivated attacks against Protestants are rarely prosecuted by local officials (Christianity Today 1990, 60-61).[13]

While the eventual constitutional changes of 1992 opened the country for greater religious freedom for all faiths in Mexico, the Catholic Church has negotiated a more preferential position. The new legislation allows for legally recognized religions to proselytize freely. However, obtaining legal recognition is not easy.

> For example, to qualify as a legal church or "religious association," a group must have been active in Mexico for at least five years and must have "well-known roots" in society. The group also must have "sufficient property" to meet church needs. "In business terms," [Roberto] Blancarte [president of the Center for Religious Studies in Mexico] says, "the government is declaring Mexico a closed market to all new religious movements" (Scott 1992a, 6. See also Gill 1995b).

Since property ownership for religious organizations, including the Catholic Church, was illegal until 1992, this essentially gives the government wide, and somewhat arbitrary, latitude in determining what religions will be legally recognized, a policy that the Catholic Church has favored its own recognition is solidly guaranteed.

A similar strategy of trying to raise the costs of proselytizing to *evangélicos* has been pursued in Argentina. Protestant growth in Argentina has been slower than in most Latin American countries, owing in large part to close church-state relations and a privileged legal status for the Catholic Church (Gill 1998, 149-71).[14] During the most recent military government (1976-83), the Catholic Church convinced the junta to enact laws banning outright a number of religious groups considered to be aggressively expansionary, including the Jehovah's Witnesses and Hare Krishna (see Foreign Broadcast Information Service 1978).[15] Decree 2037 of August 23, 1979 increased the regulatory power of the National Registry of Religion [Culto], a government agency charged with the task of registering and monitoring the activities of all religious organizations except the Roman Catholic Church, which is exempt from registering. Religious organizations were given 90 days to complete updated forms or lose legal status within the country.[16]

A modification to this law allowing for voluntary registration of religious organizations was debated in 1992 and 1993, with the Catholic Church arguing for strict definitions of what counted as religions. However, "voluntary" registration applied to those organizations that could meet one of four criteria:

1. Credibly demonstrate an effective presence in three provinces.
2. Be an official religion of state that maintains diplomatic relations with Argentina.[17]
3. Credibly demonstrate a secular presence in the country.
4. Credibly demonstrate a number of followers equivalent to 10% of the population on the province in which it is located (de Vedia 1992).

Since it was difficult for any new or small, independent religious groups (such as many Pentecostal churches) to meet any of these criteria, registration would have continued to be de facto law. The legislation debated in 1992-93 did not pass the House of Deputies, thus mandatory registration continued to be required.

Although registration gives religious organizations several advantages—e.g., exemption of religious ministers from military service, inviolability of religious temples and access to the broadcast media (Beladrich 1993) it also allows the government the power to determine what religious groups can exist within the country. While such governmental authority is common in most countries, it has caused a great deal of controversy in Argentina considering accusations by evangelical organizations that the government and Office of the Secretary of Religion is heavily pro-Catholic (*El Puente* 1995; Porcel 1993). Part of this controversy has involved media and government concerns over religious groups seen to be a "health hazard" because of their use of "mind control" and "spiritual healing" (see Frigerio 1996). Legislation was finally passed in 1995 with the approval of the Catholic Church that prohibited anyone designated as a religious minister from practicing medicine (Senado de la Nación 1995, 856), which effectively burdens Pentecostal (and other) churches that practice faith healing.

While the Catholic Church has been successful in placing costly barriers in front of evangelical religions in some cases, thereby slowing (but not preventing) the growth of Protestantism, this strategy has become increasingly less reliable as countries liberalize politically and society becomes more religiously pluralistic. Many politicians view evangelical Protestants as a potentially powerful and unified voting bloc and thus are reluctant to alienate them with anti-evangelical legislation (Gill 1995a). The electoral successes of Jorge Serrano (Guatemala) and Alberto Fujimori (Peru) were, in part, attributed to evangelical support (Berryman 1994, 10). Likewise, Ernesto Samper's presidential victory in Colombia owed much to the non-Catholic vote, and, to thank this group of supporters, Samper's Liberal party strengthened the constitutional right of religious freedom and declared that Roman Catholicism was no longer the country's official religion.[18] Samper's courting of Protestant support angered many within the Catholic hierarchy (Brooke 1994). *Evangélico* political activity has also been increasing in Mexico, a situation that has not gone unnoticed by the ruling elite (Delgado 1995).

If raising the costs of competitive entry into the religious marketplace is becoming an increasingly difficult strategy to rely on, the Catholic Church still has recourse to government subsidies that can be used to lower their production costs in some areas (e.g., building maintenance) and allow bishops to divert resources to other areas (e.g., Catholic charities, seminaries). This strategy has been quite evident in Mexico. Following the Mexican Revolution (1910-20), all religious buildings were seized and became property of the state. Not surprisingly, this initially created a great deal of tension between the Catholic Church and the state. But as relations improved under the administration of Lázaro Cárdenas (1934-40), the Church was allowed to use its former property to hold religious services and train clergy, free of charge. Constitutional and other legal changes in 1992 once again made it legal for religious organizations to own property, and all new churches built by the Catholic Church since that time are funded from the Church's coffers. However, the episcopacy has not asked the state to return its properties expropriated in the 1920s because doing so would mean transference of maintenance costs to the Church (as opposed to the state), something the Church simply cannot afford.[19] The rent-free use of state property represents a huge subsidy for the Catholic Church, which if ended would put a sizeable strain on its budget and make it less competitive with the low-cost operations of *evangélicos*.

Likewise in Argentina, the government is legally committed to paying the Catholic Church an annual stipend of approximately US $8.5 million (Criterio 1996, 39). Though this only amounts to less than 1 percent of the Church's total budget, it is 1 percent that non-Catholic religions do not enjoy. During the early 1990s, Nicaraguan President Violeta Chamorro gave the Catholic Church government land free of charge to reconstruct its national cathedral, damaged in a 1972 earthquake (Ruether 1993).[20] Throughout Latin America, Catholic bishops have been known to lobby hard for financial subsidization for parochial schools, charities, and other Catholic services (cf. Serbin 1995). The ability of the Church to rely upon this form of assistance is increasingly jeopardized by the fiscal crises that governments are facing in the region and the increasing reluctance of many politicians to show favoritism to one particular religious denomination, especially when electoral outcomes may hinge upon the voting power of religious minorities. With both protection and subsidization becoming increasingly unreliable options in the "battle with the sects," the Church has found itself with only one major alternative remaining—institutional restructuring.

CATHOLIC RESPONSE II:
INSTITUTIONAL REFORM AND THE "NEW EVANGELIZATION"

In economics, if a noncompetitive firm can no longer rely upon governmental assistance to combat more efficient entrants into the market, it has the choice of either liquidating the business or restructuring the company. For the Catholic Church, which considers its mission to be beholden to God (not stockholders), the former option is simply not conceivable.[21] Thus, if we are correct in assuming that evangelical Protestantism represents a serious threat to the Church and that other means of forestalling this advance are not working well, we should expect to see an increasing effort on the part of the ecclesiastical hierarchy to reform its institution in ways that are meant to keep people committed to the Catholic faith and reevangelize those who have strayed from the flock or have only nominal loyalty. This is what the theme of "New Evangelization" that dominated the 1992 Santo Domingo Conference of Latin American bishops was all about—institutional restructuring.

The introduction of institutional reforms to deal with competitive threats dates back to the early 1900s when various national Catholic Churches promoted the creation of *círculos obreros* (labor unions) and Catholic Action groups to deal with the appearance of socialist organizers (Gill 1998, 32-36 and 126-30). Many of these groups formed the basis (or served as inspiration) for what would later become the *comunidades eclesiales de base* (CEBs), or Christian base communities. CEBs were a radical innovation in the Catholic Church that emphasized greater lay involvement in religious services, participation of active Catholics in social activities (e.g., land rights movements), and tended toward greater decentralization within the ecclesiastical hierarchy (although clergy were still the primary organizers of these groups). These small communities resembled, and were in part a response to, Protestant missionary organizations in their emphasis on lay involvement and social activities such as Bible readings and literacy campaigns (Gill 1998, 100-04; Cook 1985).

In the contemporary period (1990s), the movement towards institutional (pastoral) reform has taken the form of the "New Evangelization," the theme of the 1992 Santo Domingo conference. This call to refocus the Latin American Church's resources and energy to winning back the faithful dates back to the pope's comments in Santo Domingo in 1984 (Conferencia Episcopal Argentina 1990, 10-11) and is a direct response to the "preoccupation of John Paul II about the sects" (Comisión Nacional de Ecumenismo 1989, 96). To understand how the "New Evangelization" represents a restructuring of the institutional Church and its priorities, it is useful to quote extensively from the official concluding document of the Fourth General Conference of Latin American Bishops held in Santo Domingo.[22] In general, the document states

> The expression "new evangelization" does not mean reevangelizing. In Latin America, the point is not to act as though there were no first evangelization but, rather, to start from the many rich values it has left in place and proceed to complement them by *correcting for previous shortcomings*. . . . It means taking up the magnificent endeavor of energizing Latin American Christianity. [24. Emphasis added.]

> Our situations require new approaches to evangelization. . . . [W]e must draw on imagination and creativity so that the gospel will reach everyone in a pedagogical and compelling way. [29]

Perhaps the most preeminent restructuring goal of "new evangelization" is to reach those who have had minimal contact with the institutional Church as a way of forestalling defections to alternative faiths.

> Prayer groups, apostolic movements, new forms of life and of contemplative spirituality, as well as various expressions of popular religiosity are spreading within the Church. . . . Interest in the Bible is growing, thus demanding a biblical pastoral activity adequate to offer the laity criteria for responding to the subtle accusations and appeals of a fundamentalist interpretation or to the tendency to

withdraw from life in the Church and take refuge in the sects. [38]

Achieving closer contact with the laity means putting more pastoral agents, including priests and lay catechists, in the field.

> As a rule, our dioceses do not have enough well-trained pastoral agents. Many do not yet have a genuine and clear pastoral planning process. [56]

> Hence it is absolutely necessary that we: Increase the number of people working in the various fields of pastoral action and provide them with adequate training. . . . Set in motion comprehensive, organic planning processes to encourage the involvement of all members of the people of God, of all communities, and all the various charisms. [57]

To remedy the shortage of priests, the Santo Domingo document noted that the "pope has invited us to devote attention to vocations from native peoples" [80], thus particular concern must be directed to the challenge represented by the priestly formation of those candidates who come from indigenous and African American cultures" [84]. Given that indigenous vocations have never been strongly encouraged by the Church,[23] this is a major shift in policy.

The organizational structure of the Church has also been put under scrutiny, including policies toward the deaconate.

> Our work must take the following directions: Renew parishes through structures that make it possible to subdivide pastoral activity into small church communities in which the responsibility of lay believers can come to the fore. Upgrade the formation and participation of the laity by training them to embody the gospel in the specific situations where they live or engage in activity. . . . Renew [parish] ability to display both a welcoming attitude and missionary drive toward those believers who remain afar, and multiply the physical presence of the parish by creating chapels and small communities. [60]

> We want to aid married deacons so that they may be faithful to their twofold sacramentality—that of matrimony and of holy orders—and . . . we propose to create the space necessary so that deacons may help in developing the services that the Church provides, by detecting and developing leaders, and promoting the shared responsibility of all in working toward a culture of reconciliation and solidarity. [77]

And despite the efforts of John Paul II to restrict the activities of some, politically active lay activists the Latin American bishops still endorse the concept of CEBs.

> We see a need to: Reaffirm the validity of basic Christian communi-

ties by developing in them a spirit of mission and solidarity and seeking to integrate them into the parish, the diocese, and the universal Church, in keeping with the teachings of *Evangelii Nuntiandi*. Develop plans for pastoral activity to strengthen the training of the lay leaders who weave these communities in close communion with the pastor and the bishop. [63]

When they lack a clear ecclesiological foundation and are not sincerely seeking communion, such communities cease being ecclesial and may fall victim to ideological or political manipulation. [62]

The Church in Latin America, at the behest of the Vatican, is trying to both decentralize its operations to reach more parishioners at the grassroots level and give the clergy autonomy to innovate organizationally, but at the same time increase hierarchical control over the clergy via the expansion of dioceses. This juggling act is not unlike the restructuring of an inefficient firm that seeks to promote innovation on the shop floor while simultaneously monitoring the productivity of its employees.

Promoting institutional reform has been on the top of John Paul II's agenda since attending the 1979 Third General Conference of the Latin American Bishops in Puebla, Mexico. Data on Church personnel and institutional structure indicate that most Latin American episcopacies have made significant strides in this direction, though the overall news remains mixed. Table 1 reveals the weakness in pastoral outreach as most countries have less than two priests for every 10,000 people. Moreover, there has been a significant decline in the ratio of priests to population from 1977 to 1997, most significantly influenced by high population growth rates, an aging clergy, and the inability to replace retiring clergy at a one-to-one ratio. However, the Catholic Church has made dramatic progress in recruiting seminarians under John Paul II's tenure as pope.[24] The number of seminarians to total population tripled for Latin America as a whole between 1977 and 1997. The replacement ratios, which can be read as the number of seminarians in training that are available to replace one retiring priest, reinforce the notion that the Catholic Church has made substantial headway in promoting future personnel needs. However, replacement ratios for all countries are less than 1.0, indicating that the Church is still losing ground in trying to meet the needs of a growing population. For example, the Argentine Church in 1997 could only replace roughly 34 percent of its retiring priests with new clergy, a situation that does not bode well for head-to-head competition with an expanding evangelical ministry. The shrinking ranks of the clergy means that the Church will be under greater pressure to rely upon foreign priests and lay activists if it wants to pursue effectively the objectives of the "new evangelization."

TABLE 1
CATHOLIC PERSONNEL IN LATIN AMERICA

	Priests per 10,000 population					Seminarians per 10,000 population					Replacement Ratio				
	1977	1982	1987	1992	1997	1977	1982	1987	1992	1997	1977	1982	1987	1992	1997
Argentina	1.93	1.84	1.85	1.76	1.73	0.13	0.34	0.65	0.69	0.59	0.07	0.18	0.35	0.39	0.34
Bolivia	1.45	1.33	1.36	1.29	1.48	0.14	0.15	0.29	0.53	0.74	0.09	0.11	0.21	0.41	0.50
Brazil	1.16	1.21	1.03	0.94	1.00	0.09	0.34	0.44	0.41	0.44	0.08	0.28	0.42	0.43	0.44
Chile	1.96	1.74	1.85	2.08	1.65	0.15	0.37	0.86	0.64	0.54	0.08	0.21	0.46	0.31	0.33
Colombia	2.02	1.92	1.95	1.93	1.97	0.40	0.43	0.89	1.18	1.24	0.20	0.22	0.46	0.61	0.63
Costa Rica	1.98	1.86	1.94	1.96	2.16	0.43	0.49	1.24	1.07	0.91	0.22	0.26	0.64	0.55	0.42
Cuba	0.21	0.20	0.21	0.21	0.21	0.05	0.04	0.05	0.03	0.05	0.23	0.21	0.23	0.13	0.26
Ecuador	1.88	1.72	1.66	1.51	1.53	0.11	0.11	0.32	0.52	0.66	0.06	0.07	0.19	0.34	0.43
El Salvador	1.04	0.79	0.75	0.85	0.93	0.11	0.20	0.25	0.47	0.57	0.11	0.25	0.33	0.55	0.62
Guatemala	1.21	1.01	0.83	0.75	0.81	0.15	0.12	0.39	0.51	0.54	0.13	0.12	0.47	0.67	0.67
Honduras	0.80	0.59	0.59	0.55	0.54	0.08	0.07	0.11	0.24	0.18	0.10	0.12	0.19	0.43	0.34
Mexico	1.69	1.38	1.35	1.34	1.34	0.42	0.38	0.56	0.68	0.73	0.25	0.28	0.42	0.51	0.54
Nicaragua	1.44	1.24	1.07	0.84	0.79	0.17	0.22	0.15	0.32	0.44	0.12	0.18	0.14	0.37	0.55
Panama	1.77	1.47	1.34	1.40	1.54	0.12	0.18	0.62	0.82	0.80	0.07	0.12	0.46	0.58	0.52
Paraguay	1.76	1.60	1.54	1.36	1.35	0.22	0.26	0.72	0.78	0.64	0.13	0.16	0.46	0.57	0.47
Peru	1.42	1.36	1.21	1.12	1.08	0.15	0.33	0.48	0.51	0.59	0.10	0.24	0.40	0.45	0.54
Uruguay	2.00	1.95	1.86	2.35	1.72	0.10	0.15	0.42	0.35	0.22	0.05	0.08	0.22	0.15	0.13
Venezuela	1.68	1.40	1.21	1.06	1.01	0.13	0.16	0.30	0.45	0.45	0.08	0.11	0.25	0.43	0.45
Latin America	1.47	1.37	1.28	1.23	1.24	0.19	0.32	0.51	0.57	0.59	0.13	0.23	0.40	0.46	0.48

Replacement ratio = (seminarians per 10,000)/(priests per 10,000).
Interpret as percentage of existing priests that can be replaced by seminarians.
Figures for Latin America represent weighted averages.
Source: *Catholic Almanac* (various years).

Table 2 indicates that the Church has been active in expanding its organizational framework. More bishops are being appointed and dioceses created all around Latin America, indicating that Church leaders are attempting to increase administrative control over smaller geographic subdivisions. Likewise, the number of parishes is increasing in every country, extending pastoral outreach to those who have not been adequately served by the Church in the past. Another indicator of the Church's attempt to touch the lives of more people is its expansion of Catholic welfare organizations (e.g., hospitals, old-age homes, and social and educational services).[25] Though table 2 does not show this, the greatest growth in Catholic welfare services has been among nurseries. The strategic logic here would be to expose new mothers to the benefits of the Catholic Church in the hopes that they and their children will develop long-term loyalties.[26]

TABLE 2
CATHOLIC INSTITUTIONAL RESOURCES

	Bishops					Parishes					Welfare Institutions			
	1977	1982	1987	1992	1997	1977	1982	1987	1992	1997	1982	1985	1988	1991
Argentina	56	67	69	77	83	1,979	2,148	2,234	2,427	2,466	810	1,025	1,326	1,559
Bolivia	16	19	20	25	30	434	NA	443	486	516	478	513	642	1,151
Brazil	228	239	305	313	308	6,033	6,423	6,872	7,605	7,966	5,290	7,766	8,803	7,998
Chile	24	23	29	35	32	784	803	815	849	919	1,676	1,783	2,046	1,676
Colombia	43	45	57	65	74	1,972	2,216	2,367	2,813	3,094	1,365	1,861	2,102	1,984
Costa Rica	4	5	5	8	7	145	163	176	216	227	133	143	152	147
Cuba	6	5	6	6	10	227	221	231	234	247	8	8	8	8
Ecuador	21	22	24	22	30	635	700	820	974	1,041	485	805	963	2,090
El Salvador	6	5	6	13	11	220	235	230	247	269	68	149	171	126
Guatemala	14	13	15	19	18	326	336	348	378	390	706	874	792	721
Honduras	6	5	7	7	7	114	124	122	126	143	91	108	363	101
Mexico	71	77	75	88	84	3,586	3,700	4,258	4,802	5,177	1,545	2,969	3,396	3,207
Nicaragua	6	6	9	10	8	173	185	181	202	198	83	88	95	96
Panama	6	7	6	8	11	127	136	144	179	175	28	56	62	66
Paraguay	9	14	15	15	17	236	260	282	324	325	345	535	548	646
Peru	36	40	44	63	47	1,160	1,144	1,250	1,306	1,407	757	1,130	2,915	4,272
Uruguay	10	10	11	12	13	NA	224	222	226	233	351	391	426	408
Venezuela	28	28	33	34	34	915	967	1,002	1,064	1,080	264	307	343	384
Latin America	590	630	736	820	824	19,066	19,985	21,997	24,458	25,873	16,465	22,496	27,141	28,631

Sources: *Catholic Almanac* (various years) for bishop and parish data.
Wilkie, *Statistical Abstract of Latin America* Vol. 32 (1995) for welfare data.
Catholic welfare institutions include hospitals, dispensaries, leprosarias, hospices,
orphanages, nurseries, educational centers, and other.

Despite efforts of bishops to reform their institution in a way that will make it more efficient at evangelizing parishioners and competitive with evangelical Protestantism, the Church is a large institution with an extended historical investment in a particular message. This creates sizeable barriers to effective reform. Considering that increasing clergy to match the expansion of the *evangélico* ministry is one of the Church's top priorities, it would seem logical to relax the celibacy requirements for the clergy and allow greater female involvement in administering the sacraments.[27] However, part of the Catholic theological message has been built around the doctrine of priestly celibacy and a male-dominated clergy. As Ekelund, et. al. note, since religion is a pure credence good,[28] "the acceptance of the Church as divinely sanctioned arbiter of earthly disputes . . . [derives] from the credibility of the religious doctrines promulgated by the Church of Rome" (1996, 26). Rapid changes in long-standing doctrines raise the possibility that parishioners will start doubting the credibility of the Church itself. The problem then is not so much with the issue of celibacy per se, but with the ability of the Church to maintain a consistent spiritual message. In recent years, Anglicans in both the Great Britain and the United States have witnessed a parishioner outflow to other faiths (primarily Catholic) due to dramatic changes in similar religious doctrines. It is likely that the Vatican understands this dilemma and is resisting changes in its celibacy and male clergy doctrines based on strategic considerations as much as ideological commitments.

The ability of the Catholic Church to expand its grassroots operations to counter evangelical growth also is limited by a major obstacle—the desire (or need) to maintain hierarchical control. Following Vatican Council II, which sought to liberalize the Church internally, grassroots Catholic organizations (e.g., CEBs) in Latin America began to openly challenge the ecclesiastical hierarchy. Lay activists and parish priests frequently endorsed and participated in revolutionary movements. Many of these movements extolled a Marxist worldview, something that Church leaders had long opposed. Reestablishing hierarchical control over these "renegade" groups has been a priority of the current papacy not only because of John Paul II's conservative ideology, as some have argued (e.g., Tangeman 1995), but because of the strategic need to preserve a consistent (hence credible) doctrine as indicated above. However, this argument ignores one of the greatest organizational strengths of the Catholic Church relative to their *evangélico* counterparts—the ability to offer a diverse array of "Catholicisms" under one institutional umbrella. It is remarkable to think that the Church can retain the loyalty of ultraconservative Catholics (e.g., members of Opus Dei) as well as left-wing liberation theologians. Granted, both the left and right struggle with one another to redefine the goals and objectives of the Church, but they do so while remaining Catholic. The Catholic Church may be able to retain a larger portion of the Latin American population in the long run largely because of this "diversity within unity." The promotion of "charismatic Catholicism" to appeal to parishioners who prefer more "Pentecostal" forms of worship (to the chagrin of more traditionalist clergy) is another example of how Church leaders are diversifying their product to meet the diverse tastes of their "customers" (cf. Nuñez and Taylor 1989, 283-307). All told, while the Church faces a number of institutional and doctrinal obstacles to institutional restructuring, making any significant changes relatively costly, it appears as if the Catholic episcopacy has begun to engage in long-term reforms. These reforms, most notably the push to increase membership in the religious vocations, will likely increase the active religious participation of a wider group in society.

CONCLUSION

In Latin America, a fierce battle currently rages as to who will provide for the souls of the population as we enter into the next century. The Catholic Church has long had the distinction of being the "sole provider" of spirituality to the region. Now, its monopoly position is being challenged in such a dramatic fashion that most bishops no longer take for granted the Catholicness of their flock. While this has provoked some episcopacies to seek limits on the religious freedom of evangelical churches, increased competition has had the beneficial impact of prodding the Catholic clergy into paying closer attention to the spiritual needs and desires of the people under their care. As politicians respond to the growing electoral clout of the *evangélicos*, demands for religious liberty and equal treatment under the law are likely to be taken more seriously. Not only will there be many "soul providers," but with the Catholic Church learning to live in an environment of increased religious pluralism, Latin America will likely undergo a spiritual renewal the likes of which it has never seen before.

NOTES

1 The author thanks Ivan Barron and Frank Donahoe for their excellent and timely research assistance.

2 It should be noted that although most research on evangelical Protestantism has been generated in the past decade, the phenomenon itself is not new. The beginning of rapid growth among evangelical denominations can be dated back to the 1930s and 1940s in countries such as Brazil and Chile. A number of other Central and South American countries witnessed the takeoff of Protestantism in the 1950s and 1960s. Damboriena (1963), Willems (1967) and Lalive d'Epinay (1967), were among the first scholars to write extensively on this subject, although their works did not gain widespread attention until the 1990s.

3 This in no way should be construed as a criticism of the excellent work that has been done to date on Latin American Protestantism. Given the complex nature of this phenomenon, it is difficult for any scholar to explore all dimensions of this topic. The objective of a scholarly community and of edited works such as this one is to provide a wide array of perspectives on the topic.

4 This chapter will focus largely on evangelical Protestantism defined loosely and broadly to mean any non-Catholic, Christ-centered religion that has an aggressive proselytizing mission. This definition includes Pentecostals (the majority of Latin American Protestants), Baptists, Seventh-Day Adventists, Mormons, Jehovah's Witnesses, and various nondenominational Christian organizations. Many social scientists and theologians undoubtedly will disagree with this broad definition and the inclusion of so many religions. However, for purposes of this paper this broad definition is suitable for rhetorical simplicity. In Latin America it is common to lump all non-Catholic, Christian (or quasi-Christian) churches into one category and call them *evangélicos*, a moniker used frequently by a variety of evangelical Protestants themselves (Stoll 1993, 3). Finally, what is said here with regards to Catholic responses to *evangélicos* is generally applicable to non-Christian religions in the region

(e.g., Umbanda, Spiritism). Many of these religions blend indigenous and African beliefs and practices with Catholicism to form unique brands of popular religiosity. The Catholic Church, especially parish priests, have been more willing to tolerate (and even promote) these forms of popular religiosity as a way of bringing people closer to the Catholic Church even though they are not officially Catholic in a doctrinal sense. Relations with *evangélicos*, which often identify themselves in contradistinction to Catholicism, are not as ecumenical.

5 The term "sects" (*sectas*) in Latin America refers to a wide range of non-Catholic religious groups including Pentecostals, Seventh-Day Adventists, Mormons, Jehovah's Witnesses, Spiritists and Afro-based movements such as Candomblé, Santería, and Umbanda. See Conferencia Episcopal Latinoamericana (1984) for an official Catholic coneptualization of the term "sects" in Latin America.

6 While this certainly is not the only analytical framework useful for understanding religious behavior and institutions, the "religious economy" school has been successful in explaining a wide range of phenomena. For an introduction to this approach see Young (1997), Iannaccone (1995), and Warner (1993).

7 The "ceteris paribus" clause controls for the demand preferences of consumers. If all consumers want one, and only one, type of religion, then that particular religious provider need not worry about competition. Demand for one brand of religion would be perfectly inelastic. Casual arguments have been made that Latin America is a "solidly" Catholic region, and that Catholicism is ingrained securely in the region's culture. Considering the undeniable growth of Protestantism, this argument is spurious, prima facie. Preferences for religious services vary among people, and demand appears to be somewhat, though not entirely, elastic (people will stick with their faith even though alternatives are available and they disagree with some aspects of their church).

8 Religious goods—e.g., eternal salvation, philosophical answers to life's difficult questions—are known as credence goods, meaning the quality of the good "is not easily determined before or after purchase" (Ekelund et. al., 1996, 13). Because of this inherent uncertainty surrounding quality, credence goods are inherently difficult to price. Given that quality perceptions will vary widely across a population, it would be difficult for priests to determine the market-clearing price for their services. Voluntary contributions solve this problem by allowing consumers to determine their own price based on their quality perceptions and demand for elasticity. Given that the voluntary payment mechanism for pricing religious goods is the most efficient way to capture revenue for this activity, it is difficult to speak of religious goods as being "sold." Nonetheless, clerics do set prices for many of their services that involve a tangible quantity of time and effort on their part (e.g, baptisms, weddings).

9 This support comes both in the form of financial resources (including assistance from Catholic charities such as CARE) and personnel (Stoll 1990, 35). In many Latin American countries, more than half the male clergy are foreigners from the United States or Europe (see Gill 1998, 86).

10 A firm interested in maximizing market share will be more sensitive to competition than a profit-maximizing firm. Although competitive entrants compete away monopoly rents, the established firm can still maintain a positive profit margin under lost market share. However, for an organization principally interested in market share, every customer lost cuts into the ultimate goal of the firm. To my knowledge, a proselytizing, universal church is the only example of a firm where market-share maximization takes ultimate precedence over profit maximization.

11 As relations between the Catholic Church and Perón deteriorated rapidly in 1954, the president relaxed restrictions on evangelicals, even allowing for a

Baptist radio broadcast (Canclini 1972, 292-317). Concurrently, subsidies for the Catholic Church were reduced.

12 Evangelical Protestants in Latin America historically have tended to stay out of political battles, either because their theology frowned upon involvement in such worldly activities or, more likely, because engaging in political partisanship as a minority group would make them targets for repression. As *evangélicos* have become more entrenched within local and national communities, they have become more politically active, often running candidates for political office, a trend that favors the latter hypothesis for their historical apoliticism. For a discussion of the growing political activism of Protestantism see the essays in Garrard-Burnett and Stoll (1993), particularly the essays by Burdick, Freston, and Coleman, et. al.

13 Reports of violence against *evangélicos* are not uncommon in Mexico, as confirmed by my personal interviews during the spring of 1992. On top of this, the U.S. Department of State's Report on Human Rights Abuses reported that "In the highlands of Chiapas and other indigenous areas, traditional leaders sometimes acquiesced in, or actually ordered, the expulsions of Protestants belonging primarily to evangelical groups. In many cases the expulsions involved the burning of homes and crops, beatings, and, occasionally, killings" (Department of State 1997). This should not be taken as evidence that Catholic officials endorse such activities; they do not. However, widespread religious persecution that goes unpunished by the government imposes significant expected costs upon religious minorities.

14 In 1966, Argentina was the last Latin American country to eliminate the *patronato*, a legal system dating back to the colonial period wherein the government had extensive control over Church affairs in exchange for guaranteed funding. In practice, the Church had power over its own affairs by the late nineteenth century, thus the *patronato* essentially guaranteed government funding, preferential access to education, and protection from competitive religions. The Catholic hierarchy wanted to formally end the *patronato* so as to eliminate a potential legal opening for governments to meddle in the selection of bishops and other Church affairs, even though the financial privileges (minimal as they may be) were kept intact.

15 See Decree 1867 (August 31, 1976) and Decree 18 (January 7, 1977) published in the *Boletín oficial de la Republica Argentina*.

16 See Decree 2037 (August 23, 1979) published in the *Boletín oficial de la Republica Argentina*.

17 While written in broad language, this obviously referred only to the Roman Catholic Church.

18 See Ley 133 (23 de mayo de 1994). *Diario oficial* (Colombia).

19 Author interview with Archbishop Rosendo Huesca. June 17, 1995, Puebla, Mexico.

20 The funding for the actual construction of the cathedral came from Domino's Pizza magnate Tom Monaghan.

21 This is not to say that religions cannot fail and vanish. Many do. However, the massive global presence of Catholicism today makes this an unlikely scenario. Nonetheless, the Vatican faced a severe fiscal crisis in the late 1970s and early 1980s (see Della Cava 1993). One could only speculate what would happen to global Catholicism should the Holy See declare bankruptcy.

22 The following quotes refer to the document "Conclusions: New Evangelization, Human Development, Christian Culture" found in Hennelly (1993, 71-155). The references in brackets refer to the paragraph of the original document.

23 There are, of course, many exceptions (e.g., Padre Hidalgo of Mexico), but the clergy has been overwhelmingly ladino for most of the Church's Latin American history.

24 It seems somewhat paradoxical that a papacy emphasizing stricter standards for its seminarians and clergy would be successful in recruiting clergy. However, Stark and Finke (1997) demonstrate that it is exactly the strictness that attracts recruits to religious vocations. The increase in seminary students in Argentina during the mid-1980s is remarkable given that the credibility of the Catholic Church was severely weakened by its public association with the country's previous military regime (Mignone 1988).

25 The numbers for welfare institutions in table 2 decrease between 1988 and 1991 for a number of countries, but remain higher than in 1982. These numbers are particularly sensitive to random disasters that call for the creation of temporary Catholic relief services. Despite this variability, there has been a general upwards trend in Catholic welfare institutions.

26 Iannaccone (1990) has argued from an economic perspective that early and constant exposure to a religion builds a stock of religious capital among individuals thereby decreasing the likelihood they will abandon the faith in the future. As for nurseries, the Church has enhanced its "early exposure," but will have to work on making that exposure constant.

27 Stark and Finke's (1997) argument may imply the opposite, given that the Catholic vocations that maintain the most rigorous requirements have been those that have been able to retain members and even grow. They argue, using time-series data from 1948, that Vatican Council II (1962-65) created disincentives for joining religious orders in that Vatican II reduced the social distinctiveness of being a member of the clergy while subsequently maintaining a number of the costs of being in a religious vocation. It is not clear whether celibacy is viewed as a cost or as a "badge of virtuousness and purity" that would yield social benefits to the individual.

28 Ekelund, et. al. define a credence good as a good "for which 'quality' is not easily determined before or after purchase. Reputation of the supplier is the primary assurance of quality" (1996, 13).

REFERENCES

Beladrich, Norberto. 1993. "Votarían antes de manyo la ley de libertad religiosa." *Clarín* (26 de enero): 11.

Berryman, Phillip. 1994. "The Coming of Age of Evangelical Protestantism." *NACLA Report on the Americas*, XXVII (6): 6-10.

Brooke, James. 1994. "Church issue muddles vote in Colombia: Archbishop suggests blank ballots be cast." *New York Times*, 19 June: 4.

Brusco, Elizabeth. 1995. *The Reformation of Machismo: Evangelical Conversion and Gender in Colombia*. Austin: University of Texas Press.

Canclini, Santiago. 1972. *Los evangélicos en el tiempo de Perón: Memorias de un pastor bautista sobre la libertad religiosa en la Argentina*. Buenos Aires: Mundo Hispano.

Christian Century. 1991. "Mexican Crackdown." *Christian Century*, 108 (26 June–3 July): 648.

Coleman, William. 1958. *Latin American Catholicism: A Self-Evaluation*. Maryknoll, NY: Maryknoll Publications.

Comisión Nacional de Ecumenismo. 1989. *Pentecostalismo, sectas y pastoral*. Santiago: Conferencia Episcopal de Chile.

Conferencia del Episcopado Mexicano. 1996. *Proyecto Pastoral de la CEM,*

1996-2000. Internet version. http://www.cem.org.mx/2000H.htm http://www.cem.org.mx/2000H.htm. Accessed 1 February 1998.

Conferencia Espiscopal Argentina. 1990. *Líneas Pastorales para la Nueva Evangelización.* Buenos Aires: Conferencia Episcopal Argentina, Oficina del Libro.

————. 1987. *Juntos para una evangelización permanente.* Buenos Aires: Conferencia Episcopal Argentina, Oficina del Libro.

Conferencia Episcopal de Chile. 1992. *Evangélicos y Sectas: Propuestas pastorales.* Santiago: Cencosep.

Conferencia Episcopal Latinoamericana. 1991. *La Evangelización en el presente y en el futuro de América Latina: Documento de Puebla.* Santiago: Conferencia Episcopal de Chile.

————. 1984. *Las sectas en América Latina.* Buenos Aires: Editorial Claretiana.

Cook, Guillermo. 1985. *The Expectation of the Poor: Latin American Base Ecclesial Communities in Protestant Perspective.* Maryknoll, NY: Orbis.

Criterio. 1996. "Editorial: La Iglesia, el dinero y el estado." *Criterio,* LXIX (2170): 39-41.

Damboriena, Prudencio. 1963. *El protestantismo en América Latina.* Fribourg, Switzerland: FERES

Damen, Franz. 1988. *El desafío de las sectas* (Serie "Fe y Compromiso" #5). La Paz: Secretariado Nacional de Ecumenismo.

de Vedia, Bartolomé. 1992. "La ley de libertad religiosa." *La Nación* [Argentina], (7 de septiembre).

Delgado, Alvaro. 1995. "Los evangélicos promueven un partido político para participar en las elecciones de 1997." *Proceso,* 995 (27 de noviembre): 39.

Della Cava, Ralph. 1993. "Financing the Faith: The Case of Roman Catholicism." *Journal of Church and State,* 35 (1): 37-59.

Department of State. 1998. *Country Reports on Human Rights Practices for 1997.* Internet publication. http://www.state.gov/www/global/human_rights/1997_hrp_report/mexico.html. Accessed 4 February 1998.

————. 1997. *Country Reports on Human Rights Practices for 1997.* Washington, D.C.: U.S. Government Printing Office.

Ekelund, Robert et al. 1996. *Sacred Trust: The Medieval Church as an Economic Firm.* Oxford: Oxford University Press.

El Puente. 1995. "Sigue la polémica por la libertad religiosa." *El Puente* [Argentina], (mayo): 14.

Foreign Broadcast Information Service. 1978. "Jehovah's Witnesses Banned." 16 February, B3.

Frigerio, Alejandro. 1996. "Religion as a social problem: Chancing 'cult' images in Argentina." Paper presented at the 46th Annual Meeting of the Society for the Study of Social Problems, New York.

Garrard-Burnett, Virginia and David Stoll, eds. 1993. *Rethinking Protestantism in Latin America.* Philadelphia: Temple University Press.

Gill, Anthony. 1998. *Rendering Unto Caesar: The Catholic Church and State in Latin America.* Chicago: University of Chicago Press.

————. 1995a. "The Institutional Limitations to Catholic Progressivism: An Economic Approach." *International Journal of Social Economics.* 22 (9/10/11): 135-48.

————. 1995b. "The Politics of Religious Regulation in Mexico: Preliminary Observations." Paper presented at the 19th International Congress of the Latin American Studies Association, Washington D.C.

Goff, James. 1968. *The Persecution of Protestant Christians in Colombia, 1948-1958.* SONDEOS, no. 23. Cuernavaca, Mexico: CIDOC.

Hallum, Anne Motley. 1996. *Beyond Missionaries: Toward and Understanding of the Protestant Movement in Central America.* Lanham: Rowman & Littlefield.

Hurtado Cruchaga, Alberto. 1992. *Es Chile un país católico?* [1941] Santiago: Editorial Los Andes.

Iannaccone, Laurence. 1995. "Voodoo Economics?: Reviewing the Rational Approach to Religion." *Journal for the Scientific Study of Religion,* 34 (1): 76-88.

————. 1991. "The Consequences of Religious Market Structure: Adam Smith and the Economics of Religion." *Rationality and Society,* 3 (2): 156-77.

————. 1990. "Religious Participation: A Human Capital Approach." *Journal for the Scientific Study of Religion,* 29 (3): 297-314.

Lalive d'Epinay, Christian. 1969. *Haven of the Masses: A Study of the Pentecostal Movement in Chile.* London: Lutterworth Press.

Latin American Weekly Report. 1991. "Government joins 'anti-sect' drive." *Latin American Weekly Report,* (10 January): 9.

Mariz, Cecília Loreto. 1994. *Coping with Poverty: Pentecostals and Christian Base Communities in Brazil.* Philadelphia: Temple University Press.

Martin, David. 1990. *Tongues of Fire: The Explosion of Protestantism in Latin America.* Oxford: Basil Blackwell.

Mignone, Emilio. 1988. *Witness to the Truth: The Complicity of Church and Dictatorship in Argentina, 1976-1983.* Translated by Phillip Berryman. Maryknoll, NY: Orbis.

Our Sunday Visitor, Inc. (Various years.) *Catholic Almanac.* Garden City, NY: Doubleday & Co.

Pierson, Paul Everett. 1974. *A Younger Church in Search of Maturity: Presbyterianism in Brazil from 1910 to 1959.* San Antonio, TX: Trinity University Press.

Poblete, Renato. 1965. *Crisis Sacerdotal.* Santiago: Editorial del Pacífico.

Poblete, Renato and Carmen Galilea. 1984. *Movimiento Pentecostal e Iglesia Católica en medios populares.* Santiago, Chile: Centro Bellarmino.

Porcel, Bemabé. 1993. "Hay libertad de culto en Argentina?" *A Fondo,* 1 (noviembre): 5.

Ruether, Rosemary Radford. 1993. "Managua parish combats cardinal over cathedral." *National Catholic Reporter* (26 February): 16.

Scott, David Clark. 1992a. "Mexico's Churches Dispute Details of New Law on State and Religion." *Christian Science Monitor* (24 July): 6.

————. 1992b. "Christian Sects Clash in Latin America." *Christian Science Monitor* (1 April): 14.

Sembrador, Pedro (n.d.). "Las dos mejores pruebas de la falsedad del protestantismo." *Folleto E.V.C.* #78. México, D.F.: Sociedad E.V.C.

————. (n.d.). "Lo que pierde un Católico que se hace protestante." *Folleto E.V.C.* #335. México, D.F.: Sociedad E.V.C.

————. (n.d.). "Catecismo breve E.V.C. sobre el protestantismo." *Folleto E.V.C.* #340. México, D.F.: Sociedad E.V.C.

Senado de la Nación [Argentina]. 1995. *Diario de asuntos entrados.* Año XI–No. 52 (27 de junio). Buenos Aires: Dirreción Publicaciones.

Serbin, Kenneth. 1995. "Brazil: State Subsidization and the Church Since 1930." In Satya Pattnayak, ed. *Organized Religion in the Political Transformation of Latin America*. Lanham, MD: University Press of America.

Stark, Rodney and Roger Finke. 1997. "Catholic Religious Vocations: Decline and Revival." Unpublished manuscript, University of Washington and Purdue University.

Stewart-Gambino, Hannah. 1992. "Introduction: New Games, New Rules." In Edward L. Cleary and Hannah Stewart-Gambino, eds. *Conflict and Competition: The Latin American Church in a Changing Environment*. Boulder, CO: Lynne Rienner.

Stoll, David. 1993. "Introduction: Rethinking Protestantism in Latin America." In Virginia Garrard-Burnett and David Stoll, eds. *Rethinking Protestantism in Latin America*. Philadelphia: Temple University Press.

———. 1990. *Is Latin America Turning Protestant? The Politics of Evangelical Growth*. Berkeley: University of California Press.

Tangeman, Michael. 1995. *Mexico at the Crossroads: Politics, the Church, and the Poor*. Maryknoll, NY: Orbis.

Vitalis, Helmut Gnadt. 1969. *The Significance of Changes in Latin American Catholicism since Chimbote 1953*. SONDEOS no 51. Cuernavaca, Mexico: CIDOC.

Warner, R. Stephen. 1993. "Work in Progress toward a New Paradigm for the Sociological Study of Religion in the United States." *American Journal of Sociology*, 98 (5): 1044-93.

Willems, Emilio (n.d.). *Followers of the New Faith: Cultural Change and the Rise of Protestantism in Brazil and Chile*. Nashville, TN: Vanderbilt University Press.

Young, Lawrence. 1997. *Rational Choice Theory and Religion: Summary and Assessment*. New York: Routledge.

TWO

THE CATHOLIC CHURCH IN CHILE
New Political Alliances

Liesl Haas

The Chilean Catholic Church has been widely recognized for its coura-geous and unwavering defense of human rights during the seventeen-year Pinochet dictatorship. The Church's opposition to the human rights violations of the authoritarian government and its protection and support of the political opposition helped pave the way for the transition to democracy in 1989. As a result of its role under the dictatorship, the Church has enjoyed renewed political influence since the transition. But where one might expect the Church to continue to be a progressive polit-ical voice in the new democracy, the Church has emerged as a largely conservative force in Chilean politics, strongly opposing much of the social policy currently being pursued by the democratic government.

During the course of the transition and the first democratic administra-tions, new issues emerged that had been barred from public debate during the dictatorship. Due to the strength of the Chilean women's movement and progressive politicians from the Center-Left, social problems relating to women's rights, the family, and sexuality have become the focus of government policy. The Chilean Catholic Church has become alarmed at the willingness of influential political actors, including major political parties and sectors within the government, to formulate policy on topics such as sex education in the schools, reproductive rights, and divorce (currently illegal in all circumstances). The Chilean Church strongly oppos-es the liberalization of existing policy on these issues, and it finds itself a partner with the political Right in condemning the proposed policies as anti-family and destructive of the moral foundations of Chilean society.

One explanation for this change in the Church's political alliances is Pope John Paul II's replacement of many progressive bishops with conservative ones, in an attempt by the Vatican to halt the participation of the Latin American Church in left-wing politics. However, the replacement of top clergy by Rome is not the primary explanation for the Church's current conservative posture and changing political alliances. While many of the bishops currently opposing government policy were uninvolved in the struggle for human rights, not all are recent appointments.[1] Rather, new policy issues have emerged on which the Church has historically held a conservative position. It should not be surprising that the Chilean Church opposes the legalization of divorce, for example, because the Catholic Church has historically held that marriage is indissoluble. Nevertheless, the emergence of such issues has strengthened the influence of conservative factions within the Church leadership.

The Chilean Church's position as a conservative political force is highly significant for the consolidation of democracy in that country. Under the authoritarian government, the Church's allies in the struggle for human rights were the political Center and Left, which also opposed the dictatorship. In its opposition to current government policy, however, the Church has found a kindred spirit in the political Right. Ironically, with regard to much of the current social agenda in Chile, the Catholic Church locates its main support among those political elements that were most supportive of the dictatorship and are most ambivalent about the virtues of the democratic process.

The Church's arguments in defense of its traditional perspective on the family, women, and sexuality have over time come to echo much of the Right's logic on these issues. The discourse of both the Church and the Right emphasizes the destabilization of society and the moral chaos that ensues if traditional norms of sexual behavior or gender roles are liberalized. Brito (1997: 63) explains that according to this reasoning, "all dissension presupposes the rupture of ethical norms. The relativization of norms implies a 'moral weakening.'" Social order and stability are of central concern for many Chileans because of the chaos of the Allende years and the coup and dictatorship that followed. It is not unusual for the political Right to emphasize the potential for social breakdown, but, since the transition, the Church has made increasing reference to the issue as well. Far from enhancing the social stability necessary for democracy to flourish, it is arguable that this preoccupation with social and moral order has a deleterious effect: in the short-term, it stifles attempts by citizens and legislators to question the social status quo; and in the long-term, by linking the challenging of traditional norms with social destabilization, such arguments may promote intolerance and the suppression of diversity. As discussed below, the statements of the most conservative members of the Church leadership, like the political Right, have expressed ambivalence about the ability of the democratic process to safeguard moral order.

The Church's political actions since the transition have placed it in a precarious position. It emerged from the years of dictatorship with renewed political influence and a reputation as a strong force in favor of democracy. But by allying itself so closely with the Right since the transition, the Church risks being identified, together with the Right, as an obstacle in the consolidation of democracy.

THE COMPLEXITY OF THE CHURCH'S ROLE IN POLITICS

Contemporary Catholic Social Doctrine translates uneasily into traditional Left-Right political distinctions. On a number of social issues, the Church situates itself left of the political center; for instance, in its support of the unionization of workers, its concern for the environment, and its opposition to capital punishment. However, this "pro-life" philosophy also extends to a defense by the Church of traditional gender roles, conceptions of the family, and norms of sexual conduct. For example, the Church's opposition to contraception, abortion, and divorce, and its encouragement of mothers not to work outside the home reflect its emphasis on maternity as essential to a woman's identity and reproduction as her primary social function. In contemporary democratic politics, one rarely finds such a comprehensive defense of the social status quo outside the most conservative sectors of the political Right. While the Catholic Church is not monolithic in its opinions on these issues, this is the perspective held by the majority of current Church leadership in Chile, and it concurs with the official position of the pope as well.[2]

In the wake of Vatican II (1962-1965), progressive elements in the Catholic Church rose to leadership positions in several Latin American nations, mostly notably Nicaragua, El Salvador, Brazil, and Chile. The Catholic hierarchy in these countries focused attention on the dignity and rights of the poor and marginalized and criticized the social and economic inequalities widespread throughout Latin America. In many cases these concerns translated into support for left-wing political movements. In the case of Chile, in 1973, a military coup overthrew the democratically elected Marxist government of Salvador Allende. The Church protested both the human rights abuses that followed and the regressive economic policies of the military government. Human rights abuses and economic injustice were central problems under the dictatorship (especially in the early years), and on these issues the Church placed itself firmly and courageously in opposition to the government.

When the Church came out against the dictatorship, it opened up spaces in society where other groups could organize with some degree of protection. The political Left, persecuted by the military government, found a refuge in the Church for which it remains indebted. But as the transition to democracy neared, it became clear that in important ways the Church and other progressive sectors possessed competing visions for a democratic Chile.

In the course of the dictatorship, an influential women's movement emerged which became a core part of the pro-democracy movement.[3] Along with the political Left, these women hoped that the return to democracy would mean that socially important issues previously excluded from discussion would become open for public debate, and groups previously excluded from political decision-making would have a voice in the new democracy. By contrast, while the Church supported the return to democracy, it became increasingly concerned that democracy would give political power to sectors of Chilean society whose political goals contradicted Church teaching. If this occurred, it would, the Church feared, undermine the moral structure of Chilean society. As the transition neared, the Church jockeyed for a position of influence within the future political order.

MANOEUVRES IN THE MOMENT OF TRANSITION

The moment of transition from authoritarian rule was a time of tension and uncertainty. Following the failure of the 1988 plebiscite to extend the rule of General Pinochet, elections were scheduled for November 1989. The political Right's campaign strategy focused on the potential for a return to the political instability and social chaos of the Allende years if the "forces of the Left" were to gain the Presidency. The Center-Left was represented by a broad coalition of parties that composed the bulk of the democratic opposition to the military government. In contrast to the strategy of the Right, the *Concertación* coalition emphasized the positive, inclusive nature of the future democracy.[4]

The Catholic Church at this moment had two political priorities: to encourage reconciliation between the sectors of society that supported or opposed the military government,[5] and to consolidate a role for itself in future government policy making. Brito (1997: 51) explains the significance of this particular historical moment:

> Chile has been occupied by political and religious powers since its foundation. The Church knows of this history and once again exercises this power conferred by tradition. It occupies that place just when it perceives the specific moment of pain and reparation, where it can return to analyzing, directing, instructing. After a war.

Because of the visibility of the Church and its high moral standing due to its role under the dictatorship, the attitude of the Church at this juncture was critical for setting the tone for the return to democracy.

The *Concertación* hoped that the Church would issue an optimistic statement to signal confidence in the imminent transition. In November 1989, the Chilean Episcopal Conference responded with the publication of *Certainty, Coherence, and Confidence: Message to Chilean Catholics in an Hour of Transition* (CEC 1989).

The document from the Chilean bishops outlines the Church's perspective on the obstacles, opportunities, and risks inherent in the transition. The priorities outlined are, on a number of points, consistent with the progressive bent of Church Social Doctrine, echoing the Church's concern with economic injustice, environmental degradation, and the violation of human rights. In the area of human rights, the bishops emphasize the need for reconciliation among Chileans but stress that there cannot be forgiveness without justice (CEC 1989: 21). This is a reference to the need to account for the disappeared (individuals who vanished after being taken into police custody) and hold accountable those responsible for human rights abuses.

More significantly, the document introduces several themes that will form the ideological cornerstone of the Church's later involvement in democratic politics. Primary among these is the repeated concern that increased freedom under democracy could lead to a liberalization of social norms. The document devotes a large bulk of its message to a critique of modernity and the secularization of society (CEC 1989: 45-61). A clear distinction is made between Catholic moral teaching and the ethics of secular Chilean society. The document laments the separation of personal, "individual" life, which may be religious (even when religious tenants are not taken as absolutes), from "societal" life, which is secular. Religion, the document asserts, which through centuries formed the basis for societal culture, is relegated to the libraries and museums of the new, modern society (CEC 1989: 48). The document characterizes secular society as "atheistic" (CEC 1989: 47), thus pitting modern society in direct opposition to the values espoused by the Church. Modern society is not seen as a space in which a diverse citizenry engages in debate or negotiation about ethical beliefs; it is condemned as essentially lacking a moral framework.

As part of the document's critique of modern society, the deterioration of personal morality (i.e., sexuality) is also emphasized. These sections of the document reflect the view of the most conservative elements within the Church with regard to family structure, women's roles, and sexual conduct. The dominance of conservative Church thinking in these areas is evidenced by the lack of attention paid to the social and economic contexts of those social problems the Church condemns: insufficient attention for children whose mothers work outside the home, the widespread incidence of marital separations, the existence of abortion. For example, despite the Church's preoccupation with workers rights, there is no recognition of the particular problems faced by women workers, such as unequal wages, lack of child care, or women's double labor within the home and in the workplace. The sole reference to the existence of women workers is found in the section on the family, where the document explains that the most important of all jobs is that of a mother who dedicates herself to the home, to the "support of her husband and education of her children" (31).[6] In its discussion of the sanctity of marriage, the document focuses on the negative effects that children suffer when their parents separate and stresses the need for children to be raised in stable, two-parent homes. No mention is made of the high rate of domestic abuse,[7] despite the public attention focused on the issue by the women's movement and the parties of the *Concertación*. The issue of abortion is addressed, but the document limits its discussion to thanking the Pinochet government for outlawing it completely in 1989:

> Thank God there is no talk in Chile today of authorizing, much less promoting, abortion. To the contrary, a law has just been passed which prohibits abortion in any circumstance, for which we are grateful to the past government. But the country must know that, in the case of danger, the Church will defend human life, from the moment of conception to the last breath (18-19).[8]

Having elaborated the Church's position on a broad range of issues, the bishops' message underlines the importance of unity of belief among Catholics: "one thing is a *legitimate diversity of opinions on debatable topics* and another thing [is] divisions and tensions which make dialogue difficult and sometimes break 'affective and effective' communion ... the union of the Church must be our most effective contribution to the reconciliation and union of the Chilean people" (13, italics mine). Evident in this passage is the Church's connection between consensus (or concurrence) of opinion and the future stability of Chile. The reconciliation of all Chile necessitates the suppression of disagreement among its diverse sectors—in this way the appearance of unity, as opposed to the open discussion of differences, becomes synonymous with reconciliation.[9]

Chilean Catholics, united in obedience to Church teachings, are urged to participate in all aspects of public life: "In this hour of transition to democracy that the country is living, we urge you again to participate, not only in electoral processes, but in *political life* itself" (67, italics in original). However, the document also lays the groundwork for later Church insistence that Catholic policymakers must not formulate or support laws that oppose Church teachings: "How could a man of faith refuse to communicate his faith to others and to want the truth that he believes in to penetrate and inspire all aspects of human life, private and collective?" (48). The bishops quote Christ's commandment to the apostles to spread the message of the Gospel throughout the world, and ask, "Are we to take this commandment for dead?" (48).

The document extends the argument for unity among Catholics to insist that society as a whole should conform to Church teachings. The justification for this claim is found in the Church's reference to natural law, defined in the document as "the belief in a moral order which regulates all of human conduct, the idea that life has a meaning and a purpose, and that there is a path for achieving them. . . . [Natural law] is confirmed and brought to perfection through the Gospel" (46).[10] The concept of natural law is central to the logic of the Church's involvement in Chilean politics, and it appears with increasing frequency in future Church arguments against government policy. The bishops' document warns that if society (or by inference, government policy) deviates from the tenants of natural law, "happiness, peace, and growth . . . will disappear little by little in a type of morality of pleasure that ends in the worst aberrations and can make life unbearable" (46).[11]

This passage also illustrates another major element of the Church's logic: the argument of the slippery slope. Central to Church opposition to specific policies is the belief that allowing even a minor relaxation of existing norms risks opening the door to eventual moral chaos. The possibility of the future legalization of abortion in Chile is one of the Church's greatest concerns, intensified by calls from sectors of the women's movement and the political Center-Left for public debate on the topic. As discussed below, abortion is seen as a probable eventual consequence both of sex education and the legalization of divorce.

Following the transition to democracy, of the issues mentioned in the bishops' message, the Church hierarchy focused increasingly on issues of sexual morality and the need for limits to personal freedom. Faras (1997: 298) explains why the Church's preoccupation with sexuality translates into a lack of confidence in the democratic process:

> It is necessary to consider that a large part of this polemic was produced in and by the transition from a dictatorship to a democracy. Apparently this transition was perceived by the Church and the most conservative sectors as a risk with regard to sexual conduct—thinking, perhaps, of other types of liberations that come with the end of dictatorships. Apparently democracy was seen, in its relationship to sexuality, as a danger, a threat to good customs, as the passage to the feared sexual licentiousness. In this way, one can deduce that the very repressions of a dictatorship also affected, or better put con-

trolled, those behaviors that put at risk the concept of a sexuality based . . . on Christian values.

THE CHURCH AND DEMOCRATIC POLITICS:
THE DECLARATION OF A MORAL CRISIS

In 1989, the Center-Left *Concertación* won the Presidential election and Patricio Aylwin, a Christian Democrat, assumed the Presidency in March 1990. In response to pressure from the women's movement and feminists within the *Concertación*, the government created SERNAM (*Servicio Nacional de la Mujer*), a national women's service with ministerial rank. Immediately, progressive legislators and SERNAM began to focus on modernizing Chilean law in the areas of women's rights, family law, and reproductive health. These efforts included the introduction of legislative bills to sanction domestic violence, expand the property rights of married women, create day care centers for working mothers, legalize divorce, and decriminalize abortion.[12] In addition, the government undertook the development of a comprehensive program of sex education for Chilean secondary schools. Faras notes,

> Without a doubt, the return to democracy in 1990, after long years of dictatorship, made possible the opening necessary for issues like these, relegated to the space of the private, the intimate, to have visibility in the world of the public, political, and social. The act of putting into practice a new foundational project encouraged eyes to return to issues that had a direct relationship to the structure of Chilean society (1997: 271-2).

These events seemed to confirm the worst misgivings of the Church leadership. In October 1991, Cardinal Carlos Oviedo of Santiago released a Pastoral Letter entitled "Morality, Youth, and Permissive Society." The document is divided into six chapters: human sexuality and its disfiguration; actual tendencies toward immorality; sexual education and chastity; contraception, abortion, and divorce; the formation of moral conscience and its value for society; and the Church and its moral formation. The Pastoral Letter echoes the concerns of the bishops' document discussed above. In it, the Cardinal warns of a "crisis of sexual morality" and blames modern culture for relativizing ethical norms. The reference to natural law reappears as well, as Oviedo declares that the moral order which is being undermined is "natural as much as gospel." He characterizes the government's proposed sex education program as "merely a pretext to give respectability to the promotion of promiscuity" (1991: 58). The Letter concludes by calling for "a great campaign of

moral illumination of consciences and healing of customs. This obligation is an integral part of the New Evangelization of the nation, to which
the Pope urgently calls us" (58).

Due to the powerful political influence of the Church, political
tendencies from Left to Right felt obligated to concur with the Church's
statements to the extent that they were able. None of the main parties
could risk alienating the Church by not appearing responsive to its
concerns. Despite the Pastoral Letter's emphasis on sexual morality, the
Christian Democratic party consciously downplayed this aspect in their
response, concentrating instead on the social and economic inequalities
that can lead to the physical and spiritual destruction of individuals.
Andrés Zaldívar, president of the Christian Democrats, declared that
"there are elements that begin to corrupt society, in the sense of drugs,
alcoholism, delinquency. We must search for formulas for development . . .
which are not merely cost-effective or economistic" (Brito 1997: 53).
Ricardo Lagos, Education Minister and President of the left-wing Party
for Democracy, was more direct in his disagreement with the
Archbishop's conclusions, explaining that Chilean society is adjusting to
new circumstances and stating, "there is a change in Chilean society, but
I don't believe it to be a crisis of values in the sense that [the Pastoral
Letter] mentions" (Brito 1997: 53). Gonzalez Marquez, senator and president of the Radical party, was the only major politician to assert explicitly the independence of Chilean society from Church authority. He
claimed that the Letter is the type of message that "corresponds to the
Bishop as a spiritual authority in this country, but it seems . . . that in the
contemporary world there is a new vision of what constitutes morality. . . .
[W]e are with him when he calls us to fight against drug addiction, delinquency, and terrorism" (Brito 1997: 54). Members of the women's movement strongly objected to the Cardinal's message. Nuria Nuñez of the
Women's Institute insisted:

> The Church has to . . . see what demands there are in society and
> how to provide answers. It can't respond by saying that everything
> is moral crisis, licentiousness. It has to face the very serious prob-
> lems that exist in Chile, like AIDS, teenage pregnancy, the initiation
> into sexual activity under bad conditions, clandestine abortions,
> couples in crisis (Faras 1997: 294).

In sharp contrast, the political Right ignored the Letter's criticisms of
economic disparity and social marginalization but wholeheartedly
embraced its critique of modern society as morally corrupt. The Right
recognized the clear affinity between the Church's perspective on social
issues and the Right's arguments that Chilean society was being weak-

ened by sectors within the governing coalition. Andres Allamand, president of the right-wing National Renovation Party (RN), referred specifically to the bills in Congress on divorce and abortion as examples of left-wing efforts to undermine the common good. Most pointedly, he underscored the Church's concern about the disadvantages of democracy: "It profoundly disturbs National Renovation that the restoration of democracy could begin to be assimilated by important sectors of the country not only with an atmosphere of insecurity on the part of the citizens, but with a climate of public and private immorality" (Brito 1997: 59). These sentiments were echoed by numerous other leaders from National Renovation and the other major right-wing party, the Independent Democratic Union (UDI).

Thus the political alliances took shape that would determine the Church's ideological partners in future policy debates. The political Right unequivocally declared its adherence to the Church's policy positions. The political Left, including the feminist lobby, protested the extent of Church pressure on politicians to conform to Church teaching. The Christian Democrats, historically linked to the Catholic Church and the leading party in the governing coalition, struggled with deep internal divisions over these issues. In addition, they were forced to seek a balance between their loyalty to the Church and their acknowledgment of the policy preferences of their partners in the *Concertación*.

There was profound irony in this new alliance. The Right, supporter of the coup and the institutional violence of the military regime, and past critic of Church involvement in "Leftist" politics, reemerged through its ideological alliance with the Church in a position of powerful moral authority. In the first two democratic administrations, Church involvement in politics focused on two main issues: sex education and divorce.

THE CHURCH CONFRONTS SEX EDUCATION

Early in the first democratic administration the Aylwin government announced its intention to develop a program of sex education for secondary schools, and from the beginning the Church strongly opposed government plans. Church objections centered on three interrelated arguments: that government-run sex education programs impart false values and promote promiscuity; that the issue of the program's existence and its content could not be decided democratically because moral correctness cannot be determined by majority rule; and that government-sponsored sex education amounts to totalitarianism on the part of the State. The polemic surrounding sex education provided a crucial opportunity for the political Right to solidify its political alliance with the Church and to promote itself as the defender of traditional Chilean values.

Church rejection of government plans for sex education in the schools extended to an opposition to government studies to determine the extent of sexual activity among the young. It was evident at the time of transition that Chile possessed a high rate of adolescent pregnancies, an extremely high incidence of abortion, and that AIDS cases were on the rise.[14] Therefore a high priority for the first democratic administration was to collect more information on the sexual beliefs and habits of different sectors of society. The results of numerous surveys undertaken during this time indicated a high incidence of sexual activity among young Chileans as well as widespread ignorance about the facts of human reproduction, sexually transmitted diseases, and contraception.[15] Church leaders objected vociferously to the undertaking of these studies. When the San Bernardo Hospital in Santiago released the results of one such survey, Orozimbo Fuenzalida, Bishop of San Bernardo, complained directly to the doctors involved:

> In speaking with the doctors, they told me that it was not their intention to cause moral damage. I dont believe there was evil intent on their part, but I did let them know that this survey is pedagogically bad, unacceptable for the thinking of the Church . . . it seems to me that it deals with the youth from a very base perspective. It doesnt insist on supreme and legitimate values (Farías 1997: 293).

Recognizing that most sectors of society were in favor of some form of sex education and that the government was unlikely to abandon its efforts altogether, the Church focused on critiquing the blueprints for projects that did emerge. The Church contended that the government's plans focused on information as opposed to ethical formation and that this served to encourage promiscuity. Typical of these remarks was the comment by Jorge Medina, then Bishop of Valparaiso, to the Education Ministry's report entitled "Toward a Policy of Sex Education for the Improvement of the Quality of Education": "The first and most grave thing is, in my judgment, the absence of a Christian anthropology. . . . because for us, Christians and Catholics, it is impossible to speak of sexuality, or anything, apart from the coordinates of our faith" (Faras 1997: 293). Cardinal Oviedo warned Chileans not to forget that this "real campaign to dissolve the Chilean family is accompanied by aggressive promotion of free love among the young" (*La Epoca* 1991a: 11).

The Right embraced the Church's discourse as its own. For example, RN representative to the Chamber of Deputies María Angélica Cristi referred to the government's plans as "more than anything a promotion of the 'condomization' [of sexuality] rather than instruction about what sexuality truly means as part of life, love, and procreation" (Arthur 1997: D22). The RN-sponsored "Seminar on Women, Family, and Work" concluded that in countries that had instituted sex education programs, "instead of reducing adolescent pregnancies, [sex education] has encouraged them. The reason is that it gives incentive to engage in sexual activity too early, in young people who do not have the maturity for it, through the false illusion of a 'safe sex' that does not exist, because all methods of contraception can fail, either by design or because of the user" (Cristi 1996: 1). Cristián Larroulet, of the right-wing think tank Liberty and Development, concurred that "the increase in knowledge about sexual material is tightly linked to changes toward a more liberal sexual culture" (Lagos 1997: 6).

This was contradicted by studies showing a decrease in teenage pregnancies in Chilean schools that had instituted pilot sex education programs. A program developed by the University of Chile's Adolescent Medical Center and instituted in three Santiago secondary schools for two years found that pregnancy among students in the three schools fell 33 percent, while pregnancy among secondary students in all of Santiago fell only 4.7 percent. The investigators discovered that among those students already sexually active, sex education gave them the incentive to use more effective means of birth control. Delaying the time in which adolescents initiate sexual activity is a main goal of the program, and there was no indication that the program resulted in increased numbers of students becoming sexually active (Lagos 1997: 6-7).

However, research that demonstrates the effectiveness of sex education programs failed to convince the Church or the Right that such programs are a good thing. This is in part because the arguments of the Church and the Right do not directly focus on the best way to reduce the number of teenage pregnancies (or AIDS cases), but on the best way to discourage what is believed to be morally destructive behavior. Hence there is insistence that, because the activities that lead to AIDS or teenage pregnancy are immoral, the only correct way to end the problems is to insist on chastity.[16] The Catholic Church rejects the use of contraception (other than natural methods) even for married couples, so it is not surprising that it rejects imparting information on contraception to high-school students. Promotion of the means to prevent the undesired consequences of sexual activity sidesteps what the Church and the Right see as the main point: if the consequences are bad, it's because the activity itself is wrong (giving sexually active teenagers information on contraception merely compounds the immorality of their behavior). It is important to recognize this distinction because the policy debate on this issue—as is the case with divorce—does not center on competing visions of the best way to reduce the incidence of commonly recognized social problems, per se. The *primary* goal of the Church and the Right is to defend the norms of behavior that the Church deems morally correct, with the belief that a reduction in social problems will flow from this.

Because the Church and the Right considered the moral grounding of Chilean society to be at stake, they concluded that such policy issues cannot be decided by majority rule; the government must agree to uphold traditional (Catholic) values. Archbishop Medina asserted:

> Today there exists an atmosphere . . . characterized by a false virtue of "tolerance," which encourages one on the pretext of respecting other persons, not to emit judgments nor to place legitimate constraints on attitudes that are corrosive of the person and society. So one speaks as though each one has "his" truth, by which one sidesteps the vigorous affirmation of "the" truth. So also one adopts ill-defined or complacent postures before certain conduct, a comfortable (posture) to be sure, and allowing the one who does this to be repeatedly praised, lauded, and distinguished (Rozas 1989: A2).

Another Santiago priest affirmed, "The concept of tolerance seems very unclear to me. One speaks of respect for the sexual behavior of another and, in my judgment, the true acceptance of another and my Christian commitment to him demand that I help him to be true to himself and not simply that I allow him to do (as he wants)" (Farías 1997: 293).

Again, this perspective was reflected in the discourse of the Right, as in the following example. Joaquin Lavín, UDI mayor of Santiago's wealthiest district and presidential hopeful for 2000, confronted with statistics showing that a majority of Chileans favor sex education, explained, "I don't believe that this issue should be formulated in terms of majorities or minorities. Here there are values at stake" (Bofill and Ramirez 1997: 8).

Six years after the transition, the government of Christian Democrat Eduardo Frei began the introduction into schools of a sex education program known as the *Jocas,* an acronym for Conversational Workshops about Affectivity and Sexuality. In response, oppositional discourse by the Church and the Right made repeated references to the "totalitarianism" of government-run sex education. These sectors viewed the implementation of the *Jocas* as entailing the imposition of a foreign value system on Chilean society. The following excerpt from an editorial by the president of the Youth Section of the UDI is a clear example of this perspective:

> Within the discourse about the modernity of cultures and values beats the heart of ethical totalitarianism that, openly or muffled, imposes from the State a model of sex education, a form of preventing AIDS or controlling the means of communication,[17] at once

insulting and dismissive of all of us who don't share the type of life the State wishes for us. Those of us who believe that values are not relative, that there exists an objective moral order, must never allow ourselves to adopt a posture of complicity and submission, nor allow ourselves to abandon, for ease or convenience, the defense and fortification of the Chilean family by failing to realize that day by day, [the State] is attempting to drive the country into a new kind of slavery in the name of liberty without limits (Gorosabel 1997: 8).

As the Right appropriated the "traditional values" discourse of the Church, so elements of the Church began to echo the Rights characterization of government policy as authoritarian. In response to President Frei's call for the Church to stop hiding from the grave reality of adolescent pregnancies, abortion, and AIDS, Auxiliary Bishop of Santiago Cristin Caro went so far as to accuse the government of being part of a conspiracy by industrialized nations to stem population growth in the developing world (*El Mercurio* 1996: A2).

THE CHURCH CONFRONTS DIVORCE

With the legalization of divorce in Ireland in 1996, Chile became the only nation to lack some type of legal divorce. Although the Catholic Church grants marriage annulments in specific circumstances, there is no legal way to receive a civil divorce. Divorce *a la Chilena* refers to the one method of obtaining a civil annulment: committing perjury before the Civil Registrar by claiming that one lied on some aspect of the original marriage license, thereby voiding the contract. Efforts to legalize divorce have focused on the recognition of the widespread use of perjury to gain civil annulments and the need to have the State replace this informal system with a set of logical and equitable legal guidelines to regulate the dissolution of marriage.[18]

Since the turn of the century, numerous bills have been introduced into the Congress to legalize divorce, including several since the transition to democracy, but until 1997, every bill was simply buried in Congressional committee. The latest bill introduced was qualitatively different from its predecessors in that it enjoyed support not only from the political Left, but from significant sectors of the Christian Democrats and some representatives from the Right as well. After extensive and heated debate, the bill passed the lower house of Congress in September 1997. While its passage by the Senate is far from assured, its passage by the Chamber of Deputies can nonetheless be counted a tremendous success for proponents of legalization, for this signaled the first time politicians were forced to debate the topic publicly.

The issue of divorce is especially significant with regard to the role of the Catholic Church in Chilean politics. Church discourse on divorce has been fairly consistent since the 1960s, but it has increased in intensity at key moments that coincide with the introduction of divorce bills into Congress, most recently in 1990, 1991, 1994, and 1997. The campaigns undertaken by the Church, and supported by most of the Right, to block legislative debate on divorce represent by far the most extensive and aggressive lobbying efforts by the Church to date.

Despite the Church's opposition, political representatives managed to pass the divorce bill in the Chamber of Deputies. The tactics employed by the Church and the Right included all the themes elaborated in earlier statements and lobbying efforts described above: divorce undermines the family as the basis of Chilean society; legalization of divorce will start Chilean society on a downward slide of social disintegration; divorce is contrary to natural law and therefore the issue cannot be decided democratically; and the "imposition" of a divorce law is totalitarian. In terms of lobbying tactics, the Church insisted that Catholic legislators cannot promote policy that contradicts Church teaching, and it maintained a continual lobby presence in the Congress itself and through the press. Although for the most part the Right allied itself to the Church's position, some legislators from the Right eventually rebelled against the Church's pressure on the Congress.

The increase in Church lobbying over the issue of divorce has been widely noted in Chile. A 1994 press report observed that "the issue of divorce, on which the Church has focused so strongly these past days, is not an isolated example [of Church activity in politics], but it does appear to be the most intense by the Church." The article quoted Bishop Caros declaration that the Church "cannot remain silent because the stability of marriage and the family is at stake" (Zilci 1994: 19). Bishop Medina concurred that "the introduction of divorce grants the union of man and woman a provisory status ... disposable if there are difficulties." He criticized the idea that it would be up to the couple themselves to determine the state of their union (as opposed to the Church's decision to grant them an annulment) (1995: 2).

The Right warned that divorce would weaken the family. Conservative Christian Democrat Hernán Bosselin affirmed the family as the basic unit of society and therefore indissoluble (*La Epoca* 1990: 3); RN lawyer Sara Navas insisted that divorce would lead to "free love" (Delsing 1997: 180); Hernán Büchi, UDI candidate for the presidency in 1990 and himself separated, declared that a divorce law would cause people to take marriage more lightly (*La Epoca* 1991b: 9); and RN Representative María Angélica Cristi argued that legal divorce would make it easier for spouses to abandon the home (*La Epoca* 1997a: 12).

Both the Right and the Church insisted that legalized divorce would place

Chile on a downward slide toward social disintegration. Legalization of abortion was often cited as the most extreme potential consequence, as the end point of a society lacking moral grounding. Bishop Medina reasoned:

> Behind these arguments [for divorce] . . . is the idea that the Powers of the State base their decisions on arguments relying on statistics, above and even in opposition to principles. This is extremely dangerous. If this criterion is accepted, it will be with great difficulty that a way will be found to avoid legalizing, sooner or later, abortion, genetic manipulation, and euthanasia. This is how it has happened historically: once you open the door to legislate by dispensing with principles, it is almost impossible to detain the avalanche and to resist pressures based on various types of convenience (1995: 2).

Conservative Christian Democrat Hernán Bosselin imagines a similar scenario: "If marriage falls, it is my conviction that so too falls the family. And next will come marriages of homosexuals and lesbians" (Castillo and Melndez 1994: 27). Similar to the arguments used against sex education, the Church recognized the existence of de facto separations but insisted that granting legal recognition to such situations replaced an existing evil with a greater one (Betsalel 1994: 29).

In addition to its concerns about the stability of the family, the Catholic Church's opposition to divorce stems from its theological conviction that marriage is a sacrament. The sacrament of marriage, once conferred, becomes a permanent state of being that cannot be undone at the bidding of those involved. (For this reason, the Church is able to grant annulments only by declaring that a particular union never constituted a true marriage.) The granting of sacramental status to the act of marriage is a specifically Catholic belief. Other religions, including other Christian denominations, view marriage as a solemn contract, one which under certain circumstances can be broken.[19] Thus as a matter of faith the Catholic Church could never agree to the legalization of divorce. However, in insisting that the prohibition on divorce must extend beyond Catholics to be enshrined in civil law, the Church defends its position with reference to natural law. As Bishop José Manuel Santos explained, "We believe marriage is indissoluble, not only for Catholics. Marriage is indissoluble by its inherent nature and not only because it is contrary to the Church, as is generally thought" (Delsing 1997: 180). Linares Bishop Carlos Camus reasoned that for non-Catholics, the mandates of natural law still apply because for "non-Christians as well, the obligation exists to safeguard the stability of the family as the nucleus of society" (Rojas 1991: 5). Bishop Fuenzalida proclaimed: "We wouldn't want legislators who believe themselves God, or who in their pluralist relativism believe that man has changed and that now he is god of himself and possessor of his own liberty" (1997: 10).

By contrast, Lutheran Bishop Ricardo Wagner explained that the problem with reliance on natural law is that its definitions reflect specific social and historical contexts:

> To every philosophical or pseudotheological concept of the "human being" corresponds a specific natural law. For Aristotle, for example, slavery was legitimate and in accordance with natural law. This opinion simply reflected his concept of the human being, according to which only the Greek citizen was fully human. Neither the invocation of "Christian tradition" nor that of "natural law" provides solid arguments for rejecting a judicial order that is realistic and in accordance with the needs of existing society; rather [these invocations] arise from clerical interests and ideologies. For this reason, we consider it fully justified that the State legislate on divorce (Delsing 1997: 184).

Perhaps surprisingly, the Church also rejected a legislative bill introduced by Hernán Bosselin to alter civil law to reflect more closely the teachings of the Church. The Bosselin legislation aimed to end the ability of couples to perjure their way to a civil annulment. However, in an attempt to resolve the situation in which a couple granted annulment by the Church could still not receive a civil divorce, the Bosselin bill enacted a set of conditions for civil annulment that mirrored the Church's own qualifications for annulment. The bill was opposed by the Church on the grounds that it would open the door for later broader interpretations (Rojas 1991: 6).

Because the Church considers marriage indissoluble by its nature, it rejects references to the high number of separations and illegal civil annulments and considers the opinion of the majority of Chileans irrelevant.[20] Bishop Oviedo responded to arguments that the high number of separations necessitates legal recognition, by remarking, "as if numbers were the same as values" (*La Epoca* 1991a: 11). Bishop Medina explained, "Morality is not based on statistics" (Betsalel 1994: 30). Like sex education, divorce is considered to be an issue best protected from the turbulence and unpredictability of the democratic process. Despite the evidence of opinion polls showing a high majority of Chileans in favor of divorce, Bishop Caro declared that "divorce is not a right of the citizens" (Betsalel 1994: 30).

As it had done in the past, the Church repeated its insistence that Catholic legislators cannot promote policies that contradict Church teaching. Archbishop Oviedo explained that "a Catholic representative, if he wants to be true to his faith, cannot vote in favor of divorce" (Medina 1995: 2). Bishop Medina affirmed more forcefully that "a Catholic must not ... favor any divorce law, defend it or support it. ... The Catholic cannot claim autonomy regarding material which involves the doctrine of the Church" (1995: 2). These sentiments were echoed by conservative representatives within the Chamber of Deputies. Christian Democrat Carlos Dupré, for example, exhorted his fellow representatives to vote against the divorce bill by explaining that "the Pope indicates that if we Catholics want to be true to our faith, we cannot defend and even less promote a divorce law ... There exists clear doctrine with regard to which the Christian cannot resort to the autonomy of his conscience" (Cámara de Diputados 1997a: 8).

As was seen in the case of sex education, legislative attempts to legalize divorce are characterized by the bishops as authoritarian. San Bernardo Bishop Orozimbo Fuenzalida urged the Catholics of the diocese to let their representatives know that "they have no right to impose this type of divorce law on us" (1997: 10). He encouraged Catholics not to vote for those representatives who supported the divorce bill. Bishop Francisco Errázuriz of Valparaiso insisted that "No one, including the State, can prevent an engaged couple from having the conviction that marriage, by its very nature, is a union for life—which excludes divorce—and that they make use of their liberty of conscience to contract marriage for life, refusing to contract some other type of union that is not so" (La Epoca 1997b: 2). Similar statements had long been formulated by the Right, which claimed that the divorce bill being debated in Congress dissolves marriages to such an extent "that it won't permit [couples] to reinitiate their life together" (Instituto Libertad 1991: 6).

Church lobbying tactics include direct pressure on individual representatives and a visible presence within the Congress during debates on the bill. In its encounters with representatives of the Left who had been persecuted by the military government, Church lobbyists make particular reference to the protection the Church gave the democratic opposition during this time. In effect, the Church is attempting to "collect on the bill" from its pro–human rights work under the dictatorship.[21] In many instances, those bishops at the forefront of the divorce debate are not the same bishops who fought for human rights under the dictatorship.[22] In other instances, however, the same bishops who protected members of the Left now petition them personally to vote against divorce. For example, Socialist Deputy Fanny Pollarolo explained that Bishop Carlos Camus "is very dear, [and was] very progressive in the fight against the dictatorship ... we love him a lot, but on the issue of divorce he is the worst. And he is the one who is pressuring the Socialist Deputies."[23]

Among those representatives favoring the legalization of divorce, there was strong reaction to the Church's pressure on the Congress. Socialist Deputy Isabel Allende rejected the characterization of the debate as being between those who would protect the family and those who would destroy it (Cámara de Diputados 1997b: 17). Deputy José Viera-Gallo asserted:

> This bill which introduces divorce was signed ... by persons who adhere to very distinct beliefs and political positions. Today, we are in a pluralist democracy, which accepts the [United Nations] Universal Declaration of Human Rights, which respects liberty of conscience and of religion, in which there is neither a confessional State nor official atheism (1997b: 17).

Liberal Christian Democrat Sergio Elgueta explained that in a pluralist society it is crucial to distinguish between the political community and the Church and therefore to distinguish between actions undertaken by individual Christians in accordance with their consciences and actions undertaken in the name of the Church and in communion with its leaders (Cámara de Diputados 1997c: 28).

Most significantly, however, by 1997 some members of the far Right had begun to rebel against the legislative involvement of the Church. No member of the political Right had spoken in favor of a divorce bill in the past; however, in the case of the 1997 bill, ten of the fifty-eight votes in favor of the bill came from the Right. RN Deputy Arturo Longton claimed that the Church "can offer opinions, [but] it cannot undertake actions that go beyond its own competence, especially when it is a religious power that lacks the experience of a mother or father of a family" (Vaccaro 1997: 7). UDI Deputy Iván Moreira, a past defender of the Church's positions on social issues, called on the Church to cease its "religious war" (Vaccaro 1997: 7), and he urged his fellow conservatives to reclaim their legislative independence. In his speech before Congress in defense of the divorce bill, he declared, "I am the first to defend the right of all Catholics to marry a single time and not to be legally obligated to get divorced under any circumstances. What doesn't seem right to me is that what is dogma for a minority be imposed on the majority" (Cámara de Diputados 1997c: 33).

CONCLUSIONS

The Catholic Church in Chile currently finds itself in a difficult position with regard to its role in politics. Historically, the Church enjoyed unquestioned cultural hegemony, and this influence is reflected in Chilean civil law. However, in recent years a number of factors have combined to create a much more complex and competitive political environment for the Church. Recent decades have seen a pluralization of faiths in the region, and the Catholic Church is struggling to redefine itself in this new context, in which it finds itself becoming one religious option among many.[24] The transition from dictatorship to democracy has led to the emergence of new political issues, many of which challenge existing law with regard to sexuality, gender roles, and the family. Because of the current dominance of conservatives among the Church leadership, the Church is unlikely to rethink its present position on issues such as sex education and divorce.

Bolstered by its progressive role under the dictatorship, the Church is playing an influential but controversial role in the policymaking process of the democratic government. Farías writes,

> The Church was key in calling attention to and safeguarding human rights during the dictatorship. In this it could count on the respect and support of the great majority of Chileans. In the moment of the transition to democracy, the Church used this support to exercise its power to safeguard and standardize the sexual conduct of the society, intending to establish itself as the only entity capable and deserving of regulating the sexuality of Chileans (1997: 298).

The Church has found itself in alliance with the political Right in opposing current government policy in these areas. This marks a significant change since the years of dictatorship, when the Church protected and supported the Center-Left opposition to military rule. The political Right is clearly linked in the minds of Chileans with support of the authoritarian government and with current resistance to further democratization of the government.[25] One potential consequence of the Church's ideological affinity with the Right is that it risks being identified in the minds of Chileans not with its defense of human rights but with a defense of those forces that would undermine the consolidation of democracy in Chile.

The most important challenge currently facing the Catholic Church in Chile is its struggle to situate a desire to influence public policy within the larger system of pluralist, democratic politics. An instructive example on how this balance can be achieved is found in the case of Spain, which legalized divorce in 1981. In that country, Catholic bishops clearly distinguished their role as religious leaders from the role of civil legal authorities:

> Civil law might permit the dissolution of marriage, but the Catholic knows that it is an open door which he in good conscience can never cross. He does not need legal pressure to comply. . . . It is personal conscience and not State law that must regulate the ethical and religious behavior of those citizens we affirm as Catholic. . . . We must accustom ourselves to living the demands of our faith without the support of civil legal authorities, and inclusive, in a social climate and environment which will frequently be adverse (to this faith) (Rojas 1991: 4).

The Catholic Church will no doubt continue to play an influential role in Chilean politics. However, it is crucial that the Church recognize that it is but one voice, albeit an important one, in a pluralist society. To continue to be a prominent voice in a democratic system, the Church must rely on the strength of its arguments to convince voters and policymakers of its position.

NOTES

1 For example, Bishop Carlos Camus was appointed bishop before the 1973 coup (and was strongly involved in the struggle for human rights); Bishop Orozimbo Fuenzalida and Cardinal Carlos Oviedo were also ordained as bishops prior to the coup but do not share Camus' progressive reputation; and Cardinal Jorge Medina was ordained most recently, in 1985. Medina is considered the most conservative of current bishops, with a reputation of having sympathized with the military government.

2 See Pope John Paul II's 1996 "Letter to Women," which was published in anticipation of the September 1995 International Women's Conference in Beijing.

3 Chilean feminists linked the issue of dictatorship and human rights abuses to a larger system of patriarchy endemic to Latin American society. The most notable contribution of the women's movement was this linking of political and social oppression by the authoritarian government with women's oppression in the home. The slogan of the movement became "democracy in the country and in the home" (see Frohman and Valdes 1993).

4 This was exemplified by the slogan of the prodemocracy forces: "Chile, Happiness is Coming."

5 In a 1988 plebiscite, Chileans voted on whether to extend General Pinochet's rule for an additional eight years. Fifty-five percent of the population voted "no" (in other words, this group favored an immediate transition to democracy), while 43 percent vote "si" to eight more years of military rule. These results demonstrate that Chilean society remains deeply divided over how they view the legacy of the authoritarian government.

6 Women as a group are overlooked in the document. In one section, the bishops mention the need to evangelize all groups in society, and there follows a long list of "subcultures," including those based on generational, occupational, ethnic, and class differences, but gender does not figure among these important social distinctions (55-56). Except for abortion, there is no direcrt reference to issues of women's rights, which have emerged as possible policy priorities for the new govermnment. The lack of atttention paid to women in the document is especially surprising given the support the Church had given numerous women's groups during the dictatorship. The exclusion of women from discussion in the bishops' message is evidence of the increasing dominance of conservatives among the Church leadership.

7. Domestic abuse of women is estimated to occur in 25 percent of Chilean households (Cacers, et. al. 1993: 8).

8 Prior to this law, abortion was legal if a pregnancy was deemed a threat to the mother's life or health. This "therapeutic abortion" law had been in effect for several decades. The 1989 law illegalized abortion for any reason. The bishops' statement on abortion above is particularly interesting in light of the fact that Chile has the highest rate of abortion in Latin America. Despite its illegality, it is estimated that one in three pregnancies in Chile ends in abortion (Caceres, et. al. 1993: 7-8).

9 The bishops explain that this unity among Catholics should be so strong that politicians from different political tendencies should feel closer to one another than they do to members of their own political party who do not share their faith (Conferencia Episcopal de Chile 1989:67).

10 In the twelfth century, Thomas Aquinas adapted Aristotelian notions of natural law to a specifically Christian context. This is the basis for the bishops' contention that Catholic doctrine, while considered divinely inspired, nevertheless is relevant beyond the strictly theological realm and has applications for civil law.

11 In an earlier sermon at the Santiago Cathedral, Jorge Medina, then bishop of Valparaiso, foreshadowed many of the themes of the bishops' message: "The human legislator is not completely autonomous: his action cannot exceed the limits of justice, nor can it make what is by its nature an evil [into] a good, or vice versa. Human law is under the control of the law of God, inscribed in nature, which must be served and never undermined or weakend" (August 1, 1989, quoted in *El Mercurio* 1989: A2).

12 SERNAM worked together with legislators on a number of bills; however, as a government agency, SERNAM was reticent to lend official support to the most controversial legislative initiatives, namely those on abortion and divorce. These bills were the result of Conggressional initiative alone.

13 Despite Allamand's call for politicians to adhere to the Pastoral Letter and to uphold "clear values objectively based on human nature," (Oviedo 1991: 58) when the divorce bill was put forward for a committee vote in January 1997, he abstained from voting (from author's interview with committee members, January 15, 1997). Ivan Moreira, mayor and later senator from the UDI, publicly supported the Church's political involvement early on; however, he eventually broke rank with his party to vote in favor of the divorce legislation. In a speech before Congress in January 1997, he criticized as excessive the Church's involvement in policy-making (Camara de Diputados 1997b: 30-33).

14 It is estimated that in Chile, one in three pregnancies ends in abortion. As noted above, this is considered to be the highest rate in Latin America. 38 percent of births in Chile are to teenage mothers. Between 1990 and 1993, the number of women infected with the AIDS virus more than doubled; in the population at large AIDS continues to rise at an average yearly rate of 30 percent (Caceres, et.al. 1993: 7-9; and Centro de Estudios de la Mujer 1996a: 1-4).

15 A 1991 study by the National Foundation Against AIDS (Funacs) found that 44.2 percent of adolescents admitted being sexually active. By 1996 the percentage had risen to 55.1 percent. The average age for adolescents to become sexually active was 16.8 (Lagos 1997: 6-7).

16 In 1996-1997, the Health Department developed a series of televsion spots focusing on AIDS awareness. Those stations under Church or politically conservative ownership refused to air the commercials because the use of condoms was mentioned among the methods listed to protect against AIDS.

17 This is a reference to the Health Department commercials described in endnote no. 16.

18 Pursuing a civil annulment is an expensive process: one must hire a lawyer as well as two witnesses to testify that the original marriage contract is false. For this reason, proponents of legal divorce have focused on the class bias at work in the granting of annulments: if one has the financial means, getting one's mar-

riage annulled is quite easy; if one does not have the necessary resources, it is impossible. In addition, the lack of formal divorce makes the establishment of alimony and child support payments extremely difficult. This situation is aggravated by the fact that Chilean children born outside of marriage have less right to parental financial support and inheritance than children born within marriage. In 1995, 40 percent of Chilean children were born outside of marriage, many of them to parents who had previously been married and were unable to remarry (Centro de Estudios de la Mujer 1996b: 3). Proponents of legal divorce thus argue that the lack of civil divorce disadvantages women and children.

19 The differences among Christian denominations with regard to divorce is discussed in Madrid 1996: 236.

20 According to public opinion polls cited by the Center for Research on Women, in 1996, 85 percent of Chileans were in favor of legal divorce (Centro de Estudios de la Mujer 1996b: 4).

21 In interviews with the author, this phrase "collecting on the bill" was used repeatedly by members of Congress to describe the lobbying tactics of the Church.

22 See endnote no. 1.

23 From interview with the autor. Valparaiso, Chile. January 15, 1997.

24 In 1997, a law was passed formally establishing freedom of religion in Chile, thereby granting other established denominations the same rights and official recognition as the Catholic Church.

25 For example, the Right has defended the current system of "designated Senators," which allows 9 of 45 Senators to be appointed rather than elected, against attempts by the *Concertacíon* government to make all Senators stand for election. According to the 1980 Constitution, all ex-presidents are entitled to become designated Senators. Amid tremendous public controversy, in March 1997, General Pinochet retired as head of the Army and took his place in the Senate.

REFERENCES

Arthur, Blanca. 1997. "Dos Bellas y Audaces: Las Protagonistas de la Gran Disputa de RN." *El Mercurio*, April 27: D22.

――――. 1991. "Arzobispo Oviedo advirtió de 'campaña' que pretende disolver a la familia chilena." *La Epoca*, June 10: 11.

Betsalel, Claudio. 1994. "Divorcio: Por la Ley de Dios." *Ercilla*, May 6: 29-30.

Bofill, Cristian and Pedro Ramirez. 1997. "Sexo, SIDA, Divorcio, Censura e Hipocresia, Segun Lavn." *Qué Pasa*, May 3: 4-8.

Brito, Eugenia. 1997. "El Discurso sobre 'la Crisis Moral.'" In Olga Grau, et al. eds. *Discurso, Genero, y Poder-Discursos Públicos: Chile 1978-1993.* Santiago, Chile: LOM-ARCIS.

――――. 1996. "Brunner: Estado No Debe Dar Contenido Valrico a Jocas." *El Mercurio*, September 26: A2.

Cáceres, Ana, et. al. 1993. *Cómo Les Ha Ido a las Mujeres en la Democracia?* Santiago, Chile: Instituto de la Mujer.

Castillo Vicencio, Arturo and Telmo Meléndez. 1994. "Divorcio: Polemico Desencuentro." *Ercilla*, May 6: 26-28.

Centro de Estudios de la Mujer. 1996a. "Educar o no educar . . . el dilema de la educación sexual." *Argumentos Para el Cambio*, No. 7: 1-4.

————. 1996b. "Quien Le Tiene Miedo a la Ley de Divorcio?" *Argumentos Para el Cambio*, No. 11: 1-4.

Chamber of Deputies. 1997a. *Redacción de Sesiones*, No. 42a, January 22. Valparaiso: Congreso Nacional de Chile.

————. 1997b. *Redacción de Sesiones*, No. 43a, January 22. Valparaiso: Congreso Nacional de Chile.

————. 1997c. *Redacción de Sesiones*, No. 44a, January 23. Valparaiso: Congreso Nacional de Chile.

Conferencia Episcopal de Chile. 1989. *Certeza, Coherencia, y Confiancia: Mensaje a los Catolicos Chilenos en una Hora de Transicion*. Santiago: Area de Comunicaciones de la Conferencia Episcopal de Chile.

Cristi, María Angélica. 1996. *Mecanismos Para Fortalecer La Familia*. Paper presented at Seminario Mujer, Familia y Trabajo, April 30, Santiago, Chile.

Delsing, Riet. 1997. "El Problema del Divorcio en Chile." In Olga Grau, et al., eds. *Discurso, Genero, y Poder- Discursos Púbilicos: Chile 1978-1993*. Santiago, Chile: LOM-ARCIS.

————. 1997a. "Diputada Cristi: Una ley de divorcio 'no soluciona nada.'" *La Epoca*, February 2: 12.

————. 1991b. "Diputada descalificó opinión de Büchi contraria al divorcio." *La Epoca*, June 14: 9.

————. 1990. "Dirigentes del PDC rechazaron proyecto de ley sobre divorcio." *La Epoca*, September 26: 3.

Farías, Alejandra. 1997. "Sobre Educación de la Sexualidad." In Olga Grau, et al. *Discurso, Genero, y Poder–Discursos Púbilicos: Chile 1978-1993*. Santiago, Chile: LOM-ARCIS.

Frohmann, Alicia and Teresa Valdes. 1993. *Democracy in the Country and in the Home: The Women's Movement in Chile*. Santiago, Chile: FLACSO.

Fuenzalida, Orozimbo. 1997. "Carta Sobre el Divorcio." *La Epoca*, January 28: 10.

Gorosabel, Jacinto. 1997. "Letter to the Editor." *La Epoca,* May 5: 8.

Instituto Libertad. 1991. *Boletn Semanal*, II (14): 6.

Lagos, Andrea. 1997. "Las Otras JOCAS: Revolucionario Programa de la Universidad de Chile." *La Tercera*, April 20: 6-7.

Madrid Meza, Ral. 1996. "Cuestión de Estado." *La Nación*, June 7: 36.

Medina, Jorge. 1995. *De Nuevo el Tema del Divorcio Vincular*. Valparaiso, Chile: Arzobispado de Valparaiso.

————. 1997b. "Obispo Errázuriz: divorcio vulnera derecho de pareja." *La Epoca*, September 10: 12.

Oviedo, Carlos. 1991. *Morality, Youth, and Permissive Society*. Santiago, Chile: Arzobispado de Santiago.

Rojas, Juanita. 1991. "Divorcio: Se Acabará la Mentira?" *Analisis*, No. 385: 3-8.

Rozas Vial, Fernando. 1989. "El Programa de la Concertacin y la Familia." *El Mercurio*, September 21: A2.

Vaccaro, Victor. 1997. "Denuncian presiones por divorcio." *La Tercera*, January 2: 7.

Zilci, Sonia. 1994. "Divorcio: El 'Lobby' de los Curas." *Hoy*, No. 87: 18-20.

THREE

CATHOLIC ACTIVISM IN THE 1990S
NEW STRATEGIES FOR THE NEOLIBERAL AGE

Sarah Brooks

"The Catholic Church philosophy used to be 'give men fish'; I say,
'don't give men fish—teach men to fish!'"
—Aurelio Tang Ramirez, Secretary General, CARETAS,
San Jose de Amazonas, Peru

The Catholic Church has long played a meaningful role among the
social and political institutions in Latin America. Although its presence
in the daily life of Latin Americans has endured for centuries, the nature
of Catholic expression and the form of church insertion into political
and social life have changed dramatically over time and across borders.
From the time of the conquest when missionaries stood side-by-side
with Spanish soldiers in the colonization of the Americas, through the
twentieth-century struggles for liberation from the injustices of which
the church was once a part, the Catholic presence has undergone a
continual process of redefinition of its role in society.

While these dramatic shifts bear witness to the broad range of possible interpretations of church doctrine, so too do they reveal a striking
diversity of means through which the Catholic church has chosen to
advance its theological and pastoral objectives in society. From the
sponsorship of political parties in the 1920s, to collaboration with and
later mobilization against military regimes in the 1970s and 1980s, to
the recent apolitical countenance assumed by many national churches in
the 1990s, the Catholic Church in Latin America has proven able to
respond to its social and political environment in a variety of ways.

Some scholars regard the 1990s as an exception to this history of
poignant Catholic activism in Latin America (Burdick 1993; Stoll 1994;
Coleman et.al. 1994). Citing the decline in membership of base
communities and Catholic unions, loss of institutional support, decline

in the number of street protests and strikes, and fall of its traditional political allies on the Left, these scholars generally conclude that the progressive Catholic Church in Latin America has fallen into crisis. Regarding grassroots Catholic activism as a thing of the past, studies of religion in Latin America have thus begun in recent years to emphasize the vigorous growth of Protestant churches as the principle source of religious energy at the grassroots of society (Ireland 1991; Martin 1990; Stoll 1990; Stoll & Garrard Burnett 1993).

This chapter presents an alternative to the view that Catholic activism in Latin America is in crisis (see also Levine 1995). By examining the changing *political opportunity structures* of Peru, this study suggests that transformations in the social and political context have altered the patterns of religious activism at the grassroots of society. As a consequence, finding the progressive Catholic Church in the 1990s requires that we look for it in social spaces and in roles that are fundamentally distinct from those occupied by Catholics activists in previous decades. An understanding of the structures of political opportunity in Latin American society thus opens up the conceptual possibility of our hypothesis: that the progressive base of the Catholic Church is not dead, it has only changed its form. We begin, then, with three illustrations from distinct segments of the Catholic Church in Peru that are emblematic of a new *political logic* of grassroots activism in the neoliberal age.

FINDING THE PROGRESSIVE CHURCH IN THE 1990S: THREE CASES

"Ordinary people have ideas of their own. They want to act in ways that will benefit themselves, their families, and communities, but their politics are much less crude, much more nuanced" (Levine, 1995:16).

On a cool morning in July 1995, Fr. Pete Byrne, a Catholic Maryknoll priest in Lima, Peru, emerges from a new office building in the burgeoning corporate sector of San Isidro. Fr. Byrne has been meeting with executives from the major candy, dairy, and confectionery manufacturers in Peru. Later that week, he will meet with representatives from the Peruvian National Association of Industries (SNI) and the Federation of Workers (FT). Father Byrne is not planning to start up his own business, nor is he organizing laborers. Instead, Fr. Byrne is looking for strategic partners, entities with power and resources in Peru that can help him spread the message of his movement for children's human rights. In the mid-1990s, he is looking in the right place, as multinational corporations are to be found among the most powerful institutions and actors in society, even more than the State. In previous decades, Fr. Byrne might have mobilized women and children from the *pueblos jovenes* (shantytowns that encircle Lima) to march upon the city or federal government buildings to demand political or material support for their cause. Power at one time was denominated in numbers; today it is found in market share.

On his way home from the meetings, Fr. Byrne drives past one of the newly opening gas station franchises springing up in Peru since the opening of the domestic market to foreign corporations. He observes the teams of women positioned in the lot distributing advertisements to customers and passersby. Fr. Byrne decides that these, too, could be useful allies for his movement, Pro Bien Nino-Nina, as they might easily hand out pamphlets with information on children's rights along with their advertisements. Soon he expects not only to find the message of his organization diffused throughout society on the sides of milk cartons and on candy wrappers, but perhaps also in the burgeoning networks of petroleum stations.

Indeed, multinational corporations are unlikely allies and carriers of the activist agenda of the Catholic Church in Latin America, but efforts such as those of Fr. Byrne and Pro Bien represent the emerging trend in grassroots activism in Peru. Pro Bien Nino-Nina was created in response to what Byrne perceived as the dire need for a voice and action from the Catholic Church on the question of the human rights of children. Observing that armed protest against the injustices of the social structures in Latin America seemed only to worsen the death and violence in Peru, Byrne chose to combat this injustice at what he believed to be its sources, in the culture and values of the citizens. Fr. Byrne thus crafted a new form of Catholic action that parted company with traditional methods and allies through which to diffuse his message.

This choice of strategy began with the conviction by Fr. Byrne that evangelization must not be moored to the realm of Sunday worship or parish rituals. In order to truly reach the people in a meaningful way, he decided that conversion must occur within the political, economic, social, and cultural spheres that engender the violence and injustice toward children. In this sense, Pro Bien's message of children's human rights is diffused through what Fr. Byrne regards as the "ordinary" relations of life, such as family and neighborhood relationships. By simply distributing information to raise awareness of the rights of children, Pro Bien works ultimately to motivate changes in individuals that will lead to "greater solidarity" through all levels of society.

Perhaps the most remarkable aspect of this organization is the manner in which Pro Bien utilizes the new channels and opportunities created by the economic restructuring to diffuse the message of children's human rights throughout Peru. In addition to the organizations mentioned above, the national institution to promote children in Peru, as well as the National Police, agreed to collaborate with Pro Bien in the distribution of pamphlets. This strategy, though utilizing political institutions, differs from the traditional forms of mobilization. In particular, Byrne does not seek financial support from the State, nor does he utilize the traditional political decision-making forums of power. Rather, through alliances, Pro Bien aims solely to utilize the vast distributional capacity of government agencies to advance Pro Bien's cause. Although the government officially refuses to distribute political literature, the collaboration of these institutions with Pro Bien reveal the "great lack of understanding on the part of the government" of the ultimately political and progressive objectives that underpin this movement. Although distinctly political in its ultimate objective, Pro Bien Nino-Nina utilizes strategies that depart from the traditional methods and avenues of political expression.

Elsewhere in Peru, in the town of Caraveli, a Catholic Church official is donning a hard hat to begin the inspections of the gold processing factory recently purchased by the Episcopal Commission for Social Action (CEAS). Here again, the Catholic Church is not going into business, or attempting to expand its wealth. Rather, it is implementing its social doctrine of empowering and cultivating social solidarity among the rural poor of Peru, whose economic and social resources were greatly eroded by the crisis of hyperinflation and political violence in the 1980s.

Whereas union organizing, land invasions, and collective protest movements were once the means of advancing social and economic strength of the poor, today such strategies have been taken out of reach by the recent political and economic reforms. These reforms diminished the rights of collective bargaining by workers and removed the use of subsidies and price controls as means of protecting the incomes of certain social groups. Added to the disruption of the social fabric in Peru that occurred as a consequence of the *Sendero Luminoso* (Shining Path) guerrilla insurgency, CEAS was forced to find new forms of "social action" through which to build up the social and economic groundwork of society.

CEAS was created in the 1960s to serve as a liaison between the Church and the government, and voiced the official position of the Church on political events of the day. Throughout the 1970s, CEAS carried out leadership training programs and sponsored community mobilization projects at the grassroots. In recent years, as political engagement has declined as a priority of the Church leadership, CEAS officials faced internal incentives to look for new ways to support social change in Peru.

CEAS officials developed a doctrine of *integral development* in response to the observation that the strains of economic and political crisis had tended to subordinate motives of social solidarity to individualism. They recognized, however, that their traditional role in providing leadership support for ecclesiastical base communities was no longer a viable strategy in the 1990s. The integral development program forged alliances between local Churches and nongovernmental organizations to implement development projects in rural peasant communities.

Included in this social solidarity project is what CEAS calls its ministry of mineral rights ("Pastoral Mineral"), mentioned above. This ministry began when the Church purchased a gold processing factory in the town of Caraveli, Peru. The goal of the project was to build the capacity for economic development among the members of the community. Church workers, with the help of nongovernment organizations, trained the local population to manage the processing plant and engage in productive enterprise with the goal of ending their dependence on external subsidies and government food assistance. As soon as the training was completed and the finances were on steady ground, CEAS was expecting to turn over ownership of the plant to local townspeople.

This project suggests that the response of the Peruvian Catholic Church to the political and economic upheaval in the 1990s was not simply to withdraw from political engagement, but to build a new source of empowerment at the grassroots of society. This is a form of empowerment not based in the methods of collective action popularized in the 1960s or 1970s, but grounded instead in the development of individual capacity to provide for themselves and to break the cycles of dependence in which many poor people have long been trapped.

In addition to the Pastoral Mineral, CEAS carries out solidarity programs by financing loans for small artisans and microenterprises in rural areas. In 1995, more than $350 million was invested in projects for small to midsize enterprises throughout Peru. While this may appear more consistent with the objectives of a bank than a Church ministry, CEAS members affirm that projects are chosen for funding only according to the testimony of solidarity and sense of the Church's pastoral ministry embodied in the enterprise. In this sense, the goal of liberation is recast by CEAS into a framework wherein people have the capacity to provide for themselves a basic level of well-being and dignified life merited as children of God. The unique means through which CEAS advances this struggle for liberation, moreover, substitutes investments in human capital for the models of group protest of the past.

Two hours outside of Lima, in the lush Huaura Valley, young adults from rural areas throughout Peru are finishing their afternoon classes in a six-week training program at the Institute for Rural Education (IER). Some students are in entrepreneurship and marketing classes, while others are studying hydroponics. All are being trained to compete in the newly opened agricultural market. Again, this is the unlikely setting in which we find Catholic activists in Peru in the 1990s. Each day of technical training at the IER is closed with a mass offered by former liberation theology adherents of the 1960s. Today, these Catholic activists are spending more time procuring grants from development foundations to add a shrimp cultivation facility to their institute, which they will locate just behind the hydroponics nursery.

Founded in 1961 in Peru, the IER was typical of Catholic activism in Latin America at that time. Its leaders engaged in grassroots leadership training, embraced liberation theology, and directly confronted the political issues affecting rural farm workers. In the 1960s, Catholic clergy and lay activists in the IER attempted to incorporate the rural peasantry into a political force in Peru. This was intended both to preempt the growth of communism in the region, and to provide a counterweight to the political strength of the conservative oligarchy.

In the early 1970s, the revolutionary military regime of General Juan Velasco Alvarado enacted a broad reform of the land ownership system. This law permitted peasants to claim large tracts of land from their landlords for use in personal cultivation. In response to this law, the IER leaders began to hold education and training courses for peasants, which included instruction in the precise legal procedures for invading and claiming their own land. In addition, IER courses encouraged the formation of unions, leadership training, and emphasized political involvement in one's community as the means through which to advance the rights of campesinos.

In the 1960s and 1970s, the IER received funding from the Peruvian Catholic Church, and utilized Church-owned land for its training and agricultural facilities. Although technical education in agriculture was always at the foundation of the IER's mission, it was complemented in previous decades by the emphasis given to political organizing and leadership training. The mid-1980s witnessed an important change in the source of funding and the types of programs taught by the Institute. The Church leadership withdrew financial support from the Institute, but permitted it to continue utilizing Church land.

This provoked IER's leaders to fundamentally redefine its strategy and immediate goals. Where the state and Church institutions were not disposed to provide support, the IER allied with international development and Catholic service organizations. At the same time, the IER altered its curriculum toward a greater emphasis on technical production, self-management skills, and entrepreneurship. The land invasions have been long abandoned, and rural unions and cooperatives have been splintered under a series of structural reforms enacted by President Fujimori. With the withdrawal of government subsidies under the structural adjustment programs, rural farmers were forced to pursue competitiveness rather than political ties in order to succeed. Political leadership training thus gave way to courses in agricultural technology, business management, and marketing. The prayers at the end of each day at the IER serve as reminders of the Catholic mission behind that program: human and Christian development, through self-sufficiency and technical capacitation.

It is reasonable to question whether the changing strategies for individual behavior in the 1990s embody truly political transformations, or whether any political concerns are overshadowed by the demands for survival amidst economic crisis. Whereas these grassroots strategies might be viewed simply as creative anomalies, we will suggest in the remainder of this chapter that they may be taken as well to be indications of a systematic response to the changing structures of opportunity for activism in Latin America.

GRASSROOTS CATHOLIC ACTIVISM IN THE 1990s

The history of the Catholic Church in Latin America is one of continual change and transformation. After independence, the Catholic Church commenced what became a century-long sequence of pendular swings into and out of political action. With each reinsertion, the Catholic Church's presence took a new form as it joined company with new allies. Each new shape or means of political participation corresponded to the real opportunities afforded by the political and institutional frameworks of the time. This meant that the Church could be found organizing trade unions and political parties in the 1930s and 1940s, while in the 1960s it shifted to support of street-level protests, rural land invasions, and collective means of struggle for social justice through the theology of liberation. Although the underlying message and objective of action has drawn from the basic tenets of Catholic Church doctrine, each new *form* of political insertion was shaped closely by the prevailing social and political logic of the time.

In the 1980s, the protest models and grassroots collective action that characterized the progressive Church in the 1970s began to decline in prominence. The military regimes that once were the target of struggle and protest collapsed, giving way to constitutional democracy throughout the region. Economically, the hopes of socialists were shattered as parties of the Left failed to consolidate an alternative to the liberal market model that swept the region. Within the Catholic Church, conservative factions gathered strength and increased in numbers throughout the region. As they did, their strength in the leadership of the Catholic Church enabled them to redirect institutional resources and energies away from the visible and confrontational activities of earlier decades. To many observers, the activism at the base of the Catholic Church was dead or dying.

The alternative to this scenario is the view that progressive Catholics have not entirely given up their struggle for justice, but have instead changed their mode of engagement in response to the logic and incentives of their immediate context. In this sense, we may consider the street protests, base communities, and land invasions of the 1960s and 1970s more as particular *means* of struggle, than as the embodiment of Catholic activism itself. This view opens up a broad array of possibilities for action through which progressive Catholics may diffuse their message and respond to the challenges and opportunities that confront them. This may even include engagement in technical training, forging alliances with multinational corporations, or sponsoring entrepreneurship as means of advancing Catholic doctrine in the 1990s. In order to consider that Catholic activism is indeed persevering after the decline of collective protest movements, it is important thus to distinguish in this way the underlying *objectives* of social justice from the *means* of struggle employed to achieve this.

The political and economic transformations of the past decade have generated many obstacles to grassroots mobilization. At the same time, however, these have nurtured a host of new opportunities and issues that have reinvigorated grassroots Church activism. In the next section, we will locate specific changes in the structure of political and economic opportunities that have shaped the actions of Catholic groups and organizations in recent years.

The economic crisis that gripped the "lost decade" of the 1980s ended in a wave of internationally sponsored programs of market reform and economic adjustment. These reforms, which were adopted in various degrees throughout Latin America, aimed to distance or remove the state from the center of resource distribution in society. This meant removing the control politicians had over the allocation of wealth in society, such as through state subsidies and regulations of the economy. These methods, along with control over social organizations and political institutions, were long used by governments to direct and control social and economic development in Latin America.

This sequence of economic crisis and reform altered not only the proximate goals of Catholic activism, but shaped as well the forms in which people's interests were advanced. Activism shifted away from broad group interests such as justice and civil rights, and instead focused upon more basic and immediate personal goals such as survival. Moreover, individuals' participation in broad, collective efforts were limited by the more pressing need to secure their individual and family well-being.

Survival thus became the leading goal of social expressions, and the means to ensure survival were recognized as building self-sufficiency and capacity at the individual or family level. The heavy demand of working two jobs simply to provide for their families was cited as the reason many Catholics dropped out of base communities. Before they could advance the Kingdom of God, many former activists said they had to feed their children. The immediate demands of providing for one's basic needs thus displaced the will or ability of many Catholics to participate in collective movements toward broad and distant goals such as liberation.

At the same time as participation in progressive Church movements declined, the political landscape in which these had operated was radically overturned. The demise of military regimes throughout Latin America in the 1980s removed the primary target around which collective protest movements had unified and gathered support. Concomitantly, political parties of the Left, the traditional allies for these movements in Peru, suffered from ideological and organizational divisions and were near collapse by the end of the 1980s. The restoration of democratic processes thus had the effect of diminishing the energy behind grassroots activism.

Whether the recent dramatic political and economic transformations in Latin America have meant a decline or simply a change in forms of progressive Catholic church activism is the question to which we now turn. Whereas influential scholars have suggested that Catholic activists have failed to build "enduring and effective organizations" in the context of the new freedoms and possibilities of democratic capitalism (Levine and Stoll 1995), the illustrations below suggest that it is precisely the fact that organizational forms have not endured through the years that has permitted Catholic activism to persist in the 1990s. The departure from means of expression that were useful in the past, and the utilization instead of the new opportunities of democratic capitalism, may be the key to survival for Catholic as well as other grassroots movements in Latin America.

TRANSFORMATIONS IN CATHOLIC ACTIVISM:
IMPULSES FROM WITHIN

Radical Catholic activism peaked in Peru in the 1970s, when members of grassroots movements directly challenged the entrenched structures of domination with their call to social justice and liberation for the poor. From the highest ranks of the Episcopate to the catechists in base communities, Catholics in Peru gathered in support of the struggle for liberation through land invasions, labor strikes, rural education movements, and political organization. In the period from 1976-1978, Church leaders spoke out freely on the question of injustices of economic and political power. Confirming its mission in the name of the poor, Catholic workers became intimately involved in grassroots liberation movements.

At this time, the military regime became aware that the social mobilization it had previously encouraged had grown out of its control. This provoked the military President General Morales Bermudez to unleash a period of harsh repression upon activist movements, including Catholic base communities. The scores of people killed, tortured, or who disappeared at the hands of the military were a heavy toll on the progressive Church in Peru as well as in other parts of Latin America. Activists suffered the loss of not only the individuals killed, but also the many more who abandoned hope in the usefulness of protest activism.

The impulse of Catholic activism weakened further with the fall of the military regime and the return to democracy in 1980. Whereas this might seem to be something that would have emboldened the base communities with the success of their struggle, the effect was the opposite. Conservative leaders in the Church who had not supported the confrontational strategies of liberationist groups in the 1970s had nevertheless remained silent at that time due to their even stronger opposition to the repression and power of the military governments. The existence of the military regime as a common and overarching enemy thus dwarfed the divisions within the Church leadership. After the transition to democracy, these divisions were freely expressed.

The return to democratic rule brought to light deep ideological divisions in the Church, as more conservative and reactionary members of the leadership challenged the prominence of liberation theologians in the Bishops council of Latin America. The early 1980s witnessed a concerted effort by conservative bishops to reclaim control over institutional resources and Church authority. This included efforts to silence their opposition within the Church and remove prominent activist bishops from leadership positions. A conspicuous illustration of this was the replacement of the slain liberationist Bishop Oscar Romero in El

Salvador with a conservative appointee from Rome. In South America, the prominent liberation theologian Leonardo Boff was censured by the Church and silenced for a year. Without the common enemy of the military regimes, internal splits in the Catholic Church surfaced in the 1980s and led to a strong reaction by opponents of the more confrontational grassroots activism.

In 1982, this conservative resurgence in the Church leadership was evidenced when Bishop Augusto Vargas Alzamora, the General Secretary of the Peruvian Episcopate, and Bishop Ricardo Durand Florez of Callao expelled the activist group EMO (*Equipos de Mision Obrera*) from Peru (Pena 1992). The EMO had come to symbolize the strength of Catholic protest organizers in the 1970s and thus was among the first groups to feel the effects of this ideological recoil.

The conservative backlash aimed to remove the Church from the overtly political role that some practitioners of liberation theology had taken on in previous years. Reactionary Catholics endeavored to replace the theology of liberation with a "theology of reconciliation" that would put behind it the confrontational and outwardly political activism of the previous decade. The *Sodalitium Vitae* movement was symbolic of this trend in Peru. This group tried to maintain the goal of social justice in its efforts, while casting off the activist disposition and political resonance of Catholic action in previous decades.

Moreover, the consequences of this ideological change in the leadership was felt at the grassroots in the loss of institutional resources and support for activist organizations. The recoiling of the Catholic leadership greatly demoralized the progressive Catholics who saw their efforts undermined by criticism from within their own institution. In Peru, notions of political transformation were removed from the discourse of pastoral action. Those priests who politicized Church teaching or engaged in political activities were tagged "Marxists" and subject to censorship by their bishop (Pena 1992). Leaders conveyed the unequivocal message that Catholics not only should separate their faith from politics, but also that they should advance their general welfare through individual means, such as hard work, rather than through collective action.

Community action projects in the 1980s thus assumed a less political and more economically empowering orientation. The goal of addressing the needs of the poor remained central to these projects, but Church leaders cautioned sternly against making demands on the government. The importance of private activity was explained by one bishop in the following way:

Sometimes the government does not have the capacity to [help the poor] either, and we should be prepared to provide people with help either from foreign Catholic institutions, or not necessarily Catholic, but groups who can help us with materials to build a life with dignity: water, drainage, walkways, roads—the fundamentals. These things help to provide skills for people in these communities ... women work from their homes and help themselves. They are making a contribution and at the same time they help themselves without having to wait for handouts (quoted in Pena 1992:167).

Even before the neoliberal reforms went into effect, conservative movements within the Church began to direct grassroots activities away from political involvement and toward private means of action. This leadership change equipped Catholic activists with the requisite skills to engage in *private* and *decentralized* actions. It is this type of activity that we shall suggest also conforms with the character of new political opportunity structures in the 1990s.

The 1980s thus witnessed a change in the dominant ideology guiding not only economic relations, but the leadership of the Catholic Church as well. As failed progressive economic models gave way to economic liberalism and market governance, the restoration of democracy made it possible for conservative Catholic leaders to express their opposition to activist adherents and to gain control of the Church hierarchy.

WHITHER THE ACTIVIST CHURCH?

Scholars have offered a variety of interpretations for the apparent decline of grassroots Catholic activism in Latin America. One strain of research examines the burgeoning presence of Protestant faiths to explain the sharp turn in pastoral action in the Catholic Church (Adriance 1992; Burdick 1993; Stoll 1990; Gill 1994). The flexible and progressive outreach methods of Protestant evangelicals, one view suggests, enable them to more effectively recruit members at the grassroots of society. Catholic activism, in contrast, fails insofar as it remains moored to its traditional hierarchic structure of authority (insofar as priests and parishes monopolize the center of power and worship). Even the seemingly progressive effort of the Catholic leadership toward becoming a *voice for the voiceless* has been faulted for retaining the paternalistic model of Church authority: doing things *for* the people, rather than letting them do things for themselves (Levine and Stoll 1995). These scholars thus conclude that the failure of Catholics to depart from the traditional power and authority models has undermined their capacity to maintain support and participation at the grassroots.

Other scholars have turned to the contradictions in the structure of

activist organizations in the 1970s to understand the decreasing presence of Catholic protest movements. Noting the importance of practical
forms of action in recent years (those that would pay off in some direct
and tangible form), observers attribute the growth of Protestantism at
the grassroots to their emphasis on advancing "a tangible, manageable
formula for living," which contrasts with the abstract and grand visions
of social transformation furthered by liberationists. By preaching a
theology based on personal improvement (such as changing one's drinking habits), this view suggests, Protestant churches attract members by
presenting concrete opportunities for people to change what is within
their reach and make discernible improvements in their lives. In this
sense, Levine and Stoll argue that the "crisis" of grassroots Catholic
activism owes fundamentally to a breach between the espoused goal of
empowerment of the poor, and the actual *power* claimed by those
groups (1995). The failure of collective protest movements to produce
tangible and enduring benefits for their participants is in this way
regarded as the defeat of the liberationist project.

In presenting an alternative to these views, this chapter argues that
much of the research on the "crisis" of grassroots Catholic activism
overlooks at its premise a very important concept. That is, such views
begin with the assumption that the decline in certain forms of social
expression signifies the failure of the motivating force and intention
behind those forms. In other words, it confuses the action itself with the
message and actors that bring about the action. In viewing the decline of
collective mobilization as the downfall of activism itself, scholars risk
reifying the grassroots Church as the very form of action in which its
members have previously found expression.

With caution not to view the protest groups and movements as the
Church actors or entities in themselves, we attempt to follow Teresa
Tovar and "see a plurality of subjects, whose identities are created
through their own interactions and forms of understanding, and whose
positions are therefore changeable" (Tovar 1991: 31). This conceptualization permits us to separate the phenomenon of Catholic activism
from those forms of expression in which it flourished visibly in previous
decades, such as in ecclesial base communities and collective protests.
Moreover, this view permits us to treat forms of activism as unique
strategies, chosen in response to the logic and opportunities of the
context in which they were expressed. We shall thus follow the admoni-
tion of Daniel Levine and examine not only "the people" of theory, but
also "look closely at what real people say, think and do. . .[wherein] it
becomes evident that the alternatives excluded on a conceptual level are

regularly put together in everyday life" (Levine 1995: 119).

The history of the Catholic Church bears witness to a vibrant capacity to adapt and respond to changes in its social and political context; however, the forms of Catholic expression are not driven wholly by their context. Rather, an important impulse for change is generated from within the Catholic Church itself. This emerges from the process of reflection upon and reinterpretation of its role in society to which the Church continually subjects itself. Innovations in Catholic ecclesiology (the vision of the character and role of the Church in society) have thus developed from this ongoing reflection and reconsideration, particularly as it is shaped by the many contending ideologies of Church leaders.

Thus there are parallel impulses of internal redefinition of the Church's mission and external social and political transformation that combine to continually transform Catholic theology and action. Assuming that this history has not come to an end, we may look instead to find ways in which Catholics in Latin America are adopting new strategies for survival and extension of their message to the new structures of political expression in the 1990s.

SOCIAL MOVEMENT THEORY AND
THE PROGRESSIVE CHURCH OF THE 1990S

Locating the source of change in an institution as large and internally diverse as the Catholic Church is at best a precarious task. While acknowledging the important forces compelling change within the Church, we place greater emphasis upon the conditions outside the Church that shape the incentives, motives, and possibilities for activism by members and leaders within the Church. The forms of Catholic action that are treated as "political" in this sense are those actions of a group or individuals that challenge the institutions that determine the distribution of resources in society. This political presence of the Church is embodied in many of the daily life choices of Latin American Catholics. From their decisions about family planning, to how they spend their money and time, to what they eat, the Church has influenced important choices and social behaviors of its members. These everyday practices of Church teaching are important to understanding the ways that individuals in the Church craft their understanding of Catholic doctrine to fit the array of needs, possibilities, and constraints of their time, particularly in a reality that is physically as well as ideologically distant from that of the Vatican.

The relevant aspects of the local context that shape the Church presence include the structures of political and social power. These influence the space available for and legitimacy attributed to different forms of organization, as well as the possibility for effectiveness of those forms. To understand the relationship between the Catholic Church and its social and political environment, it is useful to employ a principle of contemporary social movement theory: the notion of "political opportunity structures." Although the cultural and historical significance of the Catholic Church in Latin America certainly transcends that of a typical social movement, it is useful to consider this analogy.

In its effort to transform Latin American social conditions the Catholic Church fits well within the classic definition of a "social movement" as that which seeks "a change in certain social institutions" (Herberle 1951: 6). Indeed, the progressive mobilizing force of the Church has compelled important transformations in the basic fabric of society. As one observer notes, the activism of the Catholic Church has caused "the emergence of popular groups and of popular voices able to speak and act for themselves [that] has changed the landscape of religion, politics, and culture in contemporary Latin America" (Levine 1992: 6). In this way, the mobilizing and transforming mission of the Catholic Church has earned it a position as one of the most deep-reaching social movements in Latin America.

The structure of political and social power—the conjuncture of structures and forces external to the Church that shape the patterns of action through which members realize the doctrinal and institutional objectives of the Church—is thus important for understanding how Catholic Church doctrine is brought to life in different forms of grassroots action. The Church responds to its environment in ways that are consistent with the "political logic" of the time. With this in mind, the link between individual choice, collective action, and their impact on national politics may be more clearly understood.

Changes in the political role of the Church in recent years have taken place in the context of profound social, economic, and political transformations. Those factors external to the Church that enhance or diminish its possibilities for success will be incorporated here into the notion of political opportunity structures (McAdam 1982). Tarrow employs a parsimonious, yet useful version of this theory, defining such structures as the "consistent—but not necessarily formal, permanent, or national—dimensions of the political environment that either encourage or discourage people from using collective action" (Tarrow 1994: 18). These may include the international political and economic forces that shape the domestic balance of power.

One of the global ideologies that has most forcefully altered domestic politics throughout Latin America in recent years is "neoliberal" economic theory (Williamson 1983). This school of thought rests on a fundamental belief in the market as the most efficient, and therefore best, mechanism through which resources are allocated in society. Neoliberal reforms were prescribed throughout Latin America as a remedy for the economic crisis of the 1980s, which was ascribed to the effects of excessive intervention of the state in the economy. The authority of the government over production, regulation, and the transfer of resources in society thus became the target of reforms that aimed to bring these functions under the regulation of competitive market forces.

The impact of this model has been unrivaled by that of any other economic ideology in the past two decades. Neoliberalism was embraced by multilateral lending institutions (such as the International Monetary Fund and the World Bank), which made the extension of development aid and emergency stabilization funds contingent upon the implementation of market reforms. Given that Latin American governments relied heavily upon external financing, the economic plans promulgated by international lending institutions exerted significant weight in the domestic political arena. Insofar as market reforms brought emergency financial aid and an end to hyperinflation, national politicians favoring them gained wide support, bolstering such reforms as the dominant policy objective of the 1990s.[1]

While the international arena provides an important context for understanding political dynamics in Latin America, the nature of domestic political structures is perhaps more important for understanding the social and political strategies of the Church. Facilitating this task, Sidney Tarrow has identified three significant dimensions of political opportunity structures. The first involves the openness of access to political power. This is measured by the accessibility of formal structures of representation of local and national governments to their countries' citizens (Brinton 1965). Accessibility implies both the opportunity to express social interests in formal political structures, and the existence of some mechanism, such as elections, that compels politicians to answer to their constituents. The greater the openness of political institutions, the more likely it is that popular movements will be able to utilize political avenues and forms of expression, such as lobbying or voting, to advance their cause.

The second key dimension of political opportunity structures relates to the stability of political alignments. This can be regarded as the steadiness of alliances of power in the formal political institutions. When governing coalitions are unstable, social groups can more easily win concessions to their demands (Tarrow 1983). The stability of political arrangements relates likewise to the existence and reliability of political allies who may serve as a vehicle for advancing the message of the social movement within formal political structures. We shall see below that the response to the instability of the United Left, the political allies of Catholic activists in the 1980s, was an important stimulus of the turn to new forms of expression and action in the 1990s.

The third important dimension of political opportunity structures relates to the existence of allies or support groups to help advance the message and goals of the movement. The nature of the institutions that have been able and disposed to bolster Catholic activist organizations has changed dramatically in the past decade. Whereas most Catholic activism had drawn institutional and financial support from the Church hierarchy and from political ties, the fiscal impact and reverberations of the economic crisis of the 1980s closed off the Church and state as primary sources of support.

Catholic groups have been forced in the 1990s to adapt to the changes in their political and economic context in important ways. The groups that have survived, including those described earlier in this chapter, have succeeded in redefining their strategy and immediate goals for spreading their message in society. Doing so has required them to reconceptualize their organizational identities in a way that is consistent with the new constraints and opportunities for action in the 1990s. They have adopted new forms of mobilization and have found new allies and spaces within which to advance their collective goals. These are distinct from the spaces that Catholic activists have traditionally occupied; they are outside the parish, away from the street demonstrations, and far from the halls of formal political power.

THE NEOLIBERAL TRANSFORMATION

The state in Latin America has traditionally held control of economic development in society. The "developmental state" economic model was adopted throughout the region in the 1950s, positioning the state as the guiding hand of the economy through close direction of production, credit, currency value, and the labor market. Through the ownership of large enterprises ranging from natural-resource mining to financial services, and through the extension of price controls to different sectors of the economy, governments exercised direct control over the allocation of resources in society. By politicizing domestic economic forces, political leaders in Latin America cultivated extensive patron-client networks to maintain their support bases in society. This system entailed the exchange of material benefits, such as funding for soup kitchens or wage hikes for workers, for political support for incumbent politicians.

Political leaders were thus the people to whom citizens turned to improve their material conditions and to obtain support for their communities.

This politicization of the economy was precisely the target of neoliberal economic reforms. Allocating blame for the debt crisis of the 1980s on the interference of politics in the economy, leaders throughout Latin America adopted orthodox stabilization and adjustment programs under the guidance of multilateral lending institutions. In several countries such as Peru, these measures were adopted through the use of "emergency powers" of the president and thus involved little deliberation or input by the social groups most directly affected by the reforms. Moreover, leaders who implemented the stabilization efforts that successfully tamed hyperinflation often won broad support for the continuation of these programs.[2]

Neoliberal reforms typically combine short-term stabilization measures to halt spiraling inflation with more penetrating, long-term adjustments to the structure of the economy. By placing the market as the basis of the distribution of resources in society, these reforms aim to correct the underlying sources of inflation and inefficient production in an economy. In addition, they seek to restore the confidence of international investors, whose capital is crucial for economic growth and development in Latin America. Maintaining this investor confidence has in recent years become vital for economic stability in the developing world, as the speed with which capital, goods, and information cross borders increases. As markets for goods and capital become more closely linked, investors holding mobile assets (such as currency and equity shares) acquire the capacity to "punish" governments by quickly shifting their investments from one country to the next. This "exit option" has buttressed the position of market reforms and reinforced the constraints on government participation in economic and social relations. As politics has been removed from the organization of many realms of society, the market has taken over those realms.

"FUJISHOCK" AND NEOLIBERAL PERU

Shortly following his election in 1990, President Alberto Fujimori of Peru announced the adoption of an extensive IMF-sponsored stabilization and adjustment program. "Fujishock," as the program was called, was a fourfold plan intended to curb inflation and return the economy to productiveness. Driven by the depth of the political and economic crises of the 1980s, Fujimori suspended Congress and reversed the antineoliberal platform on which he had run for the presidency. This dramatic turn followed a period of years in which Peru had been gripped by spiraling inflation, political mismanagement, corruption, and social violence. The situation reached its low point under the administration of Aprista president Alan Garcia (1985-1990). The conditions of social and political disorder left in the wake of the Garcia regime fanned widespread social mistrust of populist economics and of politicians, and laid the groundwork for Fujimori's transformation of political power structures.

The 1990 presidential election was a contest between two political outsiders, Mario Vargas Llosa, a novelist, and Fujimori, then a university rector. Vargas Llosa campaigned on a platform of orthodox structural adjustment, while Fujimori called for a more gradual approach to reform. This disposition changed dramatically after the election. In addition to his pursuit of deep structural reform of the economy, Fujimori endeavored to remove political parties from the role of institutional intermediaries between the state and society. Aiming to establish a "democracy without intermediaries," Fujimori implemented laws to diminish the role of political parties in government, and to greatly encumber the process of party formation. Under his plan, a system of public opinion audits would gauge public approval of government policies after they were implemented, thereby circumventing any representative institutions.

President Fujimori drew upon deep public mistrust of the traditional political parties to execute a systematic weakening of the political party structure in Peru. Ideological conflicts as well as organizational discord within the United Left, an alliance of leftist political parties, catalyzed its decline in the first years of Fujimori's government. This collapse of political parties of the Left removed the main institutional vehicle through which an activist agenda could be expressed in national political structures. Political arrangements were greatly destabilized by the mid-1990s, and the opportunity for grassroots activist organizations to form political alliances in opposition to the president was greatly constrained.

The weakening of the political parties was coupled with the enhancement of the executive power under the first Fujimori regime. The April 1992 *autogolpe* ("self coup") and subsequent period of technocratic rule gave Fujimori occasion to oversee the writing of a new constitution. This strengthened tremendously the powers of the President to issue laws by decree and to control the initiation of legislation. The previously bicameral legislature was replaced with a single body, fashioned to serve essentially as a "rubber stamp" for executive policy-making. President Fujimori thus succeeded in his first term to consolidate political power around the office of the executive. The consequence of this was to close the formal political avenues through which individuals and groups could voice their interests.

These transformations in political and economic power structures during the 1990s rendered untenable the strategies of grassroots interest expression and mobilization that had typified Catholic activist organizations in the 1960s and 1970s. Supplanting the political with market forces as the organizing principle in society generated a new set of criteria for successful advancement of interests, both secular and religious, and revealed new methods and avenues for expression of group messages. At the same time as the reach of the state in society narrowed, the immense changes in the tenor and structure of politics closed many of the traditional possibilities for social activism. Grassroots groups thus turned away from political leaders as the target of protest and lobbying, and away from formal political parties as support allies. Instead, they turned their energy toward the pursuit of private, local sources of support. During the economic crisis and the implementation of neoliberal reforms, means of expression shifted from collective to more individual levels of political protest, while the proximate objectives of activism turned to the more immediate needs of survival.

Neighborhood associations or landless peasants that once turned to protests and marches to secure subsidies or relief from government leaders, now find that their energies are best spent developing productive skills or effective marketing for their cooperatives. The usefulness of cultivating political ties or expressing power in numbers has thus declined greatly in the market-dominated society. Instead, power is redefined in terms of efficiency and competitiveness, and the pivotal unit of action shifts from the community to the household level. To the extent that market dynamics replace political structures as the logic of social organization, a centrifugal tendency emerges in interest expression, spinning formerly collective efforts into an array of individual, decentralized strategies of survival.

While it may seem that this logic should hold more for economic than social or religious movements, these strategies of expression at the grassroots relate to religious interests as well. Here it is important to recall the distinction between the underlying message or objective of a group, and the concrete strategy through which it is advanced. Just as the land invasions by ecclesiastical base communities in the 1970s replaced the Catholic union activism of the 1930s, or the "Catholic Action" weeks of the 1940s, the social and political action of the Catholic Church continues to develop in a manner consistent with the logic of the time.

In the 1990s, we perceive the process of change once again. The base community leaders who once led demonstrations in front of government offices, or marched in town plazas to express their interests, are now engaged in activities such as those mentioned earlier in this chapter. The objective of securing material support for collective efforts once meant cultivating and securing ties to political leaders or members of the Church hierarchy. With these sources cut off by the economic crisis and reform, the goals of efficiency, competitiveness, or alliance with private institutions become the means of advancing a broader social agenda, given the opportunities and resources of the time.

CONCLUSION

While there is little that is novel in the concept of poor people finding ways to survive when the government is not disposed to assist them, it is indeed an unconventional notion that we can locate Catholic grassroots activism in cooperative efforts with multinational corporations or in funding microenterprise development. In this chapter we have examined important changes in national political and economic institutions in the 1990s that fundamentally redefined the relationship between state and society. Whereas many scholars have identified these changes as sources of a crisis in the progressive Catholic Church in Latin America, we have considered an alternative conceptualization. Although progressive Catholic activism has not sustained the *forms* of collective mobilization that were visible in previous decades as a means to advance its message, this does not constitute proof that progressive Catholicism is dead.

We have considered the possibility that Catholics in the 1990s are responding to their social and political landscape in the same way their predecessors did—by reading the "signs of the times." In this view, the political and economic reforms that altered the basic logic of social expression have compelled activists to shake off the traditional forms of collective mobilization that do not "fit" the political logic of the 1990s. Instead, the illustrations from Peru suggest that the abandonment of the popular protests and direct political engagement of the past may be understood not as a sign of the death of the progressive Catholic Church, but rather of its *continuing life*.

NOTES

1 It is important to note as well that there was strong opposition to the neoliberal reforms, particularly from those who stood to lose subsidies as well as those who perceived neoliberalism as a form of imperialism by international institutions. Likewise, when the heavy social costs of reform fell upon large segments of societies, politicians responded by tempering the extent to which market forces governed domestic economic relations. Despite the variations in pace and intensity with which market-oriented reforms were implemented,

by the mid-1990s neoliberalism prevailed as the dominant paradigm of economic policy in Latin America.

2   Market-oriented stabilization efforts were not without costs, most of which were borne by the most needy and politically weak segment of society: the poor. The removal of price controls, subsidies, and emplyment benefits combined to swell the ranks of the impoverished and unemployed.

REFERENCES

Adriance, Madeleine. 1994. "Base communities and rural mobilization in northern Brazil." *Sociology of Religion*, 55 (2).

Burdick, John. 1993. *Looking for God in Brazil: The Progressive Catholic Church in Urban Brazil's Religious Arena.* Berkeley: University of California.

Cleary, Edward L. and Hannah Stewart-Gambino. 1992. *Conflict and Competition: the Latin American Church in a Changing Environment.* Boulder, CO: Lynne Reinner.

Coleman, K., E. Aguilar, J. M. Sandoval, and T. Steiginga. 1990. "Protestantism in El Salvador: Conventional wisdom versus the survey evidence." In David Stoll and Virginia Garrard Burnett, eds. *Rethinking Protestantism in Latin America.* Philadelphia: Temple University.

Gill, Anthony. 1994. "Rendering unto Caesar? Religious competition and Catholic political strategy in Latin America, 1962-79." *American Journal of Political Science*, 38 (2).

Heberle, Rudolf. 1951. *Social Movements: An Introduction to Political Sociology.* New York: Appleton-Century-Crofts.

Ireland, Rowan. 1991. *Kingdoms Come: Religion and Politics in Brazil.* Pittsburgh: University of Pittsburgh Press.

Kitschelt, Herbert. 1986. "Political Opportunity Structures and Political Protest: Anti-Nuclear Movements in Four Democracies." *British Journal of Political Science*, 16 (1).

Klaiber, Jeffrey. 1977. *Religion and Revolution in Peru, 1824-1976.* South Bend, IN: University of Notre Dame Press.

Levine, Daniel, ed. 1980. *Churches and Politics in Latin America.* Beverly Hills, CA: Sage.

———. 1992. *Popular voices in Latin American Catholicism.* Princeton, NJ: Princeton University Press.

———. 1995. "On Premature Reports of the Death of Liberation Theology." *The Review of Politics*, 57 (1).

Levine, Daniel and David Stoll. 1995. "Religious Change, Empowerment, and Power: Bridging the Gap in Latin America." *Journal of Iberian and Latin American Studies*, 1 (1,2).

Mainwaring, Scott. 1986. *The Catholic Church and Politics in Brazil, 1916-1985.* Stanford, CA: Stanford University Press.

Mainwaring, Scott and Alexander Wilde, eds. 1989. *The Progressive Church in Latin America.* South Bend, IN: University of Notre Dame Press.

Martin, David. 1990. *Tongues of Fire: The Explosion of Protestantism in Latin America.* Oxford: Basil Blackwell.

McAdam, Doug. 1982. *Political Process and the Development of Black Insurgency, 1930-1970*. Chicago: University of Chicago Press.

Mc Carthy, John D. and Mayer N. Zald. 1977. "Resource Mobilization and Social Movements: A Partial Theory." *American Journal of Sociology*, 82.

O'Shaughnessy, Laura. and Luis H. Serra. 1986. *The Church and Revolution in Nicaragua*. Athens, OH: Ohio University.

Peña, Milagros. 1992. "The Sodalitium Vitae Movement in Peru: A Rewriting of Liberation Theology." *Sociological Analysis*, 53 (2).

Piven, Frances Fox and Richard A. Coward. 1979. *Poor People's Movements: Why They Succeed, How They Fail*. New York: Vintage Books.

Smith, Christian. 1991. *The Emergence of Liberation Theology: Radical Religion and Social Movement Theory*. Chicago: University of Chicago Press.

Stoll, David. 1990. *Is Latin America Turning Protestant? The Politics of Evangelical Growth*. Berkeley: University of California.

Stoll, David and Virginia Garrard Burnett, eds. 1990. *Rethinking Protestantism in Latin America*. Philadelphia: Temple University Press.

Tarrow, Sidney. 1983. "Struggling to Reform: Social Movements and Policy Change During Cycles of Protest." Occasional Paper No.15, Center for International Studies, Cornell University.

————. 1994. *Power in Movement: Social Movements, Collective Action and Politics*. Cambridge: Cambridge University Press.

Turner, R.H. 1964. "Collective Behavior." In R. Faris, ed. *Handbook of Modern Sociology*. Chicago: Rand McNally.

Tilly, Charles. 1969. "Collective Violence in European Perspective." In G. Graham Hough and Ted Gurr, eds. *The History of Violence in America*. New York: Praeger.

Williamson, John, ed. 1990. *Latin American Adjustment: How Much has Happened?* Washington, DC: Institute for International Economics.

FOUR

PROGRESSIVE THEOLOGY AND POPULAR RELIGIOSITY IN OAXACA, MEXICO[1]

Kristin Norget

While transformations within the Catholic Church and the relationship between Catholicism and the everyday life of Church members have received fairly thorough study elsewhere in Latin America, they have been relatively neglected in the social science literature on Mexico.[2] Attention to these themes is badly needed if we are to assess the promise of the newly emergent "progressive" factions within the hierarchy of the Mexican Church to act as agents of concrete social change. This article attempts to clarify the present situation of the Mexican Catholic Church through a careful examination of the contemporary relationship between the official Church reformist campaign and "popular Catholicism," a form of religiosity linked closely to the official Church but existing largely outside its sphere of control.

In the broad scheme, Catholicism in Mexico, and elsewhere in Latin America, is currently experiencing a renewal aimed at consolidating and revitalizing its institutional integrity, doctrine, and pastoral practice as it struggles to retain its status in what have historically been Catholic dominated societies. This has been part of Pope John Paul II's global "one true church" campaign (Barry 1992:252), a movement that received its original impetus from the second Vatican council in the early 1960s. Since that time, however, this reformist push in Mexico has also created the basis for growing factionalism within the Mexican clergy. The division, roughly described, is one between "progressive" clergy influenced by liberation theology (who have taken the church's exhortation for social justice and political change seriously in their vocal criticism of the State and their active role in popular organizations), and more conservative (i.e. Vatican-oriented) priests and bishops who accept certain modernizing changes in doctrine and pastoral practice, but disagree with the progressive views on the proper role of the Church in contemporary Mexican society and its relationship to the State.[3]

Understanding the views of clergy is important, as they are the disseminators of official Church policy and have a strong influence on how the Church interacts with the rest of society. Nonetheless, institutionally oriented or ideologically focused studies of religion generally are of limited utility for understanding the relationship between religion and other areas of society, especially those related to sociopolitical and economic power (Asad 1983; Bourdieu 1971). Analysis must move outside the level of official church discourse to see how this discourse intersects with everyday experience. It is through interaction with popular Catholicism that the changing face of the Mexican Catholic Church is most clearly seen. As the direct devotional expression of the poor, popular religiosity is seen by ardent liberationist clergy as a pure and authentic faith that speaks to the experience and reality of God's chosen people. But for more conservative (yet still "modern") Mexican clergy, the situation appears slightly more complex. The Church depends on the participation and devotional fervor of poorer Mexicans for its institutional survival, but as these moderate reformers seek to change certain critical elements of popular religious practice, they may wind up alienating their parishioners. Thus even within the so-called "progressivist" movement, significant variation exists in terms of the attitude which clergy take towards the largely independent "popular" religious behaviors and beliefs expressed among Oaxacans. We should not see the setting then as one involving a stark separation of theological camps. Instead, individual clergy may be seen as situated on a continuum stretching between progressive and conservative ideological poles.

This article examines some of these issues in the context of the southern Mexican city of Oaxaca de Juárez.[4] Until 1992 this diocese was under the influence of an avowedly progressive (and even "liberationist") archbishop, Bartolomé Carrasco. Although Carrasco's replacement in 1992 by a more conservative Archbishop, Hector Gonzalez, effectively diluted the liberationist edge of Carrasco's reformist campaign (especially in Oaxaca City), many of the priests already working in support of his pastoral line, especially in the indigenous rural communities, have not significantly altered their pastoral practice (Norget 1997).

My main concern here is to outline the character and content of popular Catholic religiosity in Oaxaca in order to highlight the discord that exists between it and the official Church's "progressive" agenda. My overall purpose is to question how much potential there really is for an alliance between the renewal movement and popular religiosity. Implicitly, the discussion also points to the problem of glossing over the diverse nature of "liberation theology" and "progressive" Catholic movements across Mexico and Latin America. I argue that the progressive orientation within the Church and the nature of popular religiosity must both be analyzed carefully within a local context in order to provide a fruitful understanding of the relationship between religion and cultural and sociopolitical transformation.

Known as one of the most extreme Catholic strongholds in the country (Camp 1994:83), Oaxaca is a colonial capital in what is perhaps the poorest and most ethnically diverse (e.g. indigenous) region of Mexico.[5] Fieldwork in a *colonia popular* (a neighborhood I will call Colonia San Juan) on the edge of Oaxaca during the early 1990s (and in short visits since then) has given me the opportunity to observe the effects of various forms of "renewed" Catholicism. Living in a community composed largely of first- and second-generation indigenous immigrants from rural parts of Oaxaca has also exposed me to the character of Catholic practice within both the context of Church-controlled activity and the normal flow of everyday life. Indeed, Oaxacan popular Catholicism has significant links with official Catholicism, links that throw into relief certain areas of mutual dependence between them: popular religiosity draws upon the status of official clergy or other Church representatives for some modicum of legitimacy or propriety, and clergy rely on the impassioned devotion of the masses to propel their congregations. Moreover, Oaxacan popular religion is deeply integrated into popular culture, resulting in the appearance of official religious icons or rites in settings where the official does not formally dictate (for example, in the context of folk-curing, or in many secular fiestas). Likewise, nonofficial elements, derived in many cases from indigenous traditions, infuse formal Catholic contexts, such as in the festival of *Día de los Muertos* (the Day of the Dead).

Contrary to studies that have overlooked the importance of religion in the lives of urban Oaxacans, I found the Catholic religiosity of the popular classes to have a critical role in the construction of categories of moral differentiation and social (and what might be considered ethnic) identities. Popular Catholicism thus functions for many poor, "indigenous"[6] Oaxacans as a salient tool of resistance to certain marginalizing forces. People draw upon its symbols, practice, and significance to affirm their sense of place in a rapidly changing social, political, and economic environment. A holistic and comprehensive understanding of popular Catholicism in Oaxaca is impossible, however, without paying some attention to its substantive content, to how it is learned, transmitted, and practiced, and the meanings ascribed to it in the everyday realm.

POPULAR CULTURE AND RELIGION IN OAXACA

The account presented here cannot address the historical formation of popular Catholicism in Oaxaca, which resulted from a complex syncretic process that began at the time of the Conquest, as many scholars have demonstrated (e.g. Behar 1987; Christian 1981; Nutini 1976, 1988; Lafaye 1976; Ricard 1966; Foster 1960). The multilayered significance of today's expressions of Mexican popular (or "folk") religion is the cumulative result of many centuries of development, involving mutual borrowings, adaptations, and syntheses with diverse official religious traditions. But the immediate concern is to provide a general sketch of the character of contemporary Oaxacan popular religiosity.

Religious syncretism is bound up with "the negotiation of identities and hegemonies" in any context surrounding the meeting of different cultural traditions, via trade, migration, or conquest. (Stewart and Shaw 1994:19) In situations of domination or exploitation, the politics informing religious synthesis become particularly significant; in such cases, syncretic religious forms may be seen as modes of resistance through which people subvert the significance of hegemonic practices and beliefs and assimilate them to their own meanings and agendas (Stewart and Shaw 1994). Indeed, in Oaxaca many of the features of popular religiosity are the result of unique personal and collective innovations, involving a fluid, dynamic construction of symbols and practices that at turns converge with, and then diverge from, official Catholic ideology. It is a process of ongoing negotiation between these religious forms that reveals the flexibility and potential resilience of popular religiosity when threatened from outside or above.

It is difficult, if not impossible, to arrive at a satisfactory definition of popular religion or popular Catholicism that is applicable in every setting; the character of specific popular religious expressions is determined by the particularities of the social and historical context in which they are generated. Michael Candelaria's (1981:13) definition of Latin American popular Catholicism comes close to capturing Oaxacan popular religiosity's unique character when he describes it as "a system of values and ideals, and a complex of symbolic practices, discursive and nondiscursive, enacted in ritual drama and materialized in visual images, all relating the human being to the sacred, originated and maintained by the poor and the oppressed."

Though its population is officially considered mestizo (of mixed European and indigenous ancestry), Oaxaca's enduring status as a magnet for rural migrants has lent its urban cultural landscape an indigenous, traditional flavor more typical of rural locales. Here, within the spectrum of expressions of Catholicism, socioeconomic class distinctions intersect with significant variations in religious practice. For most Oaxacans, poor and of indigenous origin, religiosity encompasses a wide array of beliefs and ritual traditions, including those considered "superstitious" and magical, with origins that may predate the arrival of Catholicism. Brought to the city by rural Oaxacans, such practices and beliefs continue to thrive, but are often unknown, or pointedly ignored, by upper-class, more mestizo Catholics, who tend more toward orthodoxy, and who often make a strong effort to distinguish themselves from "inferior," indigenous ways of life.

Moreover, in Oaxaca, popular religion embraces a distinct moral code, including pragmatic tools of spiritual aid and support invoked throughout every day's activity and consciousness. Unattached to official doctrine, popular Catholicism is made up of a wide range of practices and beliefs that people assimilate through general socialization, so that religion is largely a matter of unconscious habit (Bourdieu 1977), a part of everyday experience rather than an isolated realm of culture that may be reflected upon and rationalized. In addition, Oaxacan popular Catholicism extols the ideals and values of popular consciousness that resist assimilation or redefinition from outside. As a religiosity that is predominantly felt and lived, popular religion is used in the self-reliant creation of a social and moral landscape in which popular identities are firmly anchored. Popular religiosity in Oaxaca can therefore only be understood as religion lived by people who create, sustain, and reproduce it within a social and political reality of worsening poverty, disenfranchisement, and marginalization.

The Sacred and Moral Landscape

Popular Catholic faith in Oaxaca is concerned with the vital and intimate interaction with the supernatural domain in the course of a constructed human mapping of a moral order. The sacred in popular Catholic religiosity—consonant with positive morality and spiritual potency (blessing)—has temporal and physical dimensions that, though concrete, are open to subjective construction and manipulation. Popular Catholic rites and forms of devotion, from pilgrimages to fiestas, involve a strong emphasis on tactile transfer of spiritual blessing and what I call a performative or participatory requirement for connecting with the supernatural realm. People use objects, and even use themselves, as instruments for interacting with supernatural and sacred beings, from the saints to the dead.

While there are collective aspects of religiosity that are subject to some official control (for example, mass, certain public aspects of religious fiestas), most religious activity goes on outside of the Church's physical confines, direction, and sphere of influence. The devotional expressions of the cult of the saints falls largely within this informal category of religious worship, and forms the core of popular urban (and rural indigenous) religious practice (Marroquìn 1989; Stephen and Dow 1990; Barabas and Bartolomé 1993).

Some saints are particularly popular, and are venerated throughout Mexico. The Virgin Mary, for example, in her manifestation as Nuestra Señora de Guadalupe (Our Lady of Guadaloupe), the Patroness of Mexico, is the inspiration for a wide range of feast days and devotional cults. In fact, the Virgin's special feast day on December 12 is one of the most important fiestas of the year, and millions take part in pilgrimages to Tepeyac in Mexico City, where the Virgin is said to have first appeared in 1531. In Oaxaca, on both the festival day and the day before, thousands wait outside the Basilica de Guadalupe for a blessing at the Virgin's altar.

But in keeping with popular religion's independent orientation, some individuals or families also have their own "saint of devotion," a guardian saint from whom they request personal favors. Popular custom distinguishes the saints according to their associated specialties; there is a saint for every need—fidelity, fertility, safety in travel, luck in love, recovery of lost belongings, protection of children, and so on. The saints are also icons spatially dividing the geographical territory of both state and city; in fact, every state, pueblo, and even workplace has its own *santo patronal* (patron saint), customarily celebrated on the occasion of the annual *mayordomìa*, or saint's day fiesta.

A huge part of popular Catholic ritual activity is concerned with the fulfillment of vows or pledges (*mandas* or *promesas*) made to particular saints. Participation in a pilgrimage to a faraway shrine, bringing flowers regularly for a certain period to an image in church or at home, and other forms of devotion are common ways of satisfying such a vow. Many believe that misfortune may well befall someone who fails to honor a *promesa*, or one who makes such a vow without true faith in one's heart. The intensity of people's affection for the saints is probably due to the intimate and highly personalized relationship between these supernaturals and human beings. While the awe-inspiring omnipotence imputed to God has the effect of removing him perceptually from human access, the saints are visible, tangible, material symbols who are reputed to have human needs and qualities as well as the power to grant favors. Sacred images on household altars (or, during fiesta periods, within the church) are clothed, visited, given offerings of food and flowers, kept company, talked to, sung to, laid down, caressed and kissed much as any beloved human being. During the saints' day festival in Cuauhtemoc[7], Colonia San Juan's local parish, a small image of the Virgin Mary is taken from the church to "visit" various homes in the neighborhood. In turn, people may drop in to visit the Virgin as they would a special guest in the colonia. A saint may be the object of love, but also of avoidance, as when someone concludes the saint is unlucky for him or her.

In spite of the strong affective relationship, the saints are regarded as extremely powerful, worshipped not only for day-to-day spiritual aid, but also for the critical channel to the sacred dimension that they symbolize, and the greater power and significance represented by that realm. The saints are intermediaries between the spheres of the profane and the sacred, but they are also eminently social beings with whom one has a bond of ritual reciprocity analogous to one's relationship with a relative or *compadre* (ritual kin). The goal of this relationship is a sense of well-being as much material as it is spiritual: i.e., personal health and welfare are inseparable from notions of social balance and harmony (Lancaster 1988).

Rather than having merely an abstract or imaginary mystic quality, this sacred aspect of Oaxacan popular religiosity is tangible. Images of virgins, saints, Christ, and even the cross itself, are frequently kissed or touched with one's hand or with a piece of clothing, a flower or an herb branch, in the belief that the person or object is thus imbued with some kind of sacred essence. Devotees return from pilgrimages with mementos (scapulas, religious pendants, relics, rosary beads, or a small framed portrait of the honored saint or Virgin) that they have had blessed by a priest at the saint's shrine or have used to touch the sacred image itself. These objects are then regarded as potent talismans of a spiritual blessing that has been transferred from the realm of the sacred into that of the mundane, a kind of force or manipulable potency that may be drawn upon to satisfy material, physical, and spiritual needs. The links forged between saints and specific locales play an important role in the creation of personal and collective identities.

Further, the underlying logic of popular Catholic rituals is based upon the belief that there is a dependent relationship between the human body and the social body—a belief that also acts as a guiding principle in folk medicine. This has given rise to a popular ethical code that emphasizes the virtues of cooperation, altruism, and family loyalty. Anger, severe tension (*muina*, or *coraje*), or envy (*envìdia*) between or among family and neighbors is believed to cause harm, misfortune, or illness. (The terms mentioned themselves, in fact, refer to ailments with distinct pathologies and treatments.) In the same way, trouble with the saints (and with the dead) caused by improper behavior, such as failure to keep a vow or *promesa*, or to carry out expected ritual obligations, can have similar repercussions. A combination of Catholic symbols, practices, and beliefs also saturate folk medicine in terms of both pathology and methods of curing both physical and moral ailments (Hunt 1992; Mahar Higgins 1974).

This preoccupation with magical and practical matters appears to reflect an "ethical sub-religion" (Lancaster 1988:38). In this kind of moral economy, healing has both physical and moral/spiritual connotations that, "roughly, if unconsciously, corresponds to the social interests of the popular classes and contrasts with the religion of the elites" (Lancaster 1988:38). In Oaxaca, the critical metaphorical identification of individual and social bodies, and concern for their well-being intersects with the imperative of balance and equilibrium, predicated on the ideal of a stable social order. These principles are also symbolized by other aspects of popular religious practice, among them traditions founded on notions of cooperation, communalism, reciprocity, and social welfare.

To give an example, the annual round of Catholic festivals and life cycle rites (especially baptism, first communion, confirmation) offers contexts not only for prestige competition, but also for the symbolic reaffirmation of traditional ideals and values of communal solidarity in the context of reciprocal exchange and *convivencia* (roughly, togetherness).

Sacramental rites (i.e. baptisms, weddings, first communions, and confirmations) allow for the establishment (or reaffirmation) of *compadrazgo* (ritual godparenthood) bonds.[8] But outside the *compadrazgo* network such occasions are times for the activation of more general social ties in the form of the *guelaguetza*. The *guelaguetza*, a traditional exchange system of indigenous origin, involves individuals contributing food, small amounts of money, or other items to the family hosting a religious celebration (like a wedding or a funeral), thereby allowing them to sponsor an event that otherwise they could not afford (Whitecotton 1977:240; Williams 1979; Stephen 1991). The contribution is then reciprocated by the receiver when the giver hosts a like occasion. Quite formalized in its expression in rural areas, the *guelaguetza* takes a looser form in Oaxaca city, but is still the general, tacit rule activated at such collective ritual occasions.

This section has explained popular religious faith in Oaxaca less as a body of esoteric concepts, abstract ideas, and principles grasped with the mind, and more as a distinctive spirituality transposed concretely onto the material plane to be touched, felt, seen, experienced, and then potentially adapted to fit individual or collective perceptions, needs, and realities. While Church representatives do exercise some influence, to a great extent Oaxacan popular religiosity appears to exist in relative independence. Further, the essential principle of balanced reciprocity running through its popular moral logic is embodied in symbolic and actual mechanisms of social leveling (primarily in the form of ritual exchange) and ideals of cooperation and communalism. These rurally derived economic and religious traditions speak to a popular religious rationality that in many ways diverges from that of the contemporary progressive Church discourse of renewal and renovation.

THE NEW EVANGELIZATION

In the early 1990s, many clergy displayed the theological slant of the progressive Archbishop Bartolomé Carrasco, who had led the Oaxacan diocese since 1975. This has continued despite Carrasco's replacement by the overtly conservative Archbishop Hector Gonzalez. Most priests in Oaxaca still agree in principle with the liberationist tenets of the "Option for the Poor" and the notion of "the People's Church."[9] In Oaxaca (as elsewhere) this movement for pastoral reform has been dubbed *La Nueva Evangelizacion* (The New Evangelization). Yet the way this movement has taken form in certain contexts raises some doubts as to its transformative promise. We see this exemplified in the parish in which I lived, Cuauhtemoc.

The local priest in the parish encompassing Colonia San Juan, Padre Claudio, had been its leader for sixteen years. Along with the parish advisory board (consisting of volunteers from all seven *colonias* comprising the parish) and the local deacon, he had implemented, or permitted others to institute, certain features of the "People's Church" in Cuauhtemoc. Members of the congregation were encouraged to participate in leading lectures during mass, in ceremonies such as *Via Crucis*,[10] and in religious groups such as *Encuentros Matrimoniales* (Marriage Encounters, a group for discussing marital problems), or Bible reflection groups. Participation in such groups was promoted as part of an overall consciousness-raising effort to create a closer integration of Catholic doctrine and personal practice. Additionally, the New Evangelization included changes of ritual, exemplified by the *platicas* (catechizing talks) led by Church representatives before sacramental rites such as baptisms, first communions, confirmations, and marriages. For all of these rites, a week of attendance at talks was required not only by those undergoing the ceremony, but also usually by both parents and godparents.

Forging a more unified community was intrinsic to the pastoral plan of Cuauhtemoc. Padre Claudio referred to this campaign quite formally as "the new image of the parish," and explained the plan's ideological foundation to me:

> The idea is that the Church is not made up of little groups within the same church, but rather consists of the whole community—of any age, of any sex, of any walk of life. And it is necessary that the community is very much conscious and aware that it is the community itself that constitutes the church.

Padre Claudio reiterated this emphasis on the notion of church as community in a message appearing in one issue of the monthly parish newsletter:

> The objective of our diocese and parish pastoral program is clear: evangelize the family, youth, our indigenous people. The diocese pastoral plan and that of the parish may vary, but it is very important to organize and plan to unify fundamental pastoral criteria so as to be able to take a sure step in the spiritual and pastoral renewal of our communities. We must change our archaic conceptions regarding new ideas. Yesterday was another mode of thinking, another mentality. For example, yesterday most people believed that the church was just a place, the material building or the priest...[but] now we know that...our faith in Christ is something far deeper, more universal, and more alive in the individual himself—it consists in the entire community unified by faith, hope, and love.

Padre Claudio's words reflect the sense of renewal and revitalization that saturates the *Nueva Evangelizacion,* and its proclamation of the apostolic mission of the true and loyal Catholic believer. One of the campaign's principal stated aims was to strengthen Catholics' faith through a more profound and enriched knowledge of church doctrine. Part of this was the effort to "purify" components of popular religion that misinterpreted and/or misused Catholic symbols and tenets. Examples of such "corruption of faith" were drunkenness during church fiestas and ceremonials, the use of confession to divulge the sins of other people, and ritual overspending on *mayordomìas,* baptisms, and weddings, which are salient arenas for intense prestige competition.

Throughout Oaxaca city, I observed that the New Evangelization had adopted in many ways the charismatic proselytizing style of evangelical sects in stressing a spiritual rebirth: an abrupt "change of life," an abandonment of ideas and vices standing in the way of the individual's spiritual and social development and self-empowerment. Stoll (1990:27) claims that post-Vatican II church reforms in Latin America used Protestantism as a model, especially through emphasis on the Bible as a guide to faith and the encouragement of lay leadership. Reflecting this slant toward "orthopraxis," baptism in Cuauhtemoc was stressed as a rite entailing a strict obligation (*compromiso*) to follow the sacraments of the Church. Don Reynaldo, the parish deacon, claimed that once this was recognized, "we cannot live as we did before. We were cleansed, purified, and reborn by means of baptism. Afterwards we must not go back." A more literal application of formal doctrine to everyday existence was stressed: religion was represented as ideally being a conscious (*consciente*) aspect of one's everyday activity, exemplified by the encouragement of participation in biblical reflection groups.

Knowledge and understanding of faith were crucial aspects of the New Evangelization. Thus, the campaign's discourse, heard particularly at the Bible discussion gatherings in Cuauhtemoc and other parishes in the city, involved emphasis on a modern, dynamic church whose members were "conscious" and aware, in both personal as well as social and political terms. In keeping with the rational, modernist tone of the campaign, Padre Claudio told me that popular religion was "very good [and] an expression of faith, though not very clear or profound." Popular religion, in the priest's opinion, "should be conserved, but also should continue to be renewed, and interpreted with more consciousness." The former Archbishop Bartolomé Carrasco similarly disclosed in an interview that what most characterized popular religion was its quality of "spontaneity," conveying, perhaps pejoratively, a sense of superficiality.

Some aspects of the New Evangelization in urban Oaxaca, particularly participation in lay Catholic groups, appear to have instilled in people a sense of self-direction as church members. Women especially were able to take on public leadership roles in ways customarily denied them. It seems that a sense of empowerment had also been achieved by a deepened knowledge of the Bible. In addition, in Cuauhtemoc, involvement in gatherings such as biblical discussion groups or the parish advisory board, where local problems were shared and dissected in a sacred setting that favored altruism and reconciliation, led people to develop a sense of shared identity and a moral commitment to each other and their community.

Nonetheless, the possibility that the progressivist campaign of the New Evangelization would be translated into a more politically aggressive or "truly popular" force appeared dim. In the parish, people's reasons for participating in Bible discussion groups, the principal organized expression of the New Evangelization campaign, were varied. For most participants, almost all of whom were women, group meetings appeared to function as an important source of mutual support and advice for troubles they encountered in their daily lives. The social aspect of the gatherings following Bible discussion, hymn singing, and prayer, was particularly pronounced; those attending took the opportunity to chat and gossip. Attendance at the twice-weekly meetings was not consistent, nor did I note matters of wider political interest entering meeting discussions. People's concerns remained immediate and almost literally parochial.

The apparent failure of the New Evangelization campaign to act as a significant mobilizing platform in a broader social or political sense exemplifies the rift between official religious discourse and the everyday reality of residents of San Juan, wherein people's personal motivations for participation in Bible discussion groups or other activities did not always correspond to Church perceptions or aspirations. In addition, the New Evangelization movement was not the only source of spiritual and practical support for *colonos*, since a wide range of associations from evangelical sects (Mormons, Seventh Day Adventists, Jehovah's Witnesses), to *espirituistas*,[11] New Age groups, Alcoholics Anonymous, and even other Catholic factions such as the Charismatics actively solicited people's participation as groups with which they could fulfill their needs or interests. As Burdick (1992:172) points out for Christian Base Communities (or CEBs) in Brazil, the message of such church organizations, especially in the urban milieu, "is but one contender in a contested arena of religious and ideological alternatives."

Although Padre Claudio had seemingly adopted the progressive stance of the New Evangelization movement, the commitment to a liberationist interpretation of the campaign's agenda, as supposedly encouraged by Archbishop Carrasco, appeared to be absent. While CEBs (a presumably essential element of the liberation theology movement) exist in two other parishes in Oaxaca city (see for example McNabb and Rees 1993), by 1995 there had still not been any organized in Cuauhtemoc. Though Don Reynaldo, the deacon, told me of his eagerness to establish CEBs, he added that the lack of enthusiasm on the part of Padre Claudio and many other people in the parish made the prospects for the success of such groups dim, as they required even more commitment than the Bible reflection groups. Further, despite the existence of CEBs elsewhere in Oaxaca, the local clergy had yet to become directly involved in organized political movements (unlike other settings, where priests have taken an active part in leading indigenous organizations fighting for civil rights) (Norget 1995; Hernández Diaz 1994).

In sum, regarding the "progressive" Church discourse within the framework of the People's Church in Oaxaca, a supposedly radical program for pastoral renewal has often taken a form that has been effectively conservative. In terms of people's actual religious behavior and practice, little has changed. When I asked Maria, a poor, middle-aged woman in Cuauhtemoc, about her limited participation in local Church activities and rare attendance at mass, despite her claims of being very religious, she protested to me "Wherever one likes, God may be found" (*"Donde quiera se puede encontrar a Dios"*). Another poor elderly female neighbor provided a similarly indignant reaction to the same question: "I'm Catholic in my own way" ("*Soy catolica, a mi manera*"). Such statements of individual self-reliance were echoed repeatedly.

These assertions of independence were in part a reaction to the efforts of the local Church to define proper Catholic practice within the New Evangelization campaign. At the same time, they attest to a self-defined field of meanings in popular religiosity that constitute a challenge to Church attempts at control through the imposition of official doctrinal interpretations. Scott (1985) and Abu-Lughod (1990) have shown how disadvantaged people often participate in everyday, subtle forms of resistance, such as passive noncompliance, that never become transformed into overt confrontation. A fine line may separate an opposition of negligible significance from a challenge to the dominant order. But with Oaxacan popular religion, resistance resides implicitly in the context: the independent quality of local popular Catholic belief and practice derives from features that equip popular religiosity with the tools to defy attempts to redefine the nature of its role in everyday practice. Further, the Oaxacan popular religious logic reflects a deep entrenchment of religiosity in everyday existence that in some ways is difficult to reconcile with the church's current intentions of reform and reconsolidation. Thus, the demand for attendance at *platicas* as a sacrament prerequisite, increased participation of the laity in liturgical functions, and the incorporation of evangelization into religious rites are all attempts at achieving a revitalization of Catholicism within the New Evangelization. This makes it essential for the researcher to distinguish between traditional popular Catholicism and "evangelized" popular Catholicism, since there is no clear-cut separation between them.

The popular practices that the progressive Catholic Church in Oaxaca is attempting to "purify" are those that threaten its hegemony: religious activity of a more individualistic or independent nature that takes place outside the Church's domain of control. The cult of the saints and other religious practices centered on domestic liturgies, for example, pose a threat to the centralization of spiritual teachings and devotions. The marianist (i.e. Virgin Mary–centered) character of popular piety and the great devotion to the saints are frowned upon by both Church officials and more evangelized Catholics. Some people have been accused of being excessively idolatrous, indulging in "paganism" (with the usual connotations of ignorance and backwardness associated with indigenous identity). As one evangelized Catholic in Cuauhtemoc put it, "people will travel miles to visit the Virgin of Juquila [an extremely popular saint in Oaxaca] but they forget about God."

Perhaps most important, the points of conflict between popular Catholicism and the renewed Catholic campaign are often translated in conceptual terms as a debate between tradition (in its most negative sense) and progress. The Oaxacan progressive Church is attempting to rationalize and systematize popular religious practice without alienating the faithful in the process. Thus while the few overtly liberationist priests in Oaxaca do celebrate and encourage elements of popular tradition, other priests (even while seeming to support a progressive pastoral praxis) place more emphasis on its indigenous origins and supposed association with a naive, ignorant way of life that is an impediment to "getting ahead."

Traditional Oaxacan popular religion converges with what might be class consciousness in its relation to the substantial social and cultural transformations Oaxaca is undergoing. While it can function as a forum for prestige competition and the underscoring of internal social differentiation, popular Catholicism in Oaxaca also celebrates traditional values and the positive social virtues of collectivism, communalism, and social equilibrium, affirming the virtues of poverty and the world of the traditional. As a result, it serves as an important referent for the construction of social categories informed by a sense of moral differentiation, and as a repository for past cherished sacred values and ideals. Catholic practice in Oaxaca enriches and revitalizes certain ideals and traditions critical to people's communal identification. It sets up a dichotomous relationship with believers as the poor, moral, and traditional Oaxacans on one side, and the rich, greedy, and selfish Oaxacans on the other. As a discourse of differentiated values and morality, religion here is "not a separate set of symbols, but part of a language for talking around, and about social boundaries and their reflexes in individual entities" (Chock and Wyman 1986:17).

Such an invocation of a morally circumscribed community was heard often on popular ritual occasions, illustrated by one poor old woman's comments to me on the Day of the Dead:

> The rich who have money . . . have never followed the law of God. The rich never pay any attention to the *humildes* [the poor, humble]. This means they are not kind. They don't know *Dia de los Muertos*. We in contrast, though we are the poor and humble ones, we are kind and generous with everyone else. That is how God wishes it—that we may love each other as brothers on this material earth. But the rich are rejected according to the law of our Lord God. There above [in heaven] is the reward for everything we do here on earth.

The tenor of her words was echoed by another Oaxacan.

The humble [*humilde*] class will always go [to the graveyard] with their candles, with a little *cooperacion* [bit of money], perhaps a few flowers, but they always go with an open heart; they go in fulfillment of a debt to the person who goes to the hereafter. Those in the middle or the bourgeois classes give their presence only a little while—one or two hours, and then they just leave those who are mourning. The poor, no. The poor remain, stay awake the whole night, and are still there when dawn arrives. And the next day they are still present with the same feelings and sentiments.

The quotes exemplify the way in which religiosity provides structures of meaning that inform the conscious formulation of personal and collective identity. Charged with moral resonances, Oaxacan popular religiosity embodies a distinct way of thinking, being, and acting. At the same time it contains a covert social critique of the dominant systems of meaning by which those very popular values and modes of interaction are devalued. Rather than referring to a readily identifiable social group, implied here is a notion of an "imagined community" (Anderson 1983), the basis of a common framework of popular understandings and, perhaps, of popular consciousness.

Such self-perceptions and allegiances are revealed and affirmed through everyday popular religious practice and the vocabulary of everyday speech. In this manner, Oaxacans draw upon the system of meanings provided by popular Catholicism to shore up situationally defined boundaries of community in the face of perceived threats to the social values and ideals that constitute the distinctive nature of popular culture. Like the popular religiosity in revolutionary Nicaragua (Lancaster 1988:215), here the discourse of tradition represents an active social relation, and not just a survival from the past; it is a voice of popular identity in negotiation with a dominant discourse of modernity and progress.

Conclusion

To a certain extent, as Gimenez (1978; quoted in Rowe and Schelling 1991:70) claims, "official religion . . . confronts popular religion with a power of symbolic aggressiveness," in a confrontation concerned either with diminishing popular religious forms and/or investing them with official meaning and significance. In contemporary doctrinal and pastoral renovation in Latin America, the progressive wing of the church endorses political action and a transformation of the symbolic meaning of poverty (Levine 1986:11), but this doctrine can only be realized through the actual practice of the clergy. Within the Church's renewal campaign, the terms of change and the revision of poverty's meaning are still in the hands of the Church. While the New Evangelization and other reformist campaigns aim to bridge the gap between official and popular religion, the distinction made within church discourse and debate between the People's Church and the official institutional church is still very much part of a movement defined and impelled from above.

The New Evangelization movement in Oaxaca city is yet another example of the many attempts, over the centuries, to assimilate the potency of popular religion in various forms. Nonetheless, a rich array of expressions of religious heterodoxy, including strong devotion to personal objects of worship, as well as shamanic and messianic beliefs and practices, have existed throughout Mexico's history (and still do) in relative autonomy. Resistance has been both overt and covert.[12] Behind this defensive posture is the desire to maintain a critical resource used by many urban Oaxacans in negotiating the exigencies of daily living and affirming their perceived morally rightful place in a social and political order from which they are otherwise largely excluded.

The situation in Oaxaca regarding the relationship between the institutional Catholic Church and popular Catholicism is still relatively benign. Despite the evident distance between the institutional Church and popular religiosity's core, there is still a climate of general toleration based on mutual dependence: the official Church needs the faithful to perpetuate basic Catholic tradition, while popular Catholicism relies on the Church periodically to ratify its existence with an official stamp of approval.

From the perspective of the New Evangelization movement in Oaxaca, popular Catholic expressions have often been regarded, at times quite patronizingly, as worthy religious customs that only needed to be "purified" or accompanied by a more profound understanding of Catholic doctrine. My findings suggest that in Oaxaca, opposition to or criticism of official religion by the popular classes is not necessarily conscious or overt, in the sense of representing organized protest. Yet neither the qualities nor the demonstrated goals of popular religious practice fully harmonize with official paradigms of religious worship. The response of popular Catholicism, then, is perhaps more accurately qualified not as resistance but rather as defense of an independent field of practices, symbols, and beliefs.

Assessing the capacity of the renewed Catholic campaign to provide a platform for significant social reform is impossible without attention to the implementation of the progressive movement's agenda by particular clergy. The rhetoric of this Church reformist movement attempts to shape a mindset of individual freedom and progress through rationality, knowledge, and self-determination. But in Oaxaca, the increasing alienation, transience, and fragmentation characteristic of today's sociopolitical setting have intensified a popular discourse that articulates the desire for a reaffirmation of morally positive forms of social life firmly connected to an idealized past wherein identity has strong local roots. Here traditional popular Catholicism encompasses a critical field in which dialectics of morality and power with the larger world are part of a resilient popular consciousness confronting modernity and marginalization.

Notes

1 I thank Gregory Baum and especially Catherine LeGrand for helpful comments on an earlier version of this paper. I am also grateful to Leonard Plotnicov and Don Attwood, who provided valuable editorial advice. Responsibility for this work's present form, however, is entirely my own.

2 The attempts of Higgins (1993) and Camp (1994) are, in different ways, limited in the understanding they provide of religiosity as located in a wider political and social field.

3 The very conservative factions of the Mexican episcopate do not currently represent a current significant force in internal ecclesiastic debates (Marroquin 1992). Details of the ideological changes occurring with Vatican II, and the debate within the Church both globally and within Mexico are beyond the scope of this paper, but useful summaries may be found in Concha Malo, et al. (1986), Candelaria (1981), and Hanson (1990).

4 Ethnographic information on the city of Oaxaca may be found in Murphy and Stepick (1991) and Higgins (1993).

5 Oaxaca state's population of just over 3 million is largely rural and ethnically indigenous, divided into 570 municipios in which sixteen languages are spoken (excluding dialects) (Mexican Federal Commission of Indigenous Affairs, 1995). The predominant ethnic groups are the Zapotecs and the Mixtecs.

6 Like the term "mestizo," "indigenous" is a cultural, not a genetic, category (Nagengast and Kearney 1990; Knight 1990). Due to the negative associations of Indianness prevalent in Mexico, many individuals who are descended from non-Spanish-speaking ancestors, and are at least phenotypically indigenous, assert themselves as mestizo. "Indigenous" here is used not as a label that people deploy self-referentially to distinguish themselves, but as an ideological construct involving a social stratification system in which racial distinctions overlap to a significant extent with those of socioeconomic class.

7 Cuauhtemoc is a pseudonym, as are all proper names used in this article.

8 Fictive kin social links are often activated in times of economic need. It is also worth noting that, in Oaxaca, the idiom of *compadrazgo* kinship is also stretched to include secular life-cycle rites such as school graduations.

9 The "Option for the Poor" is based on the conviction that the church's true obligation is with the poor and oppressed classes, represented in the Bible as God's chosen people. It was formally accepted into the official ecclesiastical plan at the meeting of Latin American Bishops in Puebla in 1978. For more on the Option and the related concept of the "People's Church," see Levine

(1980) and Berryman (1987).

10 *Via Crucis* (The Way of the Cross) is an enactment of Christ's march to Calvary. In Cuauhtemoc the event was performed three times a week during the three weeks leading up to *Semana Santa* (Holy Week). Participants accompanied a male (representing Jesus) who carried a large wooden cross. At each station (where an altar was set up on the street) a passage from the Bible was read, followed by an excerpt from the guide used for the *Via Crucis*. This reading drew an explicit relation between Jesus's suffering and the problems plaguing contemporary society.

11 *Espirituistas* are individuals believed capable of healing through the manipulation of supernatural energies (See Ortiz Echániz 1984; Finkler 1985)

12 As quoted in Rowe & Schelling (1991:70)

REFERENCES

Abu-Lughod, Lila. 1990. 'The Romance of Resistance: Tracing Transformations of Power Through Bedouin Women.' *American Ethnologist*, 17(1): 41-55.

Anderson, Benedict. 1983. *Imagined Communities*. London: Verso.

Asad, Talal. 1983. 'Anthropological Conceptions of Religion: Reflections on Geertz.' *Man*, 18(2): 237-259.

Barabas, Alicia and Miguel Bartolomé, eds. 1993. *Etnicidad y pluralismo cultural: la din·mica etnica en Oaxaca*. Mexico City: Consejo Nacional por la Cultura y el Arte.

——— 1984. *El Rey Cong Hoy: tradición messianica y privación social entre los Mixes de Oaxaca*. Oaxaca: INAH.

Barry, Tom. 1992. *Mexico: A Country Guide*. Albuquerque, NM: Inter-Hemisphere Education Resource Centre.

Behar, Ruth. 1987. "Sex and Sin: Witchcraft and the Devil in Late-Colonial Mexico." *American Ethnologist*, 14 (1): 34-54.

Berryman, Phillip. 1987. *Liberation Theology: Essential Facts About the Revolutionary Movement in Latin America and Beyond*. Philadelphia: Temple University Press.

Bourdieu, Pierre. 1977. *Outline of a Theory of Practice*. Cambridge: CUP.

———. 1971. "Génese et Structure du Champ Réligieux." *Rev. Francaise de la Sociologie*, XII.

Burdick, John. 1992. "Rethinking the Study of Social Movements: The Case of Christian Base Communities in Urban Brazil." In A. Escobar and Sonia Alvarez, eds. *The Making of Social Movements in Latin America*. San Francisco: Westview Press, 171-85.

Camp, Roderic. 1994. "The Cross in the Polling Booth: Religion, Politics and the Laity in Mexico." *Latin American Research Review*, 29 (3): 69-100.

Candelaria, Michael. 1981. *Popular Religion and Liberation*. Albany, NY: SUNY Press.

Carrasco, Bartolomé. 1994. Personal interview, Iglesia de la Guadelupe, Oaxaca de Juárez, Oaxaca. XI Censo de Población y Vivienda, Mexico, 1990.

Concha Malo, Miguel, et al. 1986. *La Participacion de los Cristianos en el Proceso Popular de Liberación en Mexico*. Mexico City: Siglo XXI editores.

Chance, John. 1978. *Race and Class in Colonial Oaxaca*. Stanford, CA: Stanford

University Press.

Chock, P. and J. Wyman. 1986. *Discourse and the Social Life of Meaning*. Washington, DC: Smithsonian Institute Press.

Directorio Eclesiastico de la Arquidiocesis de Antequera-Oaxaca. 1992.

Christian, Wm. 1981. *Local Religion in Sixteenth Century Spain*. Princeton, NJ: Princeton University Press.

Dussel, Enrique. 1986. "Popular Religion as Oppression and Liberation: Hypotheses on its Past and Present in Latin America." *Concilium*, August: 82-96.

Finkler, Kaja. 1985. *Spiritist Healers in Mexico*. New York: Praeger.

Foster, George. 1960. *Culture and Conquest: America's Spanish Heritage*. New York: Cooper Square.

Foweraker, Joe. 1990. "Introduction." In J. Foweraker and A. Craig, eds. *Popular Movements and Political Change in Mexico*. Boulder, CO: Lynne Reinner, 3-20.

Geertz, Clifford. 1973. *The Interpretation of Cultures: Selected Essays*. New York: Basic Books, 87-125.

Gillow, Eulogio. 1978. *Apuntes Historicos*. Graz: Akedem.

Giménez, Gilberto. 1978. *Religion y Cultura Popular en el Anahuac*. Mexico City: CEE.

Greenberg, J.B. 1989. *Blood Ties: Life and Violence in Rural Mexico*. Tucson: University of Arizona Press.

———. 1981. *Santiago's Sword: Chatino Peasant Religion and Economics*. Berkeley: University of California Press.

Gutiérrez, G. 1973. *A Theology of Liberation: History, Politics and Salvation*. Maryknoll, NY: Orbis Books.

Hanson, Eric. 1990. *The Catholic Church in World Politics*. Princeton, NJ: Princeton University Press.

Hernández Diaz, Jorge. 1994. *Revindicaciones Etnicas y Eclesiologìa de los Pobres*. Unpublished m.s. Oaxaca: IISUABJO.

Higgins, Michael. 1993. "Quienes son los migrantes étnicos al teatro urbano del valle de Oaxaca?" In Alicia Barabas and Miguel Bartolomé, eds. *Etnicidad y Pluralismo Cultural: La Dinamica Etnica en Oaxaca*.

Hunt, Linda. 1992. "Living with Cancer in Oaxaca, Mexico: Patient and Physician Perspectives in Cultural Context." Doctoral dissertation, Harvard University.

Knight, Alan. 1990. "Racism, Revolution and Indigenismo: Mexico 1910-1940." In R. Graham, ed. *The Idea of Race in Latin America, 1870-1940*. Austin: University of Texas Press, 71-113.

Lafaye, Jacques. 1974. *Quetzacoatl and Guadelupe: The Formation of Mexican National Consciousness 1531-1813*. London: University of Chicago Press.

Lancaster, Roger. 1988. *Thanks to God and the Revolution*. New York: Columbia University Press.

Levine, Daniel H. 1986. *Religion and Political Conflict in Latin America*. Chapel Hill: University of North Carolina Press.

———. 1980. *Churches and Politics in Latin America*. Beverly Hills, CA: Sage.

Mahar Higgins, Cheleen. 1974. "Integrative Aspects of Folk and Western Medicine among the Urban Poor in Oaxaca." *Anthropological Quarterly*, 48 (1): 31-37.

Marroquín, E. 1989. *La Cruz Messiánica: una aproximación del sincretismo indigena*. Oaxaca: Palabra ediciones–UABJO.

———. 1992. *El Botin Sagrado: la din·mica religiosa en Oaxaca*. Oaxaca: IISUABJO–Comunicación Sociál.

McNabb, V. and M. Rees. 1993. "Liberation or Theology?: Ecclesistical Base Communities in Oaxaca, Mexico." *Journal of Church and State*, 35 (4): 723-749.

Murphy, A. and A. Stepick. 1991. *Social Inequality in Oaxaca*. Philadelphia: Temple University Press.

Nagengast, Carol and M. Kearney. 1990. "Mixtec Ethnicity." *Latin American Research Review*, 25 (2): 61-93.

Norget, Kristin. 1997. "The Politics of 'Liberation': The Popular Church, Indigenous Theology and Grassroots Mobilization in Oaxaca, Mexico." *Latin American Perspectives*, 24 (5): 96-127.

———. 1996. "Beauty and the Feast: Aesthetics and the Performance of Meaning in the Day of the Dead in Oaxaca, Mexico." *Journal of Latin American Lore*, 19 (1).

———. 1995. "Modernization, Globalization and the Popular Church in Oaxaca, Mexico." Paper presented at the Annual Meeting of the American Anthropological Association (AAA), Washington, DC (18 Nov.)

———. 1993. "The Day of the Dead in Oaxaca, Mexico." Unpublished doctoral dissertation, University of Cambridge, England.

Nutini, Hugo. 1988. *Todos Santos in Rural Tlaxcala*. Princeton, NJ: Princeton University Press.

———. 1976. "Syncretism and Acculturation: The Historical Development of the Cult of the Patron Saint in Tlaxcala, Morelos." *Ethnology*, 15 (3): 301-321.

Ortiz Echaniz. 1984. "La Curación Espiritualista." *Cuicuilco*, IV: 14-15.

Ricard, Robert. 1966. *The Spiritual Conquest of Mexico*. Berkeley: California Library Reprint Service.

Rowe, W. and V. Schelling. 1991. *Memory and Modernity: Popular Culture in Latin America*. London: Verso.

Scott, James. 1985. *Weapons of the Weak: Everyday Forms of Peasant Resistance*. New Haven, CT: Yale University Press.

Smith, Christian. 1996. *The Emergence of Liberation Theology*. Chicago: University of Chicago Press.

Stephen, Lynn. 1991. *Zapotec Women*. Austin: University of Texas Press.

Stephen, Lynn and James Dow. 1990. "Introduction." In L. Stephen and J. Dow, eds. *Class, Politics and Popular Religion: Religious Change in Mexico and Central America*. Washington, DC: American Anthropological Association, 1-24.

Stewart, C. and Rosalind Shaw. 1994. *Syncretism/Anti-Syncretism*. New York: Routledge.

Stoll, David. 1990. *Is Latin America turning Protestant?* Berkeley: University of California Press.

Taylor, William. 1972. *Landlord and Peasant in Colonial Oaxaca*. Stanford, CA: Stanford University Press.

Whitecotton, Joseph. 1977. *The Zapotecs: Princes, Priests and Peasants*. Norman: University of Oklahoma Press.

Williams, A.. 1979. "Cohesive Features of the Guelaguetza System in Mitla." In A. Williams, ed. *Social, Political and Economic Life in Contemporary Oaxaca*. Nashville, TN: Vanderbilt University Press.

FIVE

CEBS AND CATHOLIC
CHARISMATICS IN BRAZIL[1]

Marjo de Theije

"It is our obligation to bring the word of God to the people, to the community," said Dona Joanina, a Roman Catholic lay woman of the parish of St. Vincent, Garanhuns, a town of about 100,000 inhabitants in the northeastern Brazilian state of Pernambuco. To reach this goal, the parish's charismatic renewal movement, of which Joanina is a member, founded a day care center for street children. The monks of São Bento donated the land, located in the center of town, and all the prayer groups of the town contributed money and labor in the construction of the facility. Joanina now volunteers two days a week in the new day care center. She is a lively woman in her late forties, mother of nine children, of whom the youngest is now twelve years old. Recently Dona has enjoyed some spare time to do what she always wanted to do, but never before had time for: participating "in the things of the church," as she says. In fact, Dona Joanina is not only a regular participant of the parish's charismatic prayer group. She is also engaged in the base ecclesial community in her part of the neighborhood.

Dona Joanina combines two forms of Catholicism that are, according to many, incompatible. Base communities, on the one hand, are the expression of liberationist Catholicism, a step on the way to constructing the kingdom of God on earth. They represent an ideology of engagement with the poor and oppressed in society. According to liberation theology, the people of God should organize and apply their religious inspiration in social and political activities. In the Catholic charismatic renewal (CCR) movement, on the other hand, religious experience and individual problem solving take a central place. According to critics, this emphasis is only possible at the expense of involvement in social action (e.g., CNBB 1994: 29-30). The CCR, explained one priest in the weekly magazine *Isto É*, "is the Catholic version of Evangelical

Pentecostalism with its emphasis on miracles, exorcism, and manifestations of the Holy Ghost" (Spinoza 1997).

Thus, an image emerges in which liberationist Catholicism and charismatic Catholicism are two totally different and opposed ideologies. Mass media also transmit this dichotomized view of these movements, with newspaper headlines such as "Action divides the Church" (Folha 1990). If a church group was to start a day care center, then we would expect it to be the local base community doing it, not the CCR. Moreover, in the eyes of many observers, the CCR is not only a "different" version of Catholicism, but also a weapon in the hands of conservative bishops and priests in the battle against liberationist Catholicism. In short, people widely think that base communities and the CCR don't go together. However, in fact, Dona Joanina is no anomalous religious actor in Garanhuns. Many others also participate in different Catholic lay groups. How can we explain this behavior?

The alleged incompatibilities between liberationist and charismatic Catholicism in Latin America are hardly qualified by most anthropological and sociological fieldwork. Recent ethnographies on Brazilian religion scarcely pay attention to the CCR. Burdick (1993), Hewitt (1991), Ireland (1991), and Mariz (1994), for example, do not include the CCR in their analysis of the religious field in Brazil. Happily, several Brazilian scholars are now starting to fill this gap in our understanding of Brazilian Catholicism. The works of Benedetti (1988), Machado (1994), Mariz and Machado (1994), and Prandi and Souza (1996) offer valuable insight into this relatively new version of Catholicism that in many parishes is as important as the liberationist base communities. This recent research provides grounds for questioning the supposed antagonistic relationship between the two forms of Catholicism (e.g., Benedetti 1996; Mariz 1994). In this chapter, I argue that the CCR and base communities are not necessarily adversaries. In Garanhuns, they are quite similar in a number of ways. The typical image of the CCR can be attributed to the fact that observers usually emphasize the meaning of the movement in a national and international context, overlooking the peculiarities and distinctive traits of local elaborations of charismatic teachings. Just as the base communities are not simply liberation theology writ small, local prayer groups are not necessarily the direct expression of ideology of the national and international charismatic movement.

Addressing the question of the paradoxical behavior of Dona Joanina and her co-religionists makes a contribution to the broader assessment of the role of charismatic prayer groups and base communities in

Brazilian Catholicism. To do this, I analyze local level experience in Garanhuns. This chapter is structured in two sections. The first centers on the structural and historical factors involved in Catholic lay associations and activities. In the second section, the local actors take center stage. We ask: How do members of the base communities and the CCR construct their religious activities, and what is the meaning of these constructions?

The ethnographic data for this paper were gathered in Garanhuns between 1989 and 1994. My work focuses particularly on a neighborhood I call "Colina," the more populated section of one of the parishes of the town (and diocese) of Garanhuns. This parish, Saint Vincent, consists of a large rural area containing a number of villages and a few marginal neighborhoods of the city, and includes an estimated 30,000 inhabitants altogether. Colina is a poor neighborhood, as are so many in Garanhuns. It is a rather messy area, with piles of garbage in the streets and many run-down buildings. Few of the streets are paved. During the rainy season, the streets turn into vast mudflows that sweep along everything found in their paths. It is no coincidence that the main street, named after a local politician, is called in local vernacular, *Rua d'Areia* (Sand Street). Jobs are rare in the neighborhood. Only the municipal slaughterhouse and the Water Company offer some employment. Apart from this, there are quite a number of small workshops (particularly car repair and furniture works), some *vendas* (simple grocery shops) and several bars. Colina has two schools, but these do not offer enough seats for all the area children. During my stay, the only area health center suffered from a shortage of medicine, and for some months there were no health workers, either. For most inhabitants in the neighborhood, life is hard. It is within this context that the religious actors carry out their plans, give form to their wishes, and fulfill their social and religious obligations.

LAY GROUPS: CATHOLIC CAMPAIGNS IN PRACTICE

In the 1990s, the face of much of Brazilian Catholicism at the local level is shaped by two forms of lay associations: first, by the base ecclesial communities (CEBs), which were promoted from the 1960s onward, and, second, by the more recent groups of the charismatic renewal movement. These are generally depicted as representing antagonistic factions in Latin American Catholicism, each representing an ideology opposed to the other.

Historically viewed, neither CEBs nor charismatic prayer groups are unique in practice. In Catholicism, lay movements have always been an important means of "cultural politics" (Ortner 1989).[2] Through these kinds of groups, the clergy or other religious actors have tried to guide the laity and the religious community, and to establish specific interpretations and expressions of Catholic belief. Ortner (1989) uses the word "campaign" (of cultural politics) for this type of organized endeavor to change the religious order. The Catholic clergy as a group have historically repeatedly tried to establish specific practices and ideologies by initializing campaigns according to the prevailing ideas and policies in the national and universal church. In these attempts at reform, lay associations were often the focus of attention. Throughout the centuries, campaigns to form and reform Catholicism all left their marks on the local religious order. The contemporary variation of religious forms and meanings in Garanhuns, in which both the CEBs as well as charismatic groups play an important role, is in large part related to cultural politics carried out by different actors in the past.

The Ultramontane campaign at the end of the nineteenth century, for example, was an attempt to change both the organization and content of Catholicism in Brazil. In colonial times, the authority of the Catholic Church was weak, and much of religious life transpired outside of its jurisdiction. As De Groot (1996: 83) shows, the reform-oriented clergy of the day believed that the Church should enhance its presence among the laity in order to bring them under greater religious control (for example, in regard to the autonomy of religious feasts and popular trust in independent faith healers). To reach this goal, the Church restructured and strengthened its institutional presence, with the goal of reinforcing Catholic teachings and combatting "superstition." The creation of new lay movements was an important strategy of the Ultramontane campaign. Priests founded lay groups such as the "Apostleship of Prayer" and the "Society of Saint Vincent de Paula" in this period. The effects of all these measures seem to have been quite modest at that time, however, judged by the diocesan policy in the decades that followed. Attention shifted more explicitly to a stress on theological teachings and beliefs, but the main organizational lines of the Ultramontane campaign remained intact until the second half of the twentieth century.

From the 1960s onward, however, the liberationist campaign began to take over. As in the previous periods, one of the first steps was to increase the organizational strength of the Church to support the liberationist ideology (Smith 1991). Again, lay groups were the main means of disseminating the new ideology, but this time through the CEBs. In Garanhuns, most members of the clergy embraced the liberationist ideology at an early stage. Especially after 1974, when a new bishop was appointed, Garanhuns adopted the "option for the poor." The diocese developed a pastoral practice of evangelization that encouraged laity to participate. Increasingly, pastoral activity concentrated on the formation of CEBs. The founding and guidance of base communities became the most important pastoral goal of this era. One result was a growing influence of laity in the pastoral practice, both at the level of policy making through many kinds of commissions and pastoral groups, and at the level of everyday services in the communities, through their autonomously meeting CEBs. As the conclusion of a diocesan Assembly stated: lay groups and movements are "the motors" of pastoral action.

In the parish of Saint Vincent, to which Colina belongs, as in many other parishes of Garanhuns, liberationist Catholicism filtered into the organization of daily religious practice. The effort of the clergy and diocesan policy to create a new structure of lay organizations based on small local groups resulted in dozens of CEBs in the parish, about ten in Colina alone. People did and still do form CEBs, and live out an important part of their religious lives in these groups. These CEBs each have ten to fifteen members, who all live near each other and meet once a week in the house of one participant. One or two lay persons direct the group. Most of the time, they use the *roteiro* (meeting manual) provided by the diocesan coordination team. In this manual, texts from the Bible are printed, with examples of discussion topics and suggested appropriate prayers. Base communities have become one of the most important forms of lay activity in the parish. In everyday practice, it sometimes looks as if the CEBs *are* the parish, because they form its main aim of diocesan policy and pastoral work.[3] In many instances of Catholic celebrations, the priest relies on the CEBs to organize church life in the parish. Some active CEB leaders are also members of the Parish Council, participate in various ministries, and act as readers during mass. This all adds to the impression that CEBs are the backbone of the parish structure.

After twenty years of campaigning, CEBs and the type of lay association they stand for have become the norms in much of Brazilian Catholic practice. Most participants in any lay group are also members of one of the CEBs in the neighborhood. This does not mean, however, that CEBs are exact copies of the ideal projected for them by liberation theology. The outcome of the liberationist campaign, as of any other cultural campaign, is not predictable by taking into account the ideologies and actions only of the leaders who bring it forth. Cultural politics do not work in a direct and immediate way. Since the goal in the end is always to "change the minds of the people," many other forces are typically involved as well. In this case, the religious practice of most CEBs is far less radical and politicized than the ideology of liberation theology would propose. Also, significantly, CEBs do not bar participation in other Catholic lay groups.

In Garanhuns, CEBs are supposed to help themselves, and, consequently, they are free to shape the content of their own organizations. As a result, in Garanhuns, like in many other places in Brazil (see Burdick 1993; Hewitt 1991; Mariz 1994), most CEBs do not fulfill the ideal image of church communities suggested by liberation theology. The political and social activism of the groups is especially modest. Father Milton, for instance, tries to encourage the people of the CEBs to develop community projects beyond the strictly religious sphere. In his opinion, not all CEBs are "real CEBs," presupposed to engage in political action—in political parties, unions, or local social and economic projects to improve the life conditions of the poor. Therefore, during Mass, Father Milton calls on people to participate in the groups. In his sermons, he often discusses social problems in the parish and Brazil generally. Nevertheless, most area CEBs continue not to engage in political activism and projects.

The CEBs operate quite autonomously. Occasionally a priest visits the groups, but usually only once or twice a year. CEB leaders have a meeting every month to evaluate their work and organize for the next month. Most of the time, a priest participates in these meetings. Besides this, there is a Bible course to prepare the laity to evangelize and conscientize in which the priest and a local nun lecture on liberation theology. In these classes, they stress the link between biblical texts and everyday life, as well as the social and political consequences of being a Catholic for community life. But the influence of these measures on the daily practice of the CEBs is modest. To begin with, the leaders of the groups are not all equally convinced of the need for social and political action. Others feel they are not equipped to initiate and organize such activities. Consequently, many leaders do not transmit the teachings of the priest to their groups. Some CEBs leaders have reached the level of conscientization which diocesan policy aims at, but they often find difficulty convincing their groups to "follow" them. Finally, when both leaders and other members of their groups decide to get involved in political action, they often encounter so many problems on their way that they soon lose motivation. The result is that most groups focus primarily on prayer and Bible reading.

The second explanation for the great diversity of practices produced by the original CEB campaign relates to the character of the Catholic

Church itself. The initial invitation to participate originally attracted many people who had no ambition to become "conscientized" in ways the clergy of Garanhuns or theologians of liberation had imagined. Since the ideology claimed that no one should be excluded, however, other initiatives coming from within the community were encouraged, or at least permitted, as well. Therefore, in Colina the *Apostolado da Oracao* (Apostleship of Prayer) is an important association in the neighborhood, with over fifty members. In addition, some area women had also founded a local chapter of a group called *Legiao de Maria* (Legion of Mary). This group originated during the time of the Ultramontane campaign of the first half of the twentieth century, and reflects its goal of promoting devotional activities. With the same enthusiasm, a group of lay people started a charismatic prayer group in the neighborhood, which soon attracted the attention of Dona Joanina and many others.

Thus, the democratic, populist attitude in liberationist Catholicism opened space for "counter campaigns." At a national scale, the most important initiative of the laity in recent years has been the charismatic renewal movement, which, according to most observers, opposes liberationist Catholicism in form and content.[4] In Garanhuns, the *Renovacao Católica Carismatica* started to attract more and more participants from the early 1980s onward. The promotion of this lay movement was not part of any clerical campaign in the diocese, although on a national or international level laymen and clergy, of course, promote the charismatic movement. In terms of cultural politics, this produces multivocality at the local level. Different campaigns are at work simultaneously. They can clash, but more typically the result can be a rather peaceful coexistence, as the situation in Garanhuns suggests.

For years, the CCR has functioned in the liberationist-oriented diocese of Garanhuns without support from the local clergy. None of the priests agreed to become its official spiritual leader, though none offered major opposition to its work either. In the context of encouragement for lay initiatives that is inherent in (at least the local form of) liberation theology, the charismatics enjoyed sufficient political space to develop their activities. All the priests at least agree that having a charismatic renewal within the Church is better than losing the faithful to the Pentecostal churches in town. The priest of Colina has a pragmatic attitude about this matter. Now and then he attends a prayer meeting and uses his time to speak "to introduce a more liberationist discourse in the group," as he says. So it happened that in less than ten years the charismatic movement became a significant part of the local religious system.

In Colina, the CCR prayer group has a meeting every Monday evening in the parish church of Saint Vincent. These meetings are led by lay leaders, and community involvement is significant. All participants take part in the singing and praying, and several deliver testimonies of the work of the Holy Spirit in their personal lives. Besides this weekly meeting, many members of the prayer group engage in other activities of the CCR too, such as the pastoral of the sick. Some members even perform door-to-door evangelism. The day care center provides another activity in which several members are involved. Moreover, although the CCR group is not structurally associated with the parish, many *carismaticos* fulfill formal religious tasks, such as reading during Mass or helping organize feasts for the patron saint.

As in previous Church campaigns, the liberationist campaign used a form of lay association as a vehicle for its ideological reforms. But the campaign initiated by the liberationist clergy, when confronted with great autonomy of the laity, produced unexpected consequences. At the local level, it simply offered new opportunities for the laity to follow their own path of religious action. The founding and growth of the CCR is ironically a result of this process.

LOCAL ELABORATION: THE CONSTRUCTION OF EVERYDAY RELIGION

Dona Joanina did not think the opinions of others about the meaning of the CEB and the CCR group were very important. For her, participation in both groups is meaningful. When the charismatic group started to meet some years ago, there were initial rumors that it was Protestant-influenced. For a few weeks, this news dissuaded her from attending. But then she concluded that it would not be meeting in the parish church if it were Protestant, and she started attending the meetings. Only when her CEB has held a meeting at the same time has she missed a CCR prayer meeting. Dona Joanina and many of her co-members produce and reproduce a form of Catholicism that is idiosyncratic, yet in continuity with the Church teachings.

We have seen that, within the contemporary organization of parish life, the laity have considerable autonomy. A significant degree of religious self-sufficiency became the rule in the realization of the liberationist ideals. For the laity, the result is that they become co-responsible for parish life. It also means, however, that lay people have substantial liberty to give form and meaning to their local expressions of Catholicism. The people of Saint Vincent parish use this liberty to organize themselves in various lay associations, of which the CEBs and the CCR are considered the most important today. This shows that they are self-conscious actors in the construction of everyday Catholicism—and not merely responding to practices to which they are "exposed" (Burdick 1993:10) or reacting to things that others "offer" (Hewitt 1991:48). What are the motivations of these Catholics?

To their participants, it is a foolish question to ask why one partici- pates in the CEB, the Apostleship of Prayer, the charismatic prayer group, or the Legion of Mary. "Religion is good," they simply say. Therefore, participation in a lay group is plainly a good thing to do. Recall that Dona Joanina simply wanted to take part in "the things of the Church." A survey of eighty-three participants of the CEBs in Colina revealed very general reasons for membership, such as "I like religious things," "I like to do something religious," and "I like to hear the word of God." This general view of religious participation helps to explain why many members of CEBs are also associated with other groups such as the *Apostolado da Oracao, Conferíncia Vicentina,* or the pastoral of the sick (Mariz and Theije 1991).

Ten of the eighty-three CEB members I interviewed (12 percent) also attended the weekly prayer meeting of the charismatics, just as Dona Joanina does. The faithful in Colina see no problem in participating in both the charismatic groups and CEBs. Contradictions between the two simply do not seem to exist for these people. In a recent publication based on research in Rio de Janeiro, Mariz (1996) reports the same find- ing. She discovered an "openheartedness to other religious groups" by the members of both groups, and points to the fact that participants emphasize the common elements of the groups instead of differences (1996:24). Members of the CEBs and CCR agreed that "all things reli- gious are good." The only difference that really counts for most intervie- wees is the difference between Catholicism and other religions.

Still, members of local religious groups enjoy the opportunity to maintain their own interpretations of Catholicism. In the liberationist model of CEBs, religious self-sufficiency is the norm, just as in previous campaigns the prayer meetings of the *Apostolado da Oracao,* for exam- ple, were the norm. The character of this liberationist norm opens room for other initiatives. Liberationist Catholicism supports autonomy for the laity and a decentralization of institutional power. The result is that the laity make decisions without consulting the clergy and construct their own content for their religious groups. And this local elaboration may contradict what would be ideologically expected, as in the case of CEBs limiting themselves to devotional practices, and CCR prayer groups developing social programs for street children.

For the clergy, this is a reality that can be hard to deal with. When

Dona Joanina told about the founding of the day care center, she added: "Father Milton says the Charismatics are only occupied with praise, and do nothing for the community. But we do. We do a lot." Father Milton is indeed not very fond of the charismatic group in the parish. And the local priest of Saint Vincent is not alone in his critique of the CCR. As a follower of liberationist Catholicism, he and many like-minded Catholics accuse the CCR of offering no critical perspective or engagement in relation to the social injustices of Brazilian society. However, for Dona Joanina it is not an either/or matter. In fact, she fuses these different elements together into one united religious practice.

The question then emerges: do ideological differences between movements not matter at all? I would argue that at the local level the ideological differences between liberationist and charismatic Catholicism are far less important than often assumed. The laity give relatively little attention to ideology in their meetings. Ideological differences, although not entirely absent, are less pronounced. Dona Joanina had noticed the words of Father Milton about the lack of involvement in the community of the CCR, so she was aware of his concern. But she also claimed a solution for it, fusing liberationist and charismatic ideas into one religious practice. In Colina, as in Garanhuns in general, liberation theology has been the leading pastoral ideology for two decades. This means people have been exposed to liberationist teachings for many years now. These ideas have become part of the religious practices and beliefs of all parishioners, members of CEBs and other groups alike. Central elements in the discourses and practices of different groups become "not so different" from each other in the context in which this religious construction takes place.

There are other examples of this fusion of characteristic elements from different ideologies. Both groups have the reading and interpretation of the Scripture as an important element in their practice. The use of the Bible in the meetings of the laity was strongly stimulated in the liberationist campaign, and the charismatic groups follow the liberationist norm in this respect. Furthermore, as the CEB rituals became the standard, they influenced the contents of charismatic prayer meetings as well. Take for example the liberationist concern to "connect the Word of God to daily life" (see Lehmann 1996). This happens not only in the meetings of the CEBs, but also during the CCR prayer meetings. The form is different—in the first case initiated by a collectivist, liberationist reflection on a biblical text from the diocesan meeting manual, in the second case by a personal testimony from a fellow member of the group. The end result, however, comes out much the same.

A group of young members of the local charismatic movement further substantiates this interpretation. During the national political race in 1989 and 1990, these charismatic youngsters campaigned fanatically for the PT (Workers Party) and Lula, the presidential candidate of the PT. Several liberationist priests and lay activists also openly solicited votes for PT candidates. The fact that Catholics considered "politics" to be an expression of their religious lives was not surprising. But the militancy of these young charismatics contradicted the reputation of the CCR as politically disengaged (Spinoza 1997). Furthermore, members of the CCR are typically believed to be on the conservative side of the political spectrum (Pierucci and Prandi 1996). But the activism of these youngsters was a logical working out of their beliefs, which are shaped not only by CCR teachings, but also by the local, liberationist clergy. This combination produced a strong, progressive, politically militant movement that was proud to join forces with the liberationist clergy.

Laity at the local level even mix central ideology elements of the different groups to which they belong. Take, for example, the key idea of "liberation." In the CEBs, "liberation" carries the connotation of liberation from social injustice. In the CCR, liberation is a more personal, individual freedom from suffering (Benedetti 1988, Prandi & Souza 1996). Nevertheless, "liberation" has become part of common local religious vocabulary, and in daily usage the different meanings have merged. The content of many religious symbols is not fixed, but adapts in the process of constructing the religious community. In "liberation" the Holy Spirit becomes linked to the community, since it is the community of the people of God who strive for liberation. Dona Irací, a regular participant in both the CCR and the CEB on her street, articulated this mixture of liberationist and Charismatic Catholicism when she said: "Before, this story of community did not exist, didn't exist at all. However, to get everybody involved is very difficult. The world can only become a good world when everybody would live in community, when everybody would live in prayer groups, when everybody would participate in the groups . . . then things would be different." In this process, the CEBs and charismatic prayer groups often come to resemble each other, in both ideological meanings and social practices. The new day care center founded by the CCR serves as a concrete result of the local elaboration of charismatic belief in a context of liberationist Catholic discourse.

CONCLUSION

Because ideological and political conflict receive ample attention in the study of religion, many less contentious aspects of religious practice at the local level pass unnoticed or, worse, are misunderstood by scholars. We have paid attention not only to changes and novelties in the historic development of local Catholic culture, but also to continuities in the organization of local belief and association. The liberationist campaign of the 1970s through the 1990s, founded on the lay associations of CEBs, was in line with the logic of previous campaigns. This continuity is a factor that somewhat constrains the freedom of lay actors in the religious field to live their beliefs according to their wishes. At the same time, it creates opportunities and offers possibilities for ordinary men and women to give meaning and form to their own religious lives in what I called the local elaboration of the religious.

The experience in Colina—and certainly in many other parishes in Brazil—of continuity rather than rupture and difference, and local practice over national ideology, offers a helpful point of view. From this perspective we see that the legacy of liberation theology in the practice of everyday life is both more influential and more modest than is often believed. It is more influential because members of CEBs and charismatic prayer groups both embody several ideas and practices that can be attributed to liberation theology. But it is also more modest because not all members of CEBs prove to be the "conscientized" Catholics liberation theology calls for.

In Garanhuns, the organization of Catholicism in CEBs is now normal and many people participate simply because they "like to do something religious." The desire is the same as in a CCR group. After all, people think they "were born Catholic" and want "to stay in the Church," as some women explained. From the perspective of the parishioners, then, differences between CEBs and CCR groups are more a matter of style than content. The idea that the two movements are fundamentally opposed to each other finds little support at the local level. The local Catholic order of Colina suggests instead that participation in religious groups has more to do with Catholic practice in general, with the continuity of "being Catholic," than with specific ideological characteristics of alternative groups. It also shows that, in the construction of everyday religion within those different groups, the interpenetration of ideological elements from different ideologies takes place with great ease.

NOTES

1 An early version of this paper was presented at the Fourth BRASA Conference, November 12-15, 1997, Washington, DC; thanks to Robin Nagle and Kees (C.F.G.) de Groot for their helpful contributions to this work.

2 Cultural politics are the politics of public ideology, or as Ortner (1989) defines it, "the struggles over official symbolic representations of reality that shall prevail in a given social order at a given time." In cultural politics, the control over truth and value are at stake. For general usage, these "official symbolic representations of reality" may seem a somewhat vague notion; but it is well suited to the context of religion and the goals of various religious structures. Catholicism in particular is a religion that strives for an ideological influence shaping all spheres of society.

3 This is a point of much discussion among liberation theologians and others involved in the ideological construction of CEBs. Some would like to see the CEBs as "being church," or otherwise replacing the traditional parishes.

4 Several critical authors argue that the CCR is a new type of movement within the Church, organized differently from other groups (see, e.g., Prandi and Souza 1996; Comblin 1983; Della Cava 1990). This is, however, largely an institutional argument. For the ordinary participant in the parishes, these characteristics of the movement are not readily visible or important.

REFERENCES

Benedetti, Luiz Roberto. 1988. "Templo, praça, coração. A articulação do campo religioso católico. "Tese de doutoramento. Departamento de Sociologia. Faculdade de Filosofia, Letras e Ciências Humanas, Universidade de São Paulo.

―――. 1996. "Pentecostalismo, CEBs e Renovação Carismática." Projeto do CERIS. Unpublished manuscript.

Burdick, John. 1993. *Looking for God in Brazil. The Progressive Catholic Church in Urban Brazil's Religious Arena*. Berkeley: University of California Press.

CNBB. 1994. "Levantamento sobre a Renovação Carismática no Brasil." Trabalho apresentada na 32a Assembléia Geral da CNBB. Itaia, São Paulo.

Comblin, José. 1983. Os "Movimentos" e a Pastoral Latino-americana. *Revista Eclesiástica Brasileira* 43(170): 227-262.

Della Cava, Ralph. 1990. "The Ten-Year Crusade Towards the Third Christian Millenium: An Account of Evangelization 2000 and Lumen 2000." Conference paper no. 27. New York: The Columbia University/New York University Consortium.

Folha. 1990. "Atuação divide alas da Igreja." *Folha de São Paulo*. May 27. A-8.

De Groot, Cornelius F.G. 1996. *Brazilian Catholicism and the Ultramontane Reform, 1850–1930*. Amsterdam: Cedla.

Hewitt, W. E. 1991. *Base Christian Communities and Social Change in Brazil*. Lincoln: University of Nebraska Press.

Mariz, Cecília Loreto. 1994. *Coping with Poverty: Pentecostals and Christian Base Communities in Brazil*. Philadelphia: Temple University Press.

Mariz, Cecília Loreto and Maria das Dores C. Machado. 1994. "Sincretismo e trânsito religioso: comparando carismáticos e pentecostais." *Comunicações do ISER* 12(45): 24-34.

Mariz, Cecília Loreto and Marjo de Theije. 1991. "A santa do povo: o catolicismo dos leigos no Santuário de Santa Quitéria." *Comunicações do ISER* 10(41): 42-57.

Moore, Sally Falk. 1975. "Epilogue: Uncertainties in Situations, Indeterminacies in Culture." In Sally Falk Moore and Barbara G. Meyerhoff, eds. *Symbol and Politics in Communal Ideology. Cases and Questions.* Ithaca, NY: Cornell University Press.

Ortner, Sherry B. "Cultural Politics: Religious Activism and Ideological Transformation Among 20th Century Sherpas." *Dialectical Anthropology* 14:197-211.

Pierucci, Antônio Flávio and Reginaldo Prandi. 1996. "Religiões e voto: a eleição presidencial de 1994." In Antônio Flávio Pierucci and Reginaldo Prandi, eds. *A realidade das religiões no Brasil: religião, sociedade e política.* São Paulo: Editora Hucitec/Departamento de Sociologia da Faculdade de Filosofia, Letras e Ciências Humanas da USP.

Prandi, Reginaldo and André Ricardo de Souza. 1996. "A carismática despolitização da igreja católica." In Antônio Flávio Pierucci and Reginaldo Prandi, eds. *A realidade das religiões no Brasil: religião, sociedade e política.* São Paulo: Editora Hucitec/Departamento de Sociologia da Faculdade de Filosofia, Letras e Ciências Humanas da USP.

Smith, Christian. 1991. *The Emergence of Liberation Theology: Radical Religion and Social Movement Theory.* Chicago: University of Chicago Press.

Spinoza, Rodolfo. 1997. "Question of Faith." *Brazil.* (September).

Theije, Marjo de. 1996. "Male and Female Perspectives in Northeastern CEBs." Paper presented at the Third *Brasa* Conference. September. Cambridge, England.

Valle, Rogério and Marcelo Pitta. 1994. *Comunidades Eclesiais Católicas. Resultados Estatísticos no Brasil.* Coleção Igreja do Brasil. Petrópolis: Vozes/CERIS.

SIX

EL CLAMOR POR VENEZUELA
LATIN AMERICAN EVANGELICALISM AS A COLLECTIVE ACTION FRAME[1]

David A. Smilde

On October 12, 1996, more than two thousand demonstrators gathered in front of the Venezuelan National Congress to protest deteriorating social, economic, and political conditions. Such protests have become daily occurrences in Caracas as unions, student groups, nongovernmental organizations, and other elements of civil society make their demands known (López Maya 1997). However, this protest was unique in that it was organized by an Evangelical radio station, supported by the Federation of Pentecostal Evangelical Churches of Caracas, and attended by Caracas Evangelicals of all social classes. The participants called it the *Clamor por Venezuela*, and it showed them to be not only interested in the public life of their country, but active in it as well.

Social scientists researching Latin American Evangelicalism now criticize the "political escapist" stereotype that once dominated the literature. Some argue that this form of religious participation is political in the way it provides social power to individuals and groups, and maintain that it may have important political consequences in the future (Levine 1995; Levine and Stoll 1997; Smith 1994; Smilde 1998; Ireland 1993; Martin 1990; Williams 1997; Cleary 1997; Burdick 1993). Others have demonstrated the increasing participation of Evangelicals in electoral politics (Freston 1993; Coleman et al. 1993; Martin 1990). Here I will present a case in which Evangelicals are involved in another form of political assertion common in Latin America and especially contemporary Venezuela: public protest. To do so, I will analyze the results of qualitative interviews carried out with participants in the event, using conceptual tools from social movements theory. My central argument is that Evangelicalism provides members of the popular sectors with a "collective action frame" that mobilizes them to confront the problems of their sociopolitical context. Furthermore, this frame combines with other ideologies and forms of social action in a much more complex way than is generally appreciated.

"LA CRISIS" IN VENEZUELA AND THE GROWTH OF CIVIL SOCIETY

The current growth of Evangelical Protestantism in Venezuela[2] is just one manifestation of the expansion of civil society and the cultural-symbolic diversification accompanying the progressive unraveling of an oil-fed, state-dominated society. As late as 1990, David Martin could point to Venezuela as an example of a highly secularized society in which Evangelicalism was making little progress (Martin 1990, 52, 59, 79-80, 84, 107). Indeed, up until the end of the 1980s it provided infertile ground for Evangelical growth compared to other Latin American countries. The explanation, however, lies not in the irreligiosity of the population, but rather in the fact that Venezuela passed through the postwar population boom and period of massive urbanization typical of the region under the aegis of what has been called a "populist-rentist-paternalist-clientalist"[3] state.

Venezuela's current democratic regime was established in 1958 by political elites who above all aimed to ensure stability and the continuance of the regime—the first democratic experiment had been overthrown in 1948 and resulted in a decade of military rule. Legitimacy was achieved politically, on the one hand, by elections in which the mass public could participate and, on the other, by the establishment of autocratic parties and the formation of pacts and commission by which elites and organized interests could guarantee a disproportional voice in policy making and electoral options. Legitimacy was achieved economically by the state's ability, through oil revenues, to simultaneously attend to the consumption demands of the majority, and the accumulation demands of private capital (Crisp, Levine, and Rey 1995; Lander 1995; Salamanca 1997; Neuhouser 1992; Navarro 1995; Karl 1995).

Considering that Venezuela maintained stability through a period in which democracies in Chile, Brazil, Argentina, and a number of other Latin American countries broke down, the achievements of this model were considerable. Annual growth in the gross domestic product averaged 5 percent from 1958 to 1980. Immunization drives and health care development dramatically increased life expectancy, lowered infant mortality, and led to a threefold increase in population between 1950 and 1990. A country that was 50 percent rural and 50 percent illiterate in 1950 was almost 90 percent urban and 90 percent literate by 1990.

(Salamanca 1997). Social life was comprehensively dominated by the state. The private sector was supported by state contracts, incentives, and protections; and political parties developed clientalistic networks of patronage down to the most micro of levels. Incipient civil associations were usually co-opted by political parties—those that remained autonomous usually became mere machines for obtaining state resources (Lander 1995). Evangelicalism experienced little growth. The chapter on Caracas in a 1984 book on Latin American cities written by a North American missionary is entitled: "Caracas, Venezuela: Secular City." In it the author writes, "You wonder if success didn't dull the people's spiritual sensitivities. Something must explain why, proportionally, the city's evangelical church ranks among the smallest in any Latin [American] city" (Maust 1984, 55).

The Venezuelan development model began to unravel in the early 1980s with the drop in oil prices and resulting fiscal crisis. Successive governments postponed change as long as possible until, in 1989, under the guidance of the International Monetary Fund, a severe structural adjustment package was implemented. Growth in the GDP for the decade of the eighties was -1.1 percent (Salamanca 1997), and by the early 1990s wages were below where they were at the end of the 1960s (Crisp, Levine, and Rey 1995). The poverty rate soared from 36 percent in 1984 to 68 percent in 1991, while the rate of extreme poverty more than tripled, rising from 11 percent in 1984 to 34 percent in 1991 (Lander 1995, 123). Throughout the 1990s, these trends have only accelerated. In 1996, average Venezuelans had approximately one-fifth the buying power they had in 1985 (*El Nacional* July 1, 1996). Venezuelans of all social classes refer to the current situation as *"La Crisis."*

This economic decline has undermined the legitimacy of the state and Venezuelan society in general. The announcement of austerity measures in February 1989 resulted in *"El Caracazo"*: several days of rioting, looting, and marshal law. López Maya (1997) argues that this was the beginning of a "cycle of protest" (more than four thousand protests occurred between 1989 and 1993). Two coup attempts in 1992 by nationalist sectors of the military failed, but resulted in hundreds of deaths. Ugalde et al. (1994) argue that *El Caracazo* was also the beginning of the surge in violent crime that has reached epidemic proportions. Opinion polls frequently show crime to be the number one concern of Venezuelans (*Chicago Tribune*, July 6, 1995). Corruption, on the other hand, is seen as the number one cause of *La Crisis*. In 1993, the president was accused of the misuse of state funds, and another ex-president is still being investigated on corruption charges. Corruption is undoubtedly a problem—a recent study rated Venezuela as the most corrupt country in Latin America (*El Nacional*, June 2, 1996)—however, the public obsession with it can be explained only as the search for a villain (Levine 1994).

Politically, the hegemony of the state parties and the political pacts that once ensured stability are no longer capable of containing the demands of a highly urban population that is increasingly diverse and increasingly connected to the mass media (Lander 1995; Crisp, Levine, and Rey 1995). The emergence of an array of new social movements and civil associations in the past decade has occurred at the same time that the parties' financial resources for co-optation and clientalism have dwindled (Karl 1995; Navarro 1995). The 1993 presidential elections were the first to be won by a candidate who was not affiliated with one of the two major parties, and, at this writing (April 1998), none of the four leading candidates for the 1998 elections are affiliated with them.

Uribe and Lander write that the parties have actually been quite successful at preserving themselves, but in the process they have discarded any aspiration to ideological leadership. Increasingly, new social movements—environmental action groups, neighborhood associations, women's groups, new labor unions, religious associations, etc.—are forming new spaces for political life that lie outside the mediation of the party-state complex, and defy justification in terms of "the programmatic political rationality that was traditionally offered to the country as the path to the construction of a modern society" (Uribe and Lander 1995 [1988], 23). While they may not be significant in terms of numbers, these new social movements possess "symbolic effectiveness." By reaching the public through the mass media or through public demonstrations, a relatively small movement can affect public opinion (26).

Lander warns against the complacent view that sees civil society filling the gap left by the restructuring of the state and the withdrawal of political parties from social life, pointing out that civil associations and new social movements have largely formed among the middle and upper-middle classes. Those who are most acutely affected by the restructuring—the popular sectors—are precisely those who lack the resources and the experience to effectively organize themselves (Lander 1995, 88). Indeed, the immense obstacles confronting the development of civil society within Venezuela's popular sectors are well documented.[4]

Interestingly, it is precisely among these groups that Evangelicalism, and other popular religious forms, have experienced dramatic growth. Evangelical groups have recently made inroads among the middle and upper-middle classes, but their strength remains their ability to attend to these hard-to-mobilize lower and lower-middle classes that have been left without a voice in the current transformation. The Evangelical meaning system presents individuals with a way to get a cognitive fix on the processes that are affecting their lives, and provides a basis for forming new social relationships and overcoming the obstacles to associational mobilization. Evangelical groups primarily serve as a space where individuals can reformulate their personal lives and reestablish or strengthen primary social ties. But in the *Clamor por Venezuela* we see an example of how Evangelical leaders can mobilize their members to take part in a demonstration in which their meaning system is projected into public space.

EL CLAMOR POR VENEZUELA

During the days preceding the *Clamor*, the event was advertised from the pulpit and by word-of-mouth among the members of the church with which I was doing field research. Members slowly assembled in the sanctuary on Saturday morning, singing songs led by a teenage Christian rock band. At 11:30 the pastor said a prayer and then led the congregation on the six-block walk to the Congress building. Arriving at the *Avenida Bolívar*, one of downtown Caracas's main thoroughfares, the light read "Don't Walk." At the first break in traffic the pastor and several others dashed across the street. Others followed suit, while some walked up from the intersection to the middle of the block where it would be easier to dodge the cars in their dash across the multilaned boulevard. As the *hermanos* walked up the sidewalks they would greet passersby with a friendly "Christ loves you" and hand them Bible tracts. One woman said, *"Sin Cristo nada podemos hacer"* [Without Christ we can do nothing] with each tract she handed out. Hymn singing would be interspersed with responsive chants. *"A su nombre!"* [And to his name!] an individual would shout out. *"Gloria!"* those within earshot would respond. *"Y a Su Pueblo!"* [And to his people] he or she would continue. *"Victoria!"* [Victory] the others would respond.

As they walked up the *Avenida Universidad*, nearing the Congress, they passed a man on a side street loading boxes into his car. Watching the song-singing procession with obvious disdain, he shouted out, *"Que trabajen! Que trabajen!"* (get a job, get a job). Several Evangelical men immediately responded, "Christ loves you," smiling and laughing as they continued walking. Armando, a security guard and Evangelical for eleven years, was walking next to me. He turned to me and explained, "Some people feel bad when they feel the presence of the Holy Spirit."

In the plaza in front of the Congress a white canopy was set up. Underneath on the left side were fifteen or twenty blue fold-up chairs occupied by Evangelical dignitaries of the Caracas area. To the right a band played, with three young women singing into microphones on stands. A large banner saying, "Stand up and shine, the light has come and the glory of Jehovah has come over you" covered the majority of the back canvas wall of the canopy. To the right was another banner with a map of Venezuela painted in the tricolor formula of the Venezuelan flag. In large letters it read "Lord, Venezuela belongs to you." On the left side hung a banner saying "Spirit of Grace, come over us." In front of the canopy a small platform about a foot high with a microphone stand gave each speaker a place to have his or her say. The 2,500 or so people in attendance made a sort of semicircle around the platform, accumulating back and filling up about half of the plaza. Others sought the shade underneath the overhang of the Congress building's roof.

The pastor who organized the event gave his "testimony" about the experience. "In the past few years, God has put people [i.e. Evangelicals] in key positions." The fruits of this are already beginning to show, he said. The authorities had said that holding such an event in front of the Congress building was prohibited by the law. But through these Evangelicals in high places, "We let them [the authorities] know that we come on behalf of the highest authority." This met with applause, whistles, and hollers. Then the pastor raised his hand toward the Congress building and dramatically shouted: "Today we are raising our voices from outside. Tomorrow we will raise our voices from inside!" This met with even greater applause. When it died down, a woman began singing the National Anthem. Enrique, a bank employee, whose six-year-old son was sitting on a parked motorcycle making motorcycle noises, knelt down and said, "Shhh. Listen. You have to respect the national anthem." A full four hours of sermons, songs, prayers, and children's theater ensued.

I interviewed twenty people during the course of the event, attempting to get as diverse and random a sample as is possible in a crowd. I began with an open-ended probe, attempting to elicit their conception of the purpose of the gathering: "What is the purpose of this *Clamor por Venezuela*?" Then, given the name of the event, I asked them a more specific question to try to get at their vision of the event's impact: "What kind of impact could this event have on Venezuela?" Finally, we discussed their views of the relative importance of this type of action versus other types of action. I told them the story of the person who shouted out for Evangelicals to get to work, and asked their opinions.

Throughout the interviews I asked for clarifications and added other questions that seemed appropriate.

I will analyze the responses from these interviews using a conceptualization of "collective action frames" developed by William Gamson. Snow and Benford (1992) define collective action frames as: "Action-oriented sets of beliefs and meanings that inspire and legitimate social movement activities and campaigns." Gamson (1992) argues that collective action frames can be broken down into three principle components: injustice, agency, and identity. The *injustice* component defines conditions and actions that are unjustly creating hardship and suffering for those represented by the social movement. The *identity* component identifies the "they" who are responsible for these conditions, as well as the "we" who have the ability to do something about it. The *agency* component denotes the feeling that the movement matters and is making history, that movement participators can change the terms and conditions of their lives.

A. INJUSTICE

To get at participants' sense of moral indignation, we need to first find out what hardships are motivating them, and then find out what they identify as the causes of these hardships. The observable characteristics of the *Clamor*, as described above, evidence the organizers' focus on problems with Venezuela's political leadership. However, we cannot assume that the same issues animated those who attended.[6] Thus, I coded each response to the first, open-ended question for mentions of concrete problems.[7] These were then coded either as social problems or as problems internal to the Evangelical ethical system.[8] Almost two-thirds of the issues raised in response to this question concerned everyday social problems.[9] Consistent with the externally observable characteristics of the demonstration, the main concern was with public administration; more specifically, with corrupt and ineffective government.

In his response to question one, Rigoberto, a thirty-two-year-old construction foreman who has been an Evangelical for three years and preaches at a nearby plaza, complained that "corruption has invaded the legislative, executive, and judicial powers." Mario, a twenty-five-year-old Evangelical male, argued that the purpose of the event was, "The liberation of Venezuela. Venezuela has been totally lost, with drugs and corruption everywhere. So this *Clamor* is to ask for freedom and prosperity for Venezuela." Ronaldo, a forty-five-year-old Evangelical man from a downtown church, described Venezuela as a disaster. And with solemn resolve, he looked me in the eye and said:

"This is a country with economic blessings, with oil and iron. But our politicians haven't known how to administer [the wealth], and it hasn't reached the people. It all goes to the United States." Other social problems mentioned were: foreign oppression, capital flight, unequal distribution of wealth, lack of respect for authority, poverty, sickness, abandoned children, the economic crisis, prostitution, the decline of the family, ignorance, and unemployment. Of the problems internal to Evangelicalism, people turning their backs on God, sin, and immorality topped the list, with occasional mentions of vanity, spiritual ignorance, and witchcraft rounding it out.

The most notable feature of these responses is how little they differ from the perceptions of non-Evangelicals in Venezuelan popular sectors. They are the same social problems one hears about daily in the bus, in the bakery, or on the news. Where Evangelicals differ from non-Evangelicals is in the view of *how* these problems arise. Gamson writes that the crucial dimension in developing a sense of moral indignation is the identification of concrete actors or conditions as the causes of hardship. Evangelicalism establishes this by providing an image of the supernatural that explains the source of these problems (see Smilde 1998). For example, in his response to question two,[10] Rigoberto reasoned as follows: "We can see that [Venezuela] is a very rich and productive country. But men have the government in their hands and are doing what they please (*haciendo y deshaciendo*)." Mario added to the response mentioned above that "man can't govern because man, if he doesn't have someone who is directing him, he can't do it, avarice takes over. So he needs the Kingdom of Jesus Christ to be able to get on track (*para agarrar el hilo*)." The source of corruption, ineffective government and other social problems, in this view, is the indisicpline and irresponsibility that comes from being alienated from God.

B. IDENTITY

The construction of identity, writes Gamson, is a process of constructing a "we," in opposition to a "they." Sectarian religious movements are well-known for the strong barriers they construct between in-group and out-group. Venezuelan Evangelicals rigorously distinguish between those who, "understanding" the importance of the supernatural in this life and the next, obey what they see as Biblical mandates for good conduct, and those who do not. Here we can see this identification process applied to current sociopolitical concerns. For these Evangelicals, behind the deplorable current condition lies a political leadership that has not stayed in communion with God. These "spiritually lost" leaders constitute the principle "they."

Ronaldo said, "The *Clamor* is to pray for Venezuela, pray for Venezuela so that the Lord blesses the country, because we are seeing that there is a lot of corruption in this country. Politicians haven't looked to God and we can see that this [country] is a disaster." For Jaime, a thirty-year-old Evangelical male who attends a large middle-class Evangelical church, the alienation of politicians from God is the reason for the unjust distribution of wealth in Venezuela. "A disproportional amount of the country's wealth hasn't gone to the people. It has gone to fill the pockets of people who don't have their hands placed in the hands of the Lord[11], which would have made the money be distributed justly."

Eduardo, himself a community-level political leader in one of the working-class satellite towns east of Caracas, pointed out that they were carrying out this event in front of the Congress for a good reason. His answer makes concrete reference to what he sees as the actions that are producing the Congressmembers' alienation from God: "[This is] where the important political leaders of this country legislate. We are asking that they get out of corruption, we are raising our voices to God so that the immorality, corruption, and above all the witchcraft and Satanism among them, and the drug addiction, ends. They are the reason the country is the way it is."

Less common, but also important, was a more abstract view of the "they." Clara, who attends the same middle class Pentecostal Church as Jaime, referred to Venezuela in abstract terms. Asked about the purpose of the *Clamor*, she said they were there "so that the people of Venezuela will seek God in spirit and in truth because we are seeking vain things and not seeking the presence of God. That"s why the country is like this, in crisis." Rigoberto also explained the problem in general social terms: "When man turns to evil, follows evil, society corrupts more and more. We can see groups of children abandoned by society and we can see women who go to prostitution because they have to sell their bodies because men have turned to sin and chase behind other women. . . . When we see these things, God is not in control there, because man isn't within the will of God."

Key to the construction of a "we" is the idea that the "we" is a collective agent with the ability to change circumstances. Evangelicals believe they have the key by which the world can be changed. For example, Mario, when asked whether this event could benefit Venezuela, responded that Evangelicals had the capacity to act on behalf of the rest of the country: "It [the *Clamor*] helps Venezuela a lot because God listens to the prayers of the just, of saints. . . ." To the same question,

Henri, an enthusiastic forty-five-year-old Evangelical, responded: "Yes of course, Jesus Christ said so when He said that the Church of the Lord is the salt of the Earth and light of the world, [here] to carry out the plans for which he has given us authority." Ana Karina, the wife of Jaime, sees the task of bringing people to God as central to Evangelical identity. "As it says in the sacred scripture, we are the salt of the Earth and light of the world. We, the people of the Lord, are illuminating. We are crying out to our Father for our brothers who are still blind, who have not seen, who haven't understood the truth, for people's consciousness to be raised."

C. AGENCY

A sense of agency is the feeling that the "we" matters, that current conditions are not fixed but can be altered. While many of the comments already quoted give a sense of that feeling, in this section I cite those in which the sense of agency is more explicitly revealed. Then I cite responses that expose the Evangelical intention to convince others of the Evangelicals' power to change conditions.

The principle sense of power evident here is the idea that Evangelicals can change circumstances by directly petitioning God. "In asking God to have mercy on our country, we have faith and hope that God is going to bring about change," said Mariluz, an eighteen-year-old Evangelical woman. The vision of *how* God will bring about such changes usually amounts to God "touching the hearts" of humans, and thereby bringing them to change the actions that have caused so much suffering and misery. Susana, a sixty-year-old woman from a *barrio* south of Caracas, and an Evangelical for twenty years, nicely states the view. "We are carrying out this *Clamor por Venezuela* so that Venezuela will be for Christ, so that He will liberate those people that are there governing, [such as] the president. [We are carrying it out] so that he will give them a new heart, give them a new conscience, both them [politicians] and all of those who inhabit this country." Jaime also saw Evangelicals as those who have the ability to ask God to touch human hearts.

> God is going to give us strength and is going to clean out the Congress, clean out all those people who have the spirit of filthiness, of corruption, of avarice, so that we are all honorable. Because that is what this country needs: honor, honesty, and work. Our God provides these and we have to ask Him to open up hearts and ignite in those persons who are in there [pointing to the Congress] the conviction of being Venezuelan; honorable Venezuelans like they should be.

A closely related but subtly different idea of agency is that through this activity these Evangelicals will get people to come to God, and this in turn will make them part of the solution instead of part of the problem. Ronaldo argued, "This event could help Venezuela in the sense that it could get people to seek God, get politicians to seek God. Because the person who has God is a new creature and knows how to administer things better. In having a fear of God, he knows how to administer earthly matters as well." Enrique, a twenty-eight-year-old Evangelical of two years, told me that the participants' goal was "to tell the world that there is hope in Christ, that there is a solution for the problem of humanity, which we understand to be sin; and that if we look first to the Reign of God and His justice, everything else this country needs will come by grace."

Ana Karina argued that the impact of the event was not necessarily immediate. It could provide a stimulus that would have its effect at a later time. It could, she said, "Raise the consciousness of the people, make them reflect. Because there will be a moment when a person is alone that he begins to meditate and reflect on the Word of God, that what the Lord says is that by which we should conduct ourselves."

In a successful collective action frame, it is important not only to impart a concept of agency to movement participants, but to project to others that the "we" matters and is making history (Gamson 1995, 94). This is important not only for getting the "they" to take the movement seriously, but also is key to "frame alignment," the extension of the collective action frame to potential members (Snow et al. 1986). The participants were very conscious of projecting an image of strength and success. When asked what the purpose of the gathering was, Rigoberto responded by saying: "So that Venezuela sees that everyday more and more, the number of Christians (*el pueblo Cristiano*) keeps growing, keeps increasing and that the Evangelical church is going to take the lead." Similarly, Henri affirmed that, "God has immeasurable plans to bless our motherland in all aspects—spiritual, material and financial. Because never before has the Gospel risen as it has at this time. God has given us radio[12] and all the means of communication to make our nation great." This projection of strength and success was the primary emphasis of Enrique's comments. For example, he said:

> This is the first time in history that a demonstration like this is happening, [a demonstration] showing that we're not just a couple of nuts (*ni somos cuatro, ni somos gatos*). There are a lot of us and we are people with power. Lots of people have wanted to tell the world that the Gospel is only for poor people, people who live in a situation of crime. Although we don't deny it, and we believe that Christ can transform such people, we also believe that the Christ has begun

to do great things in this country with professionals, with bankers, with people who have position, with people who are inside the Congress of the Republic. . . . So these days we are harvesting fruit we couldn't before. For example, it used to be that when a lot of these men who are here went out to preach the Gospel they were [seen as] a bunch of crazies. But now people pass by and glorify God because they realize that there aren't crazy people here. There are a bunch of people here who really have it together (*que son cuerdas*).

Other respondents echoed the organizer's view that the event's being carried out on the front steps of Venezuela's policy-making center demonstrated the power of the Evangelical movement. Eduardo said, "This is the first time that this is permitted here in this place, in front of the Congress, in the Capital where the important political leaders of this country legislate." Others mentioned the importance of other Venezuelans seeing that Evangelicals are people who are competent to lead the country.

LOCATING THE EVANGELICAL FRAME

The close fit between the meanings produced by the Evangelicals interviewed at the *Clamor* and Gamson's three components of a collective action frame demonstrate Evangelicalism's power to mobilize. Venezuelan Evangelicals believe they have found the key to explaining the country's inability to change in the past and the possibility of change in the future. The key to this frame is its vision of the supernatural as a sphere of reality that has an important impact in "this world." The frame provides a readily identifiable "they": those who do not follow "the Way of the Lord" and thereby permit the Devil to foment death and destruction. It also points to a task that is perceived as both effective and doable: obedience to "biblical" morality and the evangelization of others. This provides them with their sense of agency.

With this basic outline of the "Evangelical frame," we can ask two more questions about it. First, does this frame displace other nonreligious forms of action? Second, how does it combine with other political discourses in Latin America?

A. ALTERNATIVE OR ADDITIONAL FRAME?

Gamson points out that mobilization is not the same as social change. Indeed, it may even prevent it. Mobilization is often the result of the "hot cognitions" of "misplaced concreteness" which direct attention away from the structural basis of hardship and suffering (Gamson 1992). Put differently, while a collective action frame may mobilize by pointing at concrete enemies and presenting doable solutions, these same characteristics may direct a movement's attention away from complex structural problems that require difficult solutions.

This very issue is one source of the polemics surrounding Evangelical growth in Latin America. Evangelicalism mobilizes, but it is often seen to sap energy from other forms of social action; a point of view evident in the "get a job" comment directed at the *hermanos* walking to the *Clamor*. I told those I interviewed about this incident, and asked their opinions. My goal was to draw out their understanding of the relationship between religious and secular action.

Several indeed responded in a way that affirmed religious action to be the most important means of seeking change. Henri said, "When man recognizes his spiritual needs, God is going to bless him spiritually and physically, because the principle objective and problem of man is located in his soul. And when humans surrender their hearts to God, He blesses them in all aspects of life, spiritual, material, physical, and social." Eduardo responded, "The only one who can free us from these problems is Jesus Christ."

As a follow-up to the street confrontation question, several times I asked the respondent's opinion of a *cacerolazo* (a pot-banging protest) that had taken place a week earlier throughout the city. Mariluz said:

> Well, that is a peaceful form of protest but unfortunately it doesn't achieve anything. They came here and had a *cacerolazo* here at the Congress; everyone had their pots and all. But the next day you didn't see any change, they didn't achieve anything. In contrast, we have faith and hope that through our clamor we are going to accomplish something.

While these responses emphasize the apparent uselessness of secular action, it is worth pointing out that Eduardo is a political leader at the community level, and Mariluz is a political-science student at one of Caracas's universities.

An alternative tendency was manifest in responses that showed religious action to be complementary to other forms of secular action, insofar as it gives strength for this worldly struggle. Clara responded that "without the will of the Lord, we can't even move a leaf, and with Him we can do anything, because He is the only one who gives us strength." Rigoberto said:

> We believe that these three types of things should be combined together: work, organization, and the spiritual dimension. It isn't work in itself [that's important], it's that man has Christ in his heart. And with Christ in his heart, and man organizing himself and working, there is going to be blessings in a nation. Because if we think

about it, he who gives us strength to work is God. Where does man's strength come from? From his Creator."

Ana Karina responded, "Of course you have to work, because the Lord is a God of order. He doesn't permit his children to stay home, as they say, waiting for Him to send everything from heaven. Everything comes through effort. In the Bible, God says to Joshua: 'Work hard and be valiant and I will always be at your side.'"

We can see from these responses that, for at least some Evangelicals, their spiritual activity complements their secular action. This corresponds with Evans-Pritchard's insights on belief in supernatural agency. Its principle function is not to replace mundane beliefs about the empirical world, but rather to compliment them. It provides answers to the questions: "why *this* kind of suffering," "why now," and "why us"; and gives supernatural legitimation for everyday secular action (Evans-Pritchard 1937; see also Levine 1992, 16).

B. ANGLO VICTORY IN THE CLASH OF CIVILIZATIONS?

David Martin places the growth of Evangelicalism in Latin America within the context of the "world-historical clash between 'Anglo' culture and Hispanic civilization" (Martin 1990, 11). In this view the "sacred canopy" provided by the integration of Catholicism into the fabric of Latin American society is now breaking up, and Evangelical Protestantism is flowing into the cracks (280). There are two problems with this view, however. First, viewing Latin Americans as the "heirs of the *reconquista*" (10) obfuscates the region's cultural history; and second, as will be seen in the data, the relationship between the Evangelical frame and the discursive context is less direct and clear than is normally assumed.

More careful historical research has shown that, virtually since independence from Spain, discursive battles have waged within Latin American countries over the most appropriate cultural model on which to base "modernization" efforts. Those who looked to advanced nations—primarily England and the United States—and disparaged the local sociocultural context were countered by those who affirmed the need to ground the task in the supposed uniqueness of Latin America (Werz 1995). In contemporary Venezuela, as well as in most of Latin America, this ideological conflict lives on in the opposition between neoconservative and nationalist discourses. The first generally sees the Iberian heritage as a cultural impediment for development, calls for changes in individual responsibility, discipline, and work habits, and affirms equality and freedom (see, for example, Rangel 1992 [1976]; Mendoza, Montaner, and Vargas Llosa 1996). The nationalist discourse,

on the other hand, speaks of the need for liberation from foreign domination; the need to find a "third path" for self-governance, between capitalism and socialism; and the urgent task of articulating a uniquely Latin
American identity. Evangelicalism, then, does not introduce this division
and debate into a homogenous cultural context. Rather, it enters a discursive context that has long been fractious and contentious.

It does cause controversy, however, as it is generally seen as reinforcing the neoconservative side of this debate. The Evangelical emphasis on
personal morality and individual salvation, the Anglo origins of most
Protestant theology and missionaries, and the chronological fact that
Evangelical growth has come on the heels of the perceived decline of the
progressive Catholic movement, have understandably led the casual
onlooker to view this growth as a win for neoconservative forces.
However, empirical scrutiny shows that the actual engagement of the
Evangelical frame with the discursive context is more complex than is
often assumed. While criticism of the local sociocultural context is
almost always an aspect of the Evangelical frame, it does not usually
broaden into a general critique of Latin culture or Latin American
nations. Furthermore, the Evangelical emphasis on the supernatural
only occasionally engages with conservative politics in any clear and
consistent manner. More frequently, it simply provides moral fervor to
an individual's preexisting political preferences. This is all the more true
when in Venezuela, as in most of Latin America, political affiliations
are largely personalistic, rather than abstract and principled.

Enrique, who provided several of the comments quoted above, has
been a key informant for me throughout my fieldwork with his church.
Since his teens he had been involved with urban revolutionary groups in
the massive *23 de Enero* housing project at the western end of Caracas.
He grew disillusioned in the early 1990s, however, as the groups
became tied to drug rings. He became an Evangelical a few months after
being shot three times by the police in a demonstration. "I still believe
in the struggle," he told me, as we sat parked in his car following a tour
of his old haunts, "only now I have a different way of going about it."
He is an intense person, and has an insatiable desire for knowledge
about current events and foreign places. He has a fascination with Cuba
that is typical of politically conscious Latin Americans of the popular
classes, and once gave me a copy of Frei Betto's *Fidel and Religion*,
asking me if I had read it the next several times I saw him. At this writing (March 1998), he is excited about former coup leader Hugo
Chavez's lead in the presidential election polls, and is discussing with
some other *hermanos* the formation of a group called *Evangélicos para*

Chavez (Evangelicals for Chavez).

Evangelicals such as Enrique are not the norm in Venezuela. But neither are they uncommon. Furthermore, their political beliefs do not seem to cause them tremendous problems with other Evangelicals. Enrique preaches in a downtown plaza on Mondays, and his more explicit social and political messages cause no stir among either those who come to listen or among the nine other people who preach there. Rather, what seems most important to them is Enrique's continual manifestation of his belief in the importance of the supernatural in the present world, and his faith in God's plan for His people.

Evangelicalism is best seen, then, as a religious frame that can be combined with any number of different political ideologies. Eduardo's thoughts illustrate the point. The purpose of the *Clamor*, he said, was

> salvation for the Republic of Bolívar, the Republic of our liberator Simón Bolívar, that God wants to liberate through the Gospel of Christ. We need all of Venezuela to be for Christ. We want Venezuela to be the cradle of liberty that God meant it to be. We want it to continue being the cradle of freedom, free from all foreign oppression and free from all spiritual ignorance. We want the Gospel of the kingdom of God to be established here in Venezuela.

In Venezuela, most nationalist discourse centers around the figure of Simón Bolívar—one of the principal leaders of the nineteenth-century independence movement who was born in Venezuela and began his struggle there. Throughout my long interview with Eduardo he referred to himself as a "Bolivarian," and used so much nationalist rhetoric that I asked him whether he was a member of the *Movimiento Bolivariano Revolucionario 200*, a nationalist movement founded by Hugo Chavez. (He said he was sympathetic but not a member.)

Nevertheless, at several points in the interview he mentioned the United States as a country that had received God's blessing because its founding fathers had been in communion with God. For example, he said:

> Here we need to establish a government led by men and women of God. We want there to be progress. But the only way for there to be progress, we are aware, is if people of God govern—like the many places in North America, in Canada, and many parts of Europe [where] men and women of God have carried out and are carrying out good government. Those men and women have provided progress for their people. Why? Because they are in contact with God (*tienen a Dios*) and are doing what the Bible says. Here they have not done what the Bible says. . . .

This quote could easily have come from a nineteenth-century proponent of the Manifest Destiny of the United States. Yet here it surfaced in an interview with a strong proponent of Venezuelan nationalism.

In these quotes from Eduardo, we can see him constructing a vehicle for his sense of outrage over current conditions in Venezuela from the symbolic forms circulating in Venezuela's economy of meaning. Nationalist, neoconservative, and Evangelical discourses are freely combined in a sort of *bricolage* (Lévi-Strauss 1966), with little attention paid to any abstract contradictions between them.

CONCLUSION

From analyzing the *Clamor por Venezuela* we can see that Evangelicals act politically not only through "everyday forms of resistance" and quiet voting. In a relatively open atmosphere such as contemporary Venezuela, Evangelical leadership and the Evangelical meaning system also have the power to mobilize the faithful into aggressive actors in the public sphere. The point here is not to romanticize a purported "view from below." Popular movements—religious or otherwise—have no "privileged" viewpoint, nor is there any teleological assurance that they will contribute to social justice or democracy (Uribe and Lander 1995 [1988]; Levine n.d.). Indeed, Gamson's theorization directs us to the potential shortcomings of Evangelicalism as a collective action frame that will lead to significant change. Rather, the point is to demonstrate that Evangelicalism, like other new social movements in Venezuela, is constructing one of many new "spaces for politics" that crosscut the dominant forms of sociopolitical action and meaning construction.

But if we must tame our expectations regarding the social consequences of Latin American Evangelicalism, we can also affirm that much criticism of it relies on a zero-sum view of the economy of meaning. Two comments can be made. First, at least in the case of Venezuela, most Latin American Evangelicals did not have strong religious convictions before they converted. Thus, adoption of the Evangelical frame usually adds meaning to converts' lives rather than replacing meaning that was there before. Second, the data presented here show that while the "Evangelical frame" *can* direct individuals away from other forms of social action, and *can* undermine alternative critical political ideologies, it does not necessarily do so. Johnston argues that we should conceive of collective action frames as "bundles of beliefs and meanings" of varying degrees of abstraction. The more abstract and encompassing beliefs and meanings are shared by movement participants and are used by them individually to organize "a multiplicity of idiosyncratic personal detail" (Johnston 1995, 236). Seen in this way, it is clear that the most central and encompassing aspect of the Evangelical frame is the belief in active supernatural forces that act according to human individuals' fulfillment of a basic ethical system (Smilde 1998). This central aspect, then, can, on an individual or group level, be attached to a range of different sociopolitical contents.

NOTES

1   This research was undertaken while on a Fulbright-Hays Doctoral Dissertation Abroad Fellowship. It greatly benefitted from comments received in presentations to the Área Sociopolitica of the Centro de Estudios de Desarrollo at the Universidad Central de Venezuela, to the Escuela de Sociología of the Universidad Católica Ándres Bello, and at the 1997 meetings of the Association for the Sociology of Religion in Toronto, Canada.

2   Patrick Johnstone's figures show that the Protestant presence more than doubled, from 2.6 percent of the population in 1986 to 5.34 percent in 1993 (Johnstone 1986, Johnstone 1993). 90 percent of the 1993 total are "Evangelical," which includes Baptists and Pentecostals. 64 percent of the total are Pentecostal (for an excellent overview of the growth of Evangelicalism in Venezuela, see Froehle 1997). In Venezuela, Pentecostals refer to themselves as *Evangélicos*, to denote their professed prioritization of the Gospel, or *Cristianos*, to denote their professed Christocentrism (empirical research, however, has demonstrated a clear tendency among Latin American Evangelicals to focus on the Pauline books rather than the Gospels. See Smilde 1997, Brusco 1995). Almost all of the respondents in this chapter are Pentecostal. However, since I am using qualitative data in which respondents' self-definition is of central importance, I will use the term "Evangelical" to refer to them.

3   This description comes from Arturo Sosa, Jesuit priest and editor of the magazine *Sic* (quoted in Lander 1995, 62).

4   The School of Social Psychology at the Universidad Central de Venezuela has as its principle research focus the problems of establishing nongovernmental organizations in the popular sectors (see Wiesenfeld and Sánchez 1995).

5   *Hermano* means "brother" in Spanish and is the most common word used to refer to fellow believers.

6   Shupe and Stacey (1982), in research with conservative Protestant groups in the United States, show that participants were animated more by strictly religious themes than by the conservative political agenda of their leaders.

7   Each respondent's answer could have a maximum of one mention of any given problem. Thus, for example, if corruption was mentioned three times in one answer it would be coded only once.

8   They were coded as social problems if they were issues that are frequently mentioned by nonevangelicals and which made sense without reference to the Evangelical ethical system. They were coded as internal to Evangelical morality if they made sense only within its ethical system. Two problems, "disobedience" and "rebellion," were placed in both categories since they could

fit in either and their usage did not provide clues as to their meaning. This coding is used to persuade the skeptic of the "this-worldly" orientation of respondents. For Evangelicals themselves, even those problems coded as internal to the Evangelical ethical system would be seen as having concrete, this-worldly effects.

9 In this section I use only the responses to question one since it is the most open-ended. It could be argued that the other two, more narrow questions themselves led respondents to make greater reference to this-worldly problems. The data, however, shows only a marginal difference. For question one the proportion of this-worldly problems to total problems was .64 (23/36), while for all other parts of the interviews it was .68 (15/22). For the interviews as a whole it was .66 (38/58).

10 While discerning what issues animating participants required confining the analysis to the first question, uncovering the perceived supernatural base can come from any part of the interview since the questions cannot be seen to have biased responses in any direction.

11 The respondent mixes metaphors here. For Venezuelan Evangelicals, having "your hands raised to the Lord," refers to the conscious attempt to maintain contact with God. "Place it in the hands of the Lord," on the other hand, generally means that one should simply follow "God"s will," trusting that he will resolve problems. The respondent uses a combination of these two metaphors.

12 In the six months previous to this event, two Evangelical radio stations opened in Caracas.

REFERENCES

Brusco, Elizabeth. 1995. *The Reformation of Machismo*. Austin, TX: University of Texas Press.

Burdick, John. 1993. *Looking for God in Brazil*. Berkeley and Los Angeles: University of California Press.

Chicago Tribune. July 6, 1995. "Venezuelans Protest Crime Wave."

Cleary, Edward. 1997. "Introduction: Pentecostals, Prominence, and Politics." In E.L. Cleary and H.W. Stewart-Gambino, eds. *Power, Politics, and Pentecostals in Latin America*. Boulder, CO: Westview Press, 1-24.

Coleman, Kenneth et al. 1993. "Protestantism in El Salvador: Conventional Wisdom Versus the Survey Evidence." In V. Garrard-Burnett and D. Stoll, eds. *Rethinking Protestantism in Latin America*. Philadelphia: Temple University Press, 20-44.

El Nacional. June 2, 1996. "Venezuela esta entre los paises mas corruptos."

———. July 1, 1996. "Profesionales deben ganar Bs. 240,000 para recuperar poder adquisitivo de 1985."

Evans-Pritchard, E. E. 1937. *Witchcraft, Oracles, and Magic among the Azande*. London: Oxford University Press.

Freston, Paul. 1993. "Brother Votes for Brother: The New Politics of Protestantism in Brazil." In V. Garrard-Burnett and D. Stoll, eds. *Rethinking Protestantism in Latin America*. Philadelphia: Temple University Press, 66-110.

Froehle, Bryan. 1997. "Pentecostals and Evangelicals in Venezuela: Consolidating Gains, Moving in New Directions." In E.L. Cleary and H.W. Stewart-Gambino, eds. *Power, Politics, and Pentecostals in Latin America*. Boulder,

CO: Westview Press.

Gamson, William. 1992. *Talking Politics*. Cambridge: Cambridge University Press.

———. 1995. "Constructing Social Protest." In Hank Johnston and Bert Klandermans, eds. *Social Movements and Culture*. Minneapolis: University of Minnesota Press.

Ireland, Rowland. 1993. "The *Crentes* of Campo Alegre and the Religious Construction of Brazilian Politics." In V. Garrard-Burnett and D. Stoll, eds. *Rethinking Latin American Protestantism*. Philadelphia: Temple University Press, 45-65.

Johnston, Hank. 1995. "A Methodology for Frame Analysis: From Discourse to Cognitive Schemata." In Hank Johnston and Bert Klandermans, eds. *Social Movements and Culture*. Minneapolis: University of Minnesota Press.

Johnstone, Patrick. 1986. *Operation World*. Kent, England: Send The Light Books and WEC International.

———. 1993. *Operation World*. Kent, England: Send The Light Books and WEC International.

Karl, Terry L. 1995. "In Search of the Lost Pact: Consensus Lost in the 1980s and 1990s." In Jennifer McCoy, Andres Serpin, William C. Smith, and Andres Stambouli, eds. *Venezuelan Democracy Under Stress*. New Brunswick, NJ: Transaction Books.

Lander, Edgardo. 1995. *Neoliberalismo, Sociedad Civil y Democracia. Ensayos sobre America Latina y Venezuela*. Caracas: Universidad Central de Venezuela.

Levine, Daniel. 1992. *Popular Voices in Latin American Catholicism*. Princeton, NJ: Princeton University Press.

———. 1994. "Good-bye to Venezuelan Exceptionalism." *Journal of Interamerican Studies and World Affairs*, 36:145-82.

———. 1995. "Protestants and Catholics in Latin America: a Family Portrait." In M. Marty and S. Appleby, eds. *Fundamentalisms Comprehended*. Chicago: University of Chicago Press.

———. n.d. "El Futuro de las Teologias," unpublished manuscript.

Levine, Daniel and David Stoll. 1997. "Bridging the Gap Between Empowerment and Power in Latin America." In Rudolph and J. Piscatori, eds. *Fading States and Transnational Religious Regimes*. Boulder, CO: Westview Press, 63-103.

López Maya, Margarita. 1997. "El Repertorio de la Protesta Popular en Venezuela, 1989-1994." In *Cuadernos del CENDES*, 36 (Sept.-Dec.):109-30.

Maust, John. 1984. *Urban Growth and God's People in Ten Latin American Cities*. Coral Gables, FL: Latin American Mission.

Martin, David. 1990. *Tongues of Fire: The Explosion of Protestantism in Latin America*. Oxford: Basil Blackwell.

Mendoza, Plinio, Carlos Montaner, and Alvaro Vargas Llosa. 1996. *Manual del Perfecto Idiota Latinoamericano*. New York: Bantam Books.

Navarro, Juan Carlos. 1995. "In Search of the Lost Pact: Consensus Lost in the 1980s and 1990s." In Jennifer McCoy, Andres Serpin, William C. Smith, and Andres Stambouli, eds. *Venezuelan Democracy Under Stress*. New Brunswick, NJ: Transaction Books.

Neuhouser, K. 1992. "Democratic Stability in Venezuela: Elite Consensus or Class Compromise?" *American Sociological Review*, 57:117-35.

Rangel, Carlos. [1976] 1992. *Del Buen Salvaje al Buen Revolucionario*. Caracas: Monte Avila Editores.

Salamanca, Luis. 1997. *Crisis de la Modernización y Crisis de la Democracia en*

Venezuela. Caracas: Universidad Central de Venezuela.

Shupe, Anson, and William Stacey. 1982. *Born Again Politics and the Moral Majority: What Social Surveys Really Show*. New York: Edwin Mellen.

Smilde, David. 1997. "The Fundamental Unity of the Conservative and Revolutionary Tendencies in Venezuelan Evangelicalism: The Case of Conjugal Relations." *Religion*, 27:343-59.

———. 1998. "Letting God Govern: Supernatural Agency in the Social Practice of Latin American Evangelicals." *Sociology of Religion*, 59(3) Fall.

———. 1999. "Nationhood, Patronage and the Conflict over New Religious Movements in Venezuela." In Paul Sigmund, ed. *Evangelization and Religious Freedom in Latin America*. Maryknoll, NY: Orbis Books.

Smith, Christian. 1994. "The Spirit and Democracy: Base Communities, Protestantism, and Democratization in Latin America." *Sociology of Religion*, 55 (2):119-43.

Snow, David et al. 1986. "Frame Alignment Processes, Micromobilization and Movement Participation." *American Sociological Review*, 51:456-81.

Snow, David, and Robert Benford. 1992. "Master Frames and Cycles of Protest." In Aldon Morris and Carol Mueller, eds. *Frontiers in Social Movement Theory*. New Haven, CT: Yale University Press.

Ugalde, Luis et al. 1994. *La Violencia en Venezuela*. Caracas: Monte Avila Editores Latinoamericana.

Uribe, Gabriela, and Edgardo Lander. [1988] 1995. "Acción Social, Efectividad Simbólica y Nuevos Ambitos de lo Político." In Edgardo Lander, ed. *Neoliberalismo, Sociedad Civil y Democracia. Ensayos sobre America Latina y Venezuela*. Caracas: Universidad Central de Venezuela.

Werz, Nicholas. 1995. *Historia del Pensamiento Sociopolitico en America Latina*. Caracas: Nuevo Planeta.

Wiesenfeld, Esther, and Euclides Sánchez, eds. 1995. *Psicología Social Comunitaria: Contribuciones Latinoamericanas*. Caracas: Fondo Editorial Tropykos.

Williams, P. 1997. "The Sound of Tambourines: The Politics of Pentecostal Growth in El Salvador." In E.L. Cleary and H.W. Stewart-Gambino, eds. *Power, Politics, and Pentecostals in Latin America*. Boulder, CO: Westview Press, 179-200.

SEVEN

THE DEFEAT OF DENOMINATIONAL CULTURE IN THE ARGENTINE EVANGELICAL MOVEMENT

Matthew Marostica

In October of 1992, three thousand Argentine pastors from a wide array of Protestant churches met together outside of the city of Córdoba in the first national conference for Protestant ministers ever held in that country. A little more than a year later, facing legislation that they interpretted as openly discriminatory against non-Catholics, many of these same pastors fashioned a unified political response to this shared threat. The culmination of this process of collective action was the creation, in 1996, of a Protestant umbrella organization, the National Evangelical Christian Council (CNCE), which represents Protestant interests before the state and which provides a leadership forum for all sectors of Argentine Protestantism.

This marked trend toward Protestant, and—most curiously—Evangelical, unity in Argentina is a departure from what observers of Latin American Evangelicals (Lalive D'Epinay 1967; Stoll 1990; Bastian 1993), as well as Protestant and Catholic ecumenical movement activists, have been observing for decades—that the region's Evangelical churches are anti-ecumenical and sectarian. The Evangelicals, having generally been taught an extreme anti-World Conference of Churches theology by their missionary founders, also understood themselves to be anti-ecumenical and denominationally centered, if not sectarian. In the past several years, however, a few analysts (Marostica 1994; Semán and Wynarzyk 1995; Cook 1997) have begun to note an undeniable movement toward unity in various segments of the Evangelical population of Latin America. Though the Evangelicals are often theologically unable to call their shared worship, common practices, and organizational integration "ecumenism," there is no question that the days of Evangelical hyperdenominationalism are waning.

This chapter examines the creation of a national Evangelical movement in Argentina. The Argentine case is important, first because it is a clear example of Latin American Evangelicals abandoning denominationalism.[1] Second, because Argentina's high-profile evangelists (Carlos Annacondia, Hector Giménez, Omar Cabrera, Claudio Freidzon, and Alfredo Mottesi) have carried the message of Evangelical unity throughout Latin America. This chapter traces the rapid shift toward unity among Argentine Evangelicals, which began in the mass crusades of Carlos Annacondia and was then extended to other Evangelicals by a series of successful evangelists.

THE GENESIS OF DENOMINATIONALISM IN ARGENTINA

Protestantism became established in Argentina in three waves: immigrant churches, missionary churches, and Pentecostal missionary churches. Whether they arrived with immigrants or were created by missionaries, Protestant churches were born with a tendency toward isolation. In the immigrant churches, this isolation was primarily linguistic and cultural. Each church served as a fortress against the larger culture, language, and dominant religion. The missionary churches of the late ninteenth century, with their emphasis on building churches, schools, and clinics, maintained close ties with the parent churches that funded these outreach programs. The last wave of missionary churches, the Pentecostals, took the tendency to isolationism to extremes, endowing it with biblically stringent, antagonistic lines of separation among Pentecostals and between them and other Protestants.

Pentecostal missionaries from the United States and Canada were the most numerous missionary force in Argentina during much of the twentieth century. The Pentecostal churches that they established in Argentina were stamped with a particular identity—the identity common to North American Pentecostals of the 1930s, 1940s, and 1950s. This historically particular identity persisted among Argentine Pentecostals well into the 1980s. Marfa Cabrera (1993), the most influential female evangelist in Argentina, describes the endurance of the missionary legacy in these terms:

> there were missionaries that taught things which later evolved in the United States. However, the organizations that they created here held onto those teachings. They remained stuck in time concerning things like hair, forms of dress, makeup, whether or not you could read a newspaper or watch television.

Indeed, the entire package of North American Pentecostal beliefs from the mid-twentieth century became "stuck in time" within the Argentine Pentecostal churches. Central to this belief system were a strict adherence to biblical inerrancy, denominationalism, social and cultural isolation, apoliticism, and severe behavioral restrictions. Decades after the missionaries who had taught the beliefs were buried under the soil of their native land, their Argentine converts held fast to this particular constellation of beliefs.

Denominationalism is perhaps the best example of the persistence of the missionary teachings. Juan Terranova (1993),[2] a pastor with more than fifty years of experience in the Argentine Evangelical community explains the effect of the missionaries on denominationalism in this way:

> The churches have always brought with them the customs of the missionaries. . . . Remember, our church is not a church that was born on its own through the study of the Bible. We owe a lot to the missionaries. They had been taught to put a lot of emphasis on their denomination and they continued with the same ideas here.

When the missionaries arrived in Argentina this "emphasis on their denomination" was greatly exaggerated by the experience of working as missionaries in an unreceptive and occasionally hostile country. The missionaries had very little success and were often pitted in direct competition for souls with missionaries from other denominations. This competition exacerbated already existing animosities from the schismatic Pentecostal culture of North America.

Strict loyalty to individual denominations was, however, only one of a whole construct of convictions that the missionaries brought to the new Pentecostal churches of Argentina. Beliefs concerning things as diverse as the precise effects of the "Second Baptism," whether or not women could wear makeup, and the relationship between religion and politics were held together in a web of belief that could not be easily broken into component parts.

This package of beliefs was supplemented by a set of practices which, while not "doctrinal" in the sense that Pentecostals understand it, were still a significant part of the larger missionary construct. These practices, often matters of style, gave a distinctive form to the evangelistic practices of the missionaries. The list of these practices includes, but certainly is not limited to:

1. Forms of evangelizing: small tent meetings, street-corner preaching, and pamphletering.
2. Music: the old Pentecostal music was Sunday School music from the U.S. translated into Spanish.

3. Structure of sermons: several long passages of the Bible linked by the pastor's own exposition of the verses was the missionary form of preaching.
4. Dress for pastors: a tie and jacket were established as the standard uniform for pastors.

These practices, just like the core doctrines and behavioral restrictions, became part of the missionary legacy. They were endowed with the same sacred status as the missionary's teachings. The missionary legacy of biblical inerrancy, denominationalism, social isolation, strict behavioral restrictions, and North American evangelistic practices amounted to an imposition of the Pentecostal variant of North American culture onto the converts to Pentecostalism in Argentina. Likening her own church's intermittently successful efforts to attract young people to the efforts of the missionaries a generation before, Marfa Cabrera (1993) said, "Perhaps we are not reaching them as well as we would like because we are too insistent on changing the way they are. We want to change the youth of today just like the missionaries wanted to change our culture when they came here from the U.S."

What is most perplexing about the persistence of the missionaries' legacy is what Cabrera is hinting at here. The missionaries were never particularly successful in reaching large numbers of Argentines, quite possibly because they were too fixed on trying to change the culture of those they had come to teach. Yet, despite their lack of success in creating church growth, the missionaries' doctrines, practices, and methods were enshrined as an inviolable whole that outlasted their period of leadership by an entire generation.

Jorge Guilles (1995), a pastor from one of the first denominations started by Argentines (the Pentecostal Christian Missionary Church), tried to explain the persistence of the missionary teachings by saying that, "those of us that were outside of the missionary denominations always used to say 'they have the manual.' The missionaries, when they did leave, also left behind materials, like manuals, which told the churches how to act and what to believe." Consequently, until Carlos Annacondia began his crusades in the early 1980s, the Pentecostal churches of Argentina sang the songs, preached the sermons, and lived the life that North American missionaries had brought with them between 1930 and 1960.

CARLOS ANNACONDIA

Carlos Annacondia, a successful small businessman and a Catholic, underwent a personal conversion to Pentecostalism in 1979 at the age of

39. His evangelistic enterprise, *Mensaje de Salvación* (Message of Salvation), began as a nondenominational church formed by his family and thirty of his employees who became converted following their boss' conversion. This group later recruited an ordained pastor from the Free Brethren Church, Jorge Gromelsky, to be their pastor.[3] Within a year of his conversion, Annacondia began to see visions of himself preaching in a *villa de emergencia* (squatter settlement). In August of 1981, he started preaching in such a settlement in Bernal (in greater Buenos Aires). Of that experience he says,

> God showed me that *villa* for an entire year, but I didn't want to go. Finally I said, 'I give up' and I went. I went into mud up to my knees but I didn't feel a thing. . . . I felt love for those people that had so many problems. God protected me; He gave me authority over that place—I cast the demons out of those people and out of that place and then one day God took me out of there and put me in a more affluent neighborhood. And I used the same message to convert the rich as I had used to convert the poor (1993).

Beginning in Bernal, Annacondia became known for his direct, confrontational style, his power to cast out evil spirits, and increasingly for his ability to heal the sick. His ministry quickly expanded beyond the initial group of converts in the *villa de emergencia*.[4] After Bernal, Annacondia began to preach in rented buildings, where he could attract a wider audience than was possible in a squatter settlement. By the end of 1983, the official statistics of *Mensaje de Salvación* indicate that approximately 6,000 people had been converted through Annacondia's preaching. At this point, Annacondia caught the attention of a group of pastors in the city of La Plata with whom he planned a crusade that both established his position within Argentine Evangelicalism and that dramatically altered the character of the Evangelical community.

ANNACONDIA AND UNITY

> When I was converted, I was converted without a pastor. Those from my business were converted and we started to pray. . . . We thought that there could only be one church of Jesus Christ; we could not comprehend that serious divisions could exist (Annacondia 1993).

At the time of his conversion, Annacondia (1993) thought, as did most Argentines, that Evangelical Christians must be all the same. "I was unfamiliar with the politics of the Church before I began to preach. If I had known about them, perhaps I would not have had the same impact on unity." Annacondia's quick conversion and the nondenominational character of the original *Mensaje de Salvación* group left them unexposed to the nuances of Argentine Evangelical culture and the missionary package of beliefs which undergirded it. The intensity of the group's first year—they were either praying, reading the Bible, or working together all the time—kept them distant from the sharp cleavages within Argentine Evangelicalism.

Then Annacondia began to understand,

> that the Pentecostals and the Baptists could not stand each other. I knew that it was a human defect; that the Devil had insinuated himself into the Church. So when I started to attract attention I made one rule regarding my participation in crusades: I always invited all of the churches in the area to join the campaign. If the pastors had a problem with that, I would not preach in that area until they could resolve their differences.

Annacondia's rule, that all of the local churches be invited to participate in his crusades, was the first real break with the community's long history of denominationalism.

The first crusade in which Annacondia imposed this rule was the crusade in La Plata, the capital of the province of Buenos Aires, in 1984. All of the churches in the city received an invitation from the organizing committee, but only eight decided to join. Those eight represented perhaps 10 percent of the Protestant churches in La Plata at that time.[5] The La Plata crusade, which was held in several open air sites around the city, lasted eight months. Annacondia preached seven nights a week, while still running his business during the day. According to *Mensaje de Salvación*, there were 50,000 "decisions for Christ" in those eight months. The La Plata crusade was the last Annacondia crusade not to be widely supported by local churches. Unity became the rule for all of his subsequent crusades.

How are we to understand Annacondia's ability to demand unity in his crusades? Annacondia (1993) himself gives a very material explanation. "Since my ministry worked in their interest, the churches were forced to comply. The Pentecostals had no choice other than to invite the Baptists." What "interested" the churches were the "fruits" that Annacondia's campaigns were leaving behind: 50,000 "decision cards" in La Plata.

During December 1985, Annacondia held his first crusade in Rosario (Argentina's second biggest city). *El Puente* (December 1985), in an article headlined "There were 55,000 Decisions for Christ," reported that

> One of the most positive aspects of this crusade was the unity of the 77 churches belonging to different denominations that participated in this

common effort, in a climate of companionship and Christian community that eliminated the walls of 'names,' 'customs,' and 'denominations.'

Echoing Annacondia's explanation of the unity in his crusades, the article continues:

> Someone said that 'when the wheat increases the fences disappear; and someone else added 'the fences disappear when the fields all belong to one owner.' One vineyard, one harvest, many workers and an immense work, all for the owner of the same, Jesus.

In more material language, we could say that the Evangelical community had come to understand that Annacondia was "delivering the goods." Or, in Olson's terms (1971), Annacondia was providing selective incentives to the pastors that overcame both the free rider problems associated with organizing crusades as well as the denominationalism characteristic of the Evangelical community of that time. The "increase in the wheat" which Annacondia was producing motivated denominations and individual pastors to put aside their differences in order to be able to attract new sheep to their folds.

The initial move toward cooperation in organizing crusades occurred very quickly. *El Puente* (August 1985) reported on the meeting that began preparations for Annacondia's first crusade in the city of Buenos Aires:

> The meeting held on July 22 in the Astral Theater constitutes one of the most important and auspicious events in recent years....That over five hundred pastors and leaders from nearly all of the denominations operating in Buenos Aires were in attendance is, without a doubt, an occurrence with few antecedents. As we said, nearly all of the Evangelical denominations were represented. Among them we can mention: Baptists, Free Brethren, Church of God, Holiness Church, Salvation Army, Nazarenes, Union of the Assemblies of God, Assemblies of God, Christian Alliance, Mennonites, Missionary Pentecostal, Christian Community, Independent Church of Christ, Christian Assembly, and many independent churches.[6]

Talking about the fruits of Annacondia's crusade in Haedo (western sector of greater Buenos Aires) in August and September of 1985, the crusade's president, Pastor Albert De Luca (*El Puente*, October 1985), says:

> In addition to the 26,584 decision cards for Christ, the crusade left many other positive things. Among them: the huge number of churches that were involved, 109 total, from many denominations. Another positive aspect was the great unity of spirit that existed during the entire crusade.

Annacondia (1993) believes that the very act of working together taught the Evangelical churches that "they had the same doctrine, the same love. That's where unity really started." These face-to-face inter-actions, what resource mobilization theory calls "micromobiliza-tion," clearly worked to subvert the Evangelicals' adherence to strict denominationalism.

AN INNOVATIVE IDEOLOGICAL FRAME

In addition to demanding unity in his crusades, and thus creating a context within which Evangelicals could interact, Annacondia also created a new set of Evangelical teachings that resonated with Argentine popular culture. His teachings were simple: God and the Devil exist and are in permanent battle with each other. By accepting Christ, individu-als gain access to the divine power they need to overcome Satan. As Annacondia (1993) puts it, "The mission of the Devil is to rob, murder, and destroy. Christ's mission is to save and give life. My mission is to confront Satan." With this message, reiterated in every crusade, Carlos Annacondia gave the Evangelical community a potent new grammar that connected the problems in the lives of poor Argentines to Satan and his demons and offered the power of Christ as a solution.

In highlighting the destructive influence of demons in people's lives, Annacondia appealed to a fundamental concern in the Argentine popu-lar sector. For many poor Argentines, demons are both terrifying and commonplace. Annacondia's personal presence as a powerful figure in the fight against "the destroyer" resonated with poor Argentines. Non-believers, believers, and pastors all came to accept Annacondia as a powerful "man of God" who could do battle with *el hombre fuerte* (the strong man, i.e. Satan).

Annacondia's message offered a new diagnosis and remedy to the problems faced by both Argentine Evangelicals and their target audience in the popular sector. In his capacity as God's representative in the battle with Satan, Annacondia also established new practices or methods for winning that battle. These new evangelistic methods soon began to have a profound impact on the churches that participated in Annacondia's crusades. The October 1985 issue of *El Puente* contains an interview with "the pastor that gathered the greatest number of fruits" from the Annacondia campaign in La Plata in 1984. The pastor, Alberto Scataglini, saw his church of 300 grow to approximately 5,000 after the crusade. Commenting on his model for retaining new believers, Scataglini warns other pastors, "your churches are not going to be the same. If you make them the same, the people will leave you. If you allow the revival of the crusade to enter your church, the people will stay."

Scataglini's warning to his fellow pastors should be understood as more than a specific recommendation on how to benefit from Annacondia's crusades. It is also a commentary on the changes that Annacondia very quickly started to produce within Argentine Evangelicalism. His claim that "your churches are not going to be the same" was prescient. Annacondia's ministry began to change the way in which Evangelicals in and around the largest Argentine cities acted in their own churches.

Annacondia did much more than simply create a micromobilizational context in which pastors and workers from different churches could interact; he directly challenged the patterns of worship and evangelization established by the missionaries. The missionaries had used street corner preaching, pamphletering, camp meetings, and Sunday School music from the United States as their means of attracting new members. From all accounts, they were boring. They did not have a message or a style with wide appeal in the Argentine popular sector.

CHANGE IN THE CHURCHES

Annacondia (1993) explains the dramatic effects that his crusades produce in their target neighborhood or city in this way:

> There are battles in the air. My crusades are long because it is through these battles that barriers are broken; chains break. . . . If you want to invade a new place, the devil is going to defend himself. The church has to be aggressive. When the church invades a city, society changes, homes change, people change.

In addition, we might add, the church itself changes.

Annacondia's crusades are, as he says, "long." Typically, Evangelical crusades in Argentina had lasted a week, perhaps two. Annacondia's first mass crusade, in La Plata, lasted eight months. The next four mass campaigns after that lasted an average of sixty days. Even now, when he has evangelized nearly all of the big and medium-sized cities in Argentina, most of his crusades last thirty to forty days.

In addition to being long, Annacondia's crusades are extremely intense. As he says, when he enters a place he goes there to do "battle," and he expects the same "aggressiveness" of the churches that participate in the crusade. In addition to the pastors that generally organize the crusade and work there nightly, the churches contribute many "workers" to the crusade. The workers seek out those that commit to Christ; they help fill out decision cards; they carry off and minister to those who are overcome during their liberation from demons; and they gather testimonies from those who have been healed. All of the pastors and workers become involved in this "battle with the devil."

The two practices in the crusades that have the greatest impact on those present are spiritual liberation and healing. When Annacondia (1993b) "liberates" the possessed of demons, he paces the stage naming different demons, his voice rising to add emphasis to the battle that he is fighting:

> Out, out, out! Every demon of Macumba, of black magic, of red magic, of spiritualism, of Judo, of Karate, of the New Age! Let go of them, let go of them, let go of them! Out, Out! Every demon of Umbanda, Out! All unholy spirits, Out!

As he continues to reproach the demons, people begin to fall to the ground, some as if fainting, others writhing and shaking. Teams of two men carry those that fall to the "liberation tent" where they are ministered to by pastors and other workers that have been trained by Annacondia's team in the techniques of spiritual liberation. While the crusade continues, those that have been liberated remain in the tent receiving comfort and prayers.

Fabian (1993), a young man who was converted in an Annacondia crusade, related his personal experience of liberation as follows:

> When I was sixteen, I began playing around with some friends, one of whom practiced Macumba (Afro-Brazilian spiritualism). One night my friend got me to drink a bit of unholy blood. After that I began to feel terribly sick in my heart—rebellious. I started to fight with my mother all the time. I had thoughts of killing her. She started to go to Annacondia's crusade in San Martín [May–June 1985] and she became converted. She told me I should go and that made me furious. One night my friends and I decided to go, just to make fun of all the crazy people. When I stepped onto the field where they were holding the crusade, I fell down. I was completely overcome. When I woke up, it was six hours later—3:00 a.m. They explained to me that I had been possessed by an evil spirit and they wanted to know what type of spirit it could be so that they could help me more. I told them about the blood. . . . Since then my mother and I never fight. My brother is now a believer. I haven't left the way of the Lord since.

Fabian's testimony is typical of the mass of new believers that entered the churches through Annacondia's crusades in the mid-1980s. Night after night, as Annacondia rebuked the demons, people fell by the hundreds and received liberation. The impact this had on the pastors and workers that cared for the liberated cannot be exaggerated.

When pastors returned to their churches following Annacondia's crusades, they began to devote a regular part of each meeting to casting out demons. In doing so, they all mimicked Annacondia's method: shouting out the names of specific demons and telling them to leave, "out! out! out! all demons of black magic, of macumba," et cetera. This practice of casting out demons through Annacondia's method continues to be extremely widespread within Argentine Evangelism.[7]

Spiritual healing also became revived as a regular practice in the churches through the Annacondia crusades. Healing was, and continues to be, one of Annacondia's primary attractions. The testimonies of people who have felt healed in his crusades appear to rival those that have received spiritual liberation. One of the most interesting of these testimonies is the recurring claim that people's tooth cavities are filled with "heavenly material in the shape of a cross or of a dove." As with the practice of liberation, Annacondia's method of spiritual healing also became common in the churches following his crusades.[9]

Spiritual liberation and healing added two appealing forms of evangelistic action to the Evangelicals' collective action repertoire. As we have noted, in the Argentine popular sector evil spirits are considered to regularly afflict peoples' lives. The possibility of overcoming those afflictions through Christ, and without visiting a *curandero* (traditional healer), created a powerful incentive to visit Annacondia's crusades.

The other tactical innovation begun by Annacondia was his decision to use a more popular style of music in his crusades. As we have already noted, Annacondia came to Evangelicalism fairly late in life. For him, the old Sunday School songs used by the missionaries held no special appeal. Beginning in 1984, he invited another recent convert, Miguel Cejas, to sing in his crusades. Cejas had originally become famous as a member of the Cuarteto Imperial, a group that played popular folkloric music. Over the years, Annacondia's team has shifted its music to fit the changing tastes of the Evangelical community.[10] However, Cejas was the first widely popular evangelist/musician in Argentina. He launched a shift to more popular music in the churches.

The intensity of Annacondia's crusades for the pastors, workers, and new believers produced a sudden and very dramatic change in the practices of the Evangelical community. Annacondia converted the Evangelical community to charismatic practices. He describes this effect of his crusades in this way:

> At first the Baptists and the Free Brethren would say that the Pentecostals were all possessed. The Pentecostals said that the Free Brethren were spiritually dead. Now in my crusades there are Bap-

tists that are the president of the crusade, even though the style of my crusades—casting out demons, speaking in tongues, healing the sick—goes against everything they used to claim they believed (1993).

This conversion to a radical form of charismatic practice extends to nearly all of the churches that have participated in Annacondia's crusades. Edgardo Surenian, a pastor from the fundamentalist and formerly noncharismatic Armenian church explains:

> Can you really imagine how we all feel about Annacondia and his effect in our churches. Look at me. I'm from the serious, quiet Armenian church. Here I am, vice-president of this crusade. I have thirty people from my church working here every night and look at what's going on here. People falling down, speaking in tongues, shaking all over from demons. This is the extreme end of the Pentecostal spectrum and here we are supporting it.[11]

Surenian went on to comment on the fact that currently Annacondia's crusades are attended by pastors, workers, and nonbelievers who are "seeking Jesus." According to Surenian, when Annacondia first appeared he attracted many believers that came to his crusades looking for the "new gifts of the spirit that [he] was offering. Now they can get those things in their own churches, so they don't have to come to the crusades." This illustrates the fundamental shift undergone by the churches that participated in Annacondia's crusade. Since as early as the mid-1980s, they adopted a new, uniformly charismatic collective identity that was sustained by a distinctive set of shared practices.

In adopting the practices that they learned in the crusades, the churches became more and more like each other and believers and pastors alike came to see themselves as members of an Argentine Evangelical Movement instead of as members of individual denominations. This new collective identity took Annacondia's demon fighting, healing, and direct appeal to Argentine popular culture as its symbolic core. Argentine Evangelicals were forced either to accept the new identity and join this unprecedented movement or to close themselves off completely from other Evangelical churches and to erect boundaries around their old missionary identity.

EVANGELICAL IDENTITIES: OLD AND NEW

For all of the changes that Annacondia's crusades brought to the Evangelical community—changes in its collective beliefs, identity, and evangelistic practices—there were some clear constraints on his ministry. Annacondia was not immediately accepted by all of the pastors in the

Evangelical community. Many of them thought that his confrontations with demons were not Biblical. When faced with this opposition, Annacondia (1993) says, "I came to them with the Bible in my hand and I showed them Jesus and His disciples casting out demons. What could they say?"

Annacondia's insight here is not limited to the specific point of whether or not spiritual liberation as he was practicing it had sufficient biblical support. The larger point is that Annacondia was limited by certain fundamental principles established by the missionary package of beliefs. As strange as Annacondia appeared to Argentine Evangelicals, his ministry responded to certain apparently unbreachable components of the missionary teachings. Foremost among these was biblical inerrancy. Recognizing this, Annacondia "came to them with the Bible in his hand."

Second, Argentine Evangelicals Christians were and are distinguished by their commitment to the Great Commission to spread the gospel to the entire world. Carlos Annacondia's crusades demonstrated that there was a more effective way to accomplish their central goal of "winning Argentina for Christ." Instead of seeking to attract new adherents by stressing the virtues of a single denomination (the missionary tactic), the churches came to believe that unity, as Annacondia says, "is the secret in order for the blessing of God to be gigantic." Or as Jorge Gromelsky (*El Puente*, August 1985) admonished the pastors gathered in the Astral Theater to kick off Annacondia's Buenos Aires crusade, "only the unity of the Body can do the work which we are hoping for."

Annacondia, uncommitted to the missionary identity and teachings, challenged denominationalism and most of its peculiar practices and doctrines. In doing so, he undermined the myth of the missionary that had undergirded the Evangelical identity in Argentina for at least sixty years. Other aspects of the missionary package of beliefs: apoliticism, withdrawal from the world, and rejection of the social gospel were all supplanted over the course of the decade that followed Annacondia's first crusades. However, these components of the missionary package of beliefs were changed through very different methods than was the basic commitment to the missionary model. They were challenged by movement activists and intelligentsia in piecemeal fashion. Once Annacondia had called into question the inerrancy of the missionary myth and introduced a more resonant ideological frame and a more compelling Evangelical identity, the myth of the missionary was exploded and movement activists could explore new ways for the movement to mesh with—as well as to challenge—Argentine society.

AFTER ANNACONDIA

In 1987, Annacondia made an important break from the routine his ministry had established between 1984 and that year:

> In 1987, God told me "Get out of Buenos Aires!" So I went to the interior and out of the country because people had begun to follow me as their spiritual leader. I had to leave so that people could become accustomed to going to church. The correct thing is for them to go to the churches. I am not a pastor; they needed a pastor.[12]

Annacondia's absence created space for the emergence of new popular figures within the Evangelical movement.

Horacio Salazar (1993), a young pastor whose church is part of the Union of the Assemblies of God, summarizes the recent history of the Argentine Church this way:

> First Annacondia's ministry appeared. Then came Giménez. Then came . . . well Omar Cabrera was around before, but he wasn't accepted by the Evangelicals. He used a clerical collar, the form of his services was not the traditional form of the Evangelicals, so he was not accepted. He put lots of emphasis on healing and, well, the Evangelicals didn't like that back then. Today it is accepted. It's the same with Giménez, he used to not be accepted and now he is accepted. This seems to happen when something new appears, there is always the fear that it's not within the doctrine. The way of doing things is new, so there is resistance.

Salazar's somewhat tentative summary of the careers of Hector Giménez and Omar Cabrera is understandable. Both of these pastors had churches,[13] large churches, when Annacondia's crusades were just beginning. Omar Cabrera, in fact, was the first Argentine to organize mass meetings which emphasized healing. However, neither Giménez nor Cabrera were accepted by other sectors of the Evangelical community until after Annacondia's successful charismaticization of the Evangelicals.

Commenting on the change that enabled their ministry to become integrated into the Evangelical Movement, Marfa Cabrera (Omar's wife) (1993b) says the following:

> That was part of the spiritual opening. Our minds are more open now. We are not so closed in our concepts. . . . It's not so much that previously the Church was opposed directly to us. But anything new was extremely suspect. Nobody wanted to try something that had not already been proven. Now I can say with fear and trembling before the Lord, that Omar is considered a wise person; pastors come to consult him; things have changed.[14]

The dominance of the missionary model had effectively closed off tactical innovation as well as changes in the collective identity of

Evangelical churches for more than forty years. As Marfa Cabrera says, "anything new was extremely suspect." Annacondia's new frame and the new Evangelical identity that emerged out of his crusades, "opened the minds" of the Evangelical community to innovative forms of collective action and pushed the nation's Evangelicals toward a definitive break with their denominational past.

TACTICAL INNOVATION

Following Annacondia's departure from Buenos Aires in 1987, a more stable model of church building was necessary to accomplish precisely what Annacondia suggested above—people had to become accustomed to going to church. In addition, the Evangelical Movement needed charismatic figures who could fill the void created by Annacondia's abrupt departure—maintaining and enhancing the collective identity created in Annacondia's crusades. Horacio Salazar suggests the creative way in which Hector Giménez and Omar Cabrera fulfilled those tasks. Salazar claims that Giménez and Cabrera demonstrated to the Argentine church that:

> we could do it better than the missionaries. Why did we need them to show us how to go about building churches in Argentina, when we Argentines were doing it better than they ever had? Did you know that Cabrera has the second largest church in the world and Giménez the third largest?

Salazar's statement, first of all, is further evidence of the shift away from the myth of the missionary that had begun with Annacondia. Giménez and Cabrera demonstrated conclusively, by building extremely large churches, that Argentine Evangelicals could accomplish the central goal of Evangelicalism—mass-scale growth—better than the missionaries had ever been able to. Their successes cemented the collective identity of the Argentine church as a national church with powerful leaders who were accomplishing God's purpose in Argentina.

In addition to reinforcing the break with the missionaries as the central figure of the Argentine Evangelical movement, Giménez and Cabrera, in creating large churches, introduced a tactical innovation into the Evangelical movement. Large churches had not been part of the collective action repertoire of the Evangelical community prior to the early 1980s. The wisdom of establishing large churches was severely questioned by the community when Giménez and Cabrera first entered the movement. In Giménez's first interview in *El Puente* ("Twenty Questions to Hector Giménez"),[16] one of the questions asked was: "When a church gets this big, is there not some danger of not attending to the personal necessities of the members?" (*El Puente*, March 1987:6)

Large churches were not part of the tactical repertoire of the founding missionaries. Consequently, they were suspect until proven otherwise. It should not surprise us that at every step the old missionary ways of doing things had to be challenged and overturned. Tactical innovations often faced severe opposition from those unwilling to part with components of the old mission methods. Giménez and Cabrera, by creating large churches, challenged one of the basic organizational principles of the old missionary model.

EXPANDING THE MOVEMENT'S APPEAL

In Annacondia's initial formulation of the movement's core teachings, spiritual liberation and healing were the two primary manifestations of the power and victory available through Christ. Giménez and Cabrera, each in their own way and in keeping with the profile of their audience, established the gospel of prosperity as the third fundamental principal of the Evangelical Movement's teachings. The gospel of prosperity extends the power of Christ into the economic sphere, the one major concern in the popular sector not addressed by Annacondia.

Just as Annacondia's contributions were constrained by the continuing adherence to biblical innerancy, the prosperity gospel, in order to be widely accepted, needed to be given a firm biblical base. Cabrera and Giménez found ample justification in the Old Testament with verses such as the following:

> Bring ye all the tithes into the storehouse, that there may be meat in mine house, and prove me now herewith, saith the Lord of hosts, if I will not open you the windows of heaven, and pour you out a blessing, that there shall not be room enough to receive it (*Malachi* 4:10)

Omar Cabrera's former exclusion from the Evangelical community was based at least in part on his strong claims regarding the prosperity gospel. From his first interview in *El Puente*:

> INTERVIEWER: Some people criticize the fact that you talk so much about the prosperity of the believer. What do you teach your followers in this regard?
>
> CABRERA: Many people think that I teach the importance of giving so that they will give to us, but the Lord knows that it is not that way. A person that does not learn to open their hand, to be generous, to be giving, will never be prosperous. This is not an invention of mine, it is a principle which God established in order to bless. When a person embraces this principle, without knowing it she is opening the win-

dow of the abundance of the heavens (*El Puente*, October 1988:8).

The message of the gospel of prosperity is that in order to be prosperous you need to tithe and to make regular donations "to the work." This gospel of prosperity was not part of the missionary teachings; the missionaries minimized discussions of worldly things. Moreover, perhaps out of a fear of rejection, they did not introduce the principle of tithing until members were fully integrated into their churches. Cabrera, in the same interview, rejects the old missionary views regarding the tithe:

> You do not need to wait two years to teach the tithe. For me, it all goes together in one package: salvation, sanctity, and giving. When you do not teach giving, you deny the possibility of receiving.

In the meetings of *Visión del Futuro*, Cabrera regularly preaches about "the law of giving." He bolsters the message we have seen already with more specific promises regarding the type of prosperity that those with "a giving spirit" will receive: a car with zero kilometers, a new business, a productive professional life, and a nice house (*una vivienda digna*). These promises—professional success or ownership of a business—reflect the goals of the upwardly mobile audience of *Visión del Futuro*.

Hector Giménez also teaches prosperity, but in his own characteristic fashion. In Giménez's church, the principles of prosperity are taught in every meeting at the moment of the offering (this is true, now, of most of the churches in the movement). The most common promise in *Ondas de Amor y Paz* regarding the offering and prosperity is, "You are going to receive one hundred times more than what you give. If you doubt that, don't give an offering. You have to give with joy and love."[17]

In addition to these straight-forward statements regarding the relationship between giving and receiving, Hector Giménez also presents a more general claim regarding accepting Christ and being prospereous. In the Giménez version of the gospel of prosperity, the very act of accepting Christ opens the pathway to prosperity. The following, taken from his Christmas address in 1992, displays this larger principle of prosperity:

> I want you to think about the manger. Think about Joseph and Mary, brothers and sisters. They were so poor that they had to lay their beautiful new baby down on a bed of straw—is that right or not? Amen. But now, think about what happened next. No sooner had Jesus come into their lives than the wise men came bearing gifts: gold, frankincense, and myrrh. Do you understand me? That's the message of the manger. When Jesus comes into your life you receive gold. Hallelujah![18]

Giménez, understanding that his audience is a sector of the population that is economically marginal, does not regularly discuss professional advancement or business ownership. The prosperity he teaches is both simpler and more diffuse than that taught by Omar Cabrera. Between the two of them, by appealing to different segments of society, they established the general principal of prosperity as the third fundamental message of the Evangelical Movement. Though churches certainly vary in the degree to which prosperity is a constant theme, at the moment of "raising the offering," the law of prosperity is now almost universally invoked.

CLAUDIO FREIDZON'S CRUSADE OF MIRACLES

Once Giménez, Cabrera, and the gospel of prosperity had been incorporated into the Evangelical movement, the shape of the movement, its fundamental teachings, and its collective identity became increasingly uniform. As the vestiges of the old missionary model were thrust aside, the different ministries and denominations within the movement came to resemble one another more and more. Moreover, the believers came to respond in remarkably similar ways to the preaching and charismatic practices of the movement's popular figures. The most compelling evidence of this is the ministry of the movement's fourth major charismatic figure, Claudio Freidzon.[19]

Freidzon's "Crusade of Miracles" ministry is based on the experience of what he calls "the new anointing" or the "fresh anointing" of the Holy Spirit, which is said to expand and renovate the believers' experience of God's power in their lives. Those that receive "the anointing" develop a heightened sensitivity to, and awareness of, the influence of the Holy Spirit. The outward manifestations that accompany this spiritual gift include: falling in the Spirit, "drunkenness in the Spirit," uncontrollable laughter, and "crying with joy."

I was present when this blessing was far from routinized, and certainly before all of the modes of interaction between Freidzon and those seeking the spiritual blessing he offered had been defined. The result was unpredictability. Once the word spread that the Holy Spirit was being manifested in new and powerful ways, any meeting that Freidzon attended was overwhelmed by those seeking his blessing. So, for example, when Freidzon announced a meeting to be held in Luna Park, an indoor arena in Buenos Aires with a capacity of approximately 12,000, more than three times that number showed up. The meetings themselves, whether in his own church or in larger venues, were nearly interminable. Perhaps because there were no firm cues between leader and followers, and because everyone was having so much fun (including Freidzon), meetings that were set for two hours would last six. Evening meetings would often last nearly until dawn.

I attended a meeting in the Obras Sanitarias arena (filled to capacity with 6,600 believers) which began at one P.M. and was scheduled to end at three P.M. Freidzon spent the entire afternoon inviting pastors and other church leaders onto the platform, where he would blow into the microphone, throw his suit jacket, lay his hands on heads, or simply wave his arms in the direction of an individual or group of individuals. The result was always the same: they would fall to the ground laughing and praising God. Those that struggled to their feet would be smitten by another wave of Freidzon's arms or a thrown jacket and fall to the ground again. The only punctuation to the falling and laughing were interruptions so that everyone could sing the music of Marcos Witt.[20] The meeting finally let out at nearly nine P.M., with everyone simply too exhausted to laugh, sing, or, perhaps ironically, fall down any more.

Freidzon's popularity and the fervor of the believers that wished to receive the new anointing resulted in one tumultuous year (August 1992–July 1993) within the Evangelical community. Thousands of believers thronged Freidzon's own church in the Belgrano neighborhood of Buenos Aires. He held meetings every Tuesday night in the Obras Sanitarias arena and began to travel to the other principal cities of Argentina, plus Uruguay, Paraguay, and Chile. Even with that, the believers demanded more access to Freidzon and the new anointing. The practice, as with the other charismatic practices that we have already seen, soon became widespread in nearly all of the churches in the movement. Pastors would visit Freidzon's crusades and then return to their own churches full of the "fresh anointing" and ready to share the same blessing with their congregations.

In April of 1993, Freidzon staged a mass meeting in the *Velez Sarsfield* soccer stadium (capacity 76,000), which he filled to overflowing. That five-hour Evangelical celebration was, perhaps, the culmination of Freidzon's meteoric rise to prominence in the Evangelical movement. While remaining extraordinarily popular in Argentina, Freidzon has gone on to become a star on the international Evangelical circuit, traveling throughout Latin America, Spain, and the Latin communities of the United States. A widely noted movement of spiritual revival in Toronto, Canada, is attributed to a Canadian pastor's visit to Freidzon's church in Buenos Aires.

FREIDZON AND THE EVANGELICAL'S CYCLE OF COLLECTIVE ACTION

Claudio Freidzon arose as a popular figure well into the current cycle of collective action in the Evangelical movement. Consequently, his framing efforts, his image, and his form of interaction with believers were even more constrained than were those of Annacondia, Giménez, or Cabrera when they first emerged as movementwide charismatic figures. Both the new collective beliefs and the new Evangelical identity had become, by the time Freidzon appeared, increasingly well-defined. As the components of the old missionary model were overthrown, new and generally uniform beliefs and practices had begun to take shape.

Freidzon, a pastor and regional administrative director of the Union of the Assemblies of God in the Federal Capital, understood those new constraints and capitalized on them. Annacondia, Giménez, and Cabrera were all outsiders who came to prominence through their demonstrated ability to reach nonbelievers. Freidzon was the first insider to establish a mass ministry; he did it by "preaching to the choir."

Unlike any of his predecessors, his ministry was not directed in any way toward "the unconverted." The new anointing was directed exclusively at believers—receiving a new anointing presupposes, of course, a first anointing. In order for Freidzon to succeed on the mass level, it was essential that a large group of believers with a well-formed collective identity already exist. Freidzon (1993) himself is well aware of the process that made his ministry possible. Regarding the changes that made available the pool of believers that would seek out the new anointing, he says,

> Over the course of the last 15 years there has been a period of growth regarding the supernatural. With the arrival of Carlos Annacondia, it was as if the Argentine people was awakened to what God can do outside of a religious liturgy, outside of the normal life of a church. Carlos Annacondia came and threw down some of the preconceptions that we had regarding God's actions and the people began to realize that God was showing us a power that we had not been seeing before. For God this power is not new, but, rather, our experience of it is new.

Freidzon's account of the changes in the Evangelical community that began with Annacondia should be familiar. He is describing the charismaticization of the Evangelical Movement. Freidzon's Crusade of Miracles both took advantage of and expanded the openness to new "movements of the Spirit" that Annacondia had initiated.

Freidzon is the first popular figure to become widely accepted based on a ministry directed at believers. All of the other popular figures gained their stature based on their proven ability to attract new adherents to the movement. Freidzon became popular solely because he offered a message that reconfirmed to believers the importance of their existing beliefs. Freidzon reflected to his followers the charismatic identity they had developed in association with Carlos Annacondia, Omar Cabrera, and Hector Giménez over the preceding decade. In Freidzon's crusades the community of believers discovered that they talked the same, worshipped the same, and responded to the same men of God.[21]

FREIDZON'S CONTRIBUTIONS TO THE EVANGELICAL MOVEMENT

Given that Freidzon's ministry functioned as a reaffirmation of the new Evangelical identity, it should not be surprising that it did not generate many innovations in the movement. Believers from all of the churches in the movement thronged to his crusades, seeking what Freidzon calls "more" of God's power, but it was a power that they already recognized and understood. The concept of the new anointing was not a contribution to the movement's teachings; it gave the community new terms with which to express its newly unified charismatic character. It did nothing to reorient the Evangelicals' understanding of the world nor of the movement's relation to the society it hoped to change.

Tactically, the new anointing is not a tool of recruitment; its target is those who already believe. The new forms with which the Holy Spirit was passed from the spiritual leaders to his followers—blowing on the microphone, throwing the suit jacket, and waving the arms—are unlikely, in themselves, to resonate with nonbelievers.[22] In fact, the fervor with which believers sought "the new anointing" severely limited Freidzon's ability to preach or to channel the phenomenon toward evangelistic ends. In any meeting he attended, the believers would demand— by laughing, by crying, by falling down—immediate access to the gift that they believed Freidzon to possess. Thus, Freidzon did not expand the movement's repertoire of collective action, but rather, he consolidated aspects of the movement's identity previously established in Carlos Annacondia's crusades and spread to new segments of the popular sector by Hector Giménez and Omar Cabrera.

Freidzon did, in one way, enrich and extend the collective identity of the movement, but he did this within the Protestant community by bringing the new charismatic practices of the Evangelical movement to sectors of the historical Protestant churches that had not previously participated in any way in the charismatic practices and identity of the movement. In a meeting that I attended in Freidzon's church in Belgrano, an Anglican Bishop was among the primary targets of the new anointing. Laughing and falling, the Bishop assured Freidzon that he would carry the anointing back to his church. Other pastors from historically noncharismatic churches invited Freidzon to come to their meetings and to share this new gift of the spirit with their traditionally staid congregations.[23] This incorporation of a portion of the historical churches into the charismatic practices of the new Evangelical movement was unexpected by both sides and highlights the degree to which a movement toward unity had been operating within the entire Protestant community in Argentina.

Both Claudio Freidzon and his wife Betty are fair-skinned, blue-eyed, well-educated, and always impeccably dressed. Betty, who like Marfa Cabrera and Irma Giménez participates on stage in the Crusade of Miracles, is an attractive mother of three with an extensive wardrobe.[24] The Freidzons are, in other words, solidly middle-class. This, in itself, does not explain their appeal in the clearly middle-class historical churches, but it would appear to be a necessary condition for it.

CONCLUSION

The creation and consolidation of the Argentine Evangelical Movement and the relativization of denominational culture inherent in it mark a clear deviation from the history of Evangelical sectarianism that has been the norm in Latin America. My account of the role of a cohort of evangelists that drove the creation, extension, and consolidation of the new movement privileges one set of actors—mass-scale evangelists—while underplaying the role of other movement activists, believers, and underlying structural factors. The move away from denominationalism was certainly more complex than this chapter indicates. However, telling the story of the creation of the Argentine Evangelical Movement through the experience of these evangelists makes sense for three reasons.

First, marking changes in the movement as they emerged in the crusades of these evangelists matches the believers' understanding of the evolution of their movement. Each evangelist introduced now well-known changes into the worship practices of the churches. Pastors that prospered in the new era of mass-scale Argentine evangelism did so because they brought the practices of the crusade into their churches. Similarly, the shift in collective identity—from being members of specific denominations to being part of a nationwide movement—was clearly driven, for the believers, by their experiences in the crusades.

Another reason to focus on the effects of evangelists like Annacondia, Cabrera, Giménez, and Freidzon is that they have all carried the message of unity and the end of denominationalism beyond Argentina to other Latin American countries. While the Argentine Protestant community may be at the forefront of unity and postdenominationalism, other Evangelical communities are being taught that same message by the very evangelists who catalyzed the relativization of denominational identity in Argentina.

The third reason for tracing the demise of denominationalism in Argentina through the careers of the Evangelical community's most sought-after men of God is to underscore the fact that the charismatic leaders are extremely important actors in the still fluid social, political, and economic life of the region. The phenomenon of individual leadership generally receives scant attention from scholars, despite the fact that powerful leaders exert disproportionate influence in many countries in the region. By highlighting the role of Carlos Annacondia and other evangelists in the creation of the Evangelical Movement in Argentina, this chapter makes a claim that scholars need to find new ways to think systematically about the role of dynamic leaders in society and politics.

NOTES

1   In Argentina, the movement toward unity has even brought the Evangelicals and the historical Protestant churches closer together. The CNE (National Evangelical Council) includes representatives from all of the major Protestant denominations and interdenominational organizations in the country. Two national meetings for pastors (held in 1992 and 1995) successfully brought together 3,000 pastors from every corner of the country and from across all of the theological and political currents in the Protestant community. In 1994, the precursor to the current National Evangelical Council successfully opposed legislation seen to be destructive of religious liberty in Argentina.

2   Juan Terranova is vice-president of the Argentine chapter of the Sociedad Bíblica. He is the pastor of a large church in Villa Ballester, Province of Buenos Aires. When this interview was conducted he was also president of CONELA, the organization for evangelizing Protestants in Latin America.

3   The Free Brethren are the most severe of the fundamentalist churches in Argentina. It was, perhaps, an early indication of Annacondia's later unifying effect that a pastor from the Free Brethren would agree to minister to an energetic group of Pentecostals. Gromelsky is now a leader within Pentecostalism; he was chosen as president of the Confederation of Evangelical Pentecostals for 1994–95.

4   The official claim of *Mensaje de Salvación* is that 100 people were converted in Bernal during the approximately eight months that Annacondia preached there.

5   This figure is taken from an article on Annacondia that appeared in the first issue of the interdenominational monthly *El Puente*, May 1985.

6   Conspicuously absent from this list are any of the "historical" churches: Methodists, Presbyterians, Anglicans, Lutherans, Congregationalists, etc. The relation of these churches to the current Evangelical Movement is much closer and more open, but at the time they had nothing to do with what they saw as the hyperfundamentalist and politically reactionary Evangelicals.

7   I witnessed approximately forty pastors or workers casting out evil spirits, and they uniformly use Annacondia's precise wording and tactics. The ubiquity of the practice is testimony to the impact that Annacondia's ministry has had on Argentine Evangelicalism.

8   The filled cavities is one of the most common testimonies of Annacondia's power within the Evangelical community. He mentioned the phenomenon in his interview with me, saying that the fillings provide "an undeniable testimony to doubting Thomases."

9   When he heals, Annacondia asks one who wishes to be healed to place a hand on the area that needs to be healed. He then proceeds to cast out the demons that produce illnesses in different parts of the body. He also names various illnesses (up to one hundred on a good night). One other method he uses is to ask those with categories of illnesses (cancer, arthritis, blood diseases, bad eyesight, back trouble) to step forward as a group to be healed.

10 Young people in the churches have gained control of the music that is used for worship. Consequently, the new Evangelical popular music is exclusively soft rock (mostly the music of the Mexican singer/songwriter/producer Marcos Witt).

11 Interview (at 3:00 A.M.), after an Annacondia crusade in the suburb of Ciudadela.

12 Interview, June 21, 1993. Annacondia's claim of having left Buenos Aires for several years is corroborated by evidence from *El Puente*, which publishes an itinerary of Annacondia's crusades every month. He lead only one crusade in greater Buenos Aires in more than two years.

13 The name of Gimenez's church is *Ondas de Amor y Paz* (Waves of Love and Peace). It is a church whose membership is mostly drawn from the lower strata of the working class and even includes some urban squatters. Cabrera's church, *Visión del Futuro* (Vision of the Future), recruits, primarily, in the formal sectors of the working class and into the lower middle-class.

14 Interview, May 27, 1993.

15 This claim, though certainly bearing the characteristic ring of Argentine self-importance, is regularly made by church-growth specialist Peter Wagner (heard by the author on November 12, 1992 in the Harvest Evangelism leadership seminar). There is some question as to which church is currently larger. Giménez' Waves of Love and Peace Church has the appearance of continued, vigorous growth, while even Cabrera admits that the growth of his Vision of the Future Church seems to be stagnating. Both churches claim to have somewhere near 100,000 members. Salazar's remarks were made to me in an interview on February 19, 1993.

16 Marcello Lafitte likes to take some credit for initially helping Giménez and Cabrera to emerge as accepted figures in the Evangelical community. This sentiment seems misplaced in regard to the Evangelical base. The believers had already wholeheartedly accepted both evangelists by the time that their "coming-out" articles appeared in *El Puente*. However, it may be the case, as Lafitte claims, that the articles helped to persuade some pastors and other recalcitrant leaders to embrace Giménez and Cabrera as part of the movement. Lafitte originally took credit for bringing them into the movement in my interview with him in 1993; he made the same claim when we met again in 1995.

17 This particular promise was made by Rubén Giménez, the number two pastor in *Ondas de Amor y Paz*, on June 11, 1993.

18 Hector Giménez gave this sermon on December 22 at the Christmas meeting

of his central church, for which they rented the beautiful Astros Theater in downtown Buenos Aires.

19 Claudio Freidzon exploded onto the Argentine Evangelical scene in August 1992. Given that my research for this project began in October 1992, I was fortunate enough to observe nearly the entire trajectory of Freidzon's rise to prominence in the movement.

20 Just as Freidzon's crusades came to dominate the Evangelical movement, Witt's music became the music used in nearly all of the churches in the movement by the end of 1992.

21 The clear difference between Freidzon's ministry and the ministries of the figures that preceded him suggest that around 1992 the Evangelical Movement had begun to move into a new developmental phase (Jowitt 1977). Jowitt suggests that after movements have taken over (transformed) their target systems or organizations, they go through a phase of consolidation. In the phase of consolidation, the movement turns inward—concretizing that which is distinctive about it, thus confirming and solidifying the collective identity of the movement's followers. Freidzon's crusades accomplished this for the Evangelical Movement. His ministry reconfirmed and consolidated the new charismatic and distinctively Argentine identity of the Evangelical Movement.

22 The tactics were occasionally confusing even to believers, or at least produced interesting, ad hoc explanations for what they were experiencing. One pastor, for example, carefully explained to his congregation that he had just returned from a Freidzon crusade and that he was full of the new anointing. He went on to explain that the anointing sticks to clothes, so that when he threw his jacket at them the anointing would pass from the jacket to them. (I heard this interpretation of the new anointing on June 25, 1993 in a Pentecostal meeting in the city of San Miguel in the province of Buenos Aires).

23 One of the most prominent pastors to have Freidzon in his church was the pastor of the Central Baptist Church of Buenos Aires, Pablo Deiros, an internationally respected theologian who teaches periodically at the Princeton Theological Seminary.

24 In more than twenty visits to the Crusade of Miracles, I never saw Betty wear the same outfit twice.

25 Guillermo O'Donnell (1995) offers an important exception to this rule in arguing that caudillo-style presidents, like Argentina's Carlos Menem and Peru's Alberto Fujimori, threaten the consolidation of representative democracy in their countries.

REFERENCES

Annacondia, Carlos. 1993. (Interview June 21).

Bastian, Jean-Pierre. 1993. "The Metamorphosis of Latin American Protestant Groups: A Sociohistorical Perspective." *Latin American Research Review* 28:2.

Cabrera, Marfa. 1993. (Interview May 23).

———. 1993. (Interview May 27).

Castells, Manuel. 1983. *The City and the Grassroots: A Cross-Cultural Theory of Urban Social Movements.* Berkeley: University of California Press.

El Puente. August 1985, p. 1.

———. October 1985, p. 8.

———. December 1985, p. 4.

Fabian. 1993. (Interview January 19).

Garrard-Barnett, Virginia, and David Stoll. 1993. *Rethinking Protestantism in Latin America*. Philadelphia: Temple University Press.

Guilles, Jorge. 1995. (Interview March 4).

Mariz, Cecília. 1995. *Coping with Poverty: Pentecostals and Christian Base Communities in Brazil*. Philadelphia: Temple University Press.

Marostica, Matthew. 1994. "La iglesia evangélica como nuevo movimiento social." *Sociedad y Religión* 12:3–16.

Martin, David. 1990. *Tongues of Fire: The Explosion of Protestantism in Latin America*. London: Basil Blackwell.

McCarthy, John D, and Mayer N. Zald. 1977. "Resource Mobilization and Social Movements: A Partial Theory." *American Journal of Sociology* 82:1212–41.

Melucci, Alberto. 1989. *Nomads of the Present: Social Movements and Individual Needs in Contemporary Society*. Philadelphia: Temple University Press.

Offe, Claus. 1985. "New Social Movements: Challenging the Boundaries of Institutional Politics." *Social Research* 52, no. 4: 817–868.

O'Donnell, Guillermo. 1994. "Delegative Democracy." *Journal of Democracy* 5:55–69.

Olson, Mancur. 1971. *The Logic of Collective Action. Public Goods and the Theory of Groups*. Cambridge: Harvard University Press.

Salazar, Horacio. 1993. (Interview January 29).

Stoll, David. 1990. *Is Latin America Turning Protestant?* Berkeley: University of California Press.

Terranova, Juan. 1993. (Interview April 17).

Wynarczyk, Hilario, and Pablo Seman. 1994. "Campo evangélico y pentecostalismo en la Argentina." In Frigerio, ed. *El Pentecostalismo en la Argentina*: 29–44.

EIGHT

WRAPPED IN THE HOLY SHAWL
THE STRANGE CASE OF CONSERVATIVE CHRISTIANS
AND GENDER EQUALITY IN LATIN AMERICA

Timothy J. Steigenga and David A. Smilde

To most observers, the suggestion that evangelical Protestantism might be linked to more progressive attitudes toward equality for women would seem absurd. In a recent study of religion and politics in the United States, white evangelical Protestants were found to take consistently more conservative positions than Catholics or other Protestants on issues ranging from abortion rights to the role of women in the workforce. With the exponential growth of evangelical Protestantism in Latin America during the past three decades,[1] we might expect to see this trend spreading in that region as well. Clearly, the rhetoric of patriarchy prevalent in North American evangelicalism is also evident in Latin America. According to Leslie Gill's 1990 study of Pentecostals in Peru, for example, "[b]elief in the innate inferiority of women is so firmly entrenched in Pentecostal ideology that many believers view the subordination of women as part of the natural order. In addition, they feel that subordination is sanctioned by God, as evidenced by the teachings of the Bible"(Gill 1990: 716).

Acknowledging the patriarchal rhetoric of many evangelicals, however, a number of authors have recently pointed to countervailing tendencies within Latin American evangelicalism. Elizabeth Brusco, Lesley Gill, Cornilia Butler Flora, Carol Ann Drogus, Cecília Loreto Mariz, and others have argued that despite the evangelical rhetoric of patriarchy, there are two important ways that the spread of evangelical Protestantism may actually support women's moral autonomy in the home and right to participation in religious organizations. First, some research suggests that evangelicalism provides women with a kind of moral autonomy that supports women's increasing independence in the domestic sphere. While evangelicals follow the patriarchal teaching of Paul regarding the headship of husbands and the submission of women, they also believe and emphasize that men and women are equally called to moral perfection and equally have the right to sanction those who sin (Drogus 1997). Cornelia Butler Flora notes that the Colombian evangelical woman "gains the confidence to confront 'sinners'— whatever their sex or social class"(Butler Flora 1976: 202). Developing this theme in their study of Pentecostalism in Brazil, Cecília Loreto Mariz and Dores Campos Machado note that, "[t]hrough conversion, men and women alike learn to see themselves as autonomous beings responsible for their own achievement. Pentecostalism therefore alters people's conceptions of individualism and individual freedom, and this implies transformation of the family and gender relations"(Loreto Mariz and Campos Machado 1997: 51).

Elizabeth Brusco describes this transformation of family and gender relations in her study of Pentecostals in Colombia. According to Brusco, conversion to Pentecostalism often leads to the breakdown of *machismo* and a new focus on the centrality of the domestic sphere. Brusco explains, "[w]ith conversion, machismo, the culturally shaped aggressive masculinity that defines the male role in much of Mestizo Colombia, is replaced by evangelical belief as the main definer of expectations in husband wife relations. . . . One outcome of conversion, then, is that the boundaries of public-male life and private-female life are redrawn and the spheres themselves are redefined" (Brusco 1993: 148).

In another study of evangelicals in Colombia, Myrna Van den Eykel provides an explanation for why males may be willing to accept the changes Brusco, Mariz, and Butler Flora describe. According to Van den Eykel, evangelical beliefs allow men to maintain their ultimate authority in principle (thus preserving the male ego), while simultaneously accepting and fostering a more egalitarian model of household politics (Van den Eykel 1986: 327-331). In his study of Brazilian evangelicals, John Burdick describes how this process might lead to greater moral autonomy for evangelical women.

> "Speaking gently" at home is among the most vital of the abilities forged by conversion. The Holy Spirit and coreligionists' prayers give a woman confidence quietly but firmly to challenge her husband's conduct. Given the Apostle Paul's rule of female subordination, this confidence may seem paradoxical. Yet it is precisely the *crente* [believer] woman's strict observance of a subordinate role, as well as her knowledge of biblical pronouncements and her feeling of being inspired by the Holy Spirit, that give her the right to "show the man the error of his ways." Her observance and knowledge, furthermore, often erode her husband's ability to dismiss her challenges" (Burdick 1993: 112).

According to these authors, then, evangelical women may gain de facto power (based on moral authority) in certain domestic situations in which they might otherwise be powerless (such as domestic abuse or infidelity).

Second, the belief in spiritual equality may also lead to increased opportunity for associational participation for women outside of the home. Cornilia Butler Flora argues that among the Colombian evangelicals she studied, women take part in organizing and leading church gatherings and in evangelizing. "The doctrine of the priesthood of all believers tells the working-class woman that her voice and activity are equally necessary in the working out of God's plan" (Butler Flora 1976: 202). While official positions of authority in many evangelical churches are generally reserved for men, Elizabeth Brusco suggests that women are often more influential and active in their churches than are their male counterparts (Brusco, 1993: 148).[2] Jorge E. Maldonado supports this position, noting the important roles played by evangelical women in Venezuela and Brazil as teachers, counselors, evangelists, and pastors (Maldonado 1993: 224-231). Furthermore, David Smilde has noted that proscriptions on holding official church positions among evangelicals are readily circumvented if the woman feels she is truly "called by God" (Smilde 1994: 52).

These authors argue that beliefs and practices within Latin American evangelicalism can undermine machismo by providing a base for female authority within the home and for female associational participation. The logical question to ask is, what impact the equality and autonomy experienced in the household and the religious realm might have at the level of larger society? According to David Martin, evangelicalism permits changes to incubate on the level of culture until they are ready to effect change in society at large (Martin 1990). Here we set out to see if evangelicalism is currently having an impact on views of gender equality in the political realm.

Our study makes use of survey data collected in Costa Rica and Guatemala during the summer of 1993, as well as qualitative interviews conducted in Venezuela in 1996. We address three primary questions: 1) Are there significant differences in attitudes toward gender equality between religious groups?; 2) What sort of religious factors might explain attitudes toward gender equality?; and 3) Why might these religious factors effect attitudes toward gender equality? In short, we conclude that religious affiliation is not a good predictor of attitudes toward gender equality in the Latin American political sphere. Rather, certain religious beliefs are better predictors of such attitudes *across religious affiliations*. We follow this with qualitative data that show how and why certain religious beliefs may effect attitudes towards gender equality among *both evangelicals and Catholics in Latin America*.

THE LATIN AMERICAN RELIGIOUS LANDSCAPE

The terminology for religious groups operating in Latin America has generated much confusion. Thus, before proceeding to the data, we must define what we mean by the terms we use. The Spanish word *evangélico* connotes one who follows the *evangélico*, or Gospel (i.e. the first four books of the New Testament, which tell the story of Jesus). It is commonly used in Latin America to refer to all Protestant groups. Following the Latin American usage, we will refer to all Protestants as evangelicals. However, we group evangelicals into two basic categories: Pentecostal and Mainstream.

Mainstream evangelicals such as the Baptists, Methodists, Presbyterians, Lutherans, and Mennonites, are some of the oldest Protestant denominations in Latin America. Mainstream evangelicals tend to accept the major doctrines of the Christian faith, such as salvation through Christ, the divine inspiration of scripture, belief in the trinity, and the gift of grace. They are also more likely than their Pentecostal counterparts to interpret some passages in scripture as merely metaphorical and to reject dispensationalist[3] or millennialist conceptions, as well as manifestations of individual charisma through glossolalia (speaking in tongues), spirit possession, and revelation through dreams and visions.

Pentecostal Protestantism in Central America grew out of the missionary efforts of the Assemblies of God, the Church of God, Four Square Gospel Church, and parachurch organizations such as Campus Crusade for Christ and Youth with a Mission. These are now paralleled by numerous successful autonomous Pentecostal movements. Pentecostals are clearly the most numerous and visible of the Protestant groups active in Latin America. Like mainstream Protestants, Pentecostals accept the basic truth claims of Christian faith. However, they place great emphasis on four basic ideas: 1) accepting Jesus Christ as one's personal savior, usually through a dramatic personal conversion referred to as being "born again"; 2) perfectionism, the idea that Christians must fight against "the flesh" and that which is "worldly," not in order to "earn" salvation, but rather to be in communion with Jesus Christ; 3) the belief that Holy Spirit can possess the body through glossolalia, divine healing (via the laying on of hands), or other charismatic acts; and 4) millennialism, the belief that Jesus will soon return and usher in a millennium of messianic rule.[4] Pastors in Pentecostal churches are often charismatic individuals who use a highly dramatic and narrative style of preaching and witnessing. Worship services in Pentecostal churches are characterized by aggressive participation in singing and prayer, an oral liturgy, and personal testimonies from individual church members.

A final category sometimes referred to as evangelicals includes Mormons, Jehovah's Witnesses, and Seventh-Day Adventists. For the purposes of this study we will refer to these groups as sects. These groups represent a separate category because they do not necessarily accept the core claims of Christianity or because they make claims (such as the gift of prophesy for Joseph Smith) beyond the core claims of orthodox Christianity.

As the dominant religious group in Latin America, Catholics will be considered a base category for comparison with different evangelical groups. A final group, those who profess no religious affiliation, has been included as a further baseline for comparing the effects of any religious affiliation on attitudes toward gender equality.

QUESTION 1:
ARE THERE SIGNIFICANT DIFFERENCES IN ATTITUDES TOWARD GENDER EQUALITY BETWEEN RELIGIOUS GROUPS?

Data were collected for the first portion of the study by UNIMER (an established research firm based in San Jose, Costa Rica) during July and August of 1993. A total of 405 usable interviews were collected in five cantons of greater San Jose, Costa Rica and three cantons of Heridia, Costa Rica. In Guatemala, a total of 404 interviews were conducted in greater Guatemala City as well as in Antigua and the immediately surrounding villages of the Department of Sacatepequez. In Costa Rica, interviews were completed for 76 Catholics, 122 mainstream Protestants, 131 Pentecostal Protestants, 45 members of sects, and 31 religiously nonaffiliated individuals. In Guatemala, interviews were completed for 85 Catholics, 38 mainstream Protestants, 233 Pentecostals, 23 members of sects, and 25 individuals with no religious affiliation.[5] The sample consisted of 411 women and 398 men, with each religious group split relatively evenly between genders.[6]

In order to measure attitudes toward gender equality, we compared mean scores for religious groups on levels of agreement (1 = strongly disagree, 2 = disagree, 3 = agree, and 4 = strongly agree) with the following statement: "Women should enjoy all of the political rights and responsibilities that men do." Comparing mean scores for religious groups we found few significant differences. The mean score on agreement with this statement for the religiously nonaffiliated was significantly higher than the mean score for sect members, *but no other significant differences emerged.*

When we compared percentages of respondents who agreed or strongly agreed that women deserve all the political rights and responsibilities that men have, once again, we found that differences between religious groups were not pronounced. While Catholics and Pentecostals have the highest levels of agreement (76.9% and 76.7% respectively), and sect members the lowest (66.7%), differences between religious groups were not great.

These findings do little to support the notion that evangelical Protestantism is making sweeping changes in attitudes toward gender equality in the political sphere. While conversion and membership in evangelical organizations may empower women in the home and in the realm of religious organizations, this does not translate directly into the public realm. To answer our first question, Protestants *do not* appear to be significantly different from Catholics or the nonaffiliated in terms of their attitudes toward gender equality.

QUESTION 2:
WHAT SORT OF RELIGIOUS FACTORS MIGHT EXPLAIN ATTITUDES TOWARD GENDER EQUALITY?

In order to answer our second question we added both background variables and variables measuring religious beliefs in multivariate analysis. Although measures of individual and family income were included in the survey instrument, the number of respondents willing to answer these questions was very low, creating the need for alternative SES indicators. The following variables have been included in the model as control variables: education (grouped into eight categories ranging from "none" to "postgraduate"), occupation (grouped into seven categories ranging from "economically inactive" to "professional manager"), age (measured by the absolute number years of age at the respondent's last birthday), gender (as a dummy variable with males coded as 1), a rural versus urban distinction, a distinction between respondents who have children and those who do not, and a measure of literacy based on whether or not the respondents read the newspaper.

The multivariate analysis also includes five items measuring religious beliefs. Specifically, we focused on statements designed to measure theological conservatism and millennialism. In studies in the United States, theological conservatism and millennialism have been found to be important religious variables affecting political attitudes (Jelen 1991: 49). We have used a scale measuring theological conservatism based on respondent reports that they strongly disagree, disagree, agree, or strongly agree with the following three statements:

1. God created the world in six days of twenty-four hours each.
2. The Bible is inspired by God and must be accepted literally word for word.
3. In order to be saved, I must believe that Jesus Christ died for our sins.

Millennialist theology characterizes much of Latin American evangel-icalism. Millenialist evangelicals hold that "the Devil is the prince of this world." They readily find examples in their social context and in the mass media for Bible passages that speak of the "signs of the end times" such as war, natural disasters, and disease (see especially Matthew 24:3-11); and "the character of men in the last days" including crime, corruption, the breakdown of the family, and other antisocial behavior (see especially II Timothy 3:1, as well as the book of Revelations). Evangelicals are to prepare for the end by maintaining themselves in purity and preaching the Word to those who have not accepted Jesus. Jesus will return and usher in a millennium of rule for his people: most Pentecostals profess allegiance to such beliefs. But there is a great vari-ety among churches and individuals according to the importance they place on this aspect of their belief.

Given that a millennialist perspective is often accompanied by an emphasis on personal piety and self-control, we might expect a passive orientation toward "worldly" political action (Deiros 1992). Measures of millennialist beliefs were obtained by asking respondents if they strongly disagreed, disagreed, agreed, or strongly agreed with the following two statements:

1. There are many "signs of the end times" that signify that Christ will return soon.
2. Christians should not be concerned about this world because Christ will return soon to establish his kingdom.

As expected, our regression analysis (see Appendix 1) showed that a number of background variables have a significant effect on agreement with the statement that women should enjoy all of the political rights and responsibilities that men do. Living in Costa Rica (as compared to Guatemala), having higher educational achievement, and reading the paper frequently are all positively and significantly related to agreement. Women are also more likely to agree than men.

In terms of religious affiliation, we found that belonging to a sect, mainstream Protestant church, or a Pentecostal church has a negative relationship to agreement with the statement about women's rights and responsibilities. Like our earlier findings, these data suggest no link between Protestantism and more positive attitudes toward gender equality in the Latin American political sphere.

However, our findings on religious beliefs suggest that we need to look beyond simple religious affiliation to understand the impact of religion on gender attitudes. Two measures of theological conservatism (the responses concerning biblical literalism and Christ's death for our sins) had positive and significant effects on agreement with the statement that women should enjoy all the political rights and responsibilities that men do. One measure of millennialism (that Christ will return soon) had a negative and significant effect on agreement.

The finding that millennialism is associated with less acceptance of gender equality corresponds with the conventional wisdom about religious conservatives. We might expect the fire-and-brimstone preacher who warns of the imminent return of Christ to be relatively unconcerned about gender equality. The findings on theological conservatism, however, are more surprising. Agreement that the Bible must be interpreted literally and that Jesus Christ died for our sins were *significantly and positively related to agreement that women should enjoy all of the political rights and responsibilities that men do*. In separate regressions, we found this relationship to hold true both in Guatemala and Costa Rica, among both men and women, and among Catholics as well as evangelicals. While most of the literature on religion and gender in Latin America focuses on religious affiliation, our findings suggest that it is conservative religious beliefs that are the most important religious variables effecting attitudes toward gender equality. What is it about these religious beliefs that makes Latin American religious conservatives (both Catholic and Protestant) more likely to support the idea of women's political rights and responsibilities? In the following section we attempt to answer this question by presenting the results of qualitative interviews with Pentecostals and conservative Catholics in Venezuela.

QUESTION 3:
WHY WOULD THEOLOGICAL CONSERVATIVES SUPPORT GENDER EQUALITY?

In order to answer this question, we conducted interviews in Caracas, Venezuela, during June and July of 1996 that used the same questions as the survey, but in open-ended form. The interviews presented are from those who answered "strongly agree" to the questions designed to measure theological conservatism. Among these conservative Christians we see three principle convictions that could provide a basis for the support of gender equality in the political sphere.

First, these conservative Christians emphasized the idea that all humans are created in God's image and, therefore, God does not differentiate between them. Juan, a retired executive of an oil company and a lay participant in the Cursillas movement of the Catholic Church, said he strongly agreed with the idea that women should have all the political rights and responsibilities men have. When we asked him, "why do you strongly agree?", he replied: "The only difference [woman] has with man is that she is a woman. But she is a being just like man. And Man [humankind] was created in the image and likeness of God, so she should be treated in like manner."[7]

Many of those interviewed noted, whether speaking of race, ethnicity, social status, or gender, that God does not distinguish between persons (James 2:1); and that in Christ there is neither Jew nor Greek, slave nor freeman, male nor female (Galatians 3:28). After answering strongly agree to the question of women's political rights, Marcos, a thirty-year-old warehouse worker who is a member of a Caracas Pentecostal Church, said:

> Because God doesn't distinguish between persons. So whatever privileges men have the woman also has, because God doesn't leave anyone out. Everyone, man or woman, has the same rights in the Lord to enjoy, to elect, to be in agreement with something. Men or women.[8]

Julieta, a twenty-five-year-old woman who teaches Bible study at a Pentecostal Church in Caracas said, "God doesn't distinguish between men and women in carrying out political positions in society."[9] Flor, the wife of Juan (mentioned above), has been involved in the Cursillista movement for thirty years. In a separate and private interview, when she was asked why she strongly agreed that women deserve all of the political rights and responsibilities that men have, she stated: "God himself did not differentiate between man and women. Yes, I think that women should have as many opportunities as men."[10]

A second basis for supporting the idea of women's political rights among conservative Christians comes in the importance they give to the message of Romans 13, ("Let everyone obey the authorities that are over him, for there is no authority except from God, and all authority that exists is established by God"). In this case, the theologically conservative who teach and practice strict adherence to Biblical norms may also be strict adherents to legal norms, including the norm of equal political rights and responsibilities for women. Since God made the laws of this world, and the law gives women the same rights as men, Christians are obliged to support women's rights. This idea was reflected in a follow-up question we asked. After the response recorded above, we asked Marcos, "Can a woman be a Senator or a Mayor or anything like that?" Marcos replied, "Yes, she should have the right because God tells us we have to subject ourselves to the laws he has placed by means of men; we should subject ourselves to the laws of this world."

Also, since God does not distinguish between men and women, and he places those who rule in office, he may well place a women in power. Guadalupe, a fifty-seven-year-old evangelical woman in Caracas stated, "well the Word [Bible] says that the Lord doesn't distinguish between persons. And if the Lord wants to put one of his children as Mayor, glory to God."[11]

The third aspect of the Biblical message that provides a basis for such egalitarianism is simply the Biblical example. Many point out that Jesus treated men and women as equals, and throughout the Bible there are examples of women playing important roles. Ramiro, an unemployed thirty-five-year-old construction worker, was interviewed after he finished preaching at noontime in a downtown Caracas plaza.

He agreed that women should have the same political rights and opportunities as men:

> Yes, I think they can because Christ gave importance to the woman. While man devalued her, Christ valued her. We can see countries where there are women that have become president, such as Violeta de Chamorro, and we can see here for example in our country, we have a mayor called Irene Saez who was Miss Universe and she has been doing all kinds of things. . . . As long as men corrupt, God can raise up a woman. We can see the case in which God used Ruth, a woman. He used Deborah. We have examples that are biblical. That's why I believe that yes, she can have a [political] position.[13]

Julieta, whom we met above, said that women could carry out all of the roles of men. When asked if she felt that as a human or as a Christian, she answered, "as a human," then added, "[b]ut as a Christian also I believe that the woman carries out a large role among people and society because look at Esther. God used her in a difficult moment of crisis that the people of Israel were going through. God used her, being a woman, so that her people could be liberated, you see?"[14]

CONCLUSION

Are evangelicals in Latin America more likely than members of other religious groups to believe in a general principle of equal political rights and responsibilities between genders? Our findings suggest that they are not. We found no significant differences between religious groups on agreement with the statement that "women should enjoy all the political rights and responsibilities that men do." However, a closer examination of the data, including measures of religious beliefs associated with evangelical Protestantism (millennialism and theological conservatism), suggests that the issue is more complicated. We found countervailing tendencies among those who held these conservative religious beliefs. On one hand, millennialism was associated with less favorable attitudes toward women's rights, a finding that fits the conventional wisdom about conservative Christians. On the other hand, two measures of theological conservatism (biblical literalism and the belief that Christ died for our sins) had a significantly positive relationship to agreement with the statement on women's rights and responsibilities.

In qualitative interviews with conservative Christians (both Catholic and Protestant), we found three principle convictions that could afford a base for the support of gender equality in the political sphere. First, these individuals hold the strong belief that all humans are created in God's image and therefore God does not differentiate between them. Second, the message contained in Romans 13 suggests that legal norms, including the norm of equal political rights and responsibilities for women, must be strictly followed by Christians. Third, biblical examples of women serving in important roles and of Jesus treating men and women as equals are considered examples that may still be followed today.

The results of this study, though preliminary, have important implications for the study of religion and politics. First, without making assumptions about causality, we can state that the intellectual and theological basis of an argument in favor of greater gender equality are clearly apparent in the testimonies of Latin America's conservative Christians. This may represent a mere accommodation by religious conservatives of larger cultural tendencies toward greater gender equality. However, the highly significant positive relationship between our two measures of theological conservatism and agreement with the statement in support of gender equality suggest that religious variables may be having an important effect beyond the level of family and religious organization and within the realm of political ideas and political culture. The extent of these autonomous effects remains to be seen.

Second, researchers would do well to move beyond looking at religious affiliation and simple notions of "religious conservatism" to look at the content of actual beliefs and how these beliefs engage with attitudes and outlooks toward the social world. The religious beliefs we found to be important predictors of attitudes toward gender equality crossed denominational lines and had countervailing effects. The connections between religious beliefs and political beliefs are likely to be multilayered and interactive.

Third, this topic calls for further qualitative research to establish the relative importance of the religious themes developed by our respondents. For the purposes of this study we limited responses to those who self-identified as conservative Christians (according to measures of theological conservatism and millennialism), leaving open the question of less conservative Christians and the sort of religious themes that might inform these individuals' views on gender equality. Future comparative studies might probe the differences in attitudes toward gender equality between theological liberals and theological conservatives.

Finally, this study suggests that some of the most important and intriguing effects of the religious changes occurring in Latin America may not be immediately discernible at the macro level. Studies such as Butler Flora's, Brusco's, and Burdick's point to the manner in which conservative religious views may be utilized to invert power structures within gender relations at the level of family and religious organization. Our study demonstrates that some of these same religious views may translate into the realm of politics over time.

APPENDIX
PREDICTORS OF ATTITUDES TOWARD GENDER EQUALITY REGRESSED BY BACKGROUND VARIABLES, RELIGIOUS AFFILIATION, AND RELIGIOUS BELIEFS

	b	T	p=
BACKGROUND			
Country	.2710	4.129	.0000
Age	<.0001	0.330	.9737
Education	.0375	2.645	.0083
Gender	-.1289	-2.081	.0377
Occupation	.0030	0.171	.8642
Read paper	.1716	2.739	.0063
Rural context	-.0196	-0.321	.7483
Has children	-.0468	-0.643	.5203
DENOMINATIONAL AFFILIATION			
Sect	-.4969	-3.421	.0007
Mainstream	-.4285	-3.392	.0007
Catholic	-.1592	-1.278	.2016
Pentecostal	-.2363	-2.003	.0455
RELIGIOUS BELIEFS			
Doctrinal Orthodoxy			
Six-day creation	.0199	0.530	.5963
Christ died for sins	.2301	4.646	.0000
Literal interpretation	.1137	2.727	.0065
Millenialism			
Signs of end times	.0625	1.428	.1536
Christ returns soon	-.0162	-3.147	.0017
Constant	1.771	7.830	.0000
R^2		1.870	
n=		781	

NOTES

1 In a region traditionally dominated by Catholicism, Protestants now make up more than 10 percent of the population, with the majority of converts joining Pentecostal churches. See David Stoll, *Is Latin America Turning Protestant? The Politics of Evangelical Growth* (Berkeley: University of California Press, 1990), pp. 333–38.

2 Also see Carol Ann Drogus, who notes that, "Pentecostalism also offers women unaccustomed opportunities for official and unofficial leadership and new roles in the religious community" (Drogus 1997: 59).

3 Dispensationalism is the belief that history is divided into different time periods (or dispensations) each with specific tasks set out by God. Dispensationalists generally agree that during the current "dispensation" Christians are to prepare for the Second Coming (and a 1,000-year period during which Christ will bring perfect peace and justice) through massive attempts at evangelization.

4 See Donald Dayton, *Theological Roots of Pentecostalism* (Metuchen, NJ: Scarecrow Press, 1987), for a complete definition of Pentecostalism.

5 The samples for this study were drawn from lists of churches in each country. Lists of evangelical chruches were provided by the Instituto Misionologico de las Americas (IMDELA) in Costa Rica and the Servicio Evangelizador para America Latina (SEPAL) in Gueatemala. Names and locations of churches were randomly chosen from specific sampling categories of different denominations within the Pentecostal and mainline Protestant typology. Since lists of members were unavailable for most churches, we asked permission to station interviewrs outside of churches. Interviews were conducted with participants as they departed church services, or arrangements were made for subsequent interview appointments. The random sample for religiously nonaffiliated individuals was obtained through screening questions on door-to-door interviews conducted in the same neighborhoods as other interviews.

6 Catholics (79 females and 81 males), Pentecostals (187 females and 177 males), mainstream Protestants (92 females and 68 males), sect members (31 females and 37 males), and the religiously nonaffiliated (22 females and 34 males)

7 Interview conducted with Juan, 6/10/96, Caracas, Venezuela.

8 Interview conducted with Marcos, 6/5/96, Caracas, Venezuela.

9 Interview conducted with Julieta, 6/7/96, Caracas, Venezuela.

10 Interview conducted with Flor, 6/10/96, Caracas, Venezuela.

11 Interview conducted with Marcos, 6/10/96, Caracas, Venezuela.

12 Interview conducted with Guadalupe, 6/7/96, Caracas, Venezuela.

13 Interview conducted with Ramiro, 5/30/96, Caracas, Venezuela.

14 Interview conducted with Julietar, 5/30/96, Caracas, Venezuela.

REFERENCES

Alvarez, Sonia E. 1990. "Women's Participation in the Brazilian 'People's Church': A Critical Appraisal." *Feminist Studies*, 16 (2): 381-409.

Brusco, Elizabeth. 1993. "The Reformation of Machismo: Asceticism and Masculinity among Colombian Evangelicals." In Virginia Garrard-Burnett and David Stoll, eds. *Rethinking Protestantism in Latin America*. Philadelphia: Temple University Press.

Burdick, John. 1993. *Looking for God in Brazil: The Progressive Catholic Church in Urban Brazil's Religious Arena*. Berkeley: University of California Press.

Butler Flora, Cornilia. 1976. *Pentecostalism in Colombia: Baptism by Fire and Spirit*. London: Associated University Press.

———. 1975. "Pentecostal Women in Colombia: Religious Change and the Status of Working Class Women." *Journal of Interamerican Studies and World Affairs*, 17 (4): 411-25.

Deiros, Pablo. 1992. "Protestant Fundamentalism in Latin America." In Martin E. Marty and R. Scott Appleby, eds. *Fundamentalisms Observed*. Chicago: Chicago University Press, 149-54.

Drogus, Carol Ann. 1997. "Private Power or Public Power: Pentecostalism, Base Communities, and Gender." In Edward L. Cleary and Hannah W. Stewart-Gambino, eds. *Power, Politics, and Pentecostals in Latin America*. Boulder, CO:Westview Press, 55-75.

———. 1994. "Religious Change and Woman's Status in Latin America: A Comparison of Catholic Base Communities and Pentecostal Churches." *Working Paper #205*, Kellogg Institute, University of Notre Dame.

Gill, Lesley. 1990. "'Like a Veil to Cover Them': Women and the Pentecostal Movement in La Paz," *American Ethnologist*, 17 (November).

Jelen, Ted. 1991. *The Political Mobilization of Religious Beliefs*. New York: Praeger.

Maldonado, Jorge E. 1993. "Building Fundamentalism from the Family in Latin America." In Martin E. Marty and R. Scott Appleby, eds. *Fundamentalisms and Society: Reclaiming the Sciences, the Family, and Education*. Chicago: University of Chicago Press, 214-39.

Mariz, Cecília Loreto, and Dores Campos Machado. 1997. "Pentecostalism and Women in Brazil." In Edward L. Cleary and Hannah W. Stewart-Gambino, eds. *Power, Politics, and Pentecostals in Latin America*. Boulder, CO: Westview Press, 41-55.

Mariz, Cecília. 1992. "Religion and Poverty in Brazil: A comparison of Catholic and Pentecostal Communities." *Sociological Analysis*, 53: 563-70.

Martin, David. 1990. *Tongues of Fire: The Explosion of Protestantism in Latin America*. Oxford: Basil Blackwell.

Smilde, David A. 1994. "Gender Relations and Social Change in Latin American Evangelicalism." In Daniel R. Miller, ed. *Coming of Age: Protestantism in Contemporary Latin America*. New York: University Press of America, 39-65.

"The Diminishing Divide. . .American Churches, American Politics," From the Pew Research Center for the People and the Press, June 25, 1996. http://www.people–press.org/relgrpt.htm.

Van den Eykel, Myrna. 1986. "A Comparative Study of the Political and Social Activism of New Religious Groups in Colombia." Ph.D. Dissertation, George Washington University.

NINE

PENTECOSTALISM AND POLITICAL AWAKENING IN PINOCHET'S CHILE AND BEYOND

Frans Kamsteeg

Evangelical Protestantism is growing rapidly in Latin America today. Since the late 1980s both public and scholarly attention has been paid to the phenomenon. The general picture we get from scientists, Catholic observers, and the media is that the religious world of Latin America is changing and that traditional Catholic believers are transgressing age-old boundaries to begin shopping in a religious market where Pentecostal pastors are doing particularly good business. The Catholic Church is increasingly worried about Pentecostal church growth, and its bishops are publicly warning against the "advance of the sects."

Many scholarly works suggest that the vast majority of these Pentecostal churches are politically conservative and even support military regimes. This is also a widely shared belief by the general public throughout the world. The activity of a significant group of Chilean Pentecostal leaders in support of the military regime of General Pinochet has also established the image of Pentecostals as supporters of military rule. Yet in this contribution I will argue that a closer reading of Chile's recent history gives reason to rethink the supposedly conservative attitude and political behavior of Pentecostals. Things are not always as simple as they are often portrayed.

RELIGION IN THE RECENT HISTORY OF CHILE

In the early 1990s Chile's rapidly developing economy and the political redemocratization process became matters of public discussion, both nationally and internationally. The electoral defeat of the military, the return of democracy, and the legacy of thorough societal changes that the military left behind is still a puzzling question for Chileans, as well as for observers from the social sciences. Chile's changing religious panorama attracts much less attention, however, despite the fact that until a few years ago the social role of the Catholic Church received careful observation because of its active struggle for the return of democracy (see e.g. Correa and Viera-Gallo n.d.; Lowden 1993; Smith 1986: 163-166). The Church's *Vicaría de la Solidaridad* (Vicariate of Solidarity) was accepted as one of the strongest institutions—morally and politically—in the resistance to the Pinochet regime. Many Catholic grassroots communities and nongovernmental organizations (NGOs) could work only because they operated under the patronage of the Catholic Church. Together they are commonly regarded by most European relief agencies as the most important social actors in the organization of the struggle for democracy (see e.g. Hojman 1993). Although the Catholic Church continues to be the biggest religious organization in Chile, as in all Latin American countries, its social and political role has clearly diminished since the transition to democracy. The present Archbishop of Santiago is now an outspoken conservative and defender of the Vatican ethical policies. To the Chilean Bishops' Conference (CECH), the social doctrine of the Church is now mainly limited to the defense of family values and public morality.

While the attention paid to Catholicism is on the decline, the mass media and the Catholic hierarchy are showing increasing interest in its Protestant counterpart. In 1991, a research bureau of a politically conservative tendency, the *Centro de Estudios Publicos* (CEP), dedicated a substantial part of its magazine to the growth of the *evangélicos*, as Evangelical Protestants are commonly labeled (Fontaine 1991). The biggest Chilean newspaper, the conservative *El Mercurio*, subsequently published some lengthy articles on the results of the CEP survey. In 1992, the Chilean bishops' conference also paid extensive attention to the "problem of the sects" (Urrea 1992: 5, 9; see also CECH 1989). After the latest census (1992) there was public commotion when it appeared that about 13.2 percent of Chileans belonged to Protestant churches, which means that Chile is next to Brazil and Guatemala among the countries with the highest percentage of Protestants in Latin America (see e.g. Stoll 1990: 333-338). In most literature on Chile, however, the presence of so many Protestants (80 to 90 percent are Pentecostals) has gone almost unnoticed, except in some publications by local specialists (Sepúlveda 1987; Lagos 1988; Canales et al. 1991). Although ordinary Chileans are well aware of their presence, since Pentecostals come out regularly for evangelistic purposes and their social practice clearly deviates from the general cultural pattern, outsiders have very little understanding of what is really going on within these churches. During the past twenty-five years Pentecostals started to manifest themselves publicly, but they also—quite unexpectedly—developed divergent polit-ical tendencies, which I believe to be a manifestation of the growing complexity and ambiguity of Latin American religion today.

This public appearance of Pentecostalism during the years of military rule has revealed two previously "hidden" tendencies in Pentecostalism. One group of Chile's Protestants saw the regime as a vehicle to help them achieve public recognition in exchange for their unconditional support for the military. For an opposing group, the Pinochet regime stimulated the development of an incipient sense of social commitment and political consciousness. The struggle between these two tendencies in Chilean Pentecostalism—the "official," represented since 1975 by the *Consejo de Pastores* (Council of Pastors), and the "prophetic," from 1985 onward united in the *Confraternidad Cristiana de Iglesias* (CCI, Fraternity of Christian Churches)—has found its clearest expression in political issues, but is a result of the contradictions over social issues that exist within Pentecostalism all over Latin America. It is a dispute over the question of how Pentecostals are to deal with society, authority, and politics. The multiple ways of dealing with these very issues makes for much of the changing relation between religion and society in Latin America today, to which I will return at the end of this contribution. Before addressing the political pluralization process of Chilean Pentecostalism, I will give a short overview of its history and growth since 1909.

THE RISE OF PENTECOSTALISM IN CHILE

During the ninteenth century, several Protestant churches were estab-lished in Chile, such as the Anglicans (1836), Lutherans (1846), Presbyterians (1872) and Methodists (1877). They served the religious inter-ests of the mostly European immigrant community. The Baptists (1908) and the *Alianza Cristiana y Misionera* (Christian Missionary Alliance, 1897) arrived with more missionary spirit. All these churches became inserted in the urban middle-class sectors, but gained few adherents. Most of these churches initially expressed political liberalism, later moving to adopt more radical or even socialist ideologies. Their impact on the working-class sectors of the Chilean population was small. It was Pentecostalism that managed to gain adherence among the Chilean working class.

Usually, the start of Chilean Pentecostalism is put at 1909, when a spiritual revival took place within the Methodist Church. Since the movement did not start as the result of a foreign missionary initiative, it is considered an indigenous, national Pentecostalism. The conflict producing the division within the Methodist Church is commonly inter-preted as a cultural one, focusing on the prominence of experience and

on local leadership (Sepúlveda n.d.: 7; for detailed historical accounts
see also Vergara 1961 and Kessler 1967). It was a clash between the
rational Methodist discourse and ritual and the experiential religiosity
of the lower-middle-class Chileans who had slowly started to dominate
church membership. The conflict caused considerable upheaval in the
world of Chilean Protestantism, and was closely followed by the local
press (see Corporación IEP 1977). Doctrinal differences played a minor
role in the conflict, the real shift in orientation being that religious experience now became a part of the Protestant churches; they became sensitive to what Sepúlveda called "working-class culture."

After the events of 1909, the movement spread across Chile, though
it was concentrated primarily in the zone between Santiago and Southern
Concepción. It dramatically changed the map of Chilean Protestantism,
as Pentecostals soon outnumbered all other Protestant churches.
Through an endless series of schisms the movement gave birth to more
than two thousand different churches. Between 1930 and 1960, the first
period of rapid growth, membership in the Pentecostal churches grew
every decade (Sepúlveda n.d; Lalive d'Epinay 1969; Barrett 1982), reaching more than 400,000 followers by the early 1960s (5.6% of the population, source: *Censo Nacional de la Población*). Several characteristics
of Pentecostalism contributed to this growth. Here I name just three: the
emphasis on spiritualism, lay ministries, and tithing. Spiritual healing
proved very attractive to people, as did the broad availability of organizational offices to ordinary members. Theologically educated pastors
were no longer needed, as they were in the historical Protestant churches.
Neither did the Pentecostal churches depend on foreign money like most
of their Protestant predecessors; through tithing, churches could maintain themselves and their pastors. Moreover, the Pentecostal church
communities became famous for providing aid to their poor members.

Willems (1969) argues that it was the possibility for ordinary believers to become actively involved in church life and the internally democratic character of Pentecostal churches that were responsible for their
appeal. At the same time, Lalive d'Epinay (1969) maintains that much
of the old patriarchal relationship between landowner and peasant is
still reflected in the pastor–believer relation in Pentecostal churches. He
thinks that it is this continuity that makes for much of Pentecostalism's
attraction. Both Willems and Lalive d'Epinay consider that most
Pentecostals came from the stream of migrants that accompanied the
urbanization process of the twentieth century. Both authors also make
use of the Durkheimean concept of *anomie* (lack of purpose) to indicate
the position of moral and ethical insecurity migrants had to cope with in

their new, postmigration life in the big cities. They see Pentecostalism as an appropriate answer to this state of spiritual abandonment. For Willems, Pentecostal growth expresses the coming of modernity and democracy, while for Lalive d'Epinay it is the continuation of a social pattern of the past, and thus more a check on modernization and democratization than a push in that direction. Consequently, Lalive d'Epinay holds that Pentecostalism, because of its emphasis on personal salvation, has developed very weak social ethics and a rather rudimentary democratic consciousness. A brief examination of some of Pentecostalism's central ideas can help demonstrate this social ambivalence.

For several reasons, Chilean Pentecostals developed a conflictive relationship with the society around them. Because of the movement's lower-class and overtly anti-Catholic character, Pentecostals were generally looked upon with a certain disdain and hostility by the outside world. Pentecostals themselves tended (and still tend) to keep aloof from what they call "the world," which is characterized as sinful and potentially contaminating. For Pentecostals, "the world" is everything that goes against God's will. They infer from the Bible that the world we live in is an evil place. This "world" is opposed to the sacred life of the spiritual community. The withdrawal from this "world" is very often interpreted as a need to withdraw from the society in which they live. This has deeply influenced Pentecostals' social behavior, in the sense that it means avoiding contact with people working in groups and organizations oriented toward social or political demands for change. Pentecostals may live their life among their neighbors and do the same jobs as their colleagues, but they usually try to isolate themselves from their environment and search for refuge in the self-sustaining, sacred community of believers.

This tendency toward social isolation is still a position held by many Pentecostals. In this paper I argue that there are nevertheless some interesting trends within Chilean Pentecostalism. These changes are closely related to the social and political events of the 1960s, and became more visible after the political turnover of September 1973. The different reactions Pentecostals exhibited toward the military coup revealed the presence of these divergent attitudes within the Chilean Pentecostal community.

PENTECOSTALISM VERSUS PARTICIPATORY DEMOCRACY: CONFLICTING TENDENCIES

The period between 1964 and 1973 was one of rapid social change in Chile. The attempt at societal transformation that started under the government of Christian-Democrat Eduardo Frei received an even stronger impetus under the Socialist president Salvador Allende. During these nine years the government tried to incorporate the working-class masses into the political process. It was a period that witnessed attempts to stimulate participation and democratization at all levels, with the biggest impact on peasants and people from the urban working-class neighborhoods. Within a short time, a great variety of organizations had sprung up to help integrate lower-class Chileans into the process of participatory democratization (see Razeto et al. 1990). This is not the place to discuss the results of this process; I only want to emphasize that the effort to promote participation was directed at the same group of Chileans that had always been the targets of Pentecostal conversion efforts. Trade unions, the classic form of working-class organization, hardly interfered with Pentecostal conversion politics, because they were oriented to the factory, not to the neighborhood. The new social organizations, however, sought their supporters in the same spatial territory as did the Pentecostals. This could not but create a conflict, since participation in both neighborhood organizations and Pentecostal churches was very time consuming, and Pentecostalism's reaction to such worldly activity had always been very negative.

During the Frei government, Pentecostals slowly became involved in a wide range of social organizations (including trade unions, especially in the Concepción region). Most of them, however, refrained from such participation. When they did, it was often because they were explicitly asked to do so by groups in need of the specific qualities that Pentecostals were presumed to possess, such as speaking in public, leading small groups of people, impartiality, etc. Nevertheless, most Pentecostals interpreted the increasing possibilities for democratic participation as threatening to their 'microcosm' (Sepúlveda 1988: 241); mainstream Pentecostal "theology" condemned any type of relationship with this other world. During those years, the growth of Pentecostalism diminished. While it is not clear if this stagnation actually occurred because lower-class Pentecostals started to prefer the newly formed sociopolitical neighborhood organizations over religious solutions, the statistics do suggest that democratization and Pentecostal growth were not mutually supportive. No exact figures exist, but Chilean insiders maintain that the downward trend stopped at the moment of the military coup, thus confirming Pentecostalism's problematic relationship with democracy.

While Chilean Pentecostalism did not benefit overall from the democratization boom under Frei and Allende—at least not numerically—the sociopolitical changes did cause a small sector within Chile's indigenous Pentecostal community to open itself up to the process that was going on around them. The pioneer churches were the *Misión Iglesia Pentecostal*

(Pentecostal Mission Church, 1952), the *Iglesia Pentecostal de Chile* (Pentecostal Church of Chile, 1947) and the *Misión Wesleyana Nacional* (National Wesleyan Mission, 1926). In these churches, people started to search for reconciliation between the exigencies of Pentecostal faith and the challenge to take an active role in society. The 1960 and 1965 earthquakes provided good occasions to bring their awakening social responsibility into practice when they were asked to distribute relief products sent by international ecumenical agencies (particularly by the World Council of Churches, WCC). Some of the community's leaders even began to dream of an organized Protestant participation in politics. It was also in 1961 that two of the churches from within this strand of Pentecostalism (the already mentioned *Misión Iglesia Pentecostal* and *Iglesia Pentecostal de Chile*) became members of the ecumenical WCC. In the following section, we turn to this minority of Chile's Pentecostals.

CHALLENGING CLASSIC PENTECOSTALISM: THE CONFRATERNIDAD CRISTIANA DE IGLESIAS

Although Protestants joined forces to participate in the ecumenical *Te Deum* (the traditionally Catholic Thanksgiving service on Independence Day) during the Allende government, Protestant interchurch organization remained weak. This began to change following the military coup of 1973. The emergence of the *Consejo de Pastores* (1975) in support of the military (see next section) provoked a Protestant counteraction. The first attempt at organization was the *Asociación de las Iglesias Evangélicas de Chile* (AIECH, Association of Evangelical Churches in Chile), which released several public statements on "the evangelical duty to help the poor," and fought the *Consejo de Pastores'* claim of representing Chile's total Protestant population. However, it never condemned the regime publicly. During the 1980s this critical task became the hallmark of the *Confraternidad Cristiana de Iglesias* (CCI). From 1982 onwards, the CCI was "in formation," but the turbulent years of protest and the consequent repression between 1982 and 1984 postponed its official foundation. It was not until 1985 that the CCI became legally established by its participating churches, among which were several smaller Pentecostal denominations, including the leading *Misión Iglesia Pentecostal*. This new council of churches received strong international backing by the WCC, European churches, and Christian development agencies, which also supplied a portion of its funding. It was morally supported by the CLAI (*Consejo Latinoamericano de Iglesias*), an ecumenical council of Latin American churches, also established in 1985 and strongly related to and modeled on the WCC. In the

CLAI, Chilean presence was clear, and again leaders of the *Misión Iglesia Pentecostal* were among its participants.

Although the rise of the CCI is closely related to the period of military dictatorship, the CCI saw itself as a logical product of the socially turbulent years between 1964 and 1973 when social participation and ecumenism became increasingly normal, even for Pentecostal Protestant church members. The CCI considered itself the prophetic voice of Protestantism in Chile, charged with denouncing social and political abuses according to the tradition of the Old Testament prophets (Sepúlveda n.d., Ossa 1992). The military regime became the principal target of its activity.

In the first public statement by the CCI (April 1984, in the middle of a raging economic crisis and violent protests in working-class neighborhoods) it described its mission as one of, "both announcement of God's Word, and profound concern for all problems affecting the quality of human life, no matter if it concerns individuals or groups of people" (Ossa 1992: 19). In the same document, the unjust character of the economic system and its impact on the poor were denounced. Near the end of the declaration, the CCI made several demands of the military, such as upholding the right of dissent (ibid.: 20). After this first publication, several other statements were issued, especially when individual priests fell victim to oppression by the regime.

In an open letter (dated 29 August 1986) to Pinochet (CCI 1987: 27), which was personally delivered to the presidential palace by CCI leaders following a public lecture and church service, the organization gave testimony to the situation of the poor among whom they claimed their churches were working. The letter spoke of hunger, unemployment, undernourishment, disease, a deficient school system, and the social diseases springing from them, such as prostitution, drug addiction, delinquency, and suicide. Contrary to what is commonly proclaimed in Pentecostal public preaching, the blame for all this misery was put not on mankind and its "wicked nature," but on the State (i.e., the military). This situation was said to be "against God's will." "Because of this deplorable situation, people are desperately seeking relief, which has been refused to them by all the regular channels," the letter continues, "and finally they turn to the churches, hoping to find solutions that these churches are not destined to provide, and the State is denying them."

The church leaders continued to denounce the State's determination to prohibit to its citizens efforts to defend their rights, and they condemned the imposition of laws that "consider defenders of communal rights to be delinquents." In this particular instance, they made reference to the general protests of 1983-84 and to the Old Testament prophet, Isaiah, who exclaimed, "Woe to those who decree iniquitous decrees, and the writers who keep writing oppression" (Isaiah 10: 1). They warned that if no attention were paid to these warnings, they foresaw a spiral of violence and would hold the government responsible for the consequent bloodshed. For the subscribers to the letter the only real solution, and the only opportunity for the government "to avoid God's wrath," was:

> Opening the doors to full civil participation in the search for a consensus over the reconstruction of a land of brothers that for the moment has stopped being such a land. In the name of God, giver and supporter of life, we proclaim the urgent necessity to reestablish a participatory, pluralist, and democratic society, based on respect for human rights. (CCI 1987: 4)

The strongly worded letter was written after a month of intensive labor in the participating Protestant churches, during what was called, "the campaign of prayer for peace and reconciliation in Chile." The letter gives a clear view of how the CCI saw its role in Chilean society during the Pinochet years. CCI representatives explicitly understood themselves as prophets calling for biblical justice for humankind. Humankind was considered to comprise both the individual human being and the people as a group, a community (see also Seibert 1989: 56).

Besides these clearly political public statements, the CCI also participated in many smaller events—often in working-class neighborhoods—such as the funerals of victims of police violence, during which public letters of condemnation were spread to the media. Public statements were also made at the occasion of several murders in which police officers had been involved. In 1985, when the Chilean economy started to recover slowly from the crisis that began in 1982, a severe earthquake provoked the constitution of an Interchurch Emergency Committee. This committee, totally directed by CCI members, coordinated the WCC-sponsored relief efforts. By then, people had begun to lose interest in the protests that had defied the regime during the preceding years. Human rights' violations became less noticeable and for a while the effects of the earthquake demanded most of their attention.

The public statements and performances by the CCI and its representatives provoked strong reactions from its adversaries, especially the military. At first, the news media ignored its existence, but gradually the CCI became the target of defamation (by, for example, the major, pro-Pinochet newspaper El Mercurio) and even intimidation. The CCI office was searched and its employees were threatened.

THE CONSEJO DE PASTORES AND PINOCHET: TRADITION AND POWER

Above I briefly explained the classic position of Pentecostalism toward society and the world in general. Rejection of social involvement is usually combined with a submissive attitude toward public authorities. This does not necessarily lead to a politically conservative position: Tennekes (1985) has convincingly demonstrated that Pentecostals hardly deviate from their fellow working-class people when it comes to elections. Yet it does indicate that Pentecostals tend to be loyal to whichever government is in power. They supported Allende in defiance of their churches' leaders, but in 1973 most Pentecostals also welcomed the military coup, as did the vast majority of churches, including the Catholic Church and the non-Pentecostal Protestants. This does not mean, however, that they became supporters of Pinochet. Like most Chileans who were initially supporters of the coup, Pentecostals soon realized that it also brought many undesired consequences (Lagos 1988: 128).

To the leadership of the biggest Pentecostal church—the *Iglesia Metodista Pentecostal* (IMP, Pentecostal Methodist Church)—Pinochet was God's response to their prayers, as they made clear in several public statements made soon after the coup. They announced that "the coup by the military forces was, within the historical process of our country, the answer of God to the prayer of all believers who see Marxism as the Satanic force of darkness *par excellence*." The IMP was at that moment finishing the construction of its main temple and its leader, Bishop Javier Vásquez, invited General Pinochet to open the new building (Lagos: 154-55). Pinochet accepted the invitation, under the condition that Chile's *evangélicos* express their support for his regime. In December 1974, this last condition was met during a large meeting at the presidential Diego Portales building in Santiago, held in the presence of thirty-two, predominantly Pentecostal pastors (ibid.: 155-57). These pastors gave their support to Pinochet in the name of all Chilean Protestant churches, thus suggesting ample Protestant support for the military. This hegemonic attitude also characterized the *Consejo de Pastores*, which was constituted after this event, in 1975, by the same participating pro-Pinochet churches. The *Consejo de Pastores* (an assembly of individual pastors, not of churches) developed close relations with the regime and obtained several privileges for its members, such as free medical treatment for its pastors. It even held office within the presidential headquarters at Diego Portales. Their main public manifestation was the yearly *Te Deum*, which I will consider in more detail below.

One may wonder why the relation between this branch of Pentecostalism and the military authorities became so close, especially as most of the churches that joined the *Consejo de Pastores* had until then kept firmly to the classic isolationist Pentecostal tradition, limiting their public appearances to their weekly conversion parades and occasional evangelistic campaigns. Although the changes during the 1960s and early 1970s had made some impact on church people, church leaders rarely spoke out publicly on matters other than church affairs. How then can the hardly restrained enthusiasm of the Pentecostal clergy for Pinochet's government be explained? The now popular books by Stoll (1990) and Martin (1990) point to a widespread political conservatism among Latin American Protestants supposedly caused by United States influence, but their examples deal primarily with Central American churches that are often closely tied to their North American counterparts. Most Chilean churches, and certainly those pertaining to the *Consejo de Pastores* were only nationally organized. United States conspiracy theories on the spread of Protestantism in Latin America thus have little explanatory value in this case; we have to search for other reasons.

Pentecostalism has a long history of discrimination in Catholic Chile. Because they regard their own spiritual position as far superior to that of the Catholic Church, the Pentecostal churches have always attacked the monopolistic position of the latter. The crisis in the relationship between the Catholic Church and the military regime after the coup seemed to offer possibilities for breaking the Catholic monopoly on religious power. The IMP's invitation to Pinochet to join the first Protestant *Te Deum* in the "Evangelical cathedral" (note the appropriation of the symbol of power that the word "cathedral" represents) can therefore be interpreted as a move in a religious power struggle. Fear of the withdrawal of the existing juridical status of the churches by the government prompted the churches to join the *Consejo de Pastores* group. It was even hoped that the regime would consider changing the discriminatory legal position of the Protestant churches. The motive for Pinochet to consider the invitation was most probably the permanent conflict between the regime and the Catholic Church. In a society where religion was a major force, the regime obviously wanted as much religious legitimization as possible. Since the Catholic Church refused to give this, the regime turned to its opponents, the Pentecostals, since "the enemy of your enemy is your friend."

Pentecostal leaders also strongly rejected the Socialist government of Allende and its extended efforts at social mobilization. They saw the "social disorder," which had already started under the Frei government, as threatening the growth of their churches. It was thought that such growth, unhampered by competitive mobilizing efforts, would be best secured under the Pinochet regime. When the Pentecostal churches began to grow again after 1973, this was interpreted as proof of God's approval of the regime. As a leading progressive Pentecostal author maintains, the *Consejo de Pastores* embodied Chile's "anti-Communist, anti-ecumenist and anti-Catholic Pentecostal" tendency (Sepúlveda n.d.: 20, 21).

The main demonstration of the *Consejo de Pastores'* support for Pinochet was the *Te Deum*, celebrated from 1975 onward. This Thanksgiving service, officially held to commemorate Independence Day (September 18), always took place in the large (IMP) Evangelical cathedral. Pinochet, himself a devout Catholic, attended this service, at which the regime's blessings for Chile were counted and "God's protection for the country's benefactor" was implored, until 1989. These meetings were broadcast nationwide, year after year, confirming the image that Pentecostalism was a strong pillar of Pinochet's regime.

Pastor Francisco Anabalón, in his sermon at the first *Te Deum*—celebrated on September 7, 1975, on the eve of the second anniversary of the coup—thanked God for the "firm decision of our government to lead our nation into prosperity through the path of dignity." He also said that "we have heard our governors repeating in their declarations their respect for human rights, which the facts confirm, and their intent to take care of the well-being of all Chileans, especially those who are most in need." Anabalón further asked God's blessing for "His servant Augusto, Head of State and his honorable junta." He concluded by making a comparison between the past and the present, quoting the Apostle Paul (II Corinthians 5: 17): "Therefore, if any one is in Christ, he is a new creation; the old has passed away, behold, the new has come" (Anonymous 1978: doc. 3).

Similar allusions to the installation and support of Pinochet's regime as a sign of God's blessing were heard in all subsequent *Te Deum*s. During the 1989 version, three months before the presidential election he was to lose, General Pinochet was present for the last time. The IMP Bishop Vasquez welcomed him in the name of "the" Protestant church of Chile. Vasquez, purporting to speak for about 4.5 million *evangélicos*, repeated in a few words the principal reason for gratitude toward Pinochet: "[B]efore, we Pentecostals were not taken into consideration. . . . You, Don Augusto, have been the only President who has visited us from 1974 on." At the meeting both high authorities within the armed forces and many politicians were present, among them Pinochet's hand-picked presidential candidate Hernán Büchi and the right-wing UDI (*Unión Democrática Independiente*) party leader Jaime Guzmán. During the service, the themes of freedom, peace, and reconciliation were constantly emphasized, particularly during the sermon by Anabalón, who was still the president of the *Consejo de Pastores*. "The freedom Pinochet brought to Chile must continue to reign, and Chile's Pentecostals will work to secure this," he said. He also argued that violence had ended and peace prevailed and that Pentecostals were willing to contribute to the maintenance of this situation. The event was a last demonstration of loyalty to Pinochet and a gesture of support to his intended successor.

In 1990, a year after the presidential election, no Evangelical *Te Deum* was held, but in 1991 and 1992 the tradition was restored. On both occasions, the democratically elected President Aylwin (a Christian Democrat) was present at the service, which was still organized by the *Consejo de Pastores*. In 1992, the CCI was invited to take part in the preparation of the event for the first time. It accepted hesitantly and only "to show its good will, not to legitimate all of what had happened and been said at the foregoing *Te Deum*s," as a former CCI president confessed. This time the event was not broadcast live on television, though the President came with a representative group of politicians from both the parties in power and the conservative opposition. The liturgy of the service assigned a small role to CCI representatives, but the main part, including the sermon, was carried out by the very *Consejo de Pastores* leaders who had been showing their warm enthusiasm for Pinochet during the years before. The same Anabalón thanked God in his sermon for the fact that "division and contradiction had been overcome in the country." The general theme of his speech was reconciliation and the battle against delinquency. The concept of "reconciliation," which Aylwin's transitory government had proclaimed as the principal goal for Chile, was hard for the CCI people to digest, as they had already had to accept a great many conditions for participation in the ceremony. Several *Consejo de Pastores* leaders had declared that they would not take back anything that had been said on earlier occasions in support of the dictatorship. The fact that Romans 13 (concerning the Christian duty to obey secular governments) was also read at this occasion only served to further annoy the CCI people.

I conclude that during the Pinochet regime traditional Chilean Pentecostals became involved in politics, but this involvement acted as a source of legitimization of the regime. *The Consejo de Pastores* churches were seduced to lend themselves to the government's purposes because it meant that they were treated as conversation partners. They also hoped to gain some material benefits, which they did, and to induce the regime to improve the feeble juridical situation of the Protestant churches.

These hopes were gradually frustrated when no initiatives were taken by the regime to fulfill the promises it had made, but the yearly ceremonies of adhesion in the *Te Deum* did not stop. Ordinary church members, however, took little part in the *Consejo de Pastores'* activities, and since no clear results were achieved, other than the *Te Deum* itself, Pentecostals never became active Pinochet supporters. What was presented as the shared opinion of many churches and their members was in fact no more than the carefully designed propaganda of a few IMP leaders. These leaders hoped for power, privilege, and prestige for their churches, but within the IMP itself, with its strict hierarchical organization, the gap between the ordinary church members and their leaders remained large.

CONCLUSIONS:
THE POST-PINOCHET PERIOD AND ITS PERSPECTIVES

What can be concluded about the Pentecostal contribution to Chilean politics? It can be maintained that the military regime of Pinochet caused an acceleration in the the sociopolitical awakening of Pentecostals. Traditionally, Pentecostals came out of their religious community only for conversionist purposes. Relations with the outside world, including politics, were considered profane and therefore forbidden. The *Consejo de Pastores* churches, though in name defenders of this tradition, radically broke with it when they loudly welcomed the overthrow of the Allende government and publicly started talks with the military authorities. The subsequent declarations of support to Pinochet, expressed mainly during the *Te Deum*s, reinforced the (until then) almost unnoticed politically conservative force of Pentecostalism.

Obviously, those Pentecostals who resisted the new regime had to be much more careful. The clearly anti-Pinochet standpoint, expressed most visibly by the CCI, was rooted in an earlier break with the isolationist tradition of Pentecostalism. The sociopolitical changes Chile experienced during the Frei and Allende governments strongly influenced these churches, and this process of social (and political) consciousness-raising was only accelerated by the events after September 1973. The churches united under the CCI viewed society as a place in which they had a role to play. That role was not limited to evangelism, but also required that they make a contribution to the struggle for greater equality in social, economic, and political relations.

Yet ordinary Pentecostal church members generally did not keep pace with their leaders in this process. This holds equally for the anti- and the pro-Pinochet wings of Chilean Pentecostalism. Followers and opponents of Pinochet could be found on both sides, but fear of repercussions often made people opt for keeping silent. Anti-Pinochet people within the IMP had to add to the normal fear of repression the verdict of their religious leaders. In the CCI churches it was the other way around. Sometimes pastors got involved in activities that caused their churches to be assaulted by the police, thus placing their followers in a situation that they themselves would never have chosen.

Since practically all publicly known political statements by Pentecostals are colored by the historical context of military rule, it can be asked whether the tendencies appearing during the military regime were more than merely circumstantial. In other words, what will happen with Chile's Pentecostal community now that the military regime has gone? If we look at Chile today we see a process of political pluralization in which the extreme positions from the recent past have lost most of their attraction. This is a tendency we can also witness in Brazil and Argentina. At the same time we see Pentecostal Protestants gradually and often hesitatingly entering the political arena. Fujimori's Peru is the most significant case in point, but a similar Pentecostal involvement in politics is becoming visible in Brazil (see e.g. Ireland 1991, 1993).

Among Chilean Pentecostals there is presently little political organization. The behavior of the formerly politically active CCI is quite moderate; actually the CCI oscillates between overt crisis and weak statements. The *Consejo de Pastores* continues to be an organizational stronghold, even in the new democratic situation where it does not seem to be hindered by its past adherence to the military regime. The *Consejo de Pastores* dominates the *Comité de Coordinación Evangélica* (Evangelical Coordination Committee), which was formed under the stimulus of the Aylwin government. In this organization the *Consejo de Pastores* and the CCI are represented, together with the Baptists, Anglicans, and Methodists. Even churches that have never shown interest in any type of interchurch organization, like the *Iglesia Evangélica Pentecostal* (Evangelical Pentecostal Church), the second biggest Pentecostal church, are now considering participation. A political agreement with the government over the future juridical position of the Protestant churches is now in preparation.

More interesting than what is happening at the level of church organizations are the political preferences of individual Protestant believers. The already-mentioned CEP survey (Fontaine 1991: 102-112) shows that today Chilean *evangélicos* have clearly democratic attitudes and little more sympathy for military rule than the average Chilean. What demands our attention most, however, is their strong inclination for independent political candidates. This may explain why Protestants, especially Pentecostals, are participating so little in neighborhood organizations, which are generally associated with political games and struggles of interest between the established parties. Since at the local, neighborhood level these old political parties have been losing influence, independent candidates may be supported by Pentecostals. This already happened in some neighborhoods during the municipal elections in 1992, when several Pentecostal leaders even ran for seats. If this tendency continues, the stereotypically conservative, otherworldly Pentecostal may gradually become a thing of the past. It is, however, likely that this Pentecostal will do so on the basis of his own belief that the political struggle between good and evil is a reflection of what he generally views as "the final battle between God and the Devil."

Although it is hard to predict, it is indeed quite possible that in Chile there is such a long-term evolution in Pentecostalism toward socioreligious and political transformation, as the Chilean sociologist Manuel Ossa maintains (1991). According to him, as many as 20 percent of Chilean Pentecostals were already involved in ecumenical and sociopolitical activities during the past twenty years (ibid.: 34), a figure he believes is confirmed by the results of several quantitative surveys (Concepción 1988; SUR 1990; Vidal 1986). While my fieldwork experience—which has some overlap with Ossa's—does not provide ground to confirm that this involvement ever became very strong, it clearly contradicts Protestant political evasiveness (Kamsteeg 1998). Although *evangélicos*, more than any other group in Chilean society, think that their personal development depends more on the quality of their faith in God than on communal efforts or state intervention (Fontaine 1991: 115), this does not mean that their political consciousness is lower than the average. It is their strong moral posture that makes them averse to the performance of political parties. New parties advancing clear moral-political issues might well be able to capture a considerable part of the Pentecostal electorate.

I have argued that the stereotypical view of Pentecostals as otherworldly and politically innocent people should be reconsidered. The struggle between pro- and anti-Pinochet groups during the period of military rule was used to support this point. The outcome of this struggle is still undecided, but this particular part of Chilean history undoubtedly marks the beginning of a process in which it will become less unusual for Pentecostals to participate in the realm of politics. However, it should be emphasized that this will happen at a slower rate than predicted by the former leaders of the CCI and other ecumenical organizations (Ossa 1991). Ordinary *evangélicos* often tend to go slower and behave more independently than their leaders might wish.

REFERENCES

Anonymous. 1978. *La libertad religiosa en Chile, los evangélicos y el gobierno militar, tomo 3 anexos.* Santiago: Vicaría de la Solidaridad/UNELAM.

Anonymous. 1988. *Concepción 88. Una encuesta regional (resultados preliminarias).* Santiago: Presor, Inprode, Flacso, Cenpros.

Barrett, David B., ed. 1982. *World Christian Encyclopedia.* Nairobi: Oxford University Press, 226-230.

Canales, Manuel, Samuel Palma, and Hugo Villela. 1991. *En tierra extrana II. Para una sociología de la religiosidad popular protestante.* Santiago: SEPADE.

CCI (Confraternidad Cristiana de Iglesias). 1987. Carta abierta al general Pinochet, 29 August 1986. *Evangelio y Sociedad,* 4 (appendix).

CECh (Comisión Episcopal de Chile). 1989. *Pentecostalismo, sectas y pastoral.* Santiago: CECh.

Corporación Iglesia Evangélica Pentecostal. 1977. *Historia del avivamiento de la Iglesia Evangélica Pentecostal.* Santiago: Eben-Ezer.

Correa, Enrique and José Antonio Viera-Gallo. n.d. *Iglesia y dictadura.* Santiago: CESOC.

Fontaine Talavera, Arturo and Harald Beyer. 1991. "Retrato del movimiento evangJlico a la luz de las encuestas de opinión publica." *Estudios Publicos* 44: 63-124

Garrard-Burnett, Virginia and David Stoll, eds. 1993. *Rethinking Pentecostalism in Latin America.* Philadelphia: Temple University Press.

Ireland, Rowan. 1991. *Kingdoms Come: Religion and Politics in Brazil.* Pittsburgh: University of Pittsburgh Press.

———. 1993. "The Crentes of Campo Alegre and the Religious Construction of Brazilian Politcs." In Virginia Garrard-Burnett and David Stoll, eds. *Rethinking Pentecostalism in Latin America.* Philadelphia: Temple University Press, 45-65.

Kamsteeg, Frans. 1998. *Prophetic Pentecostalism in Chile. A Case Study on Religion and Development Policy.* Lanham, MD: The Scarecrow Press.

Kessler, Jean Baptiste August. 1967. *A Study of the Older Protestant Missions and Churches in Peru and Chile, with Special Reference to Problems of Division, Nationalism and Native Ministry.* Goes, The Netherlands: Oosterbaan & Le Cointre.

Lagos Schuffeneger, Humberto. 1988. *Crisis de la esperanza. Religión y autoritarismo en Chile.* Santiago: LAR-Presor.

Lalive d'Epinay, Christian. 1969. *Haven of the Masses. A Study of the Pentecostal Movement in Chile.* London: Lutterworth Press.

Lowden, Pamela. 1993. "The Ecumenical Committee for Peace in Chile (1973-1975): the Foundation of Moral Opposition to Authoritarian Rule in Chile." *Bulletin of Latin American Research,* 12 (2): 189-203.

Martin, David. 1990. *Tongues of Fire. The Explosion of Protestantism in Latin America.* Oxford: Basil Blackwell.

Ossa, Manuel. 1991. *Lo propio y lo ajeno. Identidad Pentecostal y Trabajo.* Santiago: Rehue.

Ossa, Manuel. 1992. *Crónica de la Confraternidad Cristiana de Iglesias (CCI).* Santiago.

Razeto, Luis, et al. 1990. *Las organizaciones económicas populares 1973-1990.* Santiago: PET.

Seibert, Ute and Pedro Correa. 1989. *Historia del protestantismo en Chile*. Santiago: Ediciones Rehue.

Sepulveda, Juan. 1987. "El nacimiento y desarrollo de las iglesias evangélicas." In Maximiliano Salinas, ed. *Historia del pueblo de Dios en Chile. La evolución del cristianismo desde la perspectivia de los pobres*. Santiago: Rehue.

———. 1988. "Pentecostalismo y Democracia. Una interpretación de sus relaciones." In Comunidad Teológica Evangélica, ed. *Democracia y Evangelio*. Santiago: Rehue, 229-250.

———. 1990. "Bases éticas para la transición a la democracia desde la perspectiva de las iglesias evangélicas." In Claudio Rammsy, ed. *Iglesia y transición en Chile*. Santiago: Rehue, 59-69.

———. n.d. *Crisis y dinámica del protestantismo actual. El caso chileno*. Santiago: mimeo.

Smith, Brian. 1986. "Chile: Deepening the Allegiance of Working-Class Sectors to the Church in the 1970s." In Daniel Levine, ed. *Religion and Political Conflict in Latin America*. Chapel Hill and London: University of North Carolina Press.

Stoll, David. 1990. *Is Latin America Turning Protestant? The Politics of Evangelical Growth*. Berkeley: University of California Press.

SUR-Profesionales. 1990. *Base actitudinal sectores marginales*. Santiago: SUR.

Tennekes, Hans. 1985. *El movimiento pentecostal en la sociedad chilena*. Amsterdam/Iquique: Subfacultad de antropología cultural de la universidad de Amsterdam/CIREN.

Urrea, Juan Carlos. 1992. *Los nuevos movimientos religiosos en America Latina*. Santiago: Ediciones Paulinas.

Vergara, Ignacio. 1962. *El protestantismo en Chile*. Santiago: Editorial del Pacifico.

Vidal, Ana M.. 1986. *El pentecostal y su actitud socio-política en el Chile de hoy*. Concepción: CEMURI.

Willems, Emilio. 1967. *Followers of the New Faith. Culture Change and the Rise of Protestantism in Brazil and Chile*. Nashville, TN: Vanderbilt University Press.

TEN

FAMILY AND REPRODUCTION AMONG PROTESTANTS IN RIO DE JANEIRO

Cecília L. Mariz and Clara Mafra

Despite great diversity among their churches, Protestants[1] have become known in Brazil for their restrictive, conservative family values as compared to those of the wider contemporary society. Pentecostal churches, especially the oldest ones such as the Assembly of God and the Christian Congregation of Brazil, stand out more than others because of their norms for conservative dress and sexual morality. Because of these norms, much of the sociological and anthropological literature has presented these churches as closed to contemporary society and unaffected by the transformations in sexual behavior and in gender relations that began in the 1960s with the emergence of the feminist movement and the increased availability of modern contraceptives (Hoffnagel 1978; Rolim 1985; Gouveia 1988). In contrast, the historical Protestant churches, which include people with greater education and income, have been considered more tolerant and flexible denominations. However, despite their relative adaptation to changes that have occurred in family life and morality, even these denominations are viewed as conservative when their sexual norms are compared to those of the contemporary Brazilian population as a whole.

Recently, there has been considerable change in Brazilian Protestantism. On the one hand, new Pentecostal churches, which have been called "neopentecostal," have emerged and have grown during the past decade (Oro 1996; Mariano 1995; Machado 1996). On the other hand, sectors of traditional historical denominations are becoming Pentecostal. Will this major denominational plurality bring diversity in relation to family values and sexual moral norms? Are Protestants changing in relation to their family lives? What are the denominational influences on this aspect of individual life?

Among Brazilian state capitals, Rio de Janeiro is the most Protestant. According to the 1991 National Census, 8.98 percent of the Brazilian population and 12.69 percent of Rio de Janeiro inhabitants are Protestant (Pentecostal and non-Pentecostal). The growth of Protestant churches in this city has been rapid. Rubem Fernandes (1992) calculated that in Rio de Janeiro's metropolitan area, 5.2 new churches were established every week between 1990 and 1991. Actually, more recent research (Pierucci and Prandi 1996) suggests a higher Protestant population: 13.3 percent of the total Brazilian population and 14.8 percent of the Rio de Janeiro population.

This chapter is based on quantitative research[2] conducted in 1994 in the Rio de Janeiro metropolitan area.[3] A representative sample of 1,332 Protestants of this area responded to a questionnaire which, among other questions, asked about gender relations and reproductive behavior. The analysis of this data aims to assess the existence of a peculiar Protestant behavior pattern in family and reproductive life. This study also seeks to discover which factors (such as belonging to a denomination or educational level and income) explain Protestant attitudes and behavior in gender relations and reproduction.

WHO ARE THE PROTESTANTS IN RIO DE JANEIRO?

Brazilians Protestants, who prefer to call themselves "*evangélicos*," belong to a large number of churches with very different values and attitudes. Our sample of 1,332 Protestants randomly selected from the Rio metropolitan area includes members from fifty-three different denominations. The majority of these (72 percent) belong to Pentecostal churches. Three denominations stand out as comprising the highest percentages of members: the Assembly of God (31 percent of the sample), the Baptist church (Brazilian Baptist Convention) (19 percent), and the Universal Church of the Kingdom of God (16 percent). Among these three, only the Baptist is non-Pentecostal. The Assembly of God constitutes the largest Protestant denomination in Brazil. In other cities and regions, its relative size is even greater than in Rio de Janeiro. The third biggest church of Rio de Janeiro, the Universal Church of the Kingdom of God was founded in 1977 by Brazilian men in this city, and has grown considerably in recent years.[4] Nevertheless, its growth in other cities and regions of Brazil is much less than in Rio de Janeiro, the city where it emerged and where its headquarters is presently located. The Baptists are also more numerous in Rio de Janeiro than in the rest of the country.

The rest of the churches are all too small to be considered individually. The remaining 34 percent of Protestants are distributed among "small Pentecostal churches" (18 percent), not counting the Assembly of God and the Universal Church; 9 percent are in other non-Pentecostal Protestant churches, which we call the "historical churches" (not including the Baptists); 7 percent are in the "renewed" churches, or historical churches that have become Pentecostal.

Protestant churches are mainly female. Women constitute 69 percent of the total number of Protestants in Rio de Janeiro. Some churches have higher female population than others. The Universal Church, for example, stands out as being composed of 81 percent women.

Regarding age structure, however, there is not much difference between the Protestants and the surrounding population as a whole; except that the cohort older than the age of fifty is slightly larger among Protestants than it is for the rest of the population. Our data suggest that the younger population is growing in Pentecostal churches. Previous research indicated the relative absence of the youth in these churches (Mariz 1994).

The majority of Protestants—61.4 percent of the women and 67.2 percent of the men—are married or cohabiting. However, 38.6 percent of Protestant women are single. About one-fifth (21.9 percent) of the Protestant women are widowed, separated, or divorced. There are many more Protestant women than men in these marital statuses: only 5.5 percent of the men are widowed, separated, or divorced.

Protestants, especially Pentecostals, are in the poorest and least educated sectors of the population. While 40 percent of Protestants have less than four years of school, only 21 percent of the whole of Rio de Janeiro's population has the same low level of instruction. On the other hand, only 26 percent of Protestants have more than nine years of school, in contrast with 47 percent of the total population of the city of Rio de Janeiro. Similarly, Protestants tend to be poorer. 58 percent of Protestants (compared to 45 percent of the whole population of the Rio de Janeiro metropolitan area) have annual incomes of about $1,560 (U.S. dollars); while 10 percent of Protestants and 25 percent of the whole population of the Rio de Janeiro metropolitan area earn more than $7,800 (U.S. dollars) per year. There is, however, an important denominational variation. While the Assembly of God and the Universal Church represent the larger proportion of members at lower levels of income and education, the historical Protestant churches (including the Baptists) are at the opposite extreme, representing a much larger proportion at higher levels. More than 60 percent of Assembly of God (*Assembléia de Deus*) and Universal church members have annual incomes of $1,560 (U.S. dollars), while 45 percent of the historical Protestant churches members have the same income. The largest difference in educational level occurs between the Universal Church members and the members of the historical Protestant church: 15 percent and 42 percent, respectively, have more than nine years of school.

FAMILY, REPRODUCTION, AND RELIGION IN BRAZIL

There are very few studies of the reproductive behavior of Protestants in Brazil. With the exception of the work of Maria das Dores Machado (1996a, 1996b), research of religion has neglected this topic. Although religious institutions are the very ones that are most concerned about sexual behavior and family issues, relatively few studies in Brazil relate religious preference to reproductive behavior. Most studies that deal with religion and reproduction in general are often concerned with the position of Roman Catholics in the face of the official teachings of their church. Lúcia Ribeiro and Solange Luçan (1992), for example, have written about the reproductive behavior of women involved in base Christian communities.

Thus there is a paucity of data available regarding religion and reproductive behavior. The qualitative studies above suggest that Catholics, even practicing Catholics, such as those that participate in Charismatic groups or base communities, tend to disregard their church norm that defines as acceptable only "natural" methods of contraception (Machado 1996a; Ribeiro and Luçan 1995). Nevertheless, among those of similar age and level of instruction, Protestants tend to accept slightly more birth control methods than do practicing Catholics (Machado 1996a).

Whereas the Roman Catholic church stands out because of its strict teachings on the use of contraceptives, approving only "natural" methods, Protestants are characterized by a diversity of positions. However, in contrast to the Catholic church, Protestantism has generally adopted a more tolerant position in relation to birth control (Machado 1996). In their countries of origin, the historical Protestant churches tend to be more open to innovation and to place greater emphasis on individual responsibility in general and on responsibility for material life. In Brazil, although there are denominations, such as the Universal Church of the Kingdom of God, which state that the ideal number of children is two and which support the use of vasectomies, other denominations do not take an official, legitimated position or one that is generalized on this subject (Machado 1996).

Reproduction is not simply an individual or purely feminine issue, and cannot be fully understood unless one considers the family and gender dynamics. Attitudes about reproduction and reproductive behavior are linked to values and attitudes about family and sexuality, and to the relationship between the sexes, which also includes responsibility for children. For this reason, in this chapter we attempt to identify the cultural values of Protestants about the roles of men and women in the family, in order to assess to what degree more egalitarian values can be related to a more positive attitude about birth control.

Religious transformations usually affect the family. Because the family is the principal locus of socialization, it is among the social units most responsible for the maintenance and reproduction of religion. Although religions generally concern themselves with family matters, in Brazil this concern is especially evident among Protestants. The cultural transformation undertaken by the Protestants involves new definitions of gender roles and the disciplining of children within the family. In this sense, family and sexuality, which have always been issues of great importance in Christianity in general, take on even more importance within Protestant belief.

The literature on Pentecostals in Latin America emphasizes that, despite maintaining a patriarchal model of the family, Pentecostals adopt a new family ethos and a new masculine role that transforms conjugal relationships (Brusco 1994; Burdick 1993; Flora 1976; Gill 1988; Mariz 1994; Machado 1996). By encouraging a restrictive sexual morality for men and women, and by emphasizing masculine responsibility along with paternity, the Protestant churches tend to strengthen the family unit. However, most related studies are restricted to qualitative methods, and take into account only a few Pentecostal denominations. This chapter also seeks to assess the extent to which these conclusions on gender relationship apply to different denominations in Rio de Janeiro.

THE AVERAGE NUMBER OF CHILDREN

In recent decades the fertility rate of the Brazilian population has dropped rapidly. For women of childbearing age the average number of children, which was 5.7 in 1970, fell to 4.35 in 1980 and to 2.58 in 1993. Protestant women in Rio de Janeiro are not very different from the national average, bearing, on the average, 2.7 children.

Unfortunately, our sample is not large enough to allow calculation of the average number of children among women of childbearing age by denomination. In order to compare between denominations, we have calculated the average number of children for all women by denomination (since there was a similar age structure for each denomination, this average may be comparable). We can thus observe the following variation in the average number of children: the smaller Pentecostal churches (3.7), the Assembly of God (3.5), the renewed churches (3.2), Baptists (3), the Universal Church (2.9), and historical Protestant churches (2.8). Those churches whose members have the highest level of education are generally those with the lowest average number of children. However, the Universal Church departs from this rule, since its members have among the smallest number of children and also the lowest level of education. The position of the Universal Church may be best understood by its members' acceptance of the antinatalist discourse of their leadership (Machado 1996a, 1996b).

Nevertheless, when we consider all the historical Protestant churches as a unit (including in this category data of the Baptist Church and of the renewed churches), and if we compare their rates with those of Pentecostal churches as a whole, we note that the former have fewer children and that they delay the beginning of reproductive life more than the latter. In the historical churches, 49.8 percent of the women of childbearing age have two children or fewer, while only 16.6 percent have five children or more. Baptist women, members of other historical churches, and members of the renewed churches stand out for bearing the first child later. Only 11.5 percent have children before the age of nineteen, and 23.1 percent have a child after the age of twenty-seven. Women of the Universal Church of the Kingdom of God, of the Assembly of God, and of other Pentecostal churches, on the other hand, start their reproductive lives earlier and have more children. It may be noted that 20.7 percent, 19.9 percent, and 18.2 percent of the women of these churches, respectively, bore the first child before being nineteen years old; and also that 21.7 percent, 26.6 percent, and 19.6 percent, respectively, bore five children or more.

When we compare people's stated ideal number of children to the actual number, we see that, in general, Protestants tend to have more children than they think is ideal. This suggests that their birth rate will probably decrease even more in the future. The majority of Protestants interviewed consider the ideal to be a maximum of two children. This is consistent for all denominations, although the Assembly of God and other Pentecostals stand out as having a lower percentage among those who consider two or fewer children ideal; and a larger percentage of those who state that the ideal would be to have more than five children. However, the Universal Church of the Kingdom of God stands out for the opposite reason. Although the members of this church have lower levels of education than the Baptist, historical, and renewed churches, their definition of the ideal number of children is very similar to these church members. The response of its members with regard to the ideal number of children may be a consequence of its antinatalist discourse.

When comparing the historical Protestant churches (including in this category the Baptists and the renewed historical churches) with the

Pentecostals, variations regarding reproductive behavior can be explained in part by the education and income of their members. In general the members of the historical Protestant churches have the highest levels of education. Delays in reproduction and marriage, along with bearing fewer children, can be explained by the greater education. The reproductive behavior of the Assembly of God, the Universal Church, and other Pentecostal churches corresponds to the pattern of the poorer classes, among whom the beginning of reproductive and sexual behavior is earlier and fertility is higher. Nevertheless, it is interesting to note that, as we have seen, despite the fact that the Universal Church of the Kingdom of God is the Protestant denomination with the lowest average level of education, its members, when compared with the members of other Pentecostal churches and the Assembly of God, tend to have lower numbers of children. In this case, denominational membership appears to have an effect independent of education and income.

CONTRACEPTIVE METHODS: PROHIBITION AND USE

The majority of the interviewees (75 percent) stated that their churches do not prohibit any contraceptive method. Ten percent did not know how to answer this question and 15 percent believed that their churches did place restrictions on some birth control methods. Among the different denominations, 7 percent of the historical churches, 5 percent of the Baptists, and 15 percent of the small Pentecostal churches stated that their churches had prohibitions against contraceptives. The numbers were much higher among the Assembly of God, with 25 percent of the interviewees feeling that such prohibitions existed. However, we have not found any literature published by the Assembly of God or any other Protestant church prohibiting contraceptive methods. Each church within a denomination, especially in the Assembly of God, can be autonomous. Thus, responses affirming the prohibition of contraceptives may reflect the position of a specific congregation or pastor, or even the position of the individual believer who responded to the question, rather than revealing an official position of that church. That would explain how respondents from the same denomination gave opposing responses. But it is also worth recalling that, in a study conducted in Recife in the 1970s, Judith Hoffnagel (1978) identified a tendency in the Assembly of God to reject birth control and family planning.

The stated lack of church prohibitions against the use of contraceptives is confirmed by the observation that 74 percent of all Protestant women of childbearing age who are married or cohabitating use contraceptives or have been sterilized. That means that the majority of the female population that is sexually active seeks to control reproduction. A similar percentage (76.7 percent) was noted by the National Study of Demographics and Public Health conducted in 1996 by the organization Family Welfare in Brazil (Benfam 1996).

Protestants also follow the general pattern of the population with regard to their choice of contraceptive method. Sterilization (60 percent) and the pill (30 percent) are the preferred means of avoiding pregnancy. The correlation between the greater use of contraceptives and higher levels of education explains the fact that the Baptist churches (76 percent) and the historical Protestant churches (81 percent) show the highest percentage of contraceptive use, but does not explain the fact that the percentage for the Universal Church (78 percent) is also high.

Tubal ligations occur more frequently among women of the denominations characterized by higher income and education. For the Baptists, this includes 47 percent of women of childbearing age, and for the historical churches 48 percent. These data concur with those of José Almino Alencar (1994), who notes that in Brazil the tubal ligation is a practice of the wealthier and more educated classes and challenges previous statements that this practice is greater among the poorer classes.

THE INFLUENCE OF RELIGIOUS VERSUS SOCIOECONOMIC FACTORS

In order to evaluate the influence of religion per se on reproductive behavior it is important to consider the timing of the conversion of the adherent. For those who have been members of a church for only a short time, religious affiliation may not have influenced the number of children they have had or their decisions concerning sterilization. We have observed, nevertheless, that although there is a representative contingent of adherents who have been in the church for fewer than ten years (43 percent), more than half (57 percent) of the Protestant population was either raised in the church (30 percent) or has already belonged to it for more than ten years (27 percent). It should be noted, however, that this percentage of recently converted varies greatly from denomination to denomination. While the largest percentage of recently converted is in the Universal Church, the smallest is in the historical churches. Based on this information, we can conclude that the influence of belonging to a church on the number of children born, age at the time of marriage, or sterilization among the members of the Universal Church may be quite affected by the length of time that the majority of the members have belonged. Nevertheless, in relation to other variables that are linked to values and perceptions, the influence of this church can still be relevant.

Religion also influences reproductive behavior when only one spouse is a member of the church, reproduction being the responsibility of both spouses. Only 51 percent of the women have husbands who are also Protestant. It is interesting to note, however, that, among those women who do not have a Protestant spouse, 24 percent stated that the spouse had been Protestant in the past, which suggests that there is a somewhat significant percentage of lapsing among the male population. On the other hand, 92 percent of Protestant men have Protestant wives. We have also observed that the proportion of Protestants whose spouses are not of the church varies according to denomination. Once again the Universal Church stands out for having a majority of its adherents in this category (56 percent), probably because it is the denomination that attracts the largest proportion of women (81 percent).

In order to verify the influence of religion on reproduction, specifically whether it has some role independent of social and economic factors, we compared the number of children of each Protestant family researched with the number of children per family in the general population of the Rio de Janeiro metropolitan area. We classified the neighborhoods researched in three socioeconomic levels according to the level of education of their inhabitants. We found that among those who live in the poorest areas, Protestant affiliation seems to decrease the number of children. Among those who live in less poor neighborhoods, Protestant affiliation seems to increase the number of children per family. Protestants in the poorest neighborhoods have 0.29 fewer children per family than the general population of those neighborhoods (1.16 compared to 1.45). Protestants in the moderately poor neighborhoods have 0.22 fewer (1.09 compared to 1.31). But Protestants in the wealthiest neighborhoods have 0.14 more children per family (1.01 compared to 0.87). This comparison, therefore, suggests that Protestant religion performs a role in reproductive behavior independent of the social and economic factor.

VALUES ABOUT GENDER RELATIONS

In order to evaluate the opinions of Protestants with regard to power and roles attributed to men and women, we offered six statements in each interview with which the respondents were asked to state whether they agreed completely, agreed partly, disagreed partly, or disagreed completely. Three statements related to the roles and the obligations of men and women in the family, and three related to sexual morality. The statements related to the obligations of men and women were: (1) "the husband should have the last word in family decisions"; (2) "the wife should take care of the house and the children, and the husband does not have any obligation to help"; (3) "the education of the children is mainly the task of the mother." For evaluating sexual morality we offered these statements : (1) "the sexual morality of men and women should be the same"; (2) "the woman should be a virgin at the time of marriage"; (3) "the man should be a virgin at the time of marriage."

In general, there is a tendency among Protestants to grant the man a superior role in the hierarchy of power in the family. Of the respondents, 59.9 percent stated that the husband should have the last word in making family decisions. However, only one-fourth of the Protestants take an extreme position on the masculine role by affirming that they agree completely with the sentence on this subject. Those who agree completely are fewer than those who disagree completely. While 24.2 percent state that they agree completely that "the husband should have the last word in family decisions," 31 percent disagree completely with this statement.

There is a tendency among a small majority of Protestants to agree that "the education of children is mainly the task of the mother." Protestants appear to value the presence of the man in the care of the house and of the children, as revealed by the high percentage (79.3 percent) of those who disagree with the sentence, "The wife should take care of the house and of the children, and the husband does not have any obligation to help." Only 13.4 percent agree completely with this, while 65.3 percent disagree completely (unfortunately, there is no similar data from the general population to compare with these responses of our interviewees). Comparing between different denominations, we noticed that although the majority of members in all denominations give the man the last word in family decisions, there are relatively fewer members of the historical churches, including the Baptists, who agree (partly or completely) with this idea. In contrast, the Universal Church has the largest percentage of those who completely agree (46.9 percent) that the last word belongs to the man. Also, this church has the highest percentage of those who agree that the man does not have any obligation to help the woman in domestic tasks or in the care of the children.

When asked if "the sexual morality of the man and the woman should be equal," the Protestants were visibly favorable: 89.3 percent agreed with this statement. However, this supposed moral equality showed itself to be fragile when these same Protestants responded to the question of the obligation of the man or the woman to be a virgin at the time of marriage. While 84.3 percent agree that the woman should come to the marriage a virgin, only 68.5 percent agree in the case of men. Nevertheless, this still shows a majority who agree with egalitarian sexual morality.

Compared to similar data from the general population, Protestants support sexual chastity. Only 18 percent of the general population affirm that a man should be a virgin when he gets married, while in the case of a woman, 43 percent share this opinion (*Folha de São Paulo* 1998).[5] Therefore, one of Protestantism's novelties is a new male sexual morality that breaks the cultural pattern dominant in Brazilian society. Even though Protestants defend a hierarchy between the sexes, defining the man as the maker of decisions, they propose equality between men and women on the level of sexual freedom. This Protestant position goes against the feminist view of sexual liberation for women, although both positions affirm equality in the exercise of sexuality. For Protestants, greater equality in sexual morality occurs by means of sexual restriction and self-control as much for men as for women (Mariz & Machado 1997).

It is important to remember that Protestants value the family and prioritize it over the interests of the individual, whether this be for women or men. Despite granting men the role of power, as the decision-maker in the family, Protestants believe that men as much as women should subordinate their interests to those of the family. Thus, according to this vision, the privileged male position in the hierarchy is not interpreted as inequality of power or as oppression, but as the result of a division of labor between men and women, who are responsible for areas of life that are defined and demarcated. This is very far from a feminist vision formulated in terms of an opposition between individual and family, with emphasis on the freedom and autonomy of the individual (Mariz and Machado 1997).

With regard to the issue of inequality between the sexes in relation to sexual morality, again the historical churches (including the Baptists and the renewed churches), whose members have more years of schooling, stand out in terms of supporting greater equality insofar as they agree most with the statements that sexual morality should be the same for men and women, and that both should be virgins at the time of marriage. There is less agreement in relation to those statements among church members with less education, that is, among Pentecostals. It is interesting to note that the members of the Universal Church stand out in terms of the greatest acceptance of inequality between the sexes, despite their apparent greater support of birth control. Thus it can be observed that a high rate of the use of birth control can occur independently of a redefinition of gender relations.

CONCLUSION

In general, this study calls into question the image of Protestants as closed to contemporary society and its family and reproductive values. Protestants, as much the Pentecostals of the Assembly of God as the others, who are presently living in Rio de Janeiro are quite different from those members of the Assembly of God in Recife, interviewed by Hoffnagel in the 1970s, who had large families and prohibited birth control.

In reproductive terms, Protestants as a whole are not generally distinct from the majority of the population. Our data tend to confirm the observations of Machado (1996a, 1996b) that among Protestants in Rio de Janeiro in the 1990s there is a great deal of tolerance with regard to methods of birth control. The faithful are free to choose. Like the general population, most Protestant women are avoiding pregnancy and do not want to have more than two children. They also prefer steriliza-tion. However, sterilization is used most frequently by women of the denominations characterized by higher levels of education and income.

Education and income are actually very important variables. The denominations whose members have the most education and income (the historical churches, including the Baptists) have the fewest children, the highest use of birth control, and the strongest support for the beliefs in gender equality in relation to both family duties and sexual morality. Nevertheless, there is an exception. Education and income do not explain the values and attitudes of the members of the Universal Church with regard to reproduction. They are the least educated and, in spite of this, use birth control as much as people from historical churches, and like them prefer the smallest number of children. Their lower level of education, however, seems to affect their attitudes toward gender roles and power relationships. In contrast to Baptist and other historical church members, great numbers of those who identified themselves as from the Universal Church support the most unequal gender relations, in terms of both sexual morality and the division of household labor. These data suggest that affiliation with the Universal Church was more important than education in explaining reproductive behavior, but not in explaining attitudes toward gender relations. The greatest equality between genders is consistently supported by those from churches whose members have the highest levels of education and income.

Unfortunately our data did not allow us to use multivariate analysis to control for education, income, and denomination in order to verify their relative statistical weight in explaining reproductive behavior and attitudes toward gender role and power relation. Neither did we find any reproductive data for the different education levels of the whole population of Rio de Janeiro that could be comparable to ours. However, our comparison of the number of Protestant children per family with a similar statistic for the whole population of their neigh-borhood suggests an interesting influence of Protestant religion in reproductive behavior. The poorest Protestants seem to have fewer children than the poorest members of the population as a whole; the opposite is true for the wealthier Protestants. This comparison suggests that affiliation with a Protestant church does affect reproductive behavior and values. The comparison between Protestant sexual morality and that of the whole population also suggests that affiliation with Protestantism creates a new pattern of values and attitudes. The defense of more gender equality in relation to sexual morality can be understood as high Protestant esteem for the nuclear family.

NOTES

1   Latin American Protestants usually refer to themselves as *evangélicos*. However, in English the term "Evangelical" refers only to a limited number of Protestant groups. To avoid confusion we will employ the category "Protestant" that in English has general meaning.

2   This research, named *Novo Nascimento* (Born Again) (Iser 1996), was a broad project that intended to study the religious, familial, and political lives of the Protestants of Rio de Janeiro. It was developed at Instuto de Estudo da Religião (ISER) in Rio de Janeiro, and was supported by the Ford Foundation, the North-South Center of University of Miami, and the World Council of Churches. The section on family and reproduction, whose data we discuss here, had the special support of the Ford Foundation. A summary of the main results of the *Novo Nascimento* project was published by Rubem Cesar Fernandes (1997), the project general coordinator. Cecília Mariz, with Clara Mafra's great help, was responsible for the section on family and reproduction.

3   This area called *Grande Rio* includes the cities of Rio de Janeiro, Nova Iguacu, Duque de Caxias, Sao Joao do Meriti, Niteroi and Sao Goncalo.

4   For more information on the Universal Church of the Kingdom of God, see Freston 1993, Ruuth 1995, Corten 1995, Lehmann 1996, and Chesnut 1997.

5   This comparison has some limits because this question was formulated differently in each of the researches. However, Datafolha's research also compares the opinion of people from different religions and also concludes that Protestants are those who most defend male and female virginity.

REFERENCES

Alencar, José Almino. 1994. "Esterilização no Brasil; o que revelam os números." *Monitor Público*, 2(1): 15-19.

Bem Fam (Sociedade Civil para o Bem-estar da família). 1996. *Pesquisa Nacional sobre Saúde Materno-Infantil e Planejamento Familiar*. Rio de Janeiro: Editora do Dept. de Educação e Comunicação da Bemfam.

———. 1992. *Pesquisa sobre Saúde Familiar no Brasil-Nordeste Brasil 1992*. Rio de Janeiro: Editora do Dept. de Educação e Comunicação da Bemfam.

Brusco, Elisabeth. 1994. "The Reformation of Machismo: Asceticism and Maculinity among Colombian Evangelicals." In V. Garrand-Burnett and David Stoll, eds. *Rethinking Protestantism in Latin America.* Philadelphia: Temple University Press.

Burdick, John. 1993. *Looking for God in Brazil.* Berkeley: University of California Press.

Chesnut, R. Andrew 1997. *Born Again.* New Brunswick, NJ: Rutgers University Press.

Corten, Andre. 1995. *Le Pentecôstime au Brésil; Émotion du pauvre et romantisme théologique.* Paris: Karthala.

Domingues, Jorge Luiz. 1995. *O Tempo da Colheita; crescimento das igrejas evangélicas no Rio de Janeiro.* Unpublished Master's thesis, IFCS and State University of Rio de Janeiro.

Fernandes, Rubem. 1992. *Censo Institucional Evangélico,* Série Texto de Pesquisa. Rio de Janeiro: Instituto de Estudos da Religião.

———. 1996. "Os Evangélicos em Casa na Igreja e na Política." *Religião e Sociedade,* 17(1): 4-15 .

Folha de São Paulo. 1998. 18 de January. Page 6/Caderno Mais.

Freston, Paul. 1993. *Protestantismo e política no Brasil: da Constituinte ao Impeachment.* Unpublished Doctoral dissertation, UNICAMP, Campinas.

Gill, L. 1990. "Like a Veil to Cover Them: Women and the Pentecostal Movement in La Paz." *American Ethnologist* 17 (4) .

Gouveia, Eliane. 1986. *O silêncio que deve ser ouvido: mulheres pentecostais em São Paulo.* Unpublished Master's thesis, Pontifical Catholic University of São Paulo.

Hoffnagel, Judith. 1978. *The Believers: Pentecostalism in a Brazilian City.* Unpublished Doctoral dissertation, Indiana University.

Hunter, J. D. 1987. *Evangelicalism; the coming generation.* Chicago: The University of Chicago Press.

IBGE/CDDI/DESIS. 1990. *Pesquisa Nacional por Amostra de Domicílio (PNAD). Participação política e Social—1988.* Rio de Janeiro: IBGE, Vol. 3.

———. 1997. *Censo Demográfico.* Rio de Janeiro: IBGE

ISER, Núcleo de Pesquisa. 1996 "Novo Nascimento," Relatório de Pesquisa. Rio de Janeiro: Instituto de Estudos da Religião.

———. 1980. "A Posição da Mulher na Comunidade Pentecostal." *Estudos Universitários; Revista de Cultura da Universidade Federal de Pernambuco* 18 (1-2): 1-18.

Lehmann, David. 1996. *Struggle for the Spirit.* Cambridge, UK: Polity Press.

Machado, Maria das Dores. 1996a. *Carismáticos e Pentecostais; adesão religiosa na esfera familiar.* Campinas: Editora Autores Associados .

———. 1996b. "Sexual Values and Family Planning among Charismatic and Pentecostal Movement in Brazil." *Reproductive Health Matters* 8 (November): 77-85

Mariano, Ricardo. 1995. *Neopentecostalismo; os pentecostais estão mudando.* Unpublished master's thesis, University of São Paulo.

Mariz, Cecília. 1994. *Coping with Poverty.* Philadelphia: Temple University Press.

Mariz, Cecília and M. Machado. 1994. "Sincretismo e Trânsito Religioso." *A Dança do Sincretismo—Comunicações do ISER*, no. 45, ano 13.

Mariz, C., M. Machado and C. Mafra. 1995. In Rosângela Oliveira and Fernanda Carneiro, eds. *Corpo; meu bem meu mal*. Rio de Janeiro: ISER.

Mariz, Cecília and M. Machado. 1996. "Pentecostalism and women in Brazil." In Edward L. Cleary and Hannah W. Stewart-Gambino, eds. *Power, Politics, and Pentecostals in Latin America*. Boulder, CO: Westview Press, 41-54.

Oro, Pedro Ari, ed. 1992. "Neo pentecostalismo." *Cadernos de Antropologia* 9.

Pierucci, Antônio Flávio and Reginaldo Prandi. 1996. *A realidade social das religiões no Brasil*. São Paulo: Editora Hucitec.

Ribeiro, Lúcia and Solange Luçan. 1995. "Reprodução e comunidades de base; dúvidas e certezas." In Rosângela Oliveira and Fernanda Carneiro, eds. *Corpo; meu bem meu mal*. Rio de Janeiro: ISER, 122-125.

Rolim, Francisco. 1985. *Pentecostais no Brasil ; uma interpretação sócio-religiosa*. Petrópolis: Vozes.

Ruuth, A. 1995. *Igreja Universal do Reino de Deus*. Estocolmo: Almqvist and Wiksell International.

ELEVEN

EXPLORING THE ARGENTINIAN CASE
Religious Motives in the Growth of
Latin American Pentecostalism

Daniel Míguez

It is by now a widely acknowledged fact that since the 1930s and 1940s Pentecostalism has expanded in different parts of Latin America, predominantly among the poor (Martin, 1990; Stoll, 1990). Explanations of why Pentecostalism has grown have very often referred to modernization. In these references, modernization has been equated with industrialization, urbanization, and democratization.

Curiously, less attention was paid to what classic texts (Parsons 1966; Wilson 1966; Berger 1967; Luckmann 1967; Bellah 1970) recognize as the main impact of modernization on religion. Namely, that religion becomes privatized and plural. When there is no official religion imposed by the state, all religions have an equal standing and may present their offers to people. Because of this, each person can freely choose his religion. When one looks, even superficially, at what has happened during these years in Latin America the image seems to leave no alternative but to associate it with such processes of privatization and pluralization. The original Catholic domination has given way to diverse forms of religiosity. Within this plural context people experienced greater freedom to move from one religion to the other, or just to create their "own thing" by mixing elements of the various options (Droogers and Rostas 1993).

This problem of not sufficiently considering the specific effects of modernization on religion appears even in some of the classic texts explaining Pentecostal growth. The initial studies by Willems (1967) and Lalive d'Epinay (1968), for example, attributed the growth of Pentecostalism to the outcome of processes of urbanization and the growth of a market economy and industry. Pentecostal churches played an adaptive role for those whose customary lifestyle was affected by these structural changes. However, they did not see in this a transformation of people's religious belief or practice. On the contrary, they tended to stress the continuity between popular Catholicism and Pentecostalism.

More recent studies on these topics, such as those of Bastian (1992, 1993), Stoll (1990) or Martin (1990, 1991), also propose that Pentecostal growth is related to changes in the political and socioeconomic terrain, and disregard transformations in the religious field itself.

These explanations are incomplete in that they put too much emphasis on political and economic causes and transformations. They fail to perceive that the privatization and pluralization of religion, and the consequent changes in religious culture are part of the explanation of Pentecostal growth in Latin America. Hence, in what follows, I show some complementary reasons why Pentecostalism grew in Latin America by looking at the processes of privatization and pluralization of the Argentinian religious field. Although I acknowledge the influence of economic and political factors, I stress processes of religious change by looking at the specific religious motives people have for joining Pentecostalism. *This motivation is defined by people's needs to find answers to transcendental questions and what they feel are appropriate ways to relate to sacred beings and forces.*

WHY PEOPLE CONVERT

In order to examine the role that privatization and pluralization have played in religious conversion in Latin America, I will present three case studies of Argentinians who converted to Pentecostalism.[1] In order to achieve at least a certain degree of representativeness, I chose cases that are not uncommon. First of all, these are cases of people who were former passive Catholics and became active Pentecostals.[2] Secondly, they belong to the popular sector.[3] Finally, researchers in other parts of Latin America have reported similar cases, showing that this kind of attitude toward religion exceeds the Argentinian frontier (cf. Droogers and Siebers 1991:6; Gill 1993; Green 1993:172 ff.).

The first case is that of Antonia. Antonia was a passive Catholic. She used to doubt God's existence. However, when her husband (a mason) died, leaving her with three children and a very low income, she began a religious quest. Given her familial tradition, the first group Antonia turned to was the Catholics. In the local parish, Antonia was aided by a social assistance group, but she was not satisfied with it because, aside from the material assistance (she received food and clothing every week), she did not find the priest's explanation of how God acted satisfactory:

> [The Father] told me that God would help me through my brothers, that I should see God's face in my brothers and turned me to that so-

cial assistance group. But that is not really believing in God, because finally you really are only believing in your brothers in that way.

Driven by this dissatisfaction, she looked for other alternatives—worshipping saints and, especially, visiting *curanderas* (faith healers). The experience was not satisfactory: "*curanderas* kept telling me that they [Saints] have powers, but no one really knew how I should ask and [also] I stood there in front of that statue and nothing happened." Looking for a more fulfilling experience Antonia kept canvassing different alternatives, until through a *curandera* she encountered an Afro-Brazilian cult (Umbanda). At first, the ritual performance of the *Mãe de Santo* (the spiritual leader in Umbanda) had convinced Antonia that she was in touch with a spiritual power source, and that through it she was going to get help: "I really thought that I was in the right direction [. . .] when she was possessed, the faces she had and the change of voice, I was really convinced she had powers." This perception had repercussions in other aspects of her life: "I did not feel so depressed any more . . . my relationship with the kids improved [i.e., she didn't hit or yell at her children so frequently]. I found a job and my economic situation was better." It is interesting to note that the same ritual elements that initially attracted Antonia became a source of deception when she experienced them in a more "complete" version. This happened when the *Mãe de Santo* invited Antonia to a group meeting: "I was very scared. All these drums, and people drunk and dancing like crazy and doing all this weird things. . . . I was told that they were devilish powers and I finally left the place." This also had consequences in other aspects of her life: "When I realized that it could be the devil that was helping me I not only became depressed, but also very frightened and angry and things went even worst with my children."

Finally, Antonia met the Pentecostals through some neighbors. She has been a very active member for the past three years, attending church two or three times a week. As was the case with Umbanda, the first thing that attracted Antonia was the ritual performance: "The first time I attended a service in the [Pentecostal] church I thought: 'now I found what I was looking for.' I felt so happy, so joyful there." She also found the doctrine convincing: "The pastor told me that there was a life after this life in which me and my husband would be reunited, I doubted this at first, but it is all there in the Bible." Antonia was attracted by other doctrinal claims that increased her self-esteem: "In church they say that we are all children of God, rich or poor, and thus for Him we all have the same value." This increase in self-esteem and confidence had consequences in other aspects of her life: "I began to feel peace in my heart and to do better with my children." Also, she received economic aid from Pentecostals, church members found Antonia's eldest son a job, and they helped her in critical moments: "I began to do better economically because here in church we all help each other."

The story of Antonia already reveals some of the criteria people use when deciding to convert to a religious group. One of the things Antonia was looking for is a satisfying doctrine and ritual. She quit the Catholic church because she was not happy with its doctrine; it was also ritual and doctrine that induced her to leave Umbanda and join the Pentecostals. Besides ritual and doctrine, Antonia was also worried about the effects that joining a group would have on her family and her ability to make a living. These effects are not independent from the way she perceives doctrine and ritual. If she perceives them correctly, she tends to improve psychologically and this has beneficial effects in other aspects of her life. When she does not feel she is connected with sacred beings and forces, she declines psychologically and this has damaging effects on her family and economic situation.

A similar pattern is perceivable in the case of Isabel and Roberto, who began a religious search when they were facing both an economic and a familial crisis. Before converting to Pentecostalism they were nonpracticing Catholics; they never attended church, "except when we married or when we were baptized." Before turning to Pentecostalism, Isabel had doubts about God's existence, and Roberto had turned to religion only at certain critical times in his life. He went on three pilgrimages when applying to the police academy, and visited a *curandera* during a difficult period in his marriage. Aside from these moments, however, religion was not central to their lives. This changed when they converted to Pentecostalism. When I interviewed Isabel and Roberto they were attending church two times a week, taking doctrinal courses, and Roberto had plans of becoming a pastor. Before reaching this stage of firm commitment a complex process took place. As with Antonia, perceptions of ritual and doctrine, and the effects that this had on their lives influenced the change of religious identity.

This can be seen in the first contact Isabel had with Pentecostalism. She was looking for a job at the time, and was very depressed because she could not find anything. As a way to combat depression she began to listen to some radio programs of Pentecostal Pastor Cabrera. This gave her a feeling of inner peace and hope, and induced her to pray for a job. Twenty days later she got a job, and attributed this to her prayers and the radio program. This did not turn her into a committed

Pentecostal, but she kept listening to the programs because they "made me [Isabel] feel good and sleep peacefully." She also began to attend a Pentecostal church from time to time.

Isabel's more profound conversion came after a marital crises. The initial process was similar to the previous one; the difference was that this time one of the pastors of the Church Isabel was attending began to visit and counsel the couple on how to work out the conflicts (specifically infidelity) they had had. Roberto did not enter church immediately. It took some time for him to become convinced. "I went and got myself a Bible to show her that what these people were saying in church was wrong. But to my surprise I found that what they were saying was correct. . . . Now I am completely convinced that this church is the right one."

The final story I will tell here is probably the type more frequently found in studies of Pentecostalism. A drunkard who overcomes his addiction through conversion and turns, not only into a committed church member, but into a completely sober Pentecostal pastor. The account shows how the process of overcoming addiction is closely linked with finding a transcendental meaning of life. Luis had a stable job as a soda deliveryman. He had no big family crisis until he fell into alcoholism. Then his familial relations began to deteriorate. Trying to solve his problem, he began a religious quest. Although he was a Catholic, he did not consult a priest. After visiting several *curanderos*, he attended a Pentecostal meeting. There he received the laying on of hands. He did not abandon his alcoholism immediately afterwards, but a complex process began: "I began to think about God more. Before that I hardly had these questions in my mind. I began to ask myself: What am I doing in this world? Why are we here? Why God this or that? I had so many questions that I wrote them down in a notebook and I said to my wife, I am going out to look for a church where they can answer me these questions." After canvassing several churches, Luis joined the congregation where I found him as a pastor with the "gift of music" (he conducted and composed the songs in church). As noted, what attracted Luis to this particular church was that he found answers to his questions even before he could ask them: "I came to this church and there was a service taking place. To my surprise, as the pastor was preaching he started answering all my questions."

THE CASES IN A THEORETICAL CONTEXT:
ANALYZING RELIGIOUS IDENTITY BUILDING

Social identity has been defined as "our understanding of who we are and who other people are" (Jenkins 1996:5). This understanding is not constructed in isolation, but through a process in which individuals interact with social groups, and incorporate the practices and visions of the group into their worldview. Thus social identity implies a sense of belonging to one social group. Because individuals participate in different social groups, they may have several types of identity: they may be fans of a football club and at the same time have an identity as members of a certain profession, etc. The particularity of religious identities is that they are constructed in relation to religious groups, and that they include, necessarily, a certain "understanding" of the transcendent. Religious identities define the relationship between the individual and the sacred forces he or she worships. This is why there are religious motives involved in a change of religious identity: people search for new answers to transcendental questions and look for new ways to relate to sacred forces. They convert (change their identity) to the group in which they find the most fulfilling answers.

Antonia and the others were not satisfied with their Catholic identities, and during certain critical periods they decided to look for a new religion. They chose the one in which they found the answers to their transcendental questions and a satisfactory way to relate to God. This implied a profound change of belief and practice: from being passive Catholics, not very convinced of God's existence, they turned into active Pentecostals. This kind of radical change is what modernity has favored.

In modern societies no group has a state-supported claim to the religious truth. Moreover, in our modern scientific society, claims to truth need to be sustained by evidence (Pluss 1988). This need gives religious identities a fluid character, as evidenced by people constantly evaluating their religious identities. In this evaluation they try to discover if sacred beings really exist, and if their religion's understanding of the transcendent is appropriate. In this there is always a certain tension between the religious leaders who define doctrine and ritual, and the followers who decide whether or not to accept it.

Acceptance depends on whether or not the ritual and doctrine provides satisfactory answers to their transcendental questions, and on how the new religion will affect other spheres of their life (e.g. familial, economic). Beyer's (1990) treatment of the performative and functional aspects of religion may help to produce such a balanced approach. Performance is related to the influence that religion may have in nonreligious dimensions of society. Beyer, following Luhmann (1982), proposes that in the modern world religion impinges on other spheres of society by acting as a moral code that influences the daily decisions these individuals make. Religion also has another dimension, what Beyer calls its specific function: "Function is the pure, sacred communication about the transcendent and the aspect that religious institutions claim for themselves" (1990:379). Therefore, religious motivation is dealt with at the level of function: where each religious group defines how to relate to sacred forces and offers answers to transcendental questions.

To Beyer, both dimensions—function and performance—are connected. Each religion's perception of the sacred influences its performance in other arenas. For example, because liberation theology interprets the Gospels as proposing social justice, it promotes political involvement in progressive movements. On the other hand, certain Evangelical groups believe that the Gospels recommend "detachment from the things of this world," and thus abstain from politics. In my view, this connection also exists at a deeper level. According to Pluss, a religion becomes performative when it convinces the followers of God's existence and willingness to intervene in their life. Thus when a person accepts a new religion, the understanding of self and how to relate to others (including sacred forces) may change. This can have a transformative effect on attitudes and practices in nonreligious spheres of life.

My problem with many of the current explanations of the growth of Pentecostalism is that they overemphasize the level of nonreligious performance by not considering religious motive.[4] A good example is provided by Mariz (1990, 1994). She finds that, for the poor and marginalized sectors of society, Pentecostalism provides a strategy for coping with the stressful situations produced by poverty. First, Pentecostalism constitutes a *psychological* strategy to cope with poverty because it gives meaning to the stressful events of life. That is, each event is planned by God, and thus every bad event has a purpose in God's plan. Second, Pentecostalism provides *cultural* strategies by giving the believer a sense of dignity. Since all men and women are children of God, no one is better or worse because of his or her wealth. Finally, the Pentecostal church also provides helpful *networks* that act as channels of assistance in times of economic need.

It is possible to discern how some of the elements mentioned by Mariz played a role in the way Antonia and the others framed their identities. In this way the "performative" role of the different religious groups becomes apparent. Antonia, for example, looked for alternatives that would help her cope with her tough economic situation; she found Catholicism satisfactory since church members helped her with food and clothing every week. Nevertheless, Antonia found that the parish did not provide enough emotional support. She then abandoned Catholicism and looked for that kind of assistance in other groups. She thought she found it in Umbanda. Mariz's perception of the psychological strategies for coping with poverty seem to be available in Umbanda. Antonia found means to overcome depression, helping her to avoid some negative conducts—yelling or hitting her children—and to assume a more positive behavior that improved her household atmosphere. However, after some time this kind of emotional support crumbled. She then turned to Pentecostalism. In Pentecostalism she found a perfect combination of emotional and material support. She found material strategies to cope with poverty. Pentecostal brothers assisted her when she was in need, e.g. they found her eldest son a job. But she also found cultural and psychological strategies to cope with poverty. The emotional support helped her get over depression and improve, once more, her household atmosphere. Also, she found a cultural strategy to cope with poverty, because Pentecostal doctrine provided a means to perceive herself as valuable in spite of her poverty.

The case of Luis and that of Isabel and Roberto also seem to support Mariz's interpretation. They joined Pentecostal churches during critical moments. Thus, according to this approach, religious identities are mainly developed in relation to their (nonreligious) performative consequences. In this view, people select religions considering only the effects they have in the nonreligious aspects of their lives. The problem that this answer gives rise to may be recognized by exploring Antonia's case further. When we compare the kind of help in nonreligious aspects Antonia received in the Catholic, the Umbanda, and Pentecostal churches, we find that these were not very different. In all three cases she found some form of material support, and in the last two she also found means to improve her household atmosphere. Thus if we rely only on the nonreligious performances, the fact that Antonia refused Catholicism and Umbanda and finally joined Pentecostalism becomes hard to explain. An explanation becomes possible only if we look at the religious motives Antonia gave for choosing among these groups.

The reasons Antonia had for not remaining a Catholic were basically religious: the priest's way of explaining how God acts and the sensations she experienced when worshipping saints, did not help Antonia to overcome her initial doubts about God's existence. Because of this, she looked to other groups for assistance. Antonia also had religious motives for joining, and then abandoning, the Umbanda group. She first thought that the *Mãe de Santo* represented a real access to spiritual sources of power, that she had found an appropriate way to relate to sacred forces. Umbanda convinced Antonia that certain kinds of sacred beings existed, and that she could relate to them through the *Mãe de*

Santo. A similar dynamic occurred when Antonia abandoned Umbanda. She found that the ritual did not match her expectations of what worshipping God should be; she felt fear and distress in that moment and interpreted these practices as devilish. This perception transformed the initial emotional support into a stressful element that triggered a process that ended with a change in Antonia's religious affiliation. When analyzing how Antonia got involved in Pentecostalism we again find an association between function and performance. Antonia accepted Pentecostal doctrine and ritual because she felt that they provided an appropriate way of connecting to God. This perception made her more self-confident, less depressed, and able to improve her household atmosphere once more.

I think these issues point to two things. First, that Antonia does not evaluate the religious statements and practices that each religious agent produces only as nonreligious performances. She is also judging them in their dimension of function. In that we can perceive religious motivation. It is only if she can accept them as an appropriate way to relate to sacred forces, and as proper answers to transcendental questions, that she can take advantage of the other strategies that the identity provides, especially of the psychological and cultural "performances" it may allow.

We can also perceive in her case that the combination of function and performance produced a change in her religious identity. From being a passive Catholic, she turned into an active Pentecostal. The case of Luis adds further prove to the importance of religious motivation. It is clear that Luis strengthened his commitment to church because he wanted to overcome his alcoholism, but his story also shows that he thinks a solution may be found only in the church where he finds answers to some of his transcendental questions. So it is in the group where answers to his religious questions are found that solutions to his health problems are also encountered.

The cases of Isabel and Roberto seem to provide a certain counterweight to my recent argument. Isabel's and Roberto's case stresses a practical attitude towards religion. It is when they face problems that they engage in a religious search, and it is to the extent that they perceive that joining a group provides solutions (to finding a job or reuniting the family) that they become committed to it. However, Isabel also seems to be considering other factors. The first thing that attracts her to Pastor Cabrera's radio programs is that they give her an inner feeling of peace. It is this feeling of connecting to some transcendental dimension that first attracts her to Pentecostalism. Roberto also seems to consider specific religious motives, since before joining the Pentecostal church he confronts what the pastor says with the Bible.

So, looking at the previous cases we may conclude that the framing of religious identities proceeds by evaluating each religious group in terms of the way they propose to connect with the sacred—the function of religion—and also the kind of performance they acquire in the nonreligious dimensions of life—the effects on personal economy, family life, health, etc. It is also clear that there are connections between these two dimensions. When people perceive that a group is proposing a correct way of connecting to the sacred, the religion will more easily have an effect in nonreligious aspects of life; and when a religion starts to have beneficial effects in nonreligious aspects of life it will more probably be accepted as a proper religion, as a proper way of connecting with the sacred. It is also clear from previous examples that people assign different weights to these factors; some are more concerned with the function of a religion (Antonia or Luis) and others with its performance (Isabel and Roberto). However, it is rare for a person to consider only one of these aspects.

CONCLUSION:
CONFRONTING THE CASES WITH DOMINANT EXPLANATIONS OF PENTECOSTAL GROWTH IN LATIN AMERICA

What the preceding sections show is that specific religious dimensions are present in religious identity building. Many authors have overlooked this and reduced religious identities to their nonreligious dimensions. In opposition to this kind of reductionism, my claim has been that people choose between religious options by looking at religion as a way to relate to sacred forces and to find answers to transcendental questions. In this chapter I have not been able to do much more than to acknowledge the existence of this religious motivation. However, these findings do suggest a different way of thinking about the causes and consequences of Pentecostal expansion.

If we look at what happened with Antonia and the others, we can see that the changes they experienced occured mainly in their religious practices and beliefs. Conversion to Pentecostalism did not result in a radical transformation of their cultural background, family life or economic status. Rather, it enabled them to overcome certain familial and economic problems that they were facing. It did, however, lead to a significant transformation of their customary religious practices and beliefs. From being passive Catholics, attending mass only once in a while, and not being very convinced of God's existence, they became quite active Pentecostals who perceived that sacred beings and forces may directly intervene in their lives. This happened as a result of the Pentecostal doctrine and rituals, and its major impact was on their religious beliefs and practices.

While there is not enough evidence to reach any definitive conclusions on how widespread this experience of religious transformation has been, it seems likely that experiences similar to those of Antonia and the others were quite common in Argentina during the 1980s. Protestants, predominantly Pentecostals, grew significantly, expanding from 3 percent to approximately 10 percent of the Argentinian population. Of those who converted 83.2 percent were nominal Catholics, who are now most likely active Pentecostals, since according to Roemers (1992) 72 percent of Argentine Pentecostals consider themselves to be religious activists. All these elements are present in Antonia's and the other's stories. Thus, we may make an informed guess and suppose that one of the main impacts of the growth of Pentecostalism in Argentina is that a whole new group of religious activists (who formerly were passive Catholics) has emerged because of Pentecostalism's ability to transform people's perception of the sacred.

NOTES

1   The evidence I present here was collected during fieldwork done in 1992 and 1994-1995 in a lower-middle-class and poor neighborhood located in the out-skirts of Buenos Aires. In those years I did interviewing and participant obser-vation in a Pentecostal congregation and a Catholic chapel of the neighborhood. The information gathered was complementary to information I gathered on the political and social institutions of the neighborhood between 1988 and 1991. My views on the religious life of the neighborhood are based on the informa-tion that sixty-five informants provided during those years of research.

2   According to Haime (1994), 83.2 percent of Pentecostal converts were for-merly nominal Catholics

3   Roemers (1992) reported that 43 percent of Pentecostals belong to the lower-middle classes, and 48 percent to the poor. In another survey Saracco found that 44 percent of the Pentecostal pastors of the sixteen more important min-istries of the country were masons or involved in casual labor. Another 54 per-cent were employees, school teachers, or blue collar workers. Of the total number of pastors, only 28 percent had finished secondary school.

4   A significant amount of literature with this kind of approach has appeared in recent years. Just to mention a few: Brusco (1995) has reported that Pente-costalism may be a means by which women deal with the reckless conduct that machismo produces in males; Ireland (1991, 1993), Burdick (1993), and Rolim (1995) have shown the ways in which Pentecostalism and political iden-tities connect.

REFERENCES

Bastian, Jean Pierre. 1992. "Les protestantismes Latino Americains: un obje a interroger et a contruire." *Social Compass*, 39 (3): 327-354.

―――. 1993"The Metamorphosis of Latin American Protestant Groups." *Latin American Research Review*, 28 (2): 33-61

Bellah, Robert. 1970. "Civil Religion in America." In *Beyond Belief: Essays on Religion in a Post-Traditional World*. New York: Harper and Row, 168-189.

Berger, Peter. 1967. *The Sacred Canopy. Elements of a Sociological Theory of Religion*. Garden City, NJ: Doubleday.

Beyer, Peter. 1990. "Privatization and the Public Influence of Religion in Global Society." In M. Feathertone, ed. *Global Culture: Nationalism, Globalization and Modernity*. London: SAGE, 373-396.

Brusco, Elizabeth. 1995. *The Reformation of Machismo. Evangelical Conversion and Gender in Colombia*. Austin: University of Texas Press.

Burdick, John. 1993. "Struggling Against the Devil: Pentecostalism and Social Movements in Urban Brazil." In. V. Garrard-Burnett and D. Stoll, eds. *Rethinking Protestantism in Latin America*. Philadelphia: Temple University Press.

Cheresky, Isidoro. 1992. *Creencias Políticas, Partidos y Elecciones*. Buenos Aires: Instituto de Investigaciones–Facultad de Ciencias Sociales.

Deiros, Pablo. 1991. "Protestant fundamentalism in Latin America." In M. Marty and R. Scott, eds. *Fundamentalisms Observed*. Chicago: University of Chicago Press, 142-196.

Droogers, Andre and Hans Siebers. 1991. "Popular Religion and Power in Latin America: An Introduction." In A. Droogers, G. Huizer, H. Siebers, eds. *Popular Power in Latin American Religions*. Saarbrucken: Verlag Breitenbach, 1-25.

Droogers, Andre and Susanna Rostas. 1993. "The Popular Use of Popular Religion in Latin America: Introduction." In A. Droogers and S. Rostas, eds. *The Popular Use of Popular Religion in Latin America*. Amsterdam: CEDLA, 1-16.

Duarte, Carlos. 1995. *Las Mil y Una Caras de la Religión. Sectas y Nuevos Movimientos Religiosos en América Latina*. Quito: CLAI.

Forni, Floreal. 1991. "Estudio comparativo de los grupos organizados para la actividad religiosa en el gran Buenos Aires (II)." *Sociedad y Religión*, 8: 15-23.

―――. 1993. "Nuevos movimientos religiosos en la Argentina." In A. Frigerio, ed. *Nuevos Movimientos religiosos y Ciencias Sociales (II)*. Buenos Aires: Centro Editor de América Latina, 7-23.

Frigerio, Alejandro. 1993. "'La Invasión de las Sectas': El Debate sobre Nuevos Movimientos Religiosos en los Medios de Comunicación en Argentina." *Sociedad y Religión*, 10/11: 10-27.

Frigerio, Alejandro and Maria Carozzi. 1992. "Las religiones afrobrasileñas en Argentina." *Cuadernos de Antropología*, 10: 39-68.

Gill, Lesley. 1993. "Religious Mobility and the Many Words of God in La Paz, Bolivia." In D. Stoll and V. Garrard-Burnett, eds. *Rethinking Protestantism in Latin America*. Philadelphia: Temple University Press, pp. 180-198.

Green, Linda. 1993. "Shifting Affiliations: Mayan Widows and Evangélicos in Guatemala." In D. Stoll and V. Garrard-Burnett, eds. *Rethinking Protes-*

tantism in Latin America. Philadelphia: Temple University Press, 159-179.

Haime, Hugo. 1994. "Parliamentary Document No. 22," Legislative Chambers of the State of Buenos Aires.

Ireland, Rowan. 1991. *Kingdoms Come. Religions and Politics in Brazil*. Pittsburgh: University of Pittsburgh Press.

————. 1993. "The crentes of Campo Alegre and the religious construction of Brazilian politics." In D. Stoll and V. Garrard-Burnett, eds. *Rethinking Protestantism in Latin America*. Philadelphia: Temple University Press, 45-65.

Jenkins, Richard. 1996. *Social Identity*. New York: Routledge.

Kniss, Fredd. 1991. "Tongues of fire." *Sociological Analysis*, 52: 217-219.

Lalive d'Epinay, Christian. 1968. *El Refugio de las Masas*. Santiago de Chile: Editorial del Pacífico.

Luckmann, Thomas. 1967. *The Invisible Religion: The Problem of Religion in Modern Society*. New York: Collier-Macmillan.

Luhmann, Nicklass. 1982. *The differentiation of Society*. New York: Columbia University Press.

Mallimaci, Fortunato. 1993. "Catolicismo integral, identidad nacional y nuevos movimientos religiosos." In A. Frigerio, ed. *Nuevos Movimientos Religiosos y Ciencias Sociales (II)*. Buenos Aires: Centro Editor de América Latina, 24-48.

Mariz, Cecília. 1990. "Igrejas pentecostais e estrategias de sobrevivencia." In J. Braga, ed. *Religiao e Cidadania*. Bahia: DEA-UFBA-EGBA, 89-112.

————. 1994. *Religion and Coping with Poverty in Brazil*. Philadelphia: Temple University Press.

Martin, David. 1990. *Tongues of Fire*. Oxford: Blackwell.

————. 1991. "Otro tipo de revolución cultural." *Estudios Públicos*, 44: 40-62.

McGuire, Meredith. 1992. *Religion: The Social Context*. Belmont: Wadsworth.

Míguez, Daniel. n.d. *Spiritual Bonfire in Argentina. The Making of a Pentecostal Identity in a Buenos Aires Suburb*. Amsterdam: Centre for the Study and Documentation of Latin America (CLASS Series). Forthcoming.

Oro, Pedro Ari. 1996. *Avanço Pentecostal e Reacâo Catolica*. Petropólis: Vozes.

Parsons, Talcott. 1966. "Religion in a Modern Pluralistic Society." *Review of Religious Research*, 7: 125-146.

Pascual, Martín. 1991. "Cultos anómicos." *Religiosidad Popular en la Argentina*. Buenos Aires: Centro Editor de América Latina.

Pluss, Jean Daniel. 1988. *Therapeutic and Prophetic Narratives in Worship*. Frankfurt: Verlag Peter Lang.

Portantiero, Juan Carlos. 1993. "Revisando el camino: las apuestas de la democracia en Sudamérica." *Sociedad*, 2: 23-44.

Roemers, Graciela. 1992. "Creyentes mas non tropo." *Revista Pagina*, 30 (January).

Roldán, Verónica. 1991. "Cultos de santificación." *Religiosidad Popular en la Argentina*. Buenos Aires: Centro Editor de América Latina, 53-61.

Rolim, Francisco. 1995. *Pentecostalismo. Brasil e América Latina*. Petrópolis: Vozes.

Santamaría, Daniel. 1991. "La cuestión de la religiosidad popular en la Argentina." *Religiosidad Popular en la Argentina*. Buenos Aires: Centro Editor de América Latina, 9-23.

Saracco, Norberto J. 1989. *Argentine Pentecostalism: Its History and Theology.* Unpublished Doctoral dissertation, University of Birmingham.

Stoll, David. 1990. *Is Latin America Turning Protestant?* Berkeley: University of California Press.

Willems, Emilio. 1967. *Followers of the New Faith.* Nashville, TN: Vanderbilt University Press.

Wynarczyk, Hilario. 1989. *Tres Evangelistas Carismáticos: Omar Cabrera, Annacondia, Giménez.* Buenos Aires. Mimeo.

Wynarczyk, Hilario and Pablo Semán, 1994. "Campo evangélico y pentecostalismo en la Argentina." In A. Frigerio, ed. *El Pentecostalismo en la Argentina.* Buenos Aires: Centro Editor de América Latina, 29-43.

Zanatta, Loris. 1996. *Del Estado Liberal a la Nación Católica. Iglesia y Estado en los Orígenes del Peronismo.* Buenos Aires: Editorial de la Universidad de Quilmes.

TWELVE

ESOTERIC LITERATURE AS A MICROCOSMIC MIRROR OF BRAZIL'S RELIGIOUS MARKETPLACE

Robert Carpenter

Prestigious book fairs often reflect current cultural trends that transcend the boundaries of a society's literary market. In August of 1995 I attended Brazil's National Book Fair in Rio de Janeiro to see how much, if at all, the exposition would reflect the burgeoning presence of esoterica in Brazilian popular culture and, indeed, esoteric influence was present to a striking degree. Out of approximately 220 total exhibits by publishers and bookstores at the exposition, at least a dozen belonged to exhibitors who explicitly presented themselves as "esoteric" proponents. Another half-dozen exhibits by major publishers prominently featured their own extensive esoteric series of books, bearing such names as *Enigmas from All Eras*, *The Arch of Time*, and *New Age*. The vast majority of the remaining stands included books unequivocally identified as being esoteric—the exceptions being those relatively few booths displaying works issued either by governmental agencies, university presses, or technically-oriented publishers. So compelling was the market demand in this particular regard that even major exhibitors affiliated directly either with the Catholic church or with Afro-Brazilian traditions also adopted the strategy of prominently displaying works featuring esoteric themes.

BRAZILIAN ESOTERIC LITERATURE IN THE CONTEXT OF EMERGING ALTERNATIVE SPIRITUALITIES IN LATIN AMERICA

This vignette from Brazil's National Book Fair exemplifies a dynamic recent development in urban Latin American culture: namely, the proliferation of *alternative spiritualities* among the region's urban middle classes and elites, and the collateral impact exerted by these traditions upon popular culture. This phenomenon has scarcely appeared on the scholarly radar screen outside of Latin America thus far, much as was the case with Pentecostalism's spread in the region prior to the 1990s. As the world crosses the threshhold of the Third Millennium, however, this emerging sector of Brazil's religious marketplace can be expected to draw increased attention from scholars tracking religious trends in the region.

What are alternative spiritualities, and what part do they play in the religious economies of Latin America? In one sense, they constitute a residual category, homologous to Timothy Miller's notion of "alternative religions" in the North American context. For Miller, alternative religions comprise all traditions situated outside the religious mainstream within a particular culture (Miller 1995: 1-3). But replacing the word "religions" in Miller's term with "spiritualities" yields a distinctive connotation, as expressed in the following capsule description by Ewert Cousins (1987: 306):

> Spirituality refers to the experiential dimension of religion in contrast with formal beliefs, external practices, and institutions; it deals with the inner depth of the person that is open to the transcendent; in traditions that affirm the divine, it is concerned with the relation of the person to the divine, the experience of the divine, and the journey of the person to a more intimate relationship with the divine.

Hence, alternative spiritualities are highly individualistic and experientially oriented approaches to the transcendent that are found outside the religious mainstream within a given cultural context. An insightful Latin American interpretation of alternative spiritualities can be found in an article by Brazilian anthropologist Luiz Eduardo Soares entitled, "Religious by Nature: Alternative Culture and Ecological Mysticism in Brazil" (Soares 1989b). In analyzing alternative culture within the Brazilian context, Soares sketches certain implications for spirituality. He identifies a Body-Spirit-Nature triad at its core, adding that Energy is the key element binding the categorys' various individual components together (124-25).

Alternative spiritualities encompass a diversified constellation of teachings and practices that address metaphysical, therapeutic, psychological, and/or ecological concerns. In addition, they include various divinatory techniques, such as different astrological, Tarot, and cabalistic systems, the I Ching, and Scandinavian runes. Specifically in Brazil, the category also includes a loose-knit array of expressions, both imported and local in origin, derived from Hinduism, Buddhism, Islam, and Japanese New Religions, as well as from Theosophy and other occult, metaphysical, and Oriental traditions.

The principal modes by which alternative spiritualities have been growing are arguably unconventional, at least in the Latin American cultural context. Their proponents have not resorted to the street-corner preaching, daily storefront healing services, processions, or massive stadium rallies that typify other religious traditions. Instead, they have relied primarily upon the sale and distribution of literature, in addition to courses, workshops, and seminars, usually on a fee-for-service basis. The prominent display of esoteric literature at the National Book Fair in Rio de Janeiro reflects this approach. My examination in this chapter of the relationship between esoteric literature, as one specific facet of alternative spiritualities, and the Brazilian religious marketplace as a whole is intended to shed some light on the exceptional capacity demonstrated by alternative spiritualities to pique the interest of the general public.

Overview and Significance of This Study

The research findings presented in this chapter are part of a larger project in which I analyze possible implications of the recent emergence of alternative spiritualities in Brazil for the overall dynamics of religious competition throughout Latin America. My purpose in narrowing the focus here strictly to the literature produced by the region's most well-developed esoteric sector is to convey the extent to which esoteric teachings and practices reflect the kaleidoscopic diversity of Brazil's overall religious marketplace. A brief examination of the authors and the content of a selected sample of esoteric texts shows just how tenuous and imprecise are the boundaries that set off Brazil's esoteric sector from some of the more established religious traditions, including Roman Catholicism, Afro-Brazilian traditions, Kardecist Spiritism, and liberal Protestantism, as well as from several quasi-religious fields. With a nod to classical esotericism's Hermetic law of correspondence between microcosm and macrocosm ("as above, so below") (Faivre 1994: 10; Hanegraaff 1998: 398), I employ the image of a microcosmic mirror to represent the manner in which esoteric literature in Brazil reflects, assimilates, and recombines elements found throughout the ambient macrocosm of the religious marketplace nationwide.

What distinctive contributions does this chapter offer to the overall study of religion in Latin America? I have already mentioned that the larger phenomenon within which esoteric literature is embedded, the dynamic growth of alternative spiritualities in Latin America, has yet to be studied in depth by scholars of religion.[1] Why is this the case? A prime reason is that the episode of religious dynamism under study here takes place, for the most part, in an unexpected quarter: namely, among Latin America's educated urban elites and middle classes (cf. Parker 1996: 156-58). Latin Americanists are accustomed to associating religious dynamism predominantly with the poor and working classes, as is the case with Pentecostal churches, Catholic Base Ecclesial

Communities, and diverse traditions based upon spirit possession. When it comes to esotericism and other expressions of alternative spirituality, however, we find profound changes occurring in patterns of religious and/or spiritual attitudes and behavior within a highly literate, well-educated segment of the population.

Another original aspect of this research is its methodological approach to contemporary esoteric literature in Brazil. The focus on the reciprocal relationship between esoteric literature and the larger religious marketplace, as well as neighboring cultural domains, employs a modified production-of-culture analytical approach, which is geared toward analyzing specific cultural products within the context of different types of multiorganizational fields (Peterson 1994; Oliven 1984). This approach entailed conducting interviews with individuals involved in various phases of the production of esoteric literature in Brazil, including authors, acquisition editors, and bookstore owners.

The importance of contextualizing Brazilian esoteric literature within the larger phenomenon of alternative spiritualities in contemporary Latin America dictates the structure of this chapter. Following a capsule description of Brazil's esoteric boom episode thus far in the next section of the chapter, I examine questions of the meaning and boundaries of esotericism in the current Brazilian context. Then I explore the most directly pertinent aspects of Brazil's religious marketplace as macrocosm before turning to some examples of esoteric literature in the final section to highlight their microcosmic implications.

ESOTERISM WITH A LATIN BEAT:
AN OVERVIEW OF BRAZIL'S ESOTERIC BOOM OF THE 1980S AND 1990S

The aggressive marketing of esoteric literature at the 1995 National Book Fair described at the outset of this chapter represented a rational response to widespread demand for esoterica in urban Brazilian culture at that time. The demand become so intense that it unleashed a veritable esoteric boom, which was first manifested in a surge in the sales of esoteric books in the latter half of the 1980s. July of 1986 might well be pinpointed as the beginning of the esoteric boom, because that is when Marion Zimmer Bradley's *The Mists of Avalon* became the first book categorized as esoteric to appear in the regular listing of bestselling books compiled by *Veja*, a national Brazilian newsmagazine.[2] *The Mists of Avalon* would remain on *Veja*'s bestseller list intermittently for the next two years, alongside translations of other esoteric works by non-Brazilian authors, including Bradley's *Web of Light* and *Web of Darkness* and Shirley MacLaine's *Out on a Limb* and *Dancing in the*

Light. The remarkable popularity of these works soon captured the attention of Brazil's largest publishing houses, which were somewhat adrift amid prolonged doldrums in the literary market. Several mainstream publishers seized the opportunity to make their debut in the esoteric market niche by inaugurating new special collections or series, joining a handful of their peers who had long specialized in esoteric/occult literature.

The esoteric market niche continued to be dominated by non-Brazilian authors until a rather unlikely challenge was mounted by Paulo Coelho, a well-known iconoclastic rock music lyricist from the early 1970s who began turning out books in the popular occult genre in the 1980s. Coelho's first two books—*The Alchemist* (1988 [1995]) and *Diary of a Magus* (1987 [1995])—made their debut on *Veja*'s bestseller list in the magazine's July 19, 1989, issue. They remained there intermittently until the list stopped appearing three years later. Coelho's initial success served as a wedge to pry open the gates to the literary market for other Brazilian authors, inasmuch as several well-known publishers were thereby prompted to assume the risk of contracting relatively unknown Brazilian writers to turn out esoteric works.[3]

Before long, prime-time television audiences found themselves being introduced to miscellaneous esoteric teachings and practices either through documentary programs or through *telenovelas*, i.e., the serial dramas and comedies that are so popular throughout Latin America. Heightened media exposure boosted consumer demand not only for esoteric literature but also for related products and services. By the mid-1990s, the boom had entered a new entrepreneurial phase, giving rise to mushrooming networks of bookstores, accessory shops, seminar and study centers, therapeutic facilities, and even consulting firms in larger cities all across Brazil. Data on these networks are limited, but anthropological research conducted in 1995 in Greater São Paulo identified more than one thousand esoteric groups and establishments within Brazil's largest metropolitan region (Magnani 1995). My own field research, which was conducted in Rio de Janeiro, the country's second-largest metropolitan region, indicates that an esoteric network of comparable expanse is thriving there, as well.

Considering the overall trajectory of Brazil's esoteric boom, the impetus it has derived from both the publishing industry and the mass media has been of crucial importance. The expansion of local, regional, and national esoteric networks in Brazilian culture has been fueled not so much by individual groups and entities gaining "converts" in a conventional sense; rather, the networks' growth is attributable primarily to their constituents' success in attracting readers, clients, patrons, customers, students, and seminar/workshop participants—in short, "consumers," of whom no lasting commitment is demanded but who furnish the wherewithal, nonetheless, to maintain the system. This evokes the "cultic milieu" profile first traced by Colin Campbell with reference to Britain and North America, in which

> [m]ore than anything else the cultic world is kept alive by the magazines, periodicals, books, pamphlets, lectures, demonstrations and informal meetings through which its beliefs and practices are discussed and disseminated. However, unlike the sectarian situation [sic] these communication media are not bounded by the framework of beliefs of a particular collectivity but are generally open (Campbell 1972: 123).

The quotation from Colin Campbell foregrounds boundary issues that have been lurking just beneath the surface throughout the entire discussion thus far. How is the term "esotericism" being used within the specific context of this study? What are its boundaries, insofar as which traditions and phenomena it encompasses and which it does not ? These boundary issues entail consideration of the connotation which the term has acquired in the contemporary Latin American cultural milieu, involving some significant changes from the classical understanding of esotericism.

WHAT IS ESOTERICISM . . .

Establishing precise parameters for the designation "esotericism" and its usage, including boundaries that serve to distinguish between that which is esoteric and that which is not, is no less formidable a task in the contemporary Brazilian case than in other cultural contexts past and present. For example, Astrology, Hermetism, Rosicrucianism, and the Theosophical Society are all unequivocally identified with the Western esoteric tradition, but many other cases are rife with ambiguity. Antoine Faivre, who has written extensively on the history of the Western esoteric tradition, contends that "the meaning of 'esotericism,' never a precise term to begin with, has begun to overflow its boundaries on all sides," particularly amid pressures generated by literary marketing and media discourse (Faivre 1994: 3). At the same time, esotericism has retained such core elements as microcosmic/macrocosmic "correspondences," the quest for concordances between distinct belief systems, and the principle of transmutation.[4]

One of the most significant modifications undergone by esotericism in modernity, distinguishing it from its classical expressions, is a radical departure from that which once was one of its core elements: hiddenness, or secrecy (Faivre 1994: 5). Esoteric cultural movements, such as the occult revival of the 1960s in western Europe and the United States and the current esoteric boom in Brazil, clearly would not have been possible if secrecy had remained an essential aspect of esotericism. Indeed, from the standpoint of most urban esoteric communities in the current Western cultural environment, secrecy is more of an impediment than an asset, insofar as it relates to the realization of their expansionary aspirations.

The Brazilian religious landscape harbors certain religious traditions that likely would be labeled "esoteric" in many other cultural contexts but constitute more ambiguous cases in Brazil because of the autonomous cultural identity they have acquired there. Prime examples include some of the more prominent Afro-Brazilian traditions, as well as Kardecist Spiritism. Andrés Rodríguez Ibarra addresses this issue explicitly in studying the esoteric network in and around Brazil's capital, Brasília. He excludes Kardecist Spiritism and Afro-Brazilian traditions from the esoteric category based on a functionalist definition of "esoteric" that is virtually synonymous with "exotic": viz., "every-thing outside the cultural patterns into which we are socialized within a given society" (Rodríguez Ibarra 1992: 29-30). With Brazil's religious field as it is presently constituted, this would require that all Oriental and, ironically enough, indigenous Brazilian traditions be classified as esoteric, along with beliefs and practices derived from classical Western esoteric traditions. On the other hand, according to Rodríguez Ibarra, any traditions deemed to fit within Brazilian patterns of socialization are to be classified as "exoteric," including Catholicism, Protestantism, the various Afro-Brazilian traditions, and Kardecism (29-30). The case studies he selects for inclusion in his ethnographic study of Brasilia's esoteric network consist of courses offered to the public in the following four areas: astrology, Gnostic philosophy, Tai Chi Chuan (exercises based on the Taoist tradition), and holism.

I should point out that this issue of excluding Afro-Brazilian tradi-tions and Kardecism from the esoteric category in Brazil is not clear-cut. In the course of the interviews that I conducted with proponents of esotericism in Brazil, I heard strong opinions expressed on both sides of the question. Some hold that esotericism's boundaries should be elastic enough to encompass elements from a wide variety of traditions, while others call for maintaining rigid distinctions between, for example, esotericism and Afro-Brazilian traditions. A separate question altogether concerns the divergent currents which exist within Umbanda—including a highly vocal minority faction that prefers to classify Umbanda as esoteric rather than as Afro-Brazilian. With due appreciation for the flexibility of the boundaries of esotericism as it is constituted in Brazil, I choose to treat Kardecism and the conventional Afro-Brazilian traditions as nonesoteric. As for the unique case of Umbanda, I treat it as straddling the boundary between esotericism and the Afro-Brazilian traditions.

. . . AND WHAT BUSINESS DOES IT HAVE THRIVING IN LATIN AMERICA'S RELIGIOUS MARKETPLACES?

Rodríguez Ibarra's aforementioned bottom line as to what qualifies as esoteric and what does not in Brazil—namely, inherent cultural patterns of socialization—highlights the inherent cultural gap between esoteric traditions and mainstream religious culture. Indeed, the esoteric networks thriving of late in São Paulo, Rio de Janeiro, and other Brazilian urban centers in many ways seem more attuned to the highly individualistic "seeker" culture and "self-spirituality" of postmodern western Europe and North America (cf. Campbell 1972 and 1982; Heelas 1982; Roof 1993; Roof, Carroll, and Roozen 1994) than to the traditionally communitarian religious culture of Latin America. This can be seen, for example, in the consumer mentality that pervades the esoteric boom much in the same way as it does the New Age movement which emerged in the Northern Hemisphere during the past two decades (cf. Heelas 1993 and 1996; Hanegraaf 1998). David J. Hess was struck by the parallel while conducting research on Kardecist Spiritism in Brazil during the initial phase of the esoteric boom in the 1980s; Hess refers to several encounters with "the world of alternative Brazilian religion, science, and medicine—a Brazilian New Age which makes that of California seem bland in comparison" (Hess 1991b: 2).

Another aspect of the various alternative traditions clustered under the esoteric umbrella in which a connection with the New Age readily comes to light is the literature associated with those traditions. According to standard usage in the Brazilian and Latin American literary markets, categories such as "esoteric" and "holistic" correspond to the broad "New Age" classification that is common parlance in the international book trade. This means that works by North American and European authors identified with New Age circles are typically marketed in Brazil as being esoteric in character,[5] with the classificatory criteria deliberately kept flexible and imprecise.

In considering the parallels and links between Brazil's esoteric boom and the international New Age movement, a cautionary note is in order. The proliferation of alternative spiritualities is not a process entirely alien to Latin American religious culture. Were this the case, it is highly unlikely that alternative spiritualities would have enjoyed as favorable a reception as has been the case. This is where the microcosmic mirror imagery from the title of this chapter weighs in. Such imagery calls attention to the connections and continuities existing between alternative spiritualities and Brazil's overall religious marketplace, as reflected in esoteric literature. In order for these connections and continuities to be fully appreciated by the reader, the next section of the chapter presents an overview of the Brazilian religious marketplace's most pertinent features.

SHIFTING CONTOURS OF THE BRAZILIAN RELIGIOUS MARKETPLACE

The following superlatives apply to the Brazilian religious marketplace: home to the world's largest Catholic population, as well as to more Pentecostals, Spiritists, and adherents of traditions derived from African religions than can be found in any other country in the world. Moreover, there are more followers of the cluster of traditions known as Japanese New Religions in Brazil than in any other country outside of Japan. Brazil's religious economy is unquestionably the most diversified in all of Latin America, and it is within this thoroughly eclectic religiocultural milieu that esotericism has been making inroads during the boom period.

The limited scope of this chapter will not permit a detailed exposition of the contemporary Brazilian religious marketplace.[6] Consequently, this section of the chapter will focus upon three aspects of Brazil's overall religious marketplace that have a direct bearing on esoteric literary production: (a) the widespread practice of combining elements pertaining to multiple traditions, (b) the recent weakening of the Catholic church's longtime hegemony, and (c) the expanding presence of publications associated with the nonesoteric traditions.

ADMIXTURE AS A TRADEMARK OF THE BRAZILIAN RELIGIOUS MARKETPLACE

The dynamics of admixture or blending pervade Brazilian culture as a whole, including its religious sphere. In a published report from an interdisciplinary research project on syncretism carried out under the auspices of the Institute for the Study of Religion (ISER) in Rio de Janeiro, Cecília Mariz and Maria das Dores C. Machado make the following sweeping assertion: "Brazilian identity has been constructed upon the idea of a syncretism, at once ethnoracial and religious, among whites, blacks, and Indians" (Mariz and Machado 1994: 26). Mariz's and Machado's assertion mirrors a pluralistic religious culture characterized by porous boundaries between distinct traditions, by a tolerance of diversity, and by a predisposition towards experimentation and innovation—all of which are deeply congruent with Brazilian cultural identity.

The term "syncretism" employed by Mariz and Machado, once routinely used in both ecclesiastical and academic literature to refer to the practice of combining elements from distinct religious traditions, is now widely dismissed as discriminatory, arbitrary, and oppressive because of the implication that "blended" traditions are inferior to ostensibly "pure" ones (Droogers 1989: 9; cf. Shaw and Stewart 1994). Nonetheless, syncretism as an analytical concept continues in use within Brazil's scholarly community. While acknowledging the syncretistic label's problematic history in both ecclesiastical and academic circles, social scientists in Brazil tend to apply it in a laudatory manner, validating their compatriots' demonstration of creativity. Consider, for example, how Pierre Sanchis situates the innate Brazilian proclivity for admixture in the religious sphere on the cutting edge of contemporary Western spirituality:

> I would like to suggest that this traditionally (as in a "premodern" sense) syncretic character of the Brazilian religious universe makes Brazil, paradoxically, a fertile field for the study of a phenomenon that observers of the most advanced societies classify as an ultra-modern development: religious eclecticism (Sanchis 1995: 124).

By "premodern" syncretism, Sanchis is alluding to two prominent forms of admixture in Brazilian religious history: folk Catholicism and Afro-Brazilian traditions. Both are rooted in the extensive and intensive process which Roger Bastide characterizes as "interpenetration" among indigenous, European, and African civilizations during Brazil's colonial period (Bastide 1978: 12-19, 109-42, 173-83). Such beginnings permanently infused Brazilian religious culture with an ethos of admixture. The only segment of Brazil's religious marketplace that has consistently and systematically resisted the blending of elements from different traditions is Protestantism; at least this has been true for its dominant Pentecostal and evangelical wings. Meanwhile, religious admixture has contributed decisively to the overall dynamism of other segments of the religious marketplace, most notably Kardecist Spiritism, Umbanda, and Japanese New Religions.

Kardecist Spiritism emerged in France in the late 1850s as a synthesis of elements from a broad array of sources—including Catholicism, Protestantism, Mesmerism, Swedenborgianism, Anglo-Saxon Spiritualism, and even Vedic religious traditions, a synthesis that Allan Kardec, the founder, defended as a rigorously scientific approach to religious belief and practice. After its arrival in Brazil in the 1860s, Kardecist Spiritism underwent a process which Hess labels as "medicalization," inasmuch as therapeutic practices received steadily increasing and ever more conspicuous emphasis (Hess 1987: 19). This reconfiguration eventually opened up new frontiers for admixture in the Brazilian sociocultural context, as Kardecist therapists discovered conceptual affinities with practitioners of various alternative therapies, such as homeopathy, parapsychology, acupuncture, and past-lives regression (Hess 1991b: 139; cf. Hess 1995).

Religious admixture has also played an influential part in the growth achieved by Japanese New Religions (JNRs) in Brazil, primarily since the 1960s. Much as Kardecism arrived in Brazil as a product of already considerable blending, the JNRs came from Japan already containing elements of Buddhism, Shinto, Confucianism, and even Christianity. Seicho-no-ie (House of Blessing or Growth), which is generally acknowledged to have amassed the largest following thus far of all the Japanese New Religions in Brazil, also includes elements derived from New Thought (Carpenter and Roof 1995: 45-46).

The foregoing examples notwithstanding, the consummate example of religious admixture in Brazil is Umbanda, which should more accurately be regarded as a cluster of traditions rather than as a single tradition. The African influence upon Umbanda is unmistakable. Nevertheless, the cluster first emerged in Brazil's most developed urban centers in the 1920s and 1930s as an eclectic synthesis—primarily of Roman Catholic, Afro-Brazilian, indigenous Brazilian and Kardecist elements, with traces of Hinduism, Buddhism, and Theosophy, as well (Ortiz 1988: 16-17; Brown 1994: 1). A major impetus for religious admixture among Umbandists stems from an ongoing struggle for preeminence between competing factions: on the one hand, those Umbanda groups and local centers who strongly identify with Afro-Brazilian traditions, and on the other hand, those Umbanda groups and local centers who identify more closely with Kardecist Spiritism (Brown 1994: 38-49; Hess 1991b: 156-58). To complicate matters further, a small but vocal esoteric contingent within Umbanda ranks claims both Western and Oriental occult traditions as a basis for the legitimacy either of certain practices or even of Umbanda itself (Brown 1994: 41-43).

Religious admixture has remained a ubiquitous feature of Brazilian religious culture throughout more than four centuries of domination by the Catholic church. The expansion of opportunities for the blending of elements from different traditions would only be expected to intensify under the impact of the next aspect of the Brazilian religious marketplace to be considered: the Catholic church's declining power and influence relative to other traditions.

THE WEAKENING OF THE CATHOLIC CHURCH'S HISTORICAL HEGEMONY IN BRAZIL

The erosion of Roman Catholicism's longstanding hegemonic status in Brazil's religious marketplace over recent decades is most evident in the dwindling of the Catholic rank and file, although this is not clearly reflected in census data. Census data on religious affiliation prior to and including 1970 consistently showed Roman Catholics accounting for at least a 90 percent share of the population, with no significant variation between censuses; even by 1980, the Roman Catholic share had dipped only slightly, to 89.2 percent. Meanwhile, the Protestant percentage had been steadily increasing—3.4 percent in 1950, 4.0 percent in 1960, 5.2 percent in 1970, 6.6 percent in 1980—whereas the composite "Spiritist" category (encompassing not only Kardecism but also Afro-Brazilian traditions and Umbanda) had been holding steady at less than 1.5 percent.[7] (This latter figure is highly misleading, inasmuch as it fails to reflect the widespread incidence of multiple religious affiliation in Brazil and therefore drastically understates the amount of participation in the various traditions lumped together by the census under the "Spiritist" category—Ribeiro de Oliveira 1977). Although more recent census data on religious affiliation is unavailable, the most recent reliable estimates, based on independent survey data gathered in 1994, show the Catholic percentage of the Brazilian population as having dropped to 75 percent (Prandi and Pierucci 1995: 1).[8] This decrease reflects that which Luiz Eduardo Soares calls a "veritable internal diaspora" (Soares, 1989b: 123), in which former Catholics by the thousands have switched their primary allegiance to evangelical Protestantism, Pentecostalism, Umbanda, Afro-Brazilian traditions, or Kardecism.

A decisive factor behind this sea change in the Brazilian religious economy was the Catholic hierarchy's shift to a more tolerant stance regarding religious pluralism. During the preconciliar period, Afro-Brazilian traditions and Umbanda were systematically denounced by the press, often at the instigation of the Catholic hierarchy, as primitive, backward, superstitious, and, in some cases, socially pathological corruptions of orthodox Roman Catholicism. Lumped together with Kardecism, they were jointly denounced by Franciscan bishop Friar Bonaventura Kloppenburg in widely circulated polemical books written to warn the Catholic faithful against the composite phenomenon designated "Spiritism" (Kloppenburg 1960 and 1961; cf. Hess 1991: 157-58).

The decade of the 1960s brought sweeping changes to the Catholic church worldwide in the wake of the Second Vatican Council (1963-65). Subsequent General Conferences of Latin American Bishops—at

Medellín, Colombia (1968), at Puebla, Mexico (1979), and at Santo Domingo, Dominican Republic (1982)—were instrumental in altering various national episcopates' longstanding posture toward non-Catholic traditions from one of discrimination to one of competitive coexistence. The Brazilian Catholic hierarchy's corresponding shift in this direction proved to be a decisive factor indeed in further opening up the country's religious marketplace (Montero 1992: 228; Hess 1991b: 157-58). On a pragmatic level, this meant simply that non-Catholic traditions faced greatly diminished interference from civil authorities and gentler forms of criticism from Catholic religious authorities than had previously been the case. But even more importantly, the shift in attitude on the part of the hierarchy drastically diminished the stigma which had formerly deterred many Catholic parishioners from investigating the claims, teachings, rituals, and practices of other religious traditions. A primary beneficiary of this development has been religious publishing across the full spectrum of the Brazilian religious marketplace.

THE IMPACT OF THE PUBLISHED WORD IN THE POSTCONCILIAR BRAZILIAN RELIGIOUS MARKETPLACE

The significant rise in the non-Catholic proportion of the population is not the only modification in Brazil's religious marketplace to have resulted from the Catholic hierarchy's adoption of a more tolerant position towards other religious traditions. Increased pluralism has dynamized the entire religious publishing sector, including that portion affiliated with the Catholic church, as the various traditions take advantage of every available avenue to compete in a lively marketplace of ideas.

Brazil's major Catholic publishing houses had traditionally specialized in a narrow range of catechetical, theological, and apologetic works which implacably advocated conservative views. But then Vozes, which had published many of Friar Bonaventura Kloppenburg's polemical attacks on non-Catholic religious traditions prior to Vatican II, assumed a pioneering role in disseminating works reflecting the newer, more progressive policy positions of the National Conference of Brazilian Bishops (CNBB) (Montero 1992: 228-29). Franciscan friar Leonardo Boff, a prolific author of books on liberation theology in his own right, assumed the key post of editor of the religion division at Vozes and pushed to expand its catalogue in new directions, including issues of social justice as well as decidedly unorthodox religious views.

Among the principal non-Catholic traditions, proponents sought to take full advantage of the space newly opened up to them in the afterglow of Vatican II through the avenue of publishing. Newspapers

distributed by Umbanda and Kardecist federations came to be prominently displayed at newsstands in major cities. Books by Umbandist
authors have reflected the full range of currents within the Umbanda
spectrum, from Africanist to Kardecist to esoteric. Literature has always
enjoyed a prestigious role within Kardecist Spiritism, owing to the tradition's self-characterization as a scientific approach to religion. A distinctive
feature of the more popular Kardecist literature is that many of the works
are ostensibly "psychographed," or channeled, by a spirit author through
a human medium (Hess 1991a: 219-20). Kardecist literary output has
expanded dramatically in the postconciliar period, as reflected in the
appearance on the scene of exclusively Spiritist bookstores and periodic
bazaar-style book fairs in larger urban centers. Protestants have followed a
similar trajectory, with their own publishing houses and bookstores. The
literature published by the Japanese New Religions, though still consisting
primarily of works in translation, has gradually assimilated a more
Brazilian perspective (cf. Nakamaki 1991; Clarke 1994).

The foregoing overview of the Brazilian religious marketplace sketches
the immediate context within which the esoteric boom has unfolded. The
prominence of admixture as both mindset and practice in Brazilian religious culture has unquestionably helped create a favorable climate for
esotericism and its innate propensity for spanning conceptual boundaries.
The timing of the boom, beginning as it did in the late 1980s, reflected the
fact that the Brazilian religious marketplace had already had ample time to
adjust to the new reality of fading Catholic hegemony and the resultant
freedom for individuals to investigate other religious options without fear
of recrimination. Related to this latter point, the esoteric boom also benefited from almost two decades in which more open competition among
religious traditions had infused fresh vigor into Brazil's literary market.

REFLECTIONS ON AND IN BRAZILIAN ESOTERIC LITERATURE

I have already addressed the issue of the indeterminacy of the boundaries
of esotericism as a philosophical/religious tradition in the Brazilian cultural
context—an indeterminacy that is compounded when we turn to the sphere
of esoteric literature. As Brazil's esoteric boom gained momentum, its literary content traversed earlier thematic boundaries. From an initial base of
popular novels and autobiographical texts drawing loosely upon classical
Western occult traditions, the literature took on a more didactic quality as
it branched out into other topical areas, including Oriental traditions,
divinatory practices from diverse cultural heritages, the Human Potential
Movement, alternative medicine, and self-help techniques.

Books designated as esoteric are published in the Brazilian market by means of several different arrangements: for example, by publishers who deal exclusively with esotericism, by publishing houses affiliated with nonesoteric religious traditions, by general interest publishers who have invested specifically in esoteric series or collections, and by general interest publishers with no specific investment in esotericism at all. For reasons of commercial viability, books that appear to be only tenuously related to esotericism are sometimes issued as part of an esoteric series. In another permutation of the relevant components, one can also find books dealing with recognizably esoteric themes and issued as part of an esoteric series, even though their authors are not closely identified with the esoteric community or network.

What this final section of the chapter will show, based on a limited sample of esoteric books, is the degree to which esoteric literature in Brazil indeed functions as a microcosmic mirror in which the diverse facets of the larger religious field we have already examined are reflected.

BESTSELLING BRAZILIAN ESOTERIC AUTHORS
PAULO COELHO'S MODERN ALCHEMY: PAPER(BACKS) INTO GOLD

The esoteric boom would likely have ended up seeing non-Brazilian authors exercising a far more dominant role than they have indeed exercised were it not for Paulo Coelho. Coelho was mentioned in the summary account of the esoteric boom earlier in the chapter as the former rock music celebrity whose stunning commercial literary success demonstrated to publishers that esoteric works by Brazilian authors could be profitable. Admittedly, Coelho's case is an anomaly within the scope of the boom, whether from the standpoint of literary talent or the standpoint of the amount of publicity or revenue that he has proved himself capable of generating. And yet, Paulo Coelho and the media attention he has been able to attract have played a key role in building the boom's momentum.

A dozen years after a short-lived but successful career in rock music in the late 1960s and early 1970s, Coelho made his inauspicious debut in the esoteric market as an author. His first book, *The Diary of a Magus* (Coelho 1987 [1995]), did not sell well until it was reissued after several years (during which time Coelho's prestige as an author had soared) under a new title, *The Pilgrimage*. But Coelho's second book, *The Alchemist* (Coelho 1988 [1995]), began a prolonged stay on the bestseller lists in Brazil within a year after its publication. Ten years and four additonal books later, Paulo Coelho had surpassed the five million mark in total volumes sold in Brazil alone, not to mention the overseas market, despite having been generally dismissed by literary critics as an inferior writer. Coelho obtained vindication to spare when *The*

Alchemist reached the top of the bestseller listings in France in late 1994; "Revenge of the Magus" was how the national newsmagazine *Veja* entitled its story announcing Coelho's landmark achievement.[9]

As for the books themselves, both are quest narratives. *The Alchemist* is an engagingly simple tale, sprinkled with references to the Hermetic tradition and to the Bible, of an Andalusian shepherd boy's journey to the pyramids of Egypt in search of personal fulfillment. *The Diary of a Magus* is an account of a modern-day trek on the classical Catholic pilgrimage route of Santiago de Compostela, punctuated by consciousness-expanding meditation exercises taught by a spiritual guide. (Each of the exercises is written up in a formulaic style apart from the flow of the text to encourage readers to practice it.) Both books incorporate elements from Catholicism and from Western occult traditions, though on a simple level that is broadly accessible. They have thus contributed to the crafting of Coelho's growing reputation as a modern-day magus, which in turn has helped to boost the popular appeal of esoteric literature vis-à-vis the Brazilian public.

MONICA BUONFIGLIO AND LATE-NIGHT CHANNELING

One Brazilian author who has unquestionably benefited from Paulo Coelho's trailblazing efforts in drawing mass media attention to Brazil's esoteric boom is Monica Buonfiglio, who has written several bestselling books since 1993. Similarly to Coelho's experience, Buonfiglio was not an instant success in her authorial debut, even though she already had a daily television program dealing with esoteric themes on a major Brazilian network. For Buonfiglio the catalyst was an appearance on an upscale, Brazilian counterpart to the "Tonight Show" or "Late Night with David Letterman" hosted by well-known comedian Jô Soares. Even though Soares made light of several of her comments during the interview, the sales of Buonfiglio's first book, *Kabbalistic Angels* (1993), began soaring heavenward the very next day, selling 250,000 copies during the next eight months (Buonfiglio 1994: 9).[10] Buonfiglio's success inspired so many other authors that the number of books on angels in Brazil's literary market quadrupled over the next two years, from thirteen to fifty-two.

Buonfiglio's work is an excellent illustration of the self-help element that is so pronounced in the esoteric boom (Birman 1993). Both *Kabbalistic Angels* and the bestselling sequel, *The Magic of Kabbalistic Angels* (1994), describe in painstaking detail the distinctive characteristics of seventy-two different angels, based on the Kabbalah, the Jewish mystical system. But the ultimate popular appeal of the books resides in Buonfiglio's precise instructions for applying the principles of correspondence in the resolution of any number of personal problems. Here we see esoteric boundary spanning encountering the pragmatic eclecticism of contemporary privatized spirituality, as Buonfiglio weaves a complex structure that combines such variables as the reader's date and time of birth with commonly used esoteric ritual accessories such as gemstones, floral essences, colored candles, incense, and talismans. For readers who desire additional information and instruction at a deeper level, Buonfiglio includes in the books the address and telephone number of the Esoteric Cultural Workshop which she owns and supervises in São Paulo and which offers courses on the various elements featured in her books.

ESOTERICISM'S IMPACT ON NONESOTERIC AUTHORS

One indication of the esoteric boom's considerable cultural penetration in Brazil is the spread of esoteric concepts across the boundaries— tenuous though they may be—that mark esotericism off from such nonesoteric sectors of the country's religious field as Catholicism and Protestantism. The different series which have been established by certain nonesoteric publishers in response to the esoteric boom turn out to be excellent windows on this boundary-spanning process through the books that their editors choose for publication.

THE GREENING OF LIBERATION THEOLOGY?

Among the books published in the Rocco publishing house's Arch of Time series, alongside works by such non-Brazilian bestselling authors as Marianne Williamson, ayurvedic healer Deepak Chopra, and psychotherapists M. Scott Peck and John Bradshaw, one immediately stands out because of the international celebrity of its two Brazilian Catholic authors. Renowned liberation theologian and former Franciscan friar Leonardo Boff was already mentioned in this chapter in connection with his work as religion editor at the Catholic-owned Vozes publishing house. He is best known worldwide, however, for the nearly yearlong "obedient silence" that was imposed upon him during 1985-86 as a disciplinary measure by the Vatican's Sacred Congregation for the Doctrine of the Faith (cf. Cox 1988) in retaliation for his questioning of certain ecclesiastical doctrines in his book, *Church: Charism and Power* (1981). Frei Betto, a Dominican friar who has exercised a prominent role in regard to lay mobilization at the grassroots level since the 1960s, is best known outside Brazil for the wide-ranging, book-length interview that he conducted with Cuban premier Fidel Castro on the topic of religion (Betto 1986).

The backgrounds of these two veteran luminaries of the progressive wing of Brazilian Catholicism would not necessarily lead one to expect them to collaborate in writing the book *The Mystical and Spirituality* (Boff and Betto 1994). Contributing alternating chapters, Boff and Betto utilize mysticism as a unifying theme to convey a postconciliar brand of ecumenicism well attuned to the boundary-spanning thrust of contemporary esotericism. Both authors affirm that all religious traditions are equally valid, as Boff suggests in the following comment on the distinctive mystical aspects of Afro-Brazilian traditions (note the resonance with Luiz Eduardo Soares's identification of Energy as a central motif of alternative spiritualities):

> The Africans have a more cosmic experience of God, linked to food, which is loaded with *axé*, the divine energy that is within everything. We Christians have something similar to *axé*: the Spirit. Everything is full of the Holy Spirit or the energies of the Spirit, which corresponds more or less to their *axé* (Boff and Betto 1994: 93).

Even though this is the only book that either Boff or Frei Betto has published in the Arch of Time series, both authors have turned their attention to more ecologically and holistically oriented themes in recent years after having built their reputations based on their prominent roles in the progressive wing of the Brazilian Catholic church during the 1970s and 1980s. For example, Leonardo Boff has even published a book through a nonesoteric publisher entitled *New Age: Planetary Civilization— Challenges to Society and to Christianity* (Boff 1994), in which he explores such topics as globalization, feminism, and the environment.

THEOSOPHICAL RESONANCE WITHIN THE PROTESTANT SPHERE

As intriguing as it is for a book co-authored by two progressive Catholics to be published in an esoteric series, even more surprising is the following book, written by Presbyterian pastor Nehemias Marien and published as part of Record's New Age collection: *Jesus, the Light of the New Age: An Eclectic and Ecumenical Perspective on the Most Revolutionary Teacher of All* (1994). Normally, one expects to encounter references to esotericism and related concepts in works by Protestant authors if and only if they are integrated into an apologetic argument designed to refute esoteric teachings. But this is no ordinary book from the word processor of a Protestant pastor. In fact, as Pastor Marien told me in an interview, he ended up paying a heavy personal price for having written this book. First, he was expelled from his Presbyterian denomination. Subsequently, in an ironic development that indicates that the elasticity of tolerance in the postconciliar Catholic church is not limitless, he was also summarily dismissed as a professor of ecumenicism at a Catholic university and as visiting professor at several Catholic seminaries.[11]

What was it about Marien's book, *Jesus, the Light of the New Age*, that provoked such a strong reaction from both Protestants and Catholics? Pastor Marien told me that his involvement in ecumenical movements over the years had gradually led him to become more interested in the study of theosophy and of esotericism in a more general sense. In fact, the invitation for him to write and publish the book had arisen after the New Age series editor had heard him speak at an esoteric conference on the new consciousness in the Northeast of Brazil. Marien expresses his esoteric sympathies quite openly in the book; he often praises theosophical ideas as part of his proposal for that which he calls an "Ecumenism for the Third Millennium" (a chapter title). One passage that assuredly was not well received by Marien's ecclesiastical peers is embedded in his discussion of astrology. After insisting that he shuns horoscopes and astral maps, Marien proposes a fanciful one-to-one correspondence between the twelve signs of the Zodiac and the sons of Jacob alongside the following critical remarks:

> [T]here will always be greater wisdom in astrological speculations than in the Church's empirical theology. In short, astrosophy [sic] leads us more reliably to the revelation of the Creator of the known universe, freeing us from the tangled thicket of systematic theology (Marien 1994: 78).

Clearly, such speculation should not be taken as indicative of any broad esoteric influence within Brazilian Protestantism, as the vehement retaliation from Marien's former denomination attests. On the other hand, he does continue to pastor an independent church in Rio de Janeiro while maintaining his involvement in interfaith gatherings marked by a distinctly esoteric aura.

Pastor Marien's story is remarkably indicative of the extent to which spiritual exploration across nominal religious boundaries persists in Brazil. Books such as the ones mentioned in this last section play a vital part in the overall process.

CONCLUSION

The explosion of esoteric literature in Brazil, within the broader context of the proliferation of alternative spiritualities, constitutes the latest innovative development to unfold in this, the most diversified religious economy in all of Latin America. As the present study shows, however, esotericism is following a growth trajectory quite unlike any previously witnessed in Brazil. None of esotericism's predecessors enjoyed access to such an unrestricted religious marketplace as the one that currently exists in Brazil. Nor were they as innately well-suited to take advantage of this opportunity as esotericism has thus far proven to be.

Why the marked difference in the case of esotericism? Part of the contrast is attributable to the nature of the esoteric phenomenon itself, and part is due to the changes that have taken place in both the religious marketplace and the broader culture in Brazil. Esotericism, unlike some of its predecessors as entrants into Brazil's religious sphere, has no inherent links with any sizable racial, ethnic, or foreign national group within the society. Consequently, esotericism as a religiocultural movement has been exempt from pressure to invest time, energy, and human and financial resources in a struggle against certain manifestations of prejudice and discrimination, as was the case with Afro-Brazilian traditions and Umbanda in the past. Esotericism's elective affinities tend instead to follow lines of socioeconomic class (middle and upper) and educational level (highly literate). This selectivity is a function not only of the learned nature of esoteric discourse but also of the relatively high financial costs incurred by those who elect to purchase esoteric textual materials, enroll in seminars or classes, avail themselves of therapies or consulting services, or acquire the pertinent accessories. Significantly, this elective affinity points to a reasonably high probability that esotericism will continue to attract a relatively wealthy, skilled, savvy, and influential constituency in its ongoing quest to secure its status in the Brazilian religious marketplace.

This leads to mention of the other aspect of esotericism's competitive advantage relative to its predecessors: a playing field in the religious marketplace more level than ever before. Not only is the Catholic constituency shrinking in size before the onslaught of Pentecostals, Umbandists, Afro-Brazilianists, and Kardecists, but the entire milieu is imbued with a basic ethos of contested coexistence emanating from Vatican II and the subsequent Latin American Bishops' Conferences—albeit sometimes with abrupt limits, as we have seen in the case of Pastor Nehemias Marien. The ecumenical spirit abroad in the Brazil's religious marketplace has been sufficiently powerful to afford esoteric cultural producers access to one of Latin America's most highly developed and vibrantly creative cultural industries in bringing their traditions to the attention of the public.

What implications does the esoteric boom hold for religion in Latin America as a whole in the near and long-term future? One prediction that I will *not* make is that esotericism will flourish in the Spanish-speaking nations to the same extent as has occurred in Brazil. The salient features of Brazilian religious culture discussed in this chapter—particularly the fundamental importance of religious admixture—do not prevail in the same manner elsewhere in Latin America. Kardecism and African-derived traditions have never undergone the kind of demographic expansion in Spanish-speaking cultures that they have achieved in Brazil. Notwithstanding esotericism's innate affinities with cultural changes occurring throughout Latin America, I have no basis for envisioning that it will have the kind of impact elsewhere that it has exerted in Brazil.

But the most significant contribution of this research to the overall study of religion in Latin America does not concern esotericism directly. Rather, it concerns the importance attributed by this study to the interaction between religious traditions and the cultural industries, be they publishing houses or the mass media. Considering the fact that religious traditions all across the spectrum in Latin America—established and emergent, mainstream and alternative—are becoming increasingly innovative and sophisticated in their use of and interaction with the cultural industries, I foresee that the insights afforded by a production-of-culture approach will become ever more valuable for understanding and analyzing new trends in the region's religious marketplaces.

Notes

1 The work published in English that focuses most directly on the phenomenon is an all-too-brief article by Paul Heelas and Leila Amaral on New Age groups and practices in Rio de Janeiro (Heelas and Amaral 1994). Noteworthy works in Portuguese include an anthropological study of the astrological network in Rio de Janeiro (Vilhena 1990) and a sociological study of Brasília's esoteric community (Rodríguez Ibarra 1992). See also Gibson Cabral da Silva 1989; Soares 1989a and 1989b; Carvalho 1992 and 1994; Amaral 1993, 1994, and 1996; Magnani 1995; and Moreira and Zicman 1994.

2 See the bestseller listing accompanying the book review of Bradley's *The Mists of Avalon* in the *Veja* issue dated July 23, 1986—João Cândido Galvão, "Távola feminina," *Veja* no. 934 (23 julho 1986): 116.

3 This point draws upon an interview conducted with Socorro Pires [pseudonym], the editor of an esoteric series at a publishing house in Rio de Janeiro. She claims that Paulo Coelho's resounding commercial success not only encouraged his publisher, Paulo Rocco, to inaugurate the new Arch of Time series in the first place but also motivated Rocco to be more patient in awaiting a return on his investment. Though most of the authors published in the Arch of Time series to date are non-Brazilian, it does include works by relatively unknown Brazilian authors, as well. Socorro Pires [pseudonym], interview by author, tape recording, Rio de Janeiro, Brazil, May 20, 1996.

4 For a thoroughgoing explanation of the continuities in modern esotericism, see Faivre 1994: 10-15, or Faivre 1992: xi-xx (cf. Hanegraaff 1998: 396-401).

5 A significant contributing factor behind the abundant supply of esoteric works in translation in Brazil's literary market has been the much lower cost of books in the New Age category compared to those in other categories in the international market. This substantial cost differential gives Brazilian publishers an additional incentive to import New Age books and market them in the esoteric

category—Socorro Pires (pseudonym), interview by author, tape recording, Rio de Janeiro, Brazil, May 20, 1996.

6 I know of no study that provides a comprehensive overview of the Brazilian religious marketplace's full, kaleidoscopic diversity at the close of the twentieth century. Coming closest to this ideal is an edited volume published in Portuguese by the Instituto de Estudos da Religião, entitled *Signs of the Times: Religious Diversity in Brazil* (Landim 1990). Another edited volume that warrants attention in this regard is *Mysticism and New Religions* (Moreira and Zicman 1994). Otherwise, the literature comprises treatments examining no more than three religious traditions (e.g., Ireland 1992; Burdick 1993; Lehmann 1996). David J. Hess's two books on Kardecist Spiritism deal explicitly with its interaction with different currents within Catholicism and Umbanda (Hess 1991b and 1994). Two articles by Carlos Rodrigues Brandão, particularly the latter (Brandão 1986 and 1993), broaden the coverage in terms of different traditions but at the cost of focusing upon a narrow range of issues.

7 For census figures on religious affiliation up through 1970, see Table II-8 in Armin K. Ludwig, *Brazil: A Handbook of Historical Statistics* (Boston: G.K. Hall & Co., 1985), 65. Regarding 1980, see Table 1.1.3, "População Residente, por Religião e Sexo, Segundo a Situação do Domicílio e Grupos de Idade," *IX Recenseamento Geral do Brasil*, 1980. Secretaria do Planejamento da Presidência da República. Rio de Janeiro: Fundação IBGE.

8 The other percentage shares cited in this study are as follows: Protestantism—13%; Kardecism—3%; Umbanda—1%; Afro-Brazilian traditions—0.5%; "Other" traditions (including Mormons, Jehovah's Witnesses, Seventh-Day Adventists, Judaism, Buddhism, Japanese New Religions, and esoteric groups)—2%; and None—5% (Prandi and Pierucci 1995); cf. "A debandada dos fiéis," *Veja* (December 25, 1991): 32-37.

9 The French edition of *The Alchemist* had reached the top of the bestseller lists compiled by *L'Express* and *Le Nouvel Observateur* toward the end of 1994, as reported in "A vingança do mago," Veja (2 janeiro 1995): 112-13.

10 Buonfiglio herself acknowledges the instantaneous takeoff in sales that *Kabbalistic Angels* experienced after the interview. Esoteric bookstore owner Lázaro Leão expressed the impact of the interview on Buonfiglio's career in the following pithy phrase: "There's Monica *before* Jô, and Monica *after* Jô—no comparison!"— Lázaro Leão [pseudonym], interview by author, tape recording, Rio de Janeiro, Brazil, September 9, 1995.

11 Pastor Nehemias Marien, interview by author, tape recording, Rio de Janeiro, Brazil, August 28, 1995.

REFERENCES

Amaral, Leila. 1993. "Os errantes da Nova Era e sua religiosidade caleidoscópica." *Caderno de Ciências Sociais* 3:4 (dezembro): 19-32.

———. 1994. "Nova Era: um movimento de caminhos cruzados." In Leila Amaral, Gottfried Küenzlen, and Godfried Danneels, eds. *Nova Era: um desafio para os cristãos*. Coleção: Atualidade em Diálogo. São Paulo: Paulinas, 11-50.

———. 1996. "As implicações éticas dos sentidos—Nova Era de comunidade." *Religião e Sociedade* 17:1/2 (agosto): 54-75.

Bastide, Roger. 1978. *The African Religions of Brazil: Toward a Sociology of the Interpenetration of Civilizations.* Translated by Helen Sebba. Baltimore: The Johns Hopkins University Press.

Betto, Frei [Carlos Alberto Libânio Christo]. 1986. *Fidel e a religião: conversas com Frei Betto.* 11ª ed. São Paulo: Editora Brasiliense.

Birman, Patrícia. 1993. "Relativismo mágico e novos estilos de vida." *Revista do Rio de Janeiro/UERJ* 1:2 (II Semestre): 44-52.

Boff, Leonardo. 1982. *Igreja: carisma e poder: ensaios de eclesiologia militante.* 3a ed. Teologia 21. Petrópolis: Editora Vozes.

————. 1994. *Nova era: a civilização planetária. Desafios à sociedade e ao cristianismo.* 2ª ed. Serie Religião e Cidadania. São Paulo: Editora Atica.

————. and Frei Betto. 1994. *Mística e espiritualidade.* 2ª ed. Coleção Arco do Tempo. Rio de Janeiro: Rocco.

Brandão, Carlos Rodrigues. 1986. "Religious Identity as a Symbolic Strategy: Brazilian Dimensions." *Social Science Information* 25:1 (1986): 229-57.

————. 1993. "Popular Faith in Brazil." In Gary Gossen, ed. *South and Meso-American Native Spirituality: From the Cult of the Feathered Serpent to the Theology of Liberation.* New York: The Crossroad Publishing Company, 436-37.

————. 1994. "A crise das instituições tradicionais produtoras de sentido." In Alberto Moreira and Renée Zicman, eds. *Misticismo e novas religiões.* 2ª ed. Petrópolis: Editora Vozes; Bragança Paulista: Instituto Franciscano de Antropologia da Universidade São Franciscano, 23-41.

Brown, Diana. 1994. *Umbanda: Religion and Politics in Urban Brazil.* New York: Columbia University Press.

Buonfiglio, Monica. 1993. *Anjos cabalísticos.* São Paulo: Oficina Cultural Esotérica Ltda.

————. 1994. *A magia dos anjos cabalísticos.* 19ª ed. São Paulo: Oficina Cultural Esotérica Ltda.

Burdick, John. 1993. *Looking for God in Brazil: The Progressive Catholic Church in Urban Brazil's Religious Arena.* Los Angeles: The University of California Press.

Campbell, Colin. 1972. "The Cult, the Cultic Milieu, and Secularization." *A Sociological Yearbook of Religion in Britain 5.* London: SCM Press, 119-36.

————. 1982. "Some Comments on the New Religious Movements, the New Spirituality and Post-industrial Society." In Eileen Barker, ed. *New Religious Movements: A Perspective for Understanding Society.* New York: The Edwin Mellen Press, 232-42.

Carpenter, Robert and Wade Clark Roof. 1995. "The Transplanting of Seicho-no-ie from Japan to Brazil: Moving beyond the Ethnic Enclave." *Journal of Contemporary Religion* 10:1 (January): 41-54.

Clarke, Peter B. 1994. "Japanese 'Old,' 'New,' and 'New, New' Religious Movements in Brazil." In Peter B. Clarke and Jeffrey Somers, eds. *Japanese New Religions in the West.* Sandgate, Folkestone, Kent: Japan Library, 150-61.

————. 1995. "The Cultural Impact of New Religions in Latin and Central America and the Caribbean with Special Reference to Japanese New Religions." *Journal of Latin American Cultural Studies* 4:1 (June): 117-26.

Coelho, Paulo. 1995. *O diário de um mago.* 107ª ed. Rio de Janeiro: Rocco.

————. 1995. *O alquimista.* Rio de Janeiro: Rocco.

Cousins, Ewert. 1987. "Spirituality in Today's World." In Frank Whaling, ed. *Religion in Today's World: The Religious Situation of the World from 1945 to the Present Day.* Edinburgh: T & T Clark, 306-34.

Cox, Harvey. 1988. *The Silencing of Leonardo Boff: The Vatican and the Future of World Christianity.* Oak Park, IL: Meyer-Stone Books.

DaMatta, Roberto. 1995. "For an Anthropology of the Brazilian Tradition or 'A Virtude Está no Meio.'" In David J. Hess and Roberto A. DaMatta, eds. *The Brazilian Puzzle: Culture on the Borderlands of theWestern World.* New York: Columbia University Press, 270-91.

de Carvalho, José Jorge. 1992. "Características do fenômeno religioso na sociedade contemporânea." In Maria Bingemer, ed. *O impacto da modernidade sobre a religião.* São Paulo: Edições Loyola, 133-95.

————. 1994. "O encontro de velhas e novas religiões: esboço de uma teoria dos estilos de espiritualidade." In Alberto Moreira and Renée Zicman, eds. *Misticismo e novas religiões.* 2ª ed. Petrópolis: Editora Vozes; Bragança Paulista: Instituto Franciscano de Antropologia da Universidade São Franciscano, 67-98.

Droogers, Andre. 1989. "Syncretism: The Problem of Definition, the Definition of the Problem." In Jerald D. Gort et al., eds. *Dialogue and Syncretism: An Interdisciplinary Approach.* Grand Rapids, MI: William B. Eerdmans Publishing Company, 7-25.

Faivre, Antoine. 1992. "Introduction I." In Antoine Faivre and Jacob Needleman, eds. *Modern Esoteric Spirituality.* World Spirituality: An Encyclopedic History of the Religious Quest, vol. 21. New York: The Crossroad Publishing Company, xi-xx.

————. 1994. *Access to Western Esotericism.* Albany: State University of New York Press.

Gibson Cabral da Silva, Magnólia. 1989. "Recentes teodicéias inspiradas na tradição oriental: conservadorismo e ou mudança social." *Revista de Cultura Vozes* 83:6 (novembro/ dezembro): 659-74.

Hanegraaff, Wouter. 1998. *New Age Religion and Western Culture: Esotericism in the Mirror of Western Thought.* SUNY Series in Western Esoteric Traditions. Albany: State University of New York Press.

Heelas, Paul. 1982. "Californian Self Religions and Socializing the Subjective." In Eileen Barker, ed. *New Religious Movements: A Perspective for Understanding Society.* New York: Edwin Mellen, 69-85.

————. 1993. "The New Age in Cultural Context: the Premodern, the Modern, and the Postmodern." *Religion* 23 (April): 103-16.

————. 1996. *The New Age: The Celebration of the Self and the Sacralization of Modernity.* Oxford and Cambridge: Blackwell Publishers.

Heelas, Paul and Leila Amaral. 1994. "Notes on the 'Nova Era': Rio de Janeiro and Environs." *Religion* 24: 173-180.

Hess, David J. 1987. "The Many Rooms of Spiritism in Brazil." *Luso-Brazilian Review* 24:2 (Winter): 15-34.

————. 1991a. "On Earth as It Is in Heaven: Spiritist Otherworldly Ethnographies." In Roberto Reis, ed. *Toward Socio-Criticism: Selected Proceedings of the Conference "Luso-Brazilian Literatures, a Socio-Critical Approach.* Tempe, AZ: Center for Latin American Studies, Arizona State University, 219-28.

————. 1991b. *Spirits and Scientists: Ideology, Spiritism, and Brazilian Culture.* University Park: The Pennsylvania State University Press.

————. 1994. *Samba in the Night: Spiritism in Brazil.* New York: Columbia University Press.

————. 1995. "Hierarchy, Heterodoxy, and the Construction of Brazilian ReligiousTherapies." In David J. Hess and Roberto A. DaMatta, eds. *The Brazilian Puzzle: Culture on the Borderlands of the Western World.* New York: Columbia University Press, 180-208.

Ireland, Rowan. 1992. *Kingdoms Come: Religion and Politics in Brazil.* Pittsburgh: Pittsburgh University Press.

Jorgensen, Danny. 1992. *The Esoteric Scene, Cultic Milieu, and Occult Tarot.* New York and London: Garland Publishing, Inc.

Kloppenburg, Boaventura. 1960. *O espiritismo no Brasil.* Petrópolis: Editora Vozes Ltda.

————. 1961. *Umbanda: orientação para os católicos.* Petrópolis: Editora Vozes Ltda.

Landim, Leilah, ed. 1990. *Sinais dos tempos: diversidade religiosa no Brasil.* Rio de Janeiro: ISER—Instituto de Estudos da Religião.

Lehmann, David. 1996. *Struggle for the Spirit: Religious Transformation and Popular Culture in Brazil and Latin America.* Cambridge, UK: Polity Press.

Lindstrom, Naomi. 1983. "Latin American Pop Occult Texts: Implicit Ideology." *Studies in Latin American Popular Culture* 2: 158-70.

Magnani, José Guilherme Cantor. 1995. "Esotéricos na cidade: os novos espaços de encontro, vivência, e culto." *São Paulo em Perspectiva* 9:2 (abril/junho): 66-72.

Marien, Nehemias. 1994. *Jesus, a luz da Nova Era: uma visão eclética e ecumênica do mais revolucionário dos mestres.* 2ª ed. Nova Era. Rio de Janeiro: Editora Record.

Mariz, Cecília, and Maria das Dores Machado. 1994. "Sincretismo e trânsito religioso: comparando carismáticos e pentecostais." In Pierre Sanchis, ed. *A dança dos sincretismos.* Special issue of *Comunicações do ISER*, no. 45, Ano 13: 24-34.

Miller, Timothy. 1995. "Introduction." In Timothy Miller, ed. *America's Alternative Religions.* SUNY Series in Religious Studies. Albany: State University of New York Press, 1-10.

Montero, Paula. 1992. "O papel das editoras católicas na formação cultural brasileira." In Pierre Sanchis, ed. *Catolicismo: modernidade e tradição*, Grupo de Estudos do Catolicismo do ISER. Catolicismo no Brasil Atual. São Paulo: Edições Loyola, 219-50.

Moreira, Alberto and Renée Zicman, eds. 1994. *Misticismo e novas religiões.* 2ª ed. Petrópolis: Editora Vozes; Bragança Paulista: Instituto Franciscano de Antropologia da Universidade São Franciscano.

Nakamaki Hirochika. 1991. "The Indigenization and Multinationalization of Japanese Religion—Perfect Liberty Kyodan in Brazil." *Japanese Journal of Religious Studies* 18:2-3 (June/ September): 213-42.

Oliven, Ruben George. 1984. "The Production and Consumption of Culture in Brazil." *Latin American Perspectives* 11:1 (Issue 40, Winter): 103-15.

Ortiz, Renato. 1988. *A morte branca do feiticeiro negro: umbanda e sociedade brasileira.* São Paulo: Editora Brasiliense.

Parker, Cristián. 1996. *Popular Religion and Modernization in Latin America: A Different Logic.* Translated by Robert R. Barr. Maryknoll, N.Y.: Orbis Books.

Peterson, Richard. 1994. "Culture Studies through the Production Perspective: Progress and Prospects." In Diana Crane, ed. *The Sociology of Culture: Emerging Theoretical Perspectives.* Oxford and Cambridge: Basil Blackwell Ltd, 163-89.

Prandi, Reginaldo and Antônio Flávio Pierucci. 1995. "As religiões no Brasil (números e perspectivas numa avaliação sociológica)." São Paulo: Departamento de Sociologia da Universidade de São Paulo (unpublished typescript).

Ribeiro de Oliveira, Pedro. 1977. "Coexistência das religiões no Brasil." *Vozes* 71:7 (setembro): 555-62.

Rodríguez Ibarra, Andrés. 1992. "Em busca da sintonia universal: o narcisismo e a procura pelo esotérico em Brasília.". Doctoral dissertation, Universidade de Brasília.

Roof, Wade Clark. 1993. *A Generation of Seekers: The Spiritual Journeys of the Baby Boom Generation.* New York: Harper-Collins Publishers.

———. Jackson Carroll and David Roozen. 1994. "The Post-War Generation: Carriers of a New Spirituality." In Wade Clark Roof, Jackson Carroll and David Roozen, eds. *The Post-War Generation and Religious Establishments: CrossCultural Perspectives.* Boulder, CO: Westview Press, 243-55.

Sanchis, Pierre, ed. 1994. *A dança dos sincretismos.* Special issue of *Comunicações do ISER*, no. 45, Ano 13.

———. 1995. "As tramas sincréticas da história: sincretismo e modernidades no espaço luso-brasileiro." *Revista Brasileira de Ciências Sociais.* 28:10 (junho): 124.

Shaw, Rosalind and Charles Stewart. 1994. "Introduction: Problematizing Syncretism." In Charles Stewart and Rosalind Shaw, eds. *Syncretism/Anti-syncretism: The Politics of Religious Synthesis.* New York: Routledge, 1-26.

Soares, Luiz Eduardo. 1989a. "Perguntar, ouvir: as 'seitas' e a invenção metafórica do espaço humano." In Leilah Landim, ed. *Sinais dos tempos: igrejas e seitas no Brasil.* Cadernos do ISER no. 21. Rio de Janeiro: ISER— Instituto de Estudos da Religião, 52-63.

———. 1989b. "Religioso por natureza: cultura alternativa e misticismo ecológico no Brasil." In Leilah Landim, ed. *Sinais dos tempos: tradições religiosas no Brasil.* Cadernos do ISER no. 22. Rio de Janeiro: ISER—Instituto de Estudos da Religião, 121-44.

Tiryakian, Edward, ed. 1974a. *On the Margin of the Visible: Sociology, the Esoteric, and the Occult.* Contemporary Religious Movements: A Wiley-Interscience Series. New York, London, Sydney, Toronto: John Wiley & Sons.

Vilhena, Luís Rodolfo. 1990. *O mundo da astrologia: estudo antropológico.* Rio de Janeiro: Jorge Zahar.

THIRTEEN

GLOBALIZATION AND RELIGIOUS CREOLIZATION AMONG THE Q'EQCHI'ES OF GUATEMALA

Hans Siebers

Globalization is a buzz word that appears time and again in the titles of seminars, congresses, and books. Despite the widespread usage of this term, however, there is still no consensus on how to define it.

Nevertheless, in spite of conceptual confusions, globalization does call attention to some specific and important contemporary issues. At the end of the twentieth century, the world has reached a stage in which people are increasingly confronted with flows of capital, goods, symbols, information, and images stemming from faraway corners of the globe (Appadurai 1990: 296-301; Hannerz 1992: 217-267). Distant places are linked in such a way that local happenings are shaped by events occurring many miles away, and individual actors can engage in interaction with others across the globe (Giddens 1990: 21-22, 64).

Authors discussing the cultural aspects of globalization (see e.g. Hannerz 1992; Robertson 1992) no longer share the simple assumptions of the former cultural imperialism thesis, according to which local actors and their cultures are wiped away to make room for a modern consumption culture imposed by Western companies and backed by Western governments (see Tomlinson 1991). They agree that globalization does not refer to the global dominance of a single homogenous culture, but that it has instead created a movement towards pluralization and heterogeneity. However, it remains unclear just how these opposing tendencies of homogeneity and heterogeneity work out in practice. Thus there is a great need to explore the concept of globalization through empirical studies.

In this article I intend to carry out just such an empirical study by concentrating on a specific group of people in Guatemala, the *Q'eqchi'es*, and on how they handle religious meanings that have their origins mainly in Europe and the United States. First, I will introduce some of the basic aspects of their life and life-world to the reader. Second, I will focus on the institutional framework through which official religious meanings must pass before they reach the Q'eqchi'es. Third, the ways in which the Q'eqchi'es deal with this information in relation to their traditional religious meanings and practices will be discussed using the term "religious creolization." Finally, I single out some basic elements for understanding the process of globalization with regard to religion. My overall task in this chapter is to show how the global flow of religious ideas and influences has a pluralizing affect on people like the Q'eqchi'es.

THE Q'EQCHI'ES: THEIR LIFE-WORLD IN A GLOBAL CONTEXT[1]

There are approximately 600,000 Q'eqchi'es living in northern Guatemala, scattered across an area of about 20,000 square kilometres. Part of this area, the heartland, consists of a mountain range whose highest peak reaches 3,000 metres above sea level. The other part is made up of lowlands which until a few decades ago were covered by tropical rain forests. The Q'eqchi'es are the primary inhabitants of this area, but a small minority of Spanish-speaking Ladinos hold the local and regional power positions (e.g., they are the landlords, merchants, government employees, army officers, etc.) The Q'eqchi'es live in some 1,600 rural communities, including coffee and cardamom plantations called fincas, independent villages, and cooperatives. Approximately one hundred of these rural communities were destroyed by army violence in the early 1980s. Some of the inhabitants were killed immediately, while others were captured by the army or fled into either Mexico or the nearby mountains. Towns in the area are limited in size and number. The largest one has about 30,000 inhabitants, and there are few Q'eqchi'es migrating to the capital or other major cities.

At first glance the Q'eqchi'es do not appear to be an obvious case for studying the impact of globalization. They live rather far away from national and international communication centers and within the Guatemalan context they are renowned for their reserved nature and closed societies. On closer inspection, however, it becomes clear that they are very much involved in global information flows. Modern health care services may be insufficient, but modern ideas about health and illness reach most of the Q'eqchi'es through government agencies and Nongovernmental organizations. These ideas and practices have their origin outside of Guatemala's borders. The same holds true for the basic methods, content, and practices of education offered to the Q'eqchi'es. They produce cash crops such as coffee and cardamom that are consumed in North America, Europe, and the Middle East. Agricultural extension workers offer them modern technology, and foreign chemical fertilizers and pesticides appear as real options for their agricultural production.

In short, global flows do not stop at the limits of the life-world of the *Q'eqchi'es*. However, it is important to note that such global flows do not reach the *Q'eqchi'es* directly. They are mediated by actors and agencies who intervene in their life-world, such as merchants, NGOs, government agencies, and radio stations.[2] For example, the opportunity to buy chemical fertilizers is offered to them by *Ladino* merchants, and scientifically elaborated agricultural technology comes to them through *Ladino* agricultural extension workers. To the *Q'eqchi'es*, global flows have "faces."

THE PRESENCE OF CHURCHES IN THE LIFE-WORLD OF THE Q'EQCHI'ES

Global religious influences are transmitted to the *Q'eqchi'es* by churches whose headquarters are also situated in various parts of the world. These influences go back to the imposition of Catholic colonialism in the sixteenth century (Van Oss 1986). Religious practices, such as the patron saint's feast, which now constitute central elements of their customary religion have their origin in this Catholic colonialism.

However, as Van Oss shows, the monastic orders had a clear interest in making sure that the indigenous peoples of Guatemala were not completely "hispanized." As long as they maintained their own linguistic and cultural characteristics, these orders were able to legitimize their prolonged presence in the highlands vis-à-vis the secular church and state officials in the capital (Van Oss 1986: 51ff, 77, 128).

At first, independence from Spain in 1821 did not change this situation dramatically. Such change had to wait until after the Liberal Reform of 1871 when almost all church personnel were expelled from the country, official religious ceremonies outside of church buildings were prohibited, and church properties were expropriated. Only one female order was allowed to stay to continue to run hospitals, and the church virtually disappeared from the life-world of the *Q'eqchi'es* (see Samandú, Siebers, and Sierra 1990: 25-27).

It was only in the 1960s that the Catholic church was able to restore its presence in the *Q'eqchi'* region. In some parts of the region pastoral work was again interrupted between 1980 and 1985 because of counter-insurgency campaigns by the army. Priests and nuns were denied access to the area because the army suspected them of harboring guerrilla sympathies. Moreover, since the 1970s the Catholic church has faced serious competition from a wide range of evangelical churches that have managed to convert between 20 and 30 percent of the *Q'eqchi'es*. In addition, the

Catholic church is itself seriously divided, with different groups and religious orders each applying their own concept of pastoral work.

Most of these churches, and the large majority of priests, nuns, and ministers, come from other parts of the world. As such, they embody the global religious influences reaching the *Q'eqchi'es*. However, the wide range of Christian denominations, and the diversity within the Catholic Church itself indicates that these global influences are highly varied.[3] Moreover, these religious specialists do not simply function as the mouthpieces of official dogma. While they are bound by the dogmas, doctrines, and official statements of their churches, which often express a modern rationalized and systematized character with a claim of universal validity, the practice of pastoral work and preaching leaves considerable room for these specialists to develop their own interpretations.

SACRAMENTALIST PASTORAL WORK

One of these groups within the Catholic church, which can be called "sacramentalist," is promoted primarily by the Salesian religious order. The Salesians stimulate *Q'eqchi'es* believers to break away from the existing religious leadership in their communities, which is centered around the *pasawink* (elderly men and women), and to leave behind their traditional religious practices. To replace the leadership of the *pasawink*, the Salesians have organized a hierarchical system of lay leaders headed by the priests, whose task is to lead the religious and social activities of the community.

Through this hierarchical structure, the Salesians promote an overtly paternalistic pastoral policy. They claim to know what the *Q'eqchi'es* should think and do, in social as well as religious matters. In religion, the Salesians stress the performance of the Mass or the "celebration of the Word" (a Mass-like meeting every Sunday without the presence of the priest), the preparation of believers who are to receive sacraments, and the celebration of special occasions such as Christmas and Holy Week. In their view, rather abstract notions of a "loving God" and "salvation" play a central role in religion. In order to reach salvation one has to listen to the Word of God, comply with the moral demands God makes on man, and stay loyal to the church.

In the social realm, the Salesians stress the importance of such moral values as sending one's children to school and to church, supporting church activities, working hard, improving the material well-being of the household, and abstaining from quarrelling and drinking. They consider loyalty to the church to be more important than loyalty to the local village, and they preach that the main task of the community of believers is to promote the salvation of the individual.

LIBERATING PASTORAL WORK

On the opposite side of the Catholic church there is a group of priests and religious people, including the Dominicans, who promote a pastoral policy that may be called "liberating" (see Samandú, Siebers, and Sierra 1990). Every priest and lay worker of course has to promote the official Catholic belief system. This means they spend much of their time serving Masses and performing the sacraments. However, in the practice of pastoral work there is considerable room for interpretation, and the people who belong to this group try to reinforce existing Q'eqchi' religious beliefs and practices, and strengthen the role of religious leaders like the *pasawink*. For instance, they try to integrate specific Q'eqchi' religious rituals into the Mass and encourage all the *pasawink* to meet, exchange knowledge on rituals and beliefs, and support each other in their work. They try to articulate the official modern Catholic belief system while still promoting traditional Q'eqchi' beliefs and practices. In their view, local cultures also contain "tokens of the Word of God." Together with representatives of the Q'eqchi'es they try to identify valuable religious meanings and practices based on both local cultures and official texts. In pastoral practice, the members of this group do not emphasise individual moral behaviour.

EVANGELICAL CHURCHES

Evangelical churches such as the *Iglesia del Nazareno*, *Asamblea de Dios*, and *Iglesia de Dios del Evangelio Completo* also work in this region. Most of these churches have their origin in the United States, but they have reached financial and organizational independence at present, and it is very rare to see a *gringo* working with them. The evangelical churches proclaim a religious discourse stressing individual relations with God and moral responsibility. This discourse rejects personalized views on nature and encourages followers to improve their economic performance. In the words of an evangelical Q'eqchi': "We pray both to God and Jesus Christ. If someone does his *k'anjel* well he will receive the blessings of God. Good *k'anjel* brings about the favors of God."

Interestingly, this respondent used the word *k'anjel*, which in Q'eqchi' has the general meaning of "effort": both in the moral and economic sense of the word. So God's favors depend on the efforts and work of the believer, and having economic success is a token of the blessing of God. Moreover, several evangelical church leaders told me that praying for the president and State officials is part of their standard service.

In general, these evangelical churches try to force a rupture with existing Q'eqchi' religion and social structures. The local community is replaced by the community of believers, which often has three or four meetings a week. However, the literature on evangelical churches points to the fact that those churches that have reached the highest levels of "indigenization" have been the most successful in finding converts among the indigenous population of Guatemala. In this case "indigenization" means the translation of Bible texts into local and regional vernacular, the training of local and regional leaders, the organization of literacy courses and the transmission of radio programmes in the various languages of Guatemala (Samandú 1989: 30-32; Samandú 1990: 81-88; Garrard 1986: 198).

THE TRANSFORMATION OF RELIGIOUS INFLUENCES BY CHURCHES IN THE REGION

Despite resistance on the part of many religious groups, they cannot avoid adapting their discourse and practices to the local cultural context. These global religious influences are mediated and transformed not only by the interpretations of the local specialists themselves, however. The very method of transmitting their interpretations to the Q'eqchi' communities also involves a high level of adaptation and modification. Priests, nuns, and ministers have only limited direct access to the local communities. They visit them a few times a year, but their main communication with these communities takes place through instructing and training local leaders (e.g., catechists). The latter are supposed to pass on to their communities what they have learned from the religious specialists.

Consequently, these religious discourses become fragmented and lose a large part of their systematized and rationalized coherence. This loss of coherence makes the discourse much less forceful and compulsory. For example, the acceptance of the moral demands of God does not necessarily oblige the Q'eqchi'es to become worried about the distinction between monotheism and polytheism. The Q'eqchi'es are encouraged to deal with external religious discourses in a very selective way.

THE Q'EQCHI'ES' RELIGIOUS CREOLIZATION

The selective transmission of religious beliefs and practices to the Q'eqchi'es is matched by the selective way in which they deal with these external religious influences. While their constantly evolving religious belief system is influenced by the teachings of these churches, the Q'eqchi'es also draw upon local customary leaders like the chinames, pasawink, and aj ilonel who encourage others in their community to perform customary rituals and respect customary religious beliefs.

Only couples who have started their own household can be chinames.

They are assisted by *mertomes*, who may be single men. *Chinames* are always organized hierarchically. The first *chinames* (*xb'enil*) command the second (*xkab'il*), the second command the third (*roxil*), and so on. In general, this hierarchy consists of about five couples, sometimes assisted by up to twenty *mertomes*. A couple is *chinam* for one or two years and then they look for substitutes who have to be confirmed by the community members as a token of the respect they merit. The tasks the *chinames* execute are twofold. First, they have their obligations towards the Catholic church. They take care of the building and the cemetery, they keep the church clean and decorate or repair it, and they organize the construction of a new one if necessary. The second task of the *chinames* is to organize customary rituals that are performed by the community as a whole, especially the feast of the patron saint. They take care of all practical matters on these occasions, but in some communities, dominated by Salesian-trained catechists, this second task is rather controversial.

A couple who have served as *chinames* and reached a respectable age are regarded as *pasawink*, or wise old men and women. In parishes run by the Dominican order, *pasawink* are consulted on every important community issue, and several of them take the lead in the performance of customary rituals. Here *pasawink* have a rather discursive role: they pray in the name of the whole community at customary rituals and they transmit knowledge of customary rituals and beliefs to the youth of the community. Sometimes, *pasawink* are also *aj ilonel*, or traditional healers. *Iloneles* are specialized in taking care of patients and healing them by way of prescribing medicinal plants and restoring the relationship between the patient and the natural and supernatural order. Sometimes, they can be suspected of being an *aj tuul*, or witch, as well.

In recent years, the movement of "Maya priests" has gained momentum and influence nationwide. They intend to restore the importance of pre-Columbian religious beliefs and rituals, and to "purify" their traditions from Christian influences. They have received considerable public recognition. The importance of Maya spirituality and sacred places is formally confirmed in the peace treaty the guerrilla movement and the government concluded at the end of 1996. The movement's Council of Elders is acknowledged by the government and granted an advisory role in the implementation of reforms in the wake of this peace treaty. In various parts of the country they are trying to extend their work to the local communities, but it still is too early to assess their local influence on the Q'eqchi' religion.

The point here is that the Q'eqchi'es draw selectively both from their own traditions and from church influences. Out of a selective adoption and adaptation of religious beliefs and practices stemming from their own traditions and these external religious influences they create their own blend of religion. For example, the symbol of the cross has meanings stemming both from church influences and from *Q'eqchi'* customs. It refers not only to Christ and His sacrifice, but also to the four corners of the universe and to the spirit of maize. Within the church, the cross is symbolic of Christ, whereas the same cross erected on a piece of land at the moment of planting maize symbolizes the spirit of a good harvest. To the *Q'eqchi'es,* religious meanings are very much context-bound.

The concept that I use to refer to this process of the selective mixing of elements stemming both from the *Q'eqchi'es'* own traditions and from transformed global religious influences is "religious creolization."[4] The *Q'eqchi'es* have a considerable range of religious practices and beliefs, but these all fall into two basic categories: a customary one and a Bible-oriented one. These two categories are both complementary and contradictory: complementary because almost all the *Q'eqchi'es* adhere to both of these principles, and contradictory because they express clearly different meanings which cannot both be true at the same time.

CUSTOMARY RELIGION

The *Q'eqchi'es* are, fundamentally, peasant farmers. They want to make their living by cultivating the land they live on. Very few *Q'eqchi'es* work as merchants or craftsmen, and even fewer live in towns. Those who have to live and work on one of the *fincas,* which occupy about one-third of the *Q'eqchi'* area, feel that they cannot reproduce their culture in this context. They are the ones who look for a piece of land in the settlement areas in El Petén, Izabal, and Belize.

Being situated in a mountainous landscape, the *Q'eqchi'es* feel that they depend on the life that is provided to them by the mountain and the valley, which is called the *Tzuultaq'a* in *Q'eqchi'.* The mountain gives them all they need to live: the maize and beans that grow out of his or her skin (some mountains are considered female, others male), and the wood to make fires and build houses. Water comes down from his or her slopes, he or she feeds their animals and grows medicinal herbs to cure diseases, and so on. To be sure, in the beginning God created everything, and in the end God is the source of all life, but in practice and in daily life it is the *Tzuultaq'a* that the *Q'eqchi'es* depend on for their survival.

In short, maize, beans, turkeys, trees, water, medicinal herbs, and so on constitute the life sent by the *Tzuultaq'a.* As a result, all these "things" are considered to be imbued with a spirit originating in the *Tzuultaq'a.* The *Tzuultaq'a* can be either benevolent or angry. This depends solely on the *Q'eqchi'es* themselves. If they fulfill their obligations toward the *Tzuultaq'a*, he or she will reciprocate. If not, he or she will punish them by not allowing their maize to grow, or by sending snakes to bite them or bad spirits to inflict illness.

The obligations of the *Q'eqchi'es* are several. In order to get the things they expect from the *Tzuultaq'a*, a variety of rituals have to be performed. For example, before the clearing of the land the community gathers to perform its *mayejak* ritual. This ritual begins with a celebration of the Word, after which the *pasawink* take the lead in what is called the *yo'lek*. The *yo'lek* is performed by the *pasawink* at sacred places on the nearby mountain, and on several of the central thirteen *Tzuultaq'a* (mountains) that can be found in the *Q'eqchi'* heartland. A *yo'lek* always has the same standard ingredients: the *pasawink* addresses all those who are considered to be important in the universe, including God, the known *Tzuultaq'a*s, the saints, the air, the moon, the sun, the village, nearby villages, the priest, the bishop, the pope, the trees, the animals, and so on. Next, he burns a type of resin called *copal pom*, lights candles, and puts the meat of a turkey on the ground as a sacrifice. Finally, he asks all of these beings, but especially the nearby mountain, to give the community permission to clear the land, to protect its members from illness, accidents, and snake bites, and to provide its members with a good harvest.

Similar rituals are performed when the maize is planted, and, at the harvest, rituals are performed in order to thank the *Tzuultaq'a* for providing the community with its crop. The *yo'lek* is also performed at times like the patron saint's feast, when the construction of a house is finished, or when a drought or flood threatens the crops, and it constitutes the main obligations of the *Q'eqchi'es* towards the *Tzuultaq'a*.

Customary rituals are performed by both the individual households and by the community as a whole, but the emphasis is clearly on the community. Even in the case of rituals performed at the household level—such as the "house-feeding" rituals that are performed after finishing the construction of a house—friends, relatives, and other villagers are invited to take part and have a meal together and a *pasawink* leads the ceremony. The unity of the community is particularly stressed at the patron saint's feast. In the eyes of the *Q'eqchi'es*, saints are nonvisible persons who can be called upon to do things like curing a disease. The patron saint symbolizes and reinforces the unity of the whole local community, which is essential in maintaining good relations with the *Tzuultaq'a*[6]. Customary rituals are mainly performed within the family and the local community, but many communities send representatives to visit some of the central thirteen mountains in the region each year to perform a *yo'lek* and, again, to ask for protection, for permission to cultivate the land, and for a good harvest.

BIBLE-ORIENTED RELIGION

The customary principle does not monopolize *Q'eqchi'* religion. There is another important religious principle that may be called Bible-oriented because it focuses on God and His Word. God has created nature, which is not imbued with life. Life has been granted to each man and woman, and in the end his or her life will return to God. In the meantime people have to comply with His demands in order to secure their well-being. These demands are: to listen to His Word, to pray frequently to God, to be loyal to the church, and to live according to the moral demands God makes on man.

It is primarily the individual who enters into relations with God and who complies with His demands. The main function of the church community is to stimulate the individual to take care of his or her relations with God. Relations with God are rather abstract in the sense that they do not deal with specific things that the believer needs, such as a good harvest of maize. By contrast, God has the general destiny of humanity in His hands. Relations with God are about the general well-being, destiny, and fate of the believer. Moreover, relations are not clearly reciprocal, because even in the case of a believer who does not comply with his or her obligations towards God, He may or may not decide to grant forgiveness.

For Catholics, the main religious practices in which this Bible-oriented principle is expressed are the celebration of the Word or the Mass on Sunday and the sacraments. The relevant evangelical practices are: the services that are held several times a week, meetings of Bible study, fasting, and special campaigns.

MIXING, MINGLING, AND ARTICULATING

The crucial point here is that the *Q'eqchi'es* perform the basic practices stemming from both customary and Bible-oriented religion. This is possible because, for the *Q'eqchi'es*, these practices and their related meanings are highly context-specific. For example, they perform customary rituals and address the *Tzuultaq'a* at central moments in the maize cycle because maize is very much related to the *Tzuultaq'a*. By contrast, while preparing young couples to become married, the catechists talk only about God and His moral demands on the couples. The *Tzuultaq'a* has no relevance at these occasions and nothing is sacrificed. The occasion-bound character of these religious beliefs enables the *Q'eqchi'es* to portray the universe as "inhabited" by many "persons" such as the mountains, the spirits of maize, the saints, and their ancestors on occasions relevant to customary practices as expressed in the *yo'lek*, while at a celebration of the Word they are willing to talk only about God. While planting their maize they conceive of their land as the skin of the *Tzuultaq'a*, whereas within the framework of negotiating with state agencies about their land titles they deal with the same land in a very instrumentalist and practical way.

Moreover, in the lives of all the *Q'eqchi'es* both Bible-oriented and customary religious practices and beliefs are important, but the exact mix is different from one local community to the other, and even from one household to the other. In some communities customary religion is clearly dominant, while in other communities the same holds true for Bible-oriented religion. In some of the former type of communities several respondents told me: "We are children of the mountain," and others said that "the Word of God is there to enrich our ways of addressing the *Tzuultaq'a*." By contrast, in one of the latter type of communities a villager told me that "the mountain is alive because he has clouds around and above him. With these clouds he worships God just like a bird who sings in praise of God. Humans should do the same."

The villagers in the latter communities find it difficult to maintain the communitarian character of customary practices. Here, customary practices are mainly performed by individual households and groups of households instead of by the community as a whole. However, in these communities even Salesian-trained catechists and evangelicals express the importance of maintaining a degree of continuity in customary practices and meanings. Despite the explicit campaigns of both sacramentalist priests and Pentecostal churches, the *Q'eqchi'* believers have been unwilling to leave behind their customary religion. For example, when planting maize the evangelical *Q'eqchi'es* go to their land, give thanks for the harvest, and ask for a good harvest and permission to cultivate the land next year, just like their fellow villagers. There is, however, discontinuity in some of the rituals they perform: they do not bury a piece of turkey in the ground as sacrifice and do not put this turkey's blood on the seed before planting it in order to "feed" the seed. Moreover, most of them told me that they pray only to God at this occasion. After coming to trust me more, however, almost all of them admitted that they also continue to address the *Tzuultaq'a* at this occasion. In short, there is continuity and change, which points to the fact that the cultural rupture the Christian churches try to enforce is not as drastic and dramatic as is often assumed in Guatemala.

Conclusions

As stated at the beginning of this chapter, globalization is often used to describe the tendency towards cultural pluralism and heterogeneity. It has a corollary theory called localization, which refers to the incorporation of information and practices from these global flows into local processes of meaning-making (Hannerz 1992: 217-267). It emphasizes the increasing demand on all individuals and groups to respond to new impulses and to reevaluate their beliefs and identities in the face of a globalizing context that questions and relativizes all preexisting cultural frames of reference.

Globalization and localization are involved in constant interplay. But this process is often described in extremely vague and abstract terms. Roland Robertson, for example, portrays globalization in terms of a constant "interpenetration of the universalization of particularism and the particularization of universalism" (Robertson 1995: 100).

The case of the *Q'eqchi'es*, their selective adaptation of both traditional and external religious elements provides a clear and concrete illustration of the interaction of the twin forces of globalization and localization. The *Q'eqchi'es* are not simple victims of a one-sided flow of religious beliefs and practices from other parts of the world. In order to reach the *Q'eqchi'es* these beliefs and practices must first pass through a series of mediating structures and institutions (e.g. the Catholic Church and various Protestant denominations, the individual priest or minister, the *pasawink*, etc.), and at each stage they are further transformed and "indigenized." This "indigenization" process is necessary, as these external beliefs and practices must be adapted to, or influenced by, *Q'eqchi'* culture in order to be acceptable to the local people. At the same time, the *Q'eqchi'es* adopt these external religious influences in a selective manner, using them in some parts of their lives and not in others.

Notes

1   The Ph.D. dissertation fieldwork that produced the data for this analysis was conducted in 1991 and 1992 (Siebers 1996).

2   For an elaboration on the concept of "intervening actors and agencies" see Long 1992.

3   For an elaboration on tendencies of pastoral work within the Catholic church in Guatemala see: Samandú, Siebers, and Sierra 1990.

4   In its original definintion, "creolization" refers to the mixing of racial categories or to the mixing of two different languages from which a third language arises. This linguistic analogy has subsequently been used to characterize cul-

tural mixing in a more general sense and the construction of new identities drawing on various cultural sources, especially in polyethnic societies (Drummond 1980). Next, the term has been applied in globalization theory in regard to the articulation of aspects stemming from the endogenous cultures of social actors on the one hand and elements coming to them from global flows of meanings on the other (Hannerz 1992: 261-267). In line with Hannerz it has also been used to depict the capacity of social actors to articulate their continuous reinvention of tradition with selectively adopted and adapted external and exogenous elements, combining the selective continuation of premodern elements with selectively adopted and adapted modern aspects, within an analysis of asymmetrical power relations (Siebers 1996: 275-307).

5 In practice, the patron saint is unable to protect the villagers against every internal conflict, though. I have come across personal conflicts in almost all the villages I visited.

REFERENCES

Appadurai, A. 1990. "Disjuncture and Difference in the Global Cultural Economy." In M. Featherstone, ed. *Global Culture: Nationalism, Globalization and Modernity*. London: SAGE, 295-310.

Drummond, L. 1980. "The Cultural Continuum: A Theory of Intersystems." *Man: The Journal of the Anthropological Institute*, 15: 352-374.

Garrard, V.C. 1986. *A History of Protestantism in Guatemala*. Doctoral disseration. Austin, Texas.

Giddens, A. 1990. *The Consequences of Modernity*. Cambridge, UK: Polity Press.

Hannerz, U. 1992. *Cultural Complexity: Studies in the Social Organization of Meaning*. New York: Columbia University Press.

Long, N. 1992. "From paradigm lost to paradigm regained?" In N. Long and A. Long, eds. *Battlefields of Knowledge. The interlocking of theory and practice in social research and development*. New York, Routledge, 16-43.

Robertson, R. 1992. *Globalization: Social Theory and Global Culture*. London: SAGE.

———. 1995. "Globalization: Time-Space and Homogeneity-Heterogeneity." In M. Featherstone, S. Lash, and R. Robertson, eds. *Global Modernities*. London: Sage, 25-44.

Samandú, L. 1989. "La Iglesia del Nazareno en Alta Verapaz: su historia y presencia en el mundo Kekchí." In *El Protestantismo en Guatemala: Cuadernos de Investigación*. Dirección General de Investigaciones, Univesidad de San Carlos de Guatemala, No. 2-89, 17-47.

———. 1990. "Estrategias evangélicas hacia la población indígena de Guatemala." In L. Samandú, ed. *Protestantismos y procesos sociales en Centroamérica*. San José, Costa Rica: EDUCA, 69-110.

Samandú, L. et al. 1990. *Guatemala: Retos de la Iglesia Católica en una sociedad en crisis*. San José, Costa Rica: DEI.

Siebers, H. 1996. *Creolization and Modernization at the Periphery: The Case of the Q'eqchi'es of Guatemala*. Doctoral dissertation, University of Nijmegen, The Netherlands.

Tomlinson, J. 1991. *Cultural Imperialism: A Critical Introduction*. London: Pinter Publishers.

Van Oss, A. 1986. *Catholic Colonialism. A Parish History of Guatemala 1524–1821*. Cambridge, UK: Cambridge University Press.

FOURTEEN

DISCOURSES ON AFRO-BRAZILIAN RELIGION
FROM DE-AFRICANIZATION
TO RE-AFRICANIZATION

Tina Gudrun Jensen

The mixing of races that began during Portugal's colonization of Brazil in the year 1500 has continued to be characteristic of the Brazilian population. The fact that Brazil is a multiethnic society has spawned a belief that racial prejudice does not exist there. This belief expresses itself as the ideology that Brazil has a "racial democracy." Umbanda, a religion that originated in the southeast of Brazil in the 1920s, has been praised as an expression of this ideology. However, Umbanda has also been seen as one of the manifestations of white supremacy. This article will examine how prejudices against the black Brazilian population were expressed through the de-Africanization of Umbanda and the religious discourse that accompanied that process. It then goes on to examine the recent shift to a re-Africanization of the Afro-Brazilian religions.[1]

THE AFRO-BRAZILIAN RELIGIONS
It is estimated that a total of 3,600,000 slaves were transported from Africa to Brazil between the sixteenth and the ninteenth centuries (Bastide 1978: 35), making Brazil the second-largest slave importer in the New World. During this period, the black slave population was actually larger than the ruling white minority. The slaves came mainly from Nigeria, Dahomey (Benin), Angola, Congo, and Mozambique. Although the institution of slavery split up families and spread these ethnic groups throughout the country, the slaves managed to maintain some links with their ethnic heritage. This was due to the fact, among other things, that the Portuguese minority used their policy of divide-and-rule to separate the slaves into different *nações*. The term *nação* (nation) refers to an ethnic group's local geographical area and their cultural traditions (for example, the Yoruba-speaking nations of Nigeria are the Nagô, Ketu, Ijeja, Egba, etc.). The unexpected conse-

quence of this division was that the concept of *nação* came to play an important role for the maintenance of the various African ethnic identities, and for the transmission of cultural and religious traditions.

The African slaves were banned from practicing their various native religions. The Roman Catholic church issued orders that the slaves should be baptized, and that they should take part in Mass and in the sacraments. In spite of the institutions of slavery and the Roman Catholic church, however, it remained possible for the slaves to communicate, transmit, and develop their cultural and religious traditions. There were various factors that helped them to maintain this continuity: the various ethnic groups continued to speak their mother tongues; there were a certain number of religious leaders among the slaves; and the link to Africa was constantly maintained through the arrival of new slaves.

Among the African religious traditions that came to influence the Afro-Brazilian religion, the cults of the *orixás* and *voduns* became particularly important. *Orixás* and *voduns* are deities of Yoruba and Jeje-speaking groups in Nigeria and Benin. In Africa, each of the deities presided over an aspect of nature, and at the same time over one family. In Brazil, as slavery split families, they came to preside over individuals. Central to the African religions as they developed in Brazil were the feasts for the *orixás* and *voduns*, which involved spirit possession and animal sacrifices.

The Afro-Brazilian religions constitute a relatively recent phenomenon in Brazilian religious history. For example, the first *Candomblé terreiro*, or house of Candomblé (literally: "a piece of land"), which is situated in the northeastern state of Bahia, is generally dated to 1830. These new religions first appeared in and around Brazil's urban areas, as the slaves there had greater freedom of movement, and were able to organize themselves into *nações*. They eventually spread all across the country and took on names such as *Catimbó, Tambor das Minas, Xangó, Candomblé, Macumba*, and *Batuques*. The most traditional and purely African of these religions, such as Candomblé, originated in the northeast of Brazil. Candomblé comes from the state of Bahia, and has long been synonymous with Afro-Brazilian religious traditions in general. From the beginning, *the pais-de-santos*[2] (Candomblé leaders) sought to re-Africanize the religion. This was possible in part because the boats traveling between Nigeria and Bahia kept the African connection alive. This continued even after the abolition of slavery in 1888. Freed slaves would travel to Yoruba areas, become initiated into the cult of the *orixás*, and then return to Brazil where they would found *terreiros* and revitalize the religious practice. As the Afro-Brazilian religions began to appear, the concept of *nação* was reinforced in significance, partly as a symbol of the transmission of local religious traditions, and partly as an ethnic identity marker.[3]

Re-Africanized or not, the Afro-Brazilian religions still bear the effects of their interactions with other religious traditions, especially Catholicism. The *orixás* and *voduns* were juxtaposed with Catholic saints,[4] and the interior of the *terreiros* possessed numerous Catholic elements, including altars and statuettes of saints, while the African religious objects were hidden away. The Afro-Brazilian religions were prohibited, and the *terreiros* were often raided by the police, so the practitioners obviously must have been attempting to increase the Catholic appearance of both the *orixás* and the *terreiros*. The syncretization with Catholicism can thus be seen as a survival strategy. Even though the abolition of slavery in 1888, the ratification of the constitution of the Brazilian Republic in 1889, and the separation of church and state in 1890 were all characterized by the same liberal spirit, the Republic still banned *o espiritismo* (spiritism). This ban was directed particularly against the Afro-Brazilian religions, which were denounced as *baixo espiritismo* (low spiritism). Implicit in this designation is a social prejudice directed against the members of these religions, who belonged to the lowest sectors of Brazilian society.

The black Brazilians did not fit into the Republic's approach to modernization. Inspired by European and North American "scientific" racial theories, the white ruling elite viewed the black population as a disgrace to the Brazilian national character (Skidmore 1974: 29). The "problem" of skin color required some sort of a solution, and the answer propounded among intellectuals and the elite in general was *embranquecimento* (whitening). The idea was that a continuous miscegenation would eventually lead to an overall whitening of the Brazilian population. It was further held that this whitening process would accelerate with the opening up of Brazil, especially to European immigrants.[5]

THE WHITE SPIRITISM

While the Afro-Brazilian religions were centered in the northeast of Brazil, the religious currents in the southeast came to be of decisive importance for the foundation of Umbanda, a new Brazilian religion. To the white intellectual bourgeoisie of the southeast, France was the exponent of the newest cultural and spiritual currents. Thus, the spiritism of Allan Kardec, which was first practiced in Paris around 1855 by the Frenchman Hippolyte Léon Denizard Rivail (1804-69), soon spread to the southeast of Brazil. This new brand of spritism mixed philosophy, science and religion. Kardec's ideas about the immortality of the soul and communication with spirits were combined with social evolutionism, the positivism of Comte, magnetism, Hindu concepts of reincarnation and karma, and the Christian teaching of charity.

Kardecism was embraced primarily by the white middle class. This included European immigrants, particularly doctors, lawyers, intellectuals, and army officers. *Espíritas* (Kardecist spiritists) were persecuted by the Catholic Church, but the separation of church and state in 1890 made it possible for Kardecist spiritism to gain ground. The republican government continued to persecute spiritist organizations because of their illegal medical practice, but in spite of this, many governors were themselves involved in the Kardecist movement, which was less stigmatized than the Afro-Brazilian spirit religions. A distinction was introduced between *baixo espiritismo*, which was related to the Afro-Brazilian religions and the black population from the lower sector, and *alto espiritismo* (high spiritism), which was related to Kardecist spiritism and the white population from the upper sectors (Negrão 1993: 23).

In Brazilian Kardecist spiritism, Kardec's notion of evolution combines with concepts of reincarnation and karma. In this particular brand of cultural evolutionism, the spirits of peoples such as the Aztecs, Chinese, and Egyptians are seen as representing highly developed civilizations, while the spirits of Africans and Brazilian Indians are viewed as inferior and belonging to inferior cultures. These inferior spirits are refused admittance to spiritist sessions. The majority of the spirits attending spiritist sessions are deceased renowned scientists, especially doctors, including those who were once practitioners of Brazilian Kardecist spiritism.

From the very beginning, Brazilian Kardecist spiritist centers offered health services to the sick and poor. There was, however, no recruitment among the lower sectors. On the contrary, the social distance between rich and poor was firmly maintained (Brown 1994: 24).

MACUMBA

Besides Kardecist spiritism, Umbanda has an important predecessor in Macumba. The term Macumba refers to the various mixtures of Afro-Brazilian and other religions that originated in southeast Brazil, especially in Rio de Janeiro. Macumba is also a derogatory term for *baixo espiritismo*. It is generally assumed that Macumba originated in and around Rio de Janeiro, where the former slave population was by and large from Congo, Angola, and Mozambique, and was grouped according to *nações*.

Macumba in Rio de Janeiro was characterized by a distinct religious eclecticism, and the fact that it diffused among ethnic groups from almost all social sectors. Among the various religious traditions that enter into Macumba are Candomblé, *Caboclo* cults,[6] and Kardecist spiritism. With

Macumba appeared two new spirit archetypes: *O Caboclo* (the Brazilian Indian) and *O Preto Velho* (the Old Black, a slave spirit), both of whom would assume great importance in the later foundation of Umbanda.

João do Rio, a journalist who described the religious eclecticism as it unfolded in Rio de Janeiro at the turn of the century, refers to numerous religious specialists who were representatives of the black population from the lower sectors. These specialists were consulted by clients, mostly from the middle sector and the elite. They practiced alongside religious specialists from the higher sectors of the population, and their clients paid well to rescue themselves from critical situations involving sickness, love, money, power, etc. (Rio 1976 [1904]).

The ethnic and social heterogeneity of both core members and clients within Macumba made it a religion that could mediate between the two antagonistic religious traditions, *baixo espiritismo* (low spiritism; Afro-Brazilian) and *alto espiritismo* (high spiritism; Kardecist). In this way Macumba anticipates Umbanda.

A RELIGIOUS INNOVATION

Umbanda has often been regarded as a great synthesis of Afro-Brazilian and Amerindian religious traditions, Kardecist spiritism, and Catholicism. Because of its syncretic and eclectic character, Umbanda has been seen as a religion that joins together Brazil's various ethnic groups and their cultural and religious traditions and thus reflects the miscegenation that makes up Brazilian society. Umbanda has in fact been regarded as an attempt to formulate a national religion, to create a democratic religion that would unite Brazil's various ethnic groups and social classes.

While Umbanda has often been referred to as an Afro-Brazilian religion, Brazilian scholars of today dispute this. The original tendency to regard Umbanda as an Afro-Brazilian religion seems to reflect a general prejudice against Afro-Brazilian religious traditions, and an inclination to folklorize them. There are still many disagreements and confusions about Umbanda among scholars. It has variously been interpreted as a religion of the black Brazilians, of the oppressed, of the European immigrants, and of the middle class. Actually, all these positions regarding Umbanda may in fact be true. Brazilian scholars today generally agree that it is a uniquely Brazilian religion, i.e., a religion that makes up a bricolage, a coherent ensemble, of almost all existing religious traditions in Brazil, and which expresses a certain "Brazilianess" (Ortiz 1980: 107-08). Just as Umbanda is seen as being mediative, inclusive, and fusionist, so is the culture and society which it reflects (Da Matta 1995). Scholars have seen Umbanda as a religion created by the middle-class, and at the same time as a religion that unites the white middle-class and the colored lower classes. By reinterpreting and distancing itself from the other Afro-Brazilian traditions through de-Africanization, whitening, and Brazilianization, Umbanda conforms with the dominant "racial democracy" ideology of Brazilian society (Ortiz 1991).

THE FOUNDING OF UMBANDA

The founder of Umbanda is often identified as a man called Zélio de Moraes from Rio de Janeiro. Zélio was white, middle-class, and the son of a Kardecist spiritist. He claimed that in 1920 the spirit of a Jesuit priest revealed itself to him and told him that he was going to be the founder of a new, genuinely Brazilian religion that would be dedicated to the two Brazilian spirits: *O Caboclo* and *O Preto Velho*. These were precisely the two Macumba spirit types that had been rejected as inferior by the Kardecist spiritists. In the mid-1920s, Zélio founded his first Umbanda center in Niteroi, and in the following years several more Umbanda centers were founded by people initiated there.

Like Zélio, the first founders of Umbanda centers were former Kardecists from the white middle class. They had found Kardecist spiritism to be inadequate, and had therefore begun to frequent the Macumba *terreiros* in the slums of Rio de Janeiro. There they acquired a taste for the African and Brazilian Indian Macumba spirits, whom they found far more competent and efficient than the Kardecist spirits in dealing with illnesses and other problems. Besides, the Macumba rituals were considered far more exciting when compared with the minimally ritualized sessions of Kardecist spiritism. If the Kardecists were inspired by certain aspects of Macumba, however, they were repelled by others, such as the animal sacrifices, the "demonic" spirits, the often coarse ritual conduct, and the lower social ambiance of the Macumba centers (Brown 1994: 38-41).

UMBANDA'S DE-AFRICANIZATION OF AFRO-BRAZILIAN RELIGIOUS TRADITIONS

Umbanda can be considered a synthesis of the different, and often antagonistic, religious traditions represented by Brazil's various ethnic and social groups. However, Umbandists have often held an ambiguous attitude towards the Afro-Brazilian religious traditions. This reflects the dominant sociocultural tendencies of Brazilian society.

Umbanda originated in a politically turbulent period that witnessed, among other phenomena, the emergence of nationalist and fascist movements. This political development culminated in 1937 with the rise of a dictatorship, *Estado Novo* (the New State). It was during those highly nationalist years that the ideology of the Brazilian racial democracy came into existence.[7] According to this ideology, which was based on racial egalitarianism, the country's various ethnic groups had all been equally important in the formation of Brazilian civilization. This ideology thus gave an impetus to the general belief that racial prejudice did not exist in Brazil. The effects of this had already begun to be felt toward the end of the 1920s with the nationalization and institutionalization of Afro-Brazilian culture. Cultural practices like the carnival and samba schools, which had been relegated to a low status because of their association with the black social classes, were now officially acknowledged as important components of the national culture (Brown 1994: 206). Brazilian scholars also began taking a serious interest in Afro-Brazilian culture, which, from the outset, was studied from a folkloristic point of view. At the same time the dictatorship abolished black movements that were fighting against racial discrimination, which continued to be deeply ingrained in the social reality.

O espiritismo, especially the "low" spiritism represented by the Afro-Brazilian religions, was still prohibited by law. During the period of the dictatorship, which also represented the formative years of Umbanda, persecution of persons involved in spiritism intensified. In all likelihood, it was the persecution of people involved in *baixo espiritismo* (e.g., the Afro-Brazilian religions) that caused the first Umbandists to identify themselves as *espíritas* (the term used by Kardecist spiritists to refer to themselves). By choosing this self-identity, Umbandists associated themselves with Kardecism and "high" spiritism. *Espírita* appears to have been a cover name that served to dissociate practitioners of the new religion from its Afro-Brazilian background, a gesture that is reminiscent of the Catholic masking of the Afro-Brazilian religions that had been going on for some time.[8]

As mentioned, the ideology of the Brazilian democracy was, and is, manifested as a white hegemony. This state of affairs revealed itself in the first attempts to legitimize Umbanda as a religion. The legitimization involved a de-Africanization and whitening of Umbanda. In 1939 some of the founders of the original Umbanda centers in Rio de Janeiro, including Zélio de Moraes, established the first Umbanda federation, *União Espírita da Umbanda do Brazil* (UEUB) (the Spiritist Union of Umbanda in Brazil). The federation was established in order to organize Umbanda as a coherent and homogeneous religion so as to obtain social legitimization. In 1941 the UEUB held its first conference on Umbanda spiritism which was an attempt to define and codify Umbanda as a religion in its own right, and as a religion that unites all religions, races, and nationalities. Still, the conference is also known for promoting further dissociation from the Afro-Brazilian religious traditions. The participants agreed to make the works of Allan Kardec the doctrinary foundation of Umbanda, while dissociating it from Macumba and other Afro-Brazilian religious traditions. Yet, the founding spirits of Umbanda, the *Caboclos* and *Pretos Velhos*, were still maintained as highly evolved spiritis. Generally speaking, the participants endeavored to legitimize Umbanda as a highly evolved religion. For instance, it was stated that Umbanda had existed as an organized religion for billions of years, and was thus ahead of all other religions.

In these endeavors to legitimize Umbanda as an original and highly evolved religion, the participants sought to cut it off from its Afro-Brazilian and African roots. The origin of Umbanda was traced to the Orient, from whence it was said to have spread to Lemuria (a "lost continent") and subsequently to Africa. In Africa, the story continued, Umbanda had degenerated into fetishism. In this form, it was brought to Brazil by the black slaves (Federação Espírita de Umbanda 1942: 44-47). The African influence on Umbanda was thus not denied, but it was regarded as a corruption of the original religious tradition, as a backward phase in its evolution. Umbanda had been exposed to African barbarianism in the shape of vulgar customs, practiced by a people with "rude costumes and ethnic and psychologic defects" (Ibid.: 116; my translation). Other ways of handling the African character of Umbanda were expressed in the acknowledgement that it originated in Africa, but in *Africa oriental* (Egypt), and thus in the more occidental and "civilized" part of the African continent (Ibid.: 114).

One of the goals of the conference was thus to trace the "genuine" roots of Umbanda to the Orient. The invention of the Oriental roots—along with the denial of the African ones—was reflected in the definition of the term *umbanda*, which is otherwise generally believed to be derived from a Bantu language. It was declared that *umbanda* came from the Sanskrit words *aum* and *bhanda*, terms that were translated as "the limit in the unlimited," "Divine Principle, radiant light, the source of eternal life, constant evolution" (Ibid.: 21-22). The participants generally endeavored to associate Umbanda with things like the European esoteric religious traditions and the new religious currents from India, represented by Vivekananda.

The African influence on Umbanda was acknowledged as a necessary evil that merely served to explain its arrival and development in Brazil. Candomblé, centered in the northeast of Brazil, was regarded as an earlier stage of Umbanda, which had developed in the southeast; Candomblé was still characterized by barbarian African rituals, and was thus associated with *magia negra* (black magic). The whitewashing of Umbanda's origin was expressed in terms like *umbanda pura* (pure Umbanda), *umbanda limpa* (clean Umbanda), *umbanda branca* (white Umbanda), and *umbanda da linha branca* (Umbanda of the white line), in the sense of "white magic". These terms were contrasted with *magia negra* (black magic) and *linha negra* (black line), which were associated with evil. Furthermore a division of spirits was established that drew a line between those *da direita* (from the right; good), represented by Umbanda, and spirits *da esquerda* (from the left; evil), represented by black magic. The only instances of positive identification with the African influence on Umbanda had to do with *Pretos Velhos* (which were seen as humble and simple, yet highly evolved, spirits), and with Africa as a suffering and heroic continent.

The participants' attitudes towards the African religious heritage were thus characterized by ambiguity. There were both positive and negative identifications, ranging from their marked attempt to dissociate themselves from the African religious traditions, to their distinctly paternalistic attitude towards Africans, whom they typified with the image of a humble slave. The black Brazilians were accepted since, after all, they had white souls.

De-Africanization in Umbanda Cosmology

The Umbandistic cosmos is divided into three levels: the astral world, the earth, and the underworld. The astral world is presided over by *deus* (god), who is followed by various *linhas* (lines). Every line is guided by an *orixá*, who often corresponds to a Catholic saint. The astral world is home to a hierarchy in which the various religious figures are ranked according to their levels of spiritual evolution. Lowest ranking are the spiritual founders of Umbanda: *Caboclos* and *Pretos Velhos*. The earth constitutes a platform for spirits that experience their human incarnations at different levels of spiritual evolution. The earth is visited by spirits from the astral world, who are incorporated by the mediums in Umbanda centers, thereby helping the human beings. The underworld, which is often called *quimbanda*, is the domain of black magic. It represents an antistructure of Umbanda. The underworld is inhabited by spirits that lived their earlier incarnations as doubtful characters (e.g., crooks, prostitutes, etc.). They are regarded as evil because of their lack of spiritual evolution. These spirits may also ascend to the earth, causing damage that the spirits from the astral world must then descend to undo.

Scholars focusing on the de-Africanization of Umbanda have sought to show how African and Afro-Brazilian religious traditions are reinterpreted in its cosmology. In Umbanda the Afro-Brazilian *orixás* have been marginalized and given less importance than in Candomblé, where the entire ceremony is centered around the *orixás*, who are incorporated by the *filhos-de-santo*. In Umbanda ceremonies, on the other hand, the *orixás* are peripheral. Due to their high position in the hierarchy, they remain in the astral spheres, and are therefore hardly ever incorporated by the mediums. It seems that the less evolved and more down-to-earth spirits, the *Caboclos* and *Pretos Velhos*, have taken up the position that the *orixás* traditionally occupy in Candomblé.

Since the nineteenth century, there has been both an oral and a written tradition concerning these two figures. The *Caboclo* is generally depicted as a representative of the unacculturated, savage, and proud indigenous population, and has become a symbol of the bygone golden age of Brazil; the *Preto Velho* has been depicted as a humble and faithful Uncle Tom–like slave. It has been emphasized that in spite of the differences between these two spirit types, they are both marked by the processes of acculturation and civilization, and share a common historical experience in having been enslaved. The replacement of the *orixás* with the *Pretos Velhos* has been interpreted as an expression of the foreign (Africa) being replaced by the national (Brazil). This replacement of the free and proud *orixás* with *Pretos Velhos*, the slaves, has furthermore been interpreted as symbolic of the transformation of the African, from being a free man in Africa to becoming a slave in Brazil. This replacement has thus been seen as an instance of the acculturation, domestication, and whitening of the African identity in its transformation into an Afro-Brazilian and national Brazilian identity (Brown 1994: 37–78).

The trickster, *Exu*, who, among other things, represents the messenger of the *orixás* in Candomblé, is another African and Afro-Brazilian religious figure who has been reinterpreted and marginalized in Umbanda. *Exu* was already associated with the devil prior to the founding of Umbanda. Within that religion, however, the devilish picture is completed. *Exu* comes to represent evil, danger, and immorality. Because of these characteristics, it seems that the early Umbandists associated *Exu* with Africans and the rebellious slaves. *Exu* was therefore segregated from Umbanda, and turned into the ruler of *quimbanda*, the underworld.

Another Umbandistic reinterpretation places *Exu* in the evolutionary order of precedence according to the Kardecist model; he is reduced to a less evolved spirit who nevertheless has the potential to evolve and become a good spirit. Some Umbandists distinguish between o *Exu pagão* (the pagan *Exu*) and *o Exu bautizado* (the baptized *Exu*), who has submitted to *doutrinação* (i.e., has learned the doctrines) and thus finds himself on the right road up the ladder of evolution. This distinction reflects some of the original ambivalent character of *Exu*, although the baptismal rite of passage that defines the distinction is, of course, new. Again, this baptism of the pagan *Exu* has been interpreted as an expression of the acculturation and domestication of the evil, dangerous, and immoral African *Exu* (Ortiz 1991: 137-144).

INCIPIENT RE-AFRICANIZATION

The breakdown of the authoritarian regime in 1945 cleared the way for democratization. This also meant that the systematic persecution of Umbandists stopped. Among Umbandists, this triggered a shift away from a common identification with the Kardecist spiritism, and opened up the possibility for several other identifications and definitions of Umbanda. This new development may be interpreted as an incipient re-Africanization of Umbanda. As an alternative to *umbanda branca* (white Umbanda), there appeared *umbanda africana* (African Umbanda). It traced its origin back to Africa, not to India, and it praised its African heritage.

The change towards democratization enabled Umbanda to become more widespread and visible in southeastern Brazil through radio programs, journals, and the foundation of several Umbanda federations.[9] In the early 1960s, despite the end of government persecution, the Catholic church led a crusade against Umbanda. Under orders from the Second Vatican Council (1962-1965), however, the Catholic church in Brazil was forced to stop the persecutions, and to enter into a dialogue with non-Christian religions. In Brazil, this resolution caused many Catholic priests to realize that the future of Catholicism in the country depended on their ability to syncretize with the Afro-Brazilian religions (Boff 1977). The Brazilian Catholic church started to adopt a liturgical pluralism by incorporating elements from Afro-Brazilian religions at certain Masses. Further, the Church started to officially acknowledge Umbanda as a religion. This change within the Brazilian Church meant that Umbanda and the other Afro-Brazilian religions could now gain a more powerful position within the overall religious field.

During the military dictatorship (1964-1985) Umbanda obtained official recognition and legitimization.[10] This may have been connected with the dictatorship's nationalistic project. Presumably, the military supported the white, Brazilian, racial-democracy interpretation of Umbanda. The regime directly supported Umbanda and used it to manipulate the masses, causing those who were in opposition to the government to despise the religion. It is very likely that the regime also used Umbanda against members of the Brazilian Catholic church, especially against clergy who opposed it.

In the 1960s, during the repressive era of the military regime, the counterculture reached Brazil from Europe and North America. Countercultural movements spread to the urban centers of southeast Brazil and were embraced by the white middle class, particularly intellectuals, students, and scholars. Left-wing movements of protest arose in sympathy for the marginalized, the poor, and the blacks. As in Europe and North America, the counterculture of the 1960s involved a search for alternatives to Western rationality. The white middle class of southeast Brazil increasingly turned to the Oriental, the mystical, and the occult in search of the origins of Brazilian culture. Their attention focused on Bahia in northeast Brazil, the cradle of Candomblé. The cultural and religious ambiance of Afro-Brazilian Bahia came to represent the last authentic remains of a true tradition in Brazil. Soon Brazilian popular culture embraced Bahia and its Afro-Brazilian cultural and religious traditions. The lyrics of popular music began to appeal to the mysteries of Candomblé, the greatest *mães-de-santos*, and the *orixás* (Prandi 1991: 71-72).

During the decade of the 1960s Afro-Brazilian culture and religion thus became increasingly less stigmatized by the white middle class from southeast Brazil. As a consequence, Candomblé started to become visible in that area.

THE SPREAD AND AFRICANIZATION OF CANDOMBLÉ IN SOUTHEAST BRAZIL

During the 1970s the hard line of the military regime underwent a relaxation, and the ban against the worship of Candomblé and other Afro-Brazilian religions was finally lifted in 1977. The number of registered Candomblé centers began to increase considerably.[11] Many new Candomblé federations were constituted, and many Umbanda federations were reorganized so as to include Candomblé centers. This development reflected Umbanda's structural Africanization and rapprochement with Afro-Brazilian religions. One of the consequences of the new recognition of Candomblé, and its structural adaptation by the Umbanda federations, was that the *pais-de-santos* of the Umbanda centers incorporated and, to a great extent, practiced Candomblé. Furthermore, Umbandist *pais-de-santos* began to travel to Bahia to be initiated in Candomblé centers. To "be made"[12] in Candomblé became a legitimization of the religious competence of Umbandist leaders. The incorporation of Candomblé into Umbanda, a synthesis which was referred to as "umbandomblé" and "candombanda," was noted with surprise by scholars, who became aware of the fact that Umbanda not only represented a distinct religious practice, but also a combination of traditions ranging from Kardecist spiritism to Candomblé (Negrão 1993: 64-66).

By 1987 the number of registered Candomblé centers in the southeastern state of São Paulo had risen to 2,500, while the number of Umbanda centers had only increased slightly after the breakdown of the military dictatorship. Those behind the spread of Candomblé in southeast Brazil were mainly Umbandist *pais-de-santos* who transformed their Umbanda centers into Candomblé centers, and who were, in many cases, followed by both core members as well as clients. Many Umbanda centers are thus in a period of transition to Candomblé and are saving up for the transformation (as Candomblé is a far more costly religion than Umbanda). While Umbandists once recruited many members from Candomblé, the tide of recruitment is now going in the opposite direction.

Another factor contributing to the spread of Candomblé in southeast Brazil is the wave of migration from the northeast, which has been increasing since the 1960s. Among the migrants have been *pais-de-santos*, who brought along their Candomblé centers or opened branches of their centers in the southeast. This transplantation and spread of Candomblé in the southeast is itself a new phenomenon. But the composition of the Candomblé followers is also new, since the black lower classes and the white middle class are about equally represented. Among white and black *pais-de-santos* the concept of *nação* has been revitalized and forms part of their religious self-images. *Pais-de-santos* trace their religious identities back to local geographic areas and cultural traditions in Africa, whereby they legitimize the purity and authenticity of their religious practices. For these new *pais-de-santos* religious genealogy is closely tied up with legitimization. In marketing a Candomblé center, it is of great importance to be able to trace one's religious career within Candomblé back to the oldest, most prestigious, and traditional Candomblé houses in Bahia.

It appears that many former Umbandist *pais-de-santos* regard Umbanda as a stage on their way to Candomblé. They consider Candomblé a more pure and aesthetic religion with strong cultural roots and traditions. Candomblé is also considered to be more magically efficacious and *mais forte* (stronger). Last, but not least, in giving their reasons for switching to Candomblé, *pais-de-santos* often state that it is no longer a stigmatized and persecuted religion (Prandi 1991: 77-90).

In the wake of the recent spread of Afro-Brazilian religions in the southeast of Brazil, there is also a process of re-Africanization going on within these religions. The endeavor to purify Candomblé of the syncretistic elements like the *Caboclos* and *Pretos Velhos*[13] represents a reversal of the process of de-Africanization and syncretization that took place within Umbanda. Accordingly, Candomblé centers are beginning to celebrate farewell feasts in honor of the Umbandistic *Caboclos* and *Pretos Velhos*. Furthermore, there are endeavors to purify Candomblé of its Catholic elements in order to return to the "genuine" traditions of Nigeria and Benin.[14] A salient expression of the Africanization of Candomblé is the cultivation of Nigerian cultural and religious traditions through the study of the Yoruba language and the mythology of the *orixás*, and through pilgrimages to Nigeria. Some of the re-Africanized *pais-de-santos* even dissociate themselves from Candomblé as an Afro-Brazilian product. Instead, they choose to name their religions *tradição do orisa* (*orixá* tradition) or *culto do orisa* (*orixá* cult).

Generally, it seems that the Afro-Brazilian religions have become more visible in the society of southeast Brazil. *Pais-de-santos* appear in the media with their own magazines and their own television and radio programs. They even appear as characters in soap operas and as fortune tellers making prognostications about events of political and social importance. Candomblé has also become a target of commercialism. The increasing number of advertisements for ritual objects and package trips to the original sacred sites of the *orixás* in Nigeria is mostly due to profane commercial interests. Their existence, however, is evidence of the interest in Candomblé. Since the 1970s Nigerian immigrants, who originally went to Brazil as exchange students, have settled down in southeast Brazil and make their living by importing and selling ritual objects from Nigeria. The first *Mercado dos orixás* (*orixá* supermarket) was established in São Paulo in 1996. Additionally, developments in the field of education reflect the growing interest in Afro-Brazilian culture and religion, and in African cultural roots. Since 1977 visiting scholars from Nigeria have offered courses in Yoruba language and culture at the state university of São Paulo. Courses like these have attracted both students, scholars, and practitioners of Candomblé. Since the end of the 1970s other educational institutions in São Paulo have also begun offering courses in Yoruba language and religion (including mythology, dance, and music for the *orixás*). These institutions function somewhat like hatcheries for the Candomblé centers (Goncalves da Silva 1995: 261-71).

THE MEANINGS OF RE-AFRICANIZATION

Scholars researching Umbanda or Candomblé currently discuss whether Candomblé is outcompeting Umbanda (i.e., whether a general shift from Umbanda to Candomblé is taking place). Although in general Umbanda is still far more widespread than Candomblé, and although its members continue to look upon Candomblé with a prejudiced attitude, Candomblé seems to be growing in the southeast of Brazil at the expense of Umbanda. Candomblé is also spreading to all sectors of Brazilian society.

Although research into the spread and re-Africanization of Afro-Brazilian religion in southeast Brazil is still incipient, divergent interpretations of this phenomena have already been advanced. The Brazilian sociologist Reginaldo Prandi has argued that a shift from Umbanda to Candomblé is taking place, and that this shift is reflective of certain social changes (Prandi 1991: 62). For Prandi, Umbanda is a religion whose social ideology reflects the society of yesterday (e.g., the modern class society that appeared in the 1920s, and was characterized by a belief in nationalism, equality, and social mobility). This type of society did not succeed. Due to the political crises and the profound social changes that occurred during the late military regime, people lost their sense of security and their belief in society and social mobility. In Prandi's view, Candomblé is more in tune with contemporary society. He characterizes Candomblé as a nonethical religion that values worldy things and focuses on the individual. Thus, Candomblé fits the hedonistic, narcissistic, postethical (in short, the postmodern) society of today (Ibid.: 186).

Another hypothesis that Prandi defends is that Candomblé, as it is being transplanted from the northeast to the southeast of Brazil, has undergone a change from an ethnic to a universal religion. Prandi assumes that the popularization of Candomblé, which has been going on through music and the mass media since the 1960s, has prepared the way for a widespread acknowledgement of Afro-Brazilian and African culture and religion. This rediscovery of Africa has attracted the white middle class to the Candomblé centers, something that has contributed to the legitimization and popularization of Candomblé. According to Prandi, Africanization has nothing to do with black skin color or Afro-Brazilian identity. Afro-Brazilian culture and religion have lost almost any ethnic identity and connection to the history of the Afro-Brazilian population. Instead, Prandi sees Africanization as a kind of intellectual-ized invention of traditions in which the return to African roots represents a search for origins and authenticity (Ibid.: 118). Prandi's arguments are indirectly supported by other arguments, which, for example, claim that Candomblé has achieved general acceptance by the dominant white sector of Brazilian society partly as a result of its having been marketed as an authentic and pure religion (Bacelar 1989: 87).

Prandi's point of view regarding Africanization represents Candomblé as an expression of culturalism. Cultural elements appear as freely floating and have lost any relation to a particular socioeconomic or political stratum of society or ethnohistorical category. Other scholars have taken an opposite road and have related the spread and Africanization of Afro-Brazilian religious traditions directly to ethnic and political issues. Thus, the North American anthropologist Diana Brown connects the growth of Candomblé in southeast Brazil with an increasing racial consciousness among Brazilians of African ancestry. Brown calls attention to the fact that the growth of Candomblé, with respect to both time and place, coincides with the appearance of cultural and political interests in African identity among black Brazilians (e.g., with the racial consciousness movements that started in the late 1960s) (Brown 1994: xxii). But Brown denies that there are clear and unambiguous explanations for the spread of Candomblé in southeast Brazil. She argues, in particular, that one has to be aware of the differences between how the white middle class and the black lower class identify with Candomblé.

The different points of view discussed here represent two interpretations of the recent growth and re-Africanization of Candomblé in southeast Brazil. One appeals to the universality and culturalism of Candomblé, the other focuses on ethnicity and politics. Under the first interpretation, Candomblé is part of a symbolic repertoire and represents but one among many cultural and religious identities in the multicultural, multireligious supermarket of modern society in which each individual is free to choose and combine the various and multifarious religious identities. The other point of view considers Candomblé to be connected with an ethnic and political consciousness and the struggle against discrimination, which has been increasing among the Afro-Brazilian population since the 1970s. Here Candomblé appears as a resource in a political struggle where the reinvention of African religious traditions may be used as a means of ethnic mobilization, and a way to raise people's consciousness and build an ethnic identity. The two points of view are not, of course, mutually exclusive. It is likely that in the eyes of the white middle class Candomblé is no longer an expression of Afro-Brazilian identity, while, at the same time, it may very well constitute a potential source of ethnic consciousness and mobilization in the Afro-Brazilian population.

During my own research on the Africanization of Candomblé in southeast Brazil, I observed that there are strong differences between the black and white Brazilians involved in Afro-Brazilian religions. Among blacks and whites there are now serious controversies over the definitions of Candomblé, Africanhood, and blackness. The most Africanized (e.g. those who study Yoruba and orixá mythology and go on pilgrimages to Africa) tend to be white Brazilians from the middle class.

They generally try to dissociate themselves from Candomblé, which they consider an "impure" Afro-Brazilian syncretistic religion. Instead, they prefer to define their religion as "Afro-descendant," naming it *tradição do orisa* (*orixá* tradition) and *culto do orisa* (*orixá* cult). There is only a small representation of black Brazilians in the religious centers of these "Afro-descendent" practicioners.

Black Brazilians, however, seem to predominate in the traditional Afro-Brazilian Candomblé centers, which also include a strong representation of participants in the Black Movement. These participants link their religious involvement to their racial consciousness and struggle against discrimination. They dissociate themselves from the more Africanized religious movements of white Brazilians, reproaching them for ignoring the social reality that black Brazilians face and for worshipping Africa alone, rather than that which connects Africa and Brazil. They point out that African culture (in a sense, Africa itself) exists within Brazil, and that the syncretized Candomblé is part of the social history and identity of black Brazilians. Despite the controversies between black and white, they do unite in federations and organizations as practicioners of Afro-Brazilian religions.

In interpreting the growth and Africanization of Afro-Brazilian religion, the culturalist and ethnic/political standpoints are not either-or, but rather a both-and reality. Both standpoints can work together. The challenge lies in acknowledging that Candomblé can no longer be viewed as an unambigious dimension. From having been regarded as a kind of "cultural ghetto," as a cultural phenomenon mainly restricted to northeast Brazil, Afro-Brazilian religion has now spread across the country, and has been adopted by a wide range of ethnic and social groups, each of whom interpret it in their own way. One of the challenges in studying Afro-Brazilian religions today seems to lie in exploring the various meanings they have taken on in the intercultural society of southeast Brazil, where race-related issues are marked by unmatched complexity and ambiguity.

In his work *Cultural Identity and Global Process*, the anthropologist Jonathan Friedman argues that when a hegemonic center begins to decline, the dominant identity becomes increasingly difficult to maintain. A crisis for the larger society leads to a weakening of the power and identity of the dominant groups that carries with it the opportunity for formerly repressed groups to strengthen their cultural identities (Friedmann 1994: 189). As modern identity fails, emergent cultural identities and ethnifications will appear as alternatives, including indigenous movements and fundamentalist religious movements. Such movements represent the emergence of a new primitivism, a search for primordial meanings (Ibid.: 79).

In explaining the turn from a de-Africanization to a re-Africanization of Afro-Brazilian religion, it makes sense to apply Friedman's theory, together with Prandi's hypothesis regarding the shift from Umbanda to Candomblé as an expression of social changes. Umbanda originated together with the modern Brazilian society as *the* Brazilian religion, bringing together the various ethnic groups of Brazil and synthesizing their beliefs. In the assimilative process of de-Africanizing and whitening, of making the Afro-Brazilian Brazilian, Umbanda conformed with the dominant ideology of this modern society. It experienced its heyday during the nationalistic military dictatorship. When the belief in the nation and in values of modern society failed during the military regime, however, alternative political, cultural, and religious identities began to appear. Simultaneously, there was a gradual relaxation of the repressive policies of the dictatorship. After the military regime finally ended in 1985, the growth in the number of Umbanda centers stagnated, while other cultural identities began to emerge. After having been repressed, Afro-Brazilian cultural and religious identity has now become an object for new forms of identity-making in an intercultural society where identity is a matter of free choice. Identification with Afro-Brazilian religion now seems to range from the white Brazilians' search for primitivism and cultural roots to the black Brazilians' claim to racial consciousness.

NOTES

1   Research for the article was made possible financially by the Danish Research Council for the Humanities.

2   The terms for male and female Candomblé leaders are *pai-de-santo* and *mãe-de-santo* (father and mother of the saint or holy one). The initiated is called *filho/filha-de-santo* (son/daughter of the saint or holy one).

3   The Candomblé *terreiros* are divided along nations like Nagô, Ketu, etc. A person who has been initiated into a Candomblé *terreiro* of one nation, is not allowed to practice in other *terreiros* belonging to other nations.

4   This phenomenon is found among all the Catholic countries of the New World to which African slaves were brought (Herskovits 1937).

5   Immigrants of black skin color were barred (Skidmore 1974: 29).

6   The *Caboclo* cults originated in Maranhão in northeast Brazil as a mixture of Amerindian, Catholic, and African religions.

7   One of the people behind this ideology was Gilbero Freyre. The ideology is expressed in his work *Casa Grande e Senzala* (1933) (translated into English as *The Masters and The Slaves: A Study in the Development of Brazilian Civilization*).

8 It is very likely that the majority of the Umbanda centers existed under cover of Kardecist spiritist centers. From 1929 to 1944 a total of forty-two umbanda centers, 651 Kardecist spiritist centers, and no Candomblé centers were registered in the southeastern state of São Paulo (Negrao 1993: 30).

9 The foundation of these Umbanda federations is clearly an expression of the need to legitimize Umbanda. The federations face several problems, however, one of them being the fact that all attempts to codify and standardize Umbanda as a homogeneous and coherent religion have failed. Each Umbanda center formulates its own doctrines and rituals and chooses eclectically from other religious traditions.

10 The nationalization of Umbanda started in 1964, when Umbanda was first included in census statistics, and when Umbandistic feasts entered the official national and local calenders, as well as tourist guides. Simultaneously, an enourmous popular literature on Umbanda began to circulate.

11 From 1974 to 1976, 357 Candomblé centers were registered in São Paulo. During the same period, 2,844 Umbanda centers and 69 Kardecist spiritist centers were registered (Negrao 1993: 31).

12 *Ser feito* ("to be made") refers to *fazer a cabeça* ("to make the head"), a designation for the initiation rite in Candomblé, which involves the tonsure of the initiate.

13 The founding spirits of Umbanda, the *Caboclos* and *Pretos Velhos*, appear in certain types of Afro-Brazilian religion.

14 At the Second World Conference on *Orixá* Tradition and Culture, held in Salvador, Bahia, in 1983, some of the leading *mães-de-santos* from Salvador issued an official statement about the de-syncretization of Candomblé.

References
Bacelar, Jeferson. 1989. *Etnicidade. Ser Negro em Salvador*, Salvador, Bahia: Ianamá (PENBA).

Bastide, Roger. 1978. *The African Religions of Brazil: Toward a Sociology of the Interpenetration of Civilizations*. London: John Hopkins University Press.

Boff, Leonardo. 1977. "Avaliação teologico-crítica do sincretismo." *Vozes* 71:7.

Brown, Diana. 1994. *Umbanda: Religion and Politics in Urban Brazil*. New York: Columbia University Press.

Da Matta, Roberto. 1995. "For an Anthropology of the Brazilian Tradition or 'A Virtude está no Meio.'" In D. Hess and R. Da Matta, eds. *The Brazilian Puzzle: Culture on the Borderlands of the Western World*. New York: Columbia University Press.

Federação Espírita de Umbanda. 1942. *Primeiro Congresso do Espiritismo de Umbanda. Trabalhos apresentados ao 1. Congresso Basileiro do Espiritism de Umbanda, reunido no Rio de Janeiro, de 19 a 26 de Outubro de 1941*. Rio de Janeiro: Jornal do Commerico.

Freyre, Gilberto. 1946. *The Masters and the Slaves: A Study in the Development of Brazilian Civilization*. New York: Alfred A. Knopf.

Friedman, Jonathan. 1994. *Cultural Identity & Global Process*. London: Sage Publications.

Gonçalves da Silva, Vagner. 1995. *Orixás da Metrópole*. Petrópolis and Rio de Janeiro: Vozes.

Herskovits, Melville. 1937. "African Gods and Catholic Saints in New World Negro Belief." *American Anthropologist 39*.

Negrão, Lísias Nogueira. 1993. *Umbanda e Questao Moral: Formação e Atualidade do Campo Umbandista em São Paulo*. Doctoral disseration. São Paulo: Universidade de São Paulo.

Ortiz, Renato. 1980. *A Consciência Fragmentada: Ensaios de Cultura Popular e Religião*. Rio de Janeiro: Paz e Terra.

———. 1991. *A Morte Branca do Feiticeiro Negro: Umbanda e Sociedade Brasieira*. São Paulo: Brasiliense.

Prandi, Reginaldo. 1991. *Os Candomblés de São Paulo*. São Paulo: Eitora HUCITEC.

Rio, Joao do. 1976. *As Religiões no Rio*. Rio de Janeiro: Edições da Organização Simões.

Skidmore, Thomas. 1974. *Black into White: Race and Nationality in Brazilian Thought*. New York: Oxford University Press.

CONTRIBUTORS

SARAH BROOKS is a Ph.D. candidate in political science at Duke University. She earned a bachelor's and master's degree in political science from the University of Chicago and from Duke University, respectively. Sarah specializes in Latin American politics, with a particular concentration on transformations in social and political institutions in the context of economic reforms. She has a forthcoming publication on changes in social protection in Latin America under globalization, and has coauthored a chapter on church politics in Latin America.

ROBERT CARPENTER is an assistant professor at the College of Biblical Studies at Oklahoma Christian University. He is completing a doctorate in Religious Studies at the University of California, Santa Barbara.

ANTHONY GILL (Ph.D. UCLA) is an assistant professor of political science at the University of Washington. He is the author of *Rendering Unto Caesar: The Catholic Church and the State in Latin America* (University of Chicago Press), as well as articles appearing in the *American Journal of Political Science* and the *International Journal of Social Economics*. Professor Gill is currently research-ing the political economy of religious liberty.

LIESL HAAS is an assistant professor of political science at the University of Western Michigan, and a doctoral student at the University of North Carolina, Chapel Hill, conducting research on the women's movement and the legislative process in democratic Chile.

TINA GUDRUN JENSEN is a Ph.D. in the Department of Anthropology at the University of Copenhagen. She studies Brazilian religion, with a focus on Umanda and Candomble. Previous publications include "Umbanda and Its Clientele" in Peter Clarke (ed.) *New Trends and Developments in African Religions*, Greenwood Press.

FRANS KAMSTEEG is a research fellow in the Department of Cultural Anthropology and a lecturer in Culture, Organization and Management Studies at the Free University in Amsterdam. His publications include: "Pentecostal Healing and Power: A Peruvian Case," in *Popular Power in Latin American Religions*, 1991; "Pastor and Disciple: The Role of Lay Followers in the Growth of the Pentecostal Church of Arequipa, Peru," in *More than Opium: An Anthropological Approach to Latin American and Caribbean Pentecostal Praxis*, forthcoming from Scarecrow Press.

CLARA MAFRA is a Ph.D. candidate in Cultural Anthropology at the Museu Nacional de Antropologia da Universidade Federal do Rio de Janeiro. She also participates in a research group known as the "Instituto de Estudio da Religião."

CECÍLIA L. MARIZ is an adjunct professor of Sociology at the Universidade do Estado do Rio de Janeiro. Her publications include *Coping with Poverty: Pentecostal and Christian Base Communities in Brazil*, Temple University Press, 1994. She has also published several articles in Brazilian and international journals.

MATTHEW MAROSTICA received his Ph.D. from the University of California at Berkeley in 1997. He is currently an instructor in Political Science at the

California State University at Hayward, and will be an instructor in Political Science at UC Berkeley in spring 1998. His most pertinent publication is "La Iglesia Evangelica Como Nuevo Movimiento Social," *Sociedad y Religion* 12 (June 1994). His dissertation research was funded by the OAS dissertation research program and the Institute for International and Area Studies at UC Berkeley.

DANIEL MÍGUEZ received his Ph.D. from the University of Amsterdam, and is currently working as an associate professor of Symbolic Anthropology and the History of Anthropological Theory at the University of the State of Buenos Aires. He has recently published articles in the *European Review of Latin American and Caribbean Studies*, as well as in several edited volumes on Pentecostalism in Latin America. He is currently working on a book about the rise of Pentecostalism in Argentina that will probably appear in 1998.

KRISTIN NORGET is an anthropologist at McGill University.

JOSHUA PROKOPY is a graduate student in Sociology at the University of North Carolina at Chapel Hill. He is studying religion, social change, and grassroots development. He has spent two years studying development and socially engaged Buddhism in Thailand while living with activist monks and lay Buddhists involved in grassroots development. He is currently conducting his master's research on resident participation in a public housing–based community center.

HANS SIEBERS received his Ph.D. from the Catholic University of Nijmegen, the Netherlands. He is the author of several books and articles on religion in Latin America. Currently he is working on a comparative project on New Age managers in the Netherlands and Mayan managers in Guatemala. The research will focus on the conditions of identity construction as a reflexive answer to a fragmented life and life-world.

DAVID A. SMILDE is a Ph.D. candidate in Sociology at the University of Chicago and a research associate in the Centro Estudios de Desarrollo at the Universidad Central de Venezuela. His research on Evangelical Protestantism in Venezuela has been supported by an international predissertation fellowship from the Social Science Research Council and by a Fullbright-Hays Dissertation Abroad Fellow-ship from the U.S. Department of Education. His published work includes: "The Fundamental Unity of the Conservative and Revolutionary Tendencies of Venezuelan Evangelicalism: The Case of Conjugal Relations," *Religion* 27:4 (October 1997); and "Letting God Govern: Supernatural Agency in the Venezuelan Pentecostal Approach to Social Change," in *Sociology of Religion* (forthcoming).

CHRISTIAN SMITH is an assistant professor of Sociology at the University of North Carolina at Chapel Hill. He is the author of *The Emergence of Liberation Theology: Radical Religion and Social Movement Theory* (University of Chicago Press, 1991), *Disruptive Religion: The Force of Faith in Social Movement Activism* (Routledge, 1996), *Resisting Reagan: The U.S. Central America Peace Movement* (University of Chicago Press, 1996), and *American Evangelicalism: Embattled and Thriving* (University of Chicago Press, 1998).

TIMOTHY J. STEIGENGA is currently serving as an assistant professor at Colby College in Waterville, Maine. From 1995 to 1997, he served as the Title VI Visiting Professor of Latin American Studies at the University of Massachusetts and the University of Connecticut. He has published articles on Latin American religion and politics in the *Latin American Research Review* and the *Review of Religious Research*. He has also been published in numerous edited volumes, including *Rethinking Protestantism in Latin America* (1993), and *Let My People Live: Faith and Struggle in Central America* (1988).

MARJO DE THEIJE is an assistant professor in the Department of Cultural Anthropology and Sociology of Development at the Free University of Amsterdam. She has done research in Brazil on the religious brotherhoods in Minas Gerais and on pilgrimage and base communities in Pernambuco. In addition to publishing articles on these topics, she is currently working on a book about Catholic lay groups in Brazil. Her publications include: "Brotherhoods Throw More Weight Around than the Pope: Catholic Traditionalism and the Lay Brotherhoods of Brazil," *Sociological Analysis* 51:2 (1991); "Charismatic Renewal and Base Communities: The Religious Participation of Women in a Brazilian Parish," in *More than Opium: An Anthropological Approach to Latin American and Caribbean Pentecostal Praxis,* forthcoming from Scarecrow Press.

INDEX